THE LIGHTS ON THE
TIPPLE ARE GOING OUT

THE LIGHTS ON THE
TIPPLE ARE GOING OUT

FIGHTING ECONOMIC RUIN IN A
CANADIAN COALFIELD COMMUNITY

Tom Langford

UBCPress · Vancouver

Printed in Canada on FSC-certified ancient-forest-free paper (100% post-consumer recycled) that is processed chlorine- and acid-free.

UBC Press is a Benetech Global Certified Accessible™ publisher. The epub version of this book meets stringent accessibility standards, ensuring it is available to people with diverse needs.

LIBRARY AND ARCHIVES CANADA CATALOGUING IN PUBLICATION

Title: The lights on the tipple are going out : fighting economic ruin in a Canadian coalfield community / Tom Langford.
Names: Langford, Tom, author
Description: Includes bibliographical references and index.
Identifiers: Canadiana (print) 20240443446 | Canadiana (ebook) 20240443578 | ISBN 9780774869287 (hardcover) | ISBN 9780774869300 (PDF) | ISBN 9780774869317 (EPUB)
Subjects: LCSH: Coal trade—Alberta—Crowsnest Pass—History—20th century. | LCSH: Coal trade—British Columbia—Elk River Valley—History—20th century. | LCSH: Deindustrialization—Alberta—Crowsnest Pass—History—20th century. | LCSH: Deindustrialization—British Columbia—Elk River Valley—History—20th century. | LCSH: Crowsnest Pass (Alta.)—Economic conditions—20th century. | LCSH: Elk River Valley (B.C.)—Economic conditions—20th century. | LCSH: Economic development—Alberta—Crowsnest Pass. | LCSH: Economic development—British Columbia—Elk River Valley.
Classification: LCC HD9554.C23 C675 2024 | DDC 338.2/7240971234—dc23

UBC Press gratefully acknowledges the financial support for our publishing program of the Government of Canada, the Canada Council for the Arts, and the British Columbia Arts Council.

This book has been published with the help of a grant from the Canadian Federation for the Humanities and Social Sciences, through the Scholarly Book Awards, using funds provided by the Social Sciences and Humanities Research Council of Canada.

UBC Press is situated on the traditional, ancestral, and unceded territory of the xʷməθkʷəy̓əm (Musqueam) people. This land has always been a place of learning for the xʷməθkʷəy̓əm, who have passed on their culture, history, and traditions for millennia, from one generation to the next.

UBC Press
The University of British Columbia
www.ubcpress.ca

Contents

Figures and Tables

Tables

Abbreviations

AFL	Alberta Federation of Labour
ALHI	Alberta Labour History Institute
BCA	BC Archives
CANDU	CANada Deuterium Uranium (nuclear reactor)
CCF	Cooperative Commonwealth Federation
CCL	Canadian Congress of Labour (1940–56)
CGE	Canadian General Electric
CLC	Canadian Labour Congress (1956–)
CMHC	Central Mortgage and Housing Corporation
CMS	Consolidated Mining and Smelting
CNI	Crows Nest Industries
CNPC	Crow's Nest Pass Coal
CNR	Canadian National Railway
COAWC	Coal Operators' Association of Western Canada (1952–71)
Cominco	The new name adopted by CMS in 1966
CPC	Communist Party of Canada
CPR	Canadian Pacific Railway
CSIS AIR	Canadian Security Intelligence Service Access-to-Information Request
DCB	Dominion Coal Board
DCOAWC	Domestic Coal Operators' Association of Western Canada
DEB	District Executive Board (of District 18, UMWA)

GNR	Great Northern Railway
GWRC	Glenbow Western Research Centre
IEB	International Executive Board (of the UMWA)
IFL	Industrial Federation of Labour (of Alberta, 1949–56)
IPCA	Indigenous Protected and Conserved Area
IWA	International Woodworkers of America
LAC	Library and Archives Canada
LCN	Lehigh Coal and Navigation
Local 2633	Coleman Local 2633, UMWA
Local 7292	Michel Local 7292, UMWA
Local 7294	Bellevue Local 7294, UMWA
Local 7295	Blairmore Local 7295, UMWA
Local 7310	Fernie Local 7310, UMWA
LPP	Labor-Progressive Party (1943–59)
MLA	Member of the Legislative Assembly
MNSHS	Michel-Natal-Sparwood Heritage Society
MRC	Miners' Rehabilitation Committee (formed in Alberta, 1954)
NDP	New Democratic Party
NES	National Employment Service
OAP	Old Age Pension
OAS	Old Age Security
PAA	Provincial Archives of Alberta
RCMP	Royal Canadian Mounted Police
TLC	Trades and Labour Congress (of Canada, 1883–1956)
UMWA	United Mine Workers of America
WCB	Workmen's [later Workers'] Compensation Board
WCBCOA	Western Canada Bituminous Coal Operators' Association (up to 1952)
WCC	West Canadian Collieries
WRF	Welfare and Retirement Fund (District 18, UMWA)

Maps

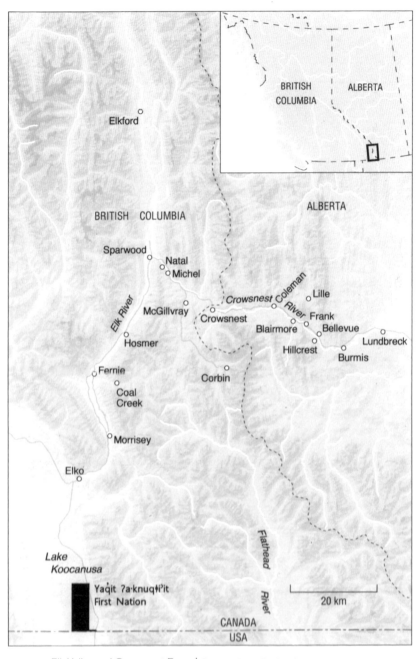

MAP 0.1 Elk Valley and Crowsnest Pass. | Cartography by Eric Leinberger.

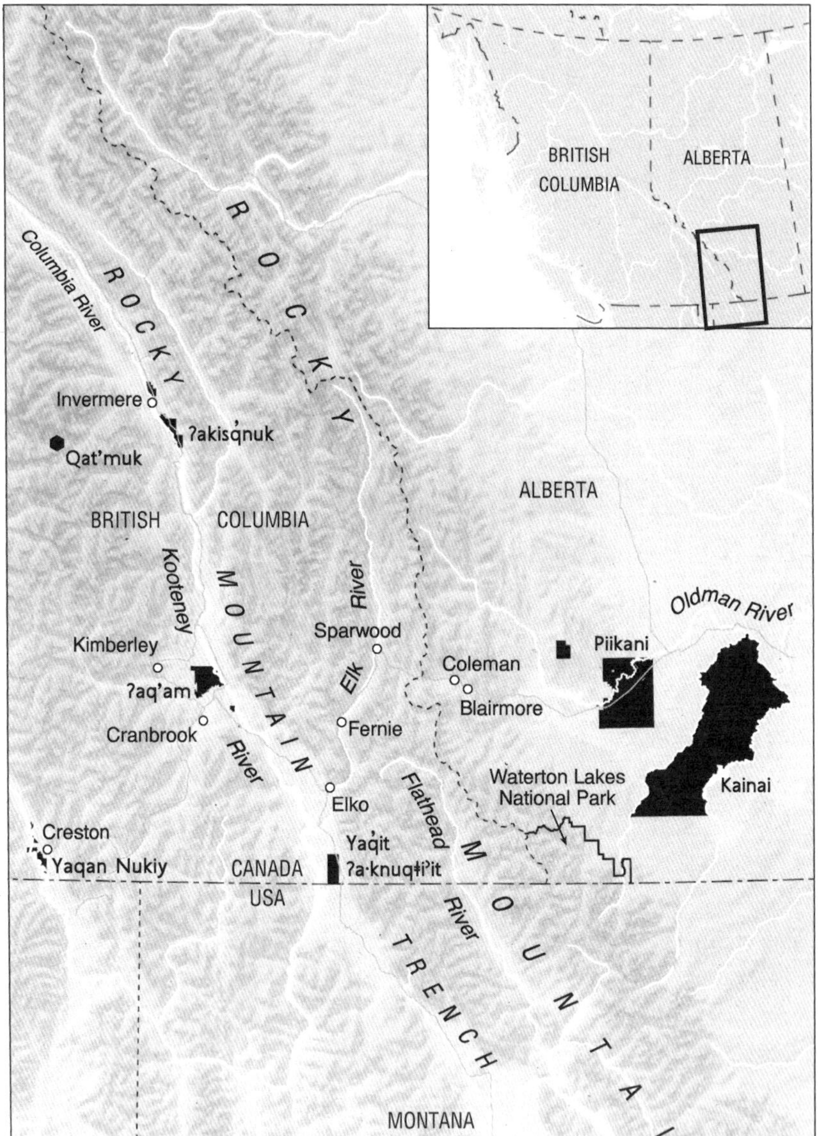

MAP 0.2 Southeastern British Columbia and Southwestern Alberta. | Cartography by Eric Leinberger.

THE LIGHTS ON THE
TIPPLE ARE GOING OUT

Introduction

*Interpretive and Comparative Perspectives on Deindustrialization
in the Crowsnest Pass and Elk Valley, 1945–68*

At the end of 1957, Robert Lilley was one of the leading citizens of Fernie,
a small city of about 3,000 residents nestled amid the Rocky Mountains
of southeastern British Columbia. The veteran coal miner was the elected
secretary-treasurer of Local 7310 of the United Mine Workers of America
(UMWA)[1] and sat as a Fernie alderman, having first been elected to city
council in late 1956 after running a campaign for which Local 7310 had
covered all expenses.[2] As an officer of his union local, Lilley worked with
a former secretary of the local and Fernie's elected provincial representative, Thomas Uphill, to raise working-class demands in the legislature
in Victoria, thereby garnering a small provincial profile. For example, in
March 1957, Uphill read a letter from Lilley in the legislature that called
on the government to continue compensation benefits after the age of
eighteen to children whose fathers had died in the mine.[3] Lilley's stature
as a union leader was significantly enhanced in November 1957 when the
president of the Calgary-based UMWA district that covered all of western Canada (District 18) appointed Lilley to the district's executive
board, representing Sub-District 8, which included the two UMWA
locals in the Elk Valley (at Fernie and Michel; see Map 0.1).[4]

Less than six years later, Lilley was featured on the front page of the
Fernie Free Press one last time. The shocking picture accompanying the
lead story of the 4 July 1963 issue is hard to fathom at first, but after
reading the caption it is clearly a body covered by a blanket lying in a
railway bed under the axle of a train car. The caption reads "the mangled
and broken body of former city alderman Bob Lilley is shown above,

FIGURE I.1 Elk River Colliery and incline to No. 9 mine, Coal Creek, British Columbia, 1958. | Photographer unknown. Courtesy of Fernie Museum and Archives, Image 1352 1.

beneath the cars and between the rails of a C.P.R. freight train minutes after he stepped onto the tracks in front of the oncoming locomotive." His suicide on 28 June 1963 was an event sure to capture the attention of the public: it occurred in the middle of the day near the passenger train station and involved a freight train carrying coal. Robert Lilley clearly had lost the will to live when he strode in front of the locomotive that day. Nevertheless, as I explain below, in the way that he ended his life, he seemed to be intent on making a final political statement: his suicide symbolized the death of Fernie as a trade union city sustained by the labour of hundreds of unionized underground coal miners. Lilley was among the ex-miners who, abandoned by their former employer and given only meagre assistance by governments and the UMWA, were unable to adjust to a new reality in which coal miners had become "yesterday's people."[5]

The mine entrances of Elk River Colliery (see Figure I.1), where Lilley had worked, were located just six kilometres outside Fernie, up the Coal Creek Valley (see Map 0.1). The closing of the colliery at the end of January 1958 came as a terrible surprise to everyone in Fernie, with the exception of the top officials of the coal company, Crow's Nest Pass Coal (CNPC), which had made the momentous decision. Fernie's citizens perhaps had been lulled to sleep by the fact that, despite the crisis in the western Canadian steam coal industry caused by the decision of the railway companies to rapidly convert their coal-powered steam locomotives to oil burners and to buy new diesel engines, the mines in the Elk Valley had maintained reasonably healthy production levels right through 1956. This was in contrast to the abysmal economic conditions in the Crowsnest Pass in Alberta, where coal production fell by 50 percent between 1952 and 1954 (see Figure I.2) and where four underground mines were shuttered between 1950 and 1956. Furthermore, the miners in Local 7310 had been disarmed about the possibility of a shutdown by the investments just made by CNPC in developing a new mine at Elk River Colliery – in late October 1957, it was already more than 1,200 feet into the side of the mountain, and a ventilation system and mechanical loaders had been installed.[6]

As secretary-treasurer of Local 7310, Robert Lilley was at the centre of the political struggles over employment rights that ensued after the closure was announced on 15 January 1958. CNPC's initial plan was to transfer most of Elk River Colliery's labour force to its operations at Michel, British Columbia, but in order to do so the company would have to lay off the 147 Alberta residents whom it had hired at Michel in recent years. The first story published by the *Fernie Free Press* on the mine

FIGURE I.2 Coal production, Crowsnest Pass and Elk Valley, 1939–59

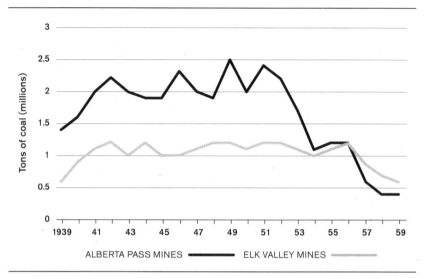

Based on data from Library and Archives Canada (hereafter LAC), RG 33/42, vol. 18, file Alberta Bituminous Coal, chart "Alberta Bituminous Coal Production by Colliery and District," and file British Columbia and Yukon, chart "British Columbia Coal Production by Collieries."

closure indicated that Lilley was "confident that company seniority would apply in transferring Elk River employees to their new jobs at Michel." District 18 officials immediately nixed this scheme, however, pointing out that the plan to displace the Alberta residents ran counter to the collective agreement since "Fernie men had no seniority" at Michel Collieries, a position supported a few days later by the Coal Operators' Association of Western Canada (COAWC).[7] Subsequently, without the authority to remove the 147 Alberta employees, CNPC immediately offered jobs at Michel to relatively few of the Elk River Colliery's workforce. As a result, overall employment at CNPC's operations in the Elk Valley declined by 270 people between 1957 and 1958 (995 to 725) and remained at the reduced level in 1959.[8]

The second employment rights case attempted to force CNPC to use seniority when hiring the limited number of Fernie miners that it needed at Michel. This matter quickly went before an independent arbitrator in Calgary. Lilley was one of the four UMWA leaders who argued that both agreement language and past precedent supported the view that "men with the longest term of service with the company in Elk River Colliery, Fernie, should be given preference of work" when the company was hiring at Michel. However, the arbitrator ruled that CNPC could "hire new men at Michel at its own discretion" since the collective agreement only allowed for the exercise of seniority rights across "mines in the same camp."[9]

The arbitrator's decision had a direct impact on Lilley, among the long-serving Fernie miners never hired at Michel Collieries. It also marked the beginning of the unravelling of his leadership role in the UMWA. Within three weeks, Lilley was bounced from the District Executive Board (DEB). The minutes of the next board meeting obliquely recorded the two events that sparked his removal: "President Boyd made an explanation to the Board as to board member Lilley's activities re the Independent Chairman while in Calgary and also the situation in which he was found in Fernie on our last visit to that district."[10]

Lilley was not the only Fernie resident to experience a personal crisis in the aftermath of the closure of Elk River Colliery. Another example appeared in the *Fernie Free Press* in early September 1959 after a fifty-four-year-old man was killed after throwing himself in front of a slow-moving Greyhound bus travelling through Fernie. A coroner's jury ruled the death a suicide after learning that the man was "depressed and reluctant to talk" when seen by a doctor a couple of hours before his death.[11] In contrast, Lilley apparently recovered from his crisis and setbacks in the spring of 1958. He carried on as secretary-treasurer of Local 7310, which still had a large membership, albeit mainly of retired and unemployed workers. Furthermore, in an unexpected development, he returned to coal mining in 1960 after the United States Steel Corporation signed a four-year option to buy the unworked coal lands of CNPC for $10 million, with a further option to buy Michel Collieries for $7 million. In the summer of 1960, Lilley was one of the handful of miners hired by the company to dig six exploratory tunnels. However, this prospecting work never turned into permanent employment since the United States Steel Corporation terminated its purchase option in late 1962 after running tests on the coking qualities of this coal at its Pennsylvania steel mills.[12]

Lilley maintained his involvement in Local 7310 at least until the final recorded membership meeting in 1961.[13] He also served a second stretch on city council after winning a by-election in May 1959. Unfortunately, his life went into a tailspin in the summer of 1961 after his wife died. Her death led him to resign from city council in the middle of a term and move to Kimberley, where his sister lived. Shortly afterward, the president of District 18 replaced Lilley as Local 7310's secretary-treasurer.[14]

Lilley eventually returned to Fernie during the first part of 1963. At that point, he no longer held any leadership position in the union or municipal government and was bereft of the support of family members in the city. Perhaps abuse of alcohol contributed to his suicide that fateful early summer day; nevertheless, his actions immediately prior to his death required physical coordination, determination, and purpose.

At about 1 p.m. on 28 June 1963, a train consisting of "two diesel units and six cars loaded with coal" was passing through Fernie. The *Fernie Free Press* reported on what transpired: "Gerald Armstrong, diesel engineer of the through freight, told police Lilley was about six railway car lengths away when he was first noticed heading directly into the path of the engine. Armstrong said he blew the whistle, rang the warning bell and applied the brakes, but the man stepped into the way of the oncoming locomotive." In the same ghoulish spirit as the photo on its front page, the paper added that, "although badly broken and mangled from the pushing and rolling beneath the engines and cars, the body remained untouched by the wheels and no limbs were severed."[15]

Perhaps Lilley was entirely oblivious of his surroundings when he stepped in front of the train engine, and therefore the fact that it was a coal train was irrelevant to the suicide, as was the fact that it occurred in a central location sure to attract public attention. Alternatively, perhaps there was political meaning in the details of his death. His life's downward spiral had begun with the sudden closure of Elk River Colliery in 1958 and the subsequent decision of the coal company to insist on its right to hire whomever it wanted at its Michel operation, thereby allowing it to sever ties with Fernie coal miners who had, for decade after decade, risked life and limb in the CNPC mines in the Coal Creek Valley. Coal mining and union leadership had been the heart of Lilley's public

life, and that life had been taken from Lilley by corporate fiat. Coal mining had also been the heart of Fernie's existence up to 1958, with the
miners' union being of sufficient economic and political power that
Fernie was widely seen as a trade union city. Lilley's suicide, if it truly
was a public performance, symbolized the death of Fernie as a union city
where miners' leaders had significant social stature. Lilley seemingly
chose a very public way to die to register his opposition to being "ren-
dered 'invisible'" by the closing of Elk River Colliery.[16]

The coverage in the *Fernie Free Press* of Robert Lilley's death occasioned the following letter to the editor from President Fred Dawson of
Local 7310:

> I was very much disappointed with the picture you had on the front
> page of your last week's *Free Press*.
>
> I think Bobby Lilley was entitled to a picture alright, but you
> could at least have put in a picture of him as a soldier (veteran of six
> years' service) or as an ex-alderman. Bob was also a good Miners'
> Union secretary-treasurer over a period of years and he has done a
> lot of good community work in Fernie.
>
> Many people feel as I do about this. After serving as a good cit-
> izen over a number of years the only picture he rated with your
> paper was a blanket and a pair of box car wheels.
>
> Hoping we do not see any more pictures of this kind, as relatives
> and friends don't like to see such things.

Joe Weber, who had run the *Fernie Free Press* since 1956 and therefore
would have been well aware of Lilley's past leadership roles in the city,
answered Dawson's letter by attempting to deflect the criticism: "While
we share to some extent Mr. Dawson's views regarding publication of
pictures such as appeared in last week's issue on the Lilley death, we did
so after all efforts to secure a 'living' picture had failed. City Hall had
none, neither had friends who were contacted. Relatives could have supplied a snapshot, but not in time for publication."[17] Of course, if it was
disrespectful and in poor taste to publish the picture of Lilley's body, the
fact that no alternative picture of Lilley was readily available does not in

any way lessen Weber's culpability. Furthermore, his editorial biases were unwittingly revealed when Weber admitted that his paper did not have on hand a photo of such an important working-class and community leader of the recent past.

The coverage in the *Fernie Free Press* of Lilley's suicide confirmed a marked change in Fernie's political dynamics in the immediate years after the closure of Elk River Colliery in 1958. It is my contention that, if Local 7310 had still been at the height of its powers (with an employed membership of more than 300 and active involvement in local and provincial political affairs), then Editor Weber might well have thought twice about antagonizing such a large mass of engaged readers. Publication of the photo, therefore, was confirmation of the death of Fernie as a trade union city where business elites stepped somewhat gingerly for fear of antagonizing a large, pro-union working class that pursued its interests through a number of local groups and initiatives, not least of which was Local 7310.

NOT YOUR EVERYDAY STORY OF MINE CLOSURES AND DEINDUSTRIALIZATION

In their sweeping historical study of the decline of the anthracite (hard coal) mining region of Pennsylvania, Thomas Dublin and Walter Licht stated that "the economic decline of coal-mining communities has been an international phenomenon across the twentieth century."[18] Whether precipitated by a major corporation's decision to switch from a coal-burning technology (as in the Crowsnest Pass and Elk Valley in the 1950s), competition from lower-cost coalfields, competition from alternative fuels such as natural gas, depletion of a particular mine's supply of readily mined coal, or a government's decision to reduce or eliminate subsidies for coal production, the decline of coalfield societies has usually proceeded rapidly, with devastating impacts on miners and their families, local businesses, and the social fabrics of once vibrant localities. Looked at from a broader perspective, closures of coal mines are instances of deindustrialization, understood as the loss of industrial employment and the long-term economic, social, and political consequences of that loss. Deindustrialization has long been a reality, or at least an ever-present worry, of life in primary resource communities.[19] More recently, it has swept through the former industrial heartland of North America as neo-liberal investment and trade policies have resulted in the shift in manufacturing many products, such as clothing and electronics, to the Global South. As a consequence, the eerie pictures of abandoned and crumbling North American factories found in recent books[20] replicate the sense of loss conveyed by images of abandoned surface buildings and equipment at coal mines shut down in the 1930s in Illinois or in the early 1960s in the Crowsnest Pass.[21]

Even the toll of psychological distress and suicide in Fernie after the closure of Elk River Colliery in 1958 is a familiar feature of other stories of deindustrialization. For instance, an early 1990s study of two Yorkshire, England, villages where coal mines had recently closed found that, "with a gradual loss of pride resulting from their inability to find a job, many former miners became isolated from former colleagues and friends ... Such men could not easily relinquish their 'breadwinner' status and struggled to cope with the collapse of their authority."[22] A second study contended that the winding down of coal mining in South Yorkshire transformed "communities characterized by cohesion and collectivity to ones signified by increasing disintegration."[23] Deindustrialization on a massive scale occurred in Youngstown, Ohio, between 1977 and 1982, when steel mill closures resulted in the loss of 50,000 jobs. The city's primary community mental health centre "saw a threefold increase in its caseload in the 1980s, with significant increases in depression, child and spouse abuse, drug and alcohol abuse, divorces, and suicide."[24] In the same vein, Steven High, in his analysis of the emotional impacts of job losses caused by the deindustrialization of manufacturing in North America, noted that "many plant shutdown stories are studded with references to marriage break-up, alcohol abuse, and suicide. Dorothy Fisher's fifty-nine-year-old husband attempted suicide three times and stopped eating, before dying of a heart attack six weeks after his Detroit plant closed."[25]

Despite the many points of similarity across multiple instances of deindustrialization, there is a pressing need for new, in-depth case studies of the phenomenon. At an analytical level, this is because of the complexity of deindustrialization: "Deindustrialization as an ongoing process of capitalism reveals itself in various iterations and elicits disparate responses in different contexts."[26] Furthermore, at the level of human interest, every closing of a mine, mill, or factory is deeply meaningful to those who lived through the hard times and struggles and to those with some sort of personal connection to the place and its inhabitants. For the current residents of the Crowsnest Pass and Elk Valley, and to the much larger diaspora living across western Canada and farther afield, the wave of underground mine closures in the years after the Second World War is of interest because it is such a significant element of many families' histories and resulted in deep and lasting changes throughout the region. As a researcher, I am similarly invested in the intrinsic features of this case through my immersion in documentary sources and interviews. I cannot help but write about these years of economic and social crisis without feeling a sense of responsibility to the coal miners and their families whose lives were turned upside down by the mine closures and who did their best to carry on and rebuild their lives. Nevertheless, this case study of deindustrialization also has multiple layers of sociological and political significance, and my goal in this book is to demonstrate that significance to readers who might not be able to find the Crowsnest Pass and Elk Valley on a map let alone have any personal connection to the area.

The focus of my research is captured in the book's subtitle: Fighting Economic Ruin in a Canadian Coalfield Community. I study the actions of groups that tried to keep mining alive in the Crowsnest Pass and Elk Valley, analyzing the successes and failures of different policy proposals, business initiatives, and political campaigns. I also study the actions of local business owners and different levels of government that strove to develop new economic foundations for the region. The "economic ruin" studied in this book is not restricted to what happens when there is no work for people; I also consider the "ruin" that results from low pay and few benefits, unsafe and unhealthy working environments, and the polluting of residential communities with coal dust, smoke, and sludge.

As an example of deindustrialization, what happened in the Crowsnest Pass and Elk Valley between 1945 and 1968 is distinctive and noteworthy for four main reasons. The first noteworthy element is that, coming out of the Second World War, the worker movement was exceptionally strong, anchored by five UMWA union locals; a number of working-class ethnocultural organizations; a long tradition of success in electing labour representatives to municipal councils, school boards, and even the BC legislature (where Thomas Uphill had been the Fernie District representative since 1920); and a left-internationalist commitment to solidarity with other worker movements that defied the stultifying nationalist ideology of the Cold War. Therefore, this case study allows us to interrogate the efficacy of the decisions made by labour leaders in the face of the crisis, assess the power of a strong worker movement to shape the course of events, and determine how that movement itself was changed as the economic crisis rapidly progressed. I address a number of specific questions. Why were there no contentious, collective protests in the Crowsnest Pass and Elk Valley similar to the underground occupation and subsequent hunger strike waged by coal miners in Decazeville, France, in 1961–62 in response to a plan to end all underground coal mining in the region?[27] Was there a backlash against the new immigrants recruited to work in the region's mines in the 1950s as production was cut back and as many veteran coal miners left the area in search of more stable employment or retired? As the economic crisis deepened throughout the 1950s and extended into the 1960s, how did the thinking and policy proposals of working-class leaders change? Which elements of the worker movement's "infrastructure of dissent"[28] attenuated during the crisis, and which elements persisted despite the hard times? Was internal union democracy negatively affected by the crisis and, if so, why? How did the "diverse connections and relations"[29] of the worker movement change between 1945 and 1968, in terms of both the networks internal to the region and the more far-reaching networks that connected Crowsnest Pass and Elk Valley miners and their organizations to workers elsewhere? How did the logic of working-class political action change – did the movement become more conservative and parochial during this crisis, an outcome that David Harvey suggests is inevitable whenever mines or factories are threatened by closure?[30]

The second noteworthy dimension of this case is the widespread support for the Communist Party of Canada (CPC, known as the Labor-Progressive Party [LPP] between 1943 and 1959) in the region. In the early 1930s, the town of Blairmore on the Alberta side of the Crowsnest Pass gained national notoriety because of its election of a pro-communist town council,[31] and Blairmore readily fits the category of a "Little Moscow," like the towns sprinkled across Western Europe in the inter-war years.[32] At the end of the Second World War, the Labor-Progressive Party had more electoral support than any other political party in the region; indeed, this was one of the few locales in Canada where support for the party exceeded that of its rival socialist party, the Cooperative Commonwealth Federation (CCF).

This study will show that the period of shrinking coal production and mine closures in the region occurred just after the Labor-Progressive Party rapidly started to lose its activist base because of Cold War pressures. Nevertheless, the party continued to play a role in the politics of deindustrialization until 1962. In tracing the fight against mine closures and economic ruin, I consider LPP contributions and contemplate how that fight might have been different if the party had maintained a robust capacity for political activism throughout the 1950s and into the 1960s.

Although the story of communist decline in this coalfield overlaps with and influences the larger story of the struggles over deindustrialization, it is significant in its own right, and I therefore analyze it in a separate chapter. The economic crisis in the steam coal industry aggravated the LPP political crisis, which in turn affected the capacity of the worker movement to respond to the economic crisis in creative and militant ways. This intertwining of crises provides a distinctive cast to the fight against mine closures.

The third noteworthy aspect of this deindustrialization is that it did not end with the total economic ruin of the region (an outcome that many residents and commentators feared in the late 1950s and early 1960s). Indeed, the story that I tell ends in 1968 with the sale of Michel Collieries and the coal-mining rights on surrounding land to the giant American firm Kaiser Steel. That company would invest $127.5 million in the late 1960s and early 1970s to develop a massive strip mine on a mountain ridge high above the historic mining villages of Natal and Michel after signing a long-term contract to sell metallurgical coal to Japanese steel companies.[33] This strip mine continues to produce metallurgical coal for the international market today, and it is one of the five strip mines that operated in southeastern British Columbia in the late twentieth century and the early twenty-first century.[34] Therefore, the closure of underground coal mines in the 1950s and early 1960s was followed by a reindustrialization in coal starting in the late 1960s, albeit with a much more capital-intensive process of production.

A twist to the reindustrialization of the region is that, although the only surviving coal company in the Alberta Pass, Coleman Collieries, signed a long-term contract with Japanese steelmakers at about the same time as Kaiser Steel, and developed new underground and strip mines to fulfill that contract, it eventually found itself unable to compete with the massive mountaintop-removal strip mines built just across the continental divide. Hence, Coleman Collieries ceased mining coal in 1980 and stopped processing thermal coal from its refuse (slack) piles in 1983.[35] Between 1983 and the time of writing (early 2023), the Alberta side of the Crowsnest Pass has been frozen in a no-mines/deindustrialized state, whereas the BC side of the region has seen the production of hundreds of millions of tons of coal. Hence, this is an unusual case of deindustrialization because, whereas one part of the original coalfield has endured an economic malaise for decades, the other part has enjoyed a robust revival that has erased memories of the economic depression of the 1950s and early 1960s.

The fourth noteworthy element of this case involves the contrasting responses from the three major governments to the declining coal industry and mine closures: the Alberta government adopted a laissez-faire, "let-the-market-decide" approach to the crisis, whereas the federal and BC governments supported the coal industry in different ways for a number of years. This study will detail how each of the three governments approached the mid-twentieth-century coal crisis as well as the end results of their respective approaches. This historical analysis has contemporary relevance since the proper response of governments to economic crises and major business failures is an ongoing matter of policy debate. A key question that I investigate here is why did Alberta's Social

Credit government refuse to introduce production subsidies or transportation subventions for the Crowsnest Pass coal industry in the 1950s and 1960s? Specifically, was Alvin Finkel correct to assert that Premier Ernest Manning sought to dismantle a worker movement that had been a thorn in the side of the Social Credit government since the late 1930s,[36] or was the Manning government's commitment to free-market orthodoxy so deep that subsidies for a struggling industry were anathema?

A CONTEXT FOR INTERPRETATION: RESISTING MINE CLOSURES AND ECONOMIC RUIN IN OTHER COALFIELDS

In this book, I investigate the fight against mine closures and economic ruin in a single coalfield. Although I provide a great deal of historical detail, my research logic is interpretive rather than descriptive; indeed, my goals are to highlight the noteworthy sociological and political dimensions of this historical case and to answer the attendant research questions. I make no attempt to systematically compare this single case to other cases, either to identify common features across the numerous fights against mine closures or to understand the factors that explain the diversity of outcomes of those fights.[37] Nevertheless, in sorting through what occurred in the Crowsnest Pass and Elk Valley and coming to interpretive conclusions, I have been influenced by a number of studies from around the world of how the residents of coalfield societies grappled with production cuts and mine closures. I concur with historian Stefan Berger that "only comparisons can help us to establish whether there were alternatives to the processes and developments which characterised the history of any one specific industrial region."[38]

In this section, I highlight five other coalfields that experienced deindustrialization, for the events in each have raised issues and caused me to question and dig deeper into what transpired in the Crowsnest Pass and Elk Valley between 1945 and 1968. Two of the comparative cases parallel the Crowsnest Pass and Elk Valley in experiencing mine closures in the 1950s and 1960s but then rebounding in the late 1960s and 1970s with new sales of metallurgical coal to Japanese steelmakers. These coalfields are in Alabama and the Australian state of Queensland. In Alabama, the number of coal miners fell from 22,000 in 1945 to 7,800 in 1960. In the coal towns in the Birmingham District in the 1950s, historian Robert Woodrum asserted, "many residents had to choose between remaining and living in dire poverty or leaving the region altogether. While UMWA members who remained underground enjoyed high wages and benefits, miners who lost jobs were transformed into a coalfield underclass ... By the mid-1950s, thousands of people who were physically able simply gave up and left the region."[39]

An important aspect of deindustrialization in the Alabama coalfield is that African American miners had a much higher rate of job loss than white miners. Woodrum argued that the UMWA bears considerable responsibility for this development. For one thing, the union "deferred to custom" and allowed companies to hire and promote only whites to operate underground coal-cutting machines while allowing strip mine operators to hire only whites to operate heavy equipment. Indeed, the UMWA in Alabama had a seniority system restricted to job classifications, meaning that long-seniority African American members who had manually mined coal had no rights to move into the new classifications created by the mechanization of production.[40] The racist hiring and laying off practices facilitated by the UMWA in Alabama in the 1950s provoke two lines of inquiry. First, were the exclusions of Indigenous people, Japanese Canadians, and Chinese Canadians from mine employment in the Crowsnest Pass and Elk Valley in the years after the Second World War facilitated by union locals that "deferred to custom" in mine hiring practices instead of standing up for the civil rights of racialized groups subjected to discrimination? Second, to what extent was the typical miner in the 1950s and 1960s operating with a conventional Anglo-Canadian identity rather than a European-cosmopolitan identity that would have facilitated a more progressive and internationalist outlook?

In the Alabama coalfield, the first long-term contract to supply metallurgical coal to Japanese steelmakers was signed by Drummond Coal in the late 1960s,[41] around the same time as Kaiser Steel signed its long-term contract to ship Elk Valley coal to Japan. A parallel process of reindustrialization took place in the Queensland coalfield in Australia in the mid- to late 1960s, spearheaded by a joint venture between the American firm

Utah Construction and the Japanese corporation Mitsubishi that developed a number of open-pit mines along with a new port facility and rail transport system.[42]

New open-pit mines in Queensland ended more than a decade of deindustrialization. At its peak in 1954, employment in the underground coal industry in Queensland was 3,700; by 1967, however, it had decreased to 1,500.[43] The historical underground coal industry in Queensland paralleled that in the Crowsnest Pass and Elk Valley in the important role of communists in union leadership. Yet, unlike in the Crowsnest Pass region, communists continued to play an important role in the Queensland Collieries Employees Union into the 1960s and led an ambitious political program against underground mine closures that included "stay-down" occupations of mines slated for closure and the organization of labour-community coalitions to fight deindustrialization.[44] This divergence forces me to reassess the staying power of the worker and socialist movements as the coal crisis roiled the Crowsnest Pass and Elk Valley.

The third comparison is the Panther Valley, Pennsylvania, located at the northern edge of Appalachia. During the first half of the twentieth century, the built environment of the Panther Valley somewhat resembled that of the Crowsnest Pass: a series of mining villages and towns strung out close to one another along the valley floor, each located near a mine opening or coal breaker.[45] The fight against mine closures and economic ruin was drawn out since the decline in anthracite production in Pennsylvania began just after the First World War and continued for the entire century; by 1990, production was a mere 3.4 percent of that in 1917.[46]

During the successive decades of deepening coal deindustrialization, many schemes were hatched to build alternative economic foundations. Therefore, this case is particularly useful as a comparison when considering the parallel schemes for economic renewal in the Crowsnest Pass and Elk Valley in the 1950s and 1960s. Small-business owners and chambers of commerce headed the efforts to reindustrialize the Panther Valley, although the working class was sometimes mobilized in support. Nevertheless, the low pay, lack of union representation, and insecurity of the jobs at newly recruited firms became key elements of a counternarrative among Panther Valley workers "that reveals the resentment that built up over decades of industrial development efforts that did little to stop economic decline."[47] In their daily lives, workers experienced how the sacrifice of worker and community rights was part of the bargain in recruiting new industries.

The struggle against mine closures came to a head in the Panther Valley in 1954 when Lehigh Coal and Navigation (LCN) shut down all its mines and breakers to put pressure on the UMWA and its six union locals in the valley to agree to a rationalization plan that aimed to eliminate 1,000 jobs. Tamaqua Local 1571 rejected the LCN plan, however, and called for equal sharing of the available work, a system that had been practised in the 1930s. After the Tamaqua local set up picket lines to prevent a return to work on the company's terms, Lehigh Coal and Navigation closed all of its mining operations, although it later leased some of its coal facilities to two new companies that operated for the balance of the 1950s. One of the new companies was even bankrolled by the UMWA to the sum of $5 million, although it too closed in 1960 because the markets for anthracite continued to shrink.[48] These events inspired three questions when thinking about my research. First, why did nothing like the Tamaqua local's militancy emerge in the Crowsnest Pass and Elk Valley in the 1950s? Second, how did political differences among UMWA locals become manifest, and did these differences ever adversely affect the fight against mine closures? Third, did the UMWA's Washington leaders offer assistance to mining families in the Crowsnest Pass and Elk Valley that approached the $5 million investment made by the union in the Panther Valley?

The final two cases are European, the first being the Aubin coal basin in south-central France, usually referred to by the name of its major town, Decazeville. The three comparative cases already introduced had privately owned coal mines (although prior to 1963 there were a few state-owned mines in Queensland[49]). In comparison, the mines in Decazeville had been nationalized immediately after the Second World War,[50] and this meant that the fight against mine closures and economic ruin focused on the central government and state bureaucrats to a much greater extent than in the Crowsnest Pass and Elk Valley, where three privately owned coal companies remained in business throughout the years of decline in the 1950s. This contrast raises two questions. Did nationalization of the mines change the economic and political reasoning behind the decisions to close them? Were the workers in the state-owned mines in Decazeville accorded greater rights and better treatment than the workers in the Crowsnest Pass and Elk Valley and, if so, why?

Throughout the 1950s, capital was invested in new heavy machinery for the open-pit mines in Decazeville, but the underground mines were not modernized, thus causing coal from those mines to become increasingly uncompetitive. During these years, the Socialist Party parliamentary deputy from Decazeville, Paul Ramadier, fought for the establishment of a new steel plant in the area but also encouraged unemployed workers to migrate to other parts of France.[51] Tellingly, he clashed with the French Communist Party over its proposal to modernize an early-twentieth-century fertilizer factory because it was a major consumer of locally produced coke. "We are dying at Decazeville," argued Ramadier, "because we want to cling with a death grip to old machines and old methods."[52] Understanding this policy conflict in Decazeville will help us to appreciate the logic behind how different groups thought the crisis in the coal industry in the Crowsnest Pass and Elk Valley could be overcome.

In 1960, the state-owned coal company, Les Charbonnages de France, proposed closing all underground coal mines in Decazeville while preserving some open-pit production capacity. This plan was realized by 1966, at which time a labour force of over 2,500 had been reduced to fewer than 500.[53] This program of closures occasioned highly contentious protests by workers and widespread regional political support, as seen in the mass resignation of 307 mayors, road blockades by peasant farmers, and a general strike on 26 January 1962. Such opposition won significant concessions from the government, including the extension of partial pension benefits to miners aged fifty to fifty-five who lost their jobs.[54] The militancy of workers and their allies in Decazeville, like the militancy of the UMWA's Tamaqua local in the Panther Valley and of the Queensland Collieries Employees Union, raises the question of why such militancy never emerged in the Crowsnest Pass and Elk Valley. Follow-up counterfactual questions are: Would worker militancy along the lines of an underground occupation of a mine have gained similar levels of sympathy and active support in western Canada as observed in south-central France in 1962? Would contentious protest actions have had any hope of changing the course of events in the Crowsnest Pass and Elk Valley?

The final comparison is the Rhondda in Wales, encompassing the large coalfield society that populated the side-by-side mountain valleys, Rhondda Fawr (large) and Rhondda Fach (small).[55] The distance from the point where the two valleys intersect, and the nearby port city of Cardiff, is only twenty-five kilometres. The Rhondda therefore had a geographic advantage in efforts to attract and keep replacement industries as mines closed – a distinctive contrast to the Crowsnest Pass and Elk Valley, where economic recruitment efforts were limited by geographic isolation.

The Rhondda was a densely populated coalfield, particularly during and just after the First World War because of the wartime expansion of production for the British navy. In 1921, the population of the two valleys was an extraordinary 163,000. As in the Panther Valley, the Rhondda experienced a prolonged, although irregular, trajectory of coal deindustrialization from 1920 to the end of the twentieth century.[56] Furthermore, the Rhondda is another coalfield society in which the communist movement was very strong during the interwar years[57] and therefore serves as an instructive contrast when mapping the strength of the communist movement in the Crowsnest Pass and Elk Valley prior to the onset of the Cold War.

Both because the Rhondda has been thoroughly studied by social scientists and because it has inspired a rich body of fiction that brings to light often hidden dimensions of life in coalfield societies, it has been especially influential in guiding my research. Indeed, two important themes owe their elaboration to work connected to the Rhondda coalfield. The first theme involves gender, a subject often taken for granted and therefore hidden from view in the documentary record of the 1950s and 1960s. In a comparison of South Wales with two other European regions with radical twentieth-century histories, Emilia in Italy and Provence in France, Philip Cooke argued, "the most notable feature shared in common by the three supposedly radical regions which I have examined is the ubiquity of patriarchy and the generally reactionary character of gender relations within them."[58] Stefan Berger arrived at a similar understanding when comparing the South Wales and Ruhr coalfield societies, noting that women were rarely present in the public sphere in either region, including in recreation and associational life. "Working-class cultures in the Ruhr and South Wales were heavily male dominated," concluded Berger, "and the ideology of 'separate spheres' was strongly entrenched in both areas."[59]

Working-class women's disadvantaged status in the Rhondda and other mining valleys in South Wales was indicated by a "death rate among women [that] lay far above that for men (as a result of frequent births, attempted abortions, or simply never getting a rest from the heavy burdens of housekeeping)."[60] This is an extraordinary statistic given the high fatality rate of underground miners. Rhys Davies grew up in the Rhondda and captured the drudgery, stress, relentlessness, and anonymity of the labour of a miner's wife in the short story "Nightgown."[61] The protagonist in the story, a fittingly nameless wife, works from dawn until well into the evening to look after the needs of her husband, Walt, and five sons, all underground coal miners. She literally dies from overwork and is able to gain a measure of dignity and individuality only in death – she is buried in a silk nightgown that she had managed to pay for by surreptitiously squeezing a few coins out of each week's household budget over the course of a year.

Women in the Rhondda might also be faced with physical violence by men, as represented in two other works of fiction. The novel *Flame and Slag*, set between the late 1950s and 1967, alludes to the routine character of violence against women in this coalfield society.[62] Meanwhile, a second short story by Rhys Davies depicts the sexual assault of a wife by her miner husband. The intensity of the violence in this story is shocking, although like most violence against women in coalfield societies it was totally hidden from public view.[63]

These reflections on women's subordination in the Rhondda inspire a number of questions about gender relations in the Crowsnest Pass and Elk Valley. How did women's experiences change during the era of underground mine closures? As more married women joined the labour force in the 1960s, was there any backlash? What is known about the extent of the violence against women during these years? To what extent were women relegated to the margins of the worker movement? Is this historical movement a flawed exemplar for worker movements of the present and future because it was so male dominated?

The second theme inspired by my reading on the Rhondda is the connection between a cosmopolitan working-class culture and the left-internationalist politics of a worker movement. A newspaper story on the Rhondda in 1897, after a period of rapid expansion of coal production and employment, opined that "we are very much of the belief that every nation under the sun ... has its representatives in one of the Rhonddas. If there is any virtue in a mixture of blood, the future Rhonddaite will, verily, be a fine specimen of humanity, perfectly cosmopolitan in his composition and world wide in his aspirations."[64] More than a century later, Stefan Berger argued that a cosmopolitan working-class culture emerged in South Wales, where "a comparatively unproblematic integration of 'foreigners' took place."[65] However, another important part of social life in the Rhondda was a pre-existing Welsh culture and a politicized Welsh identity. Therefore, the cosmopolitan working-class culture of the Rhondda was articulated with a Welsh culture of struggle and celebration that stretched many centuries into the pre-industrial past.

According to Stephen Knight, Rhys Davies believed "that the best of the modern Welsh political resistance ... in some way goes back to a native Welsh tradition that has been expressed in poetry and music, but has also, crucially, been resistant to the invaders of this anciently self-conscious region."[66] This implies that "modern strikers are linked back to the Welsh who resisted English military invasions, rather than connecting their attitudes with those of other workers of the modern world."[67]

The partial Welshness of the Rhondda was an inescapable part of daily life, given the widespread use of the Welsh language, the popularity of traditional Welsh cultural forms, and the agitation of the Welsh nationalist party, Plaid Cymru, beginning in 1925. Cultural theorist Raymond Williams grew up in Wales in the 1920s and 1930s. He argued

that native Welsh traditions were recurrently invoked in the consciousness of the residents of coalfield societies in South Wales by the distinctive geography of the valleys. Although coal mining created an "almost
invariably dark, smoke-ridden, huddled" atmosphere in which residents
lived on the valley floors, they had merely to look up to see a "profoundly
different yet immediately accessible landscape of open hills and the sky
above them." Those "open hills" frequently revealed grazing sheep.
This pastoral life, according to Williams, "is a shape which manifests
not only a consciousness of history but [also] a consciousness of alternatives, and then, in a modern form, a consciousness of aspirations and
possibilities."[68]

To the extent that Davies and Williams are correct, the worker movement in the Rhondda had nationalist roots that made it different from
the worker movement in the Crowsnest Pass and Elk Valley, where a
cosmopolitan working-class society had to find its way in a settler-
colonial context that misrepresented or ignored Indigenous history.
Indeed, by the time that settlers flooded into the region, first to build a
new branch line for the Canadian Pacific Railway (CPR) in 1897–98 and
then to work in the booming coal-mining industry that followed, the
Indigenous inhabitants had been relegated to reserves (shown in relationship to the Crowsnest Pass and Elk Valley on Map 0.2), legally
circumscribed by the Indian Act of 1876, and subjected to intrusive, de-
meaning, and sometimes abusive treatment by many government officials and Christian missionaries. The colonial subordination of the
Ktunaxa in southeastern British Columbia and two Niitsitapi (Blackfoot)
nations, the Piikani and Kainai, in southwestern Alberta persisted with
little relief well into the twentieth century and explains why Indigenous
peoples are largely absent from the events analyzed in this book.
However, recent rulings by Canadian courts and determined political
struggles by Indigenous groups and their allies have advanced a decol-
onizing process that is a vital element of Canadian politics in the twenty-
first century; this includes initiatives in the Crowsnest Pass and Elk
Valley to envision and build sustainable economic alternatives to a metallurgical coal industry whose lifespan will be truncated by innovations in
steelmaking stimulated by the climate emergency. I further sketch the

colonial context of this history in the next section. I return to present-day decolonization initiatives in the concluding chapter.

This brings us to the final set of research questions, developed from contrasting the anti-imperialist nationalism that coexisted with the development of a coalfield society in South Wales to the oppressive settler colonialism that framed the coalfield society created in the Crowsnest Pass and Elk Valley. Was left internationalism as strong a political current in the Crowsnest Pass and Elk Valley as in the Rhondda? To what extent did the left-internationalist tendencies in each worker movement grow out of a cosmopolitanism that formed by necessity because of diverse streams of labour recruitment into the coal mines? How was left politics in the Crowsnest Pass and Elk Valley ultimately different from that in the Rhondda on account of the nationalist cultural elements and a common sense of national injustice found in the Rhondda versus settlers' obliviousness of the rich Indigenous history of the Canadian region?

KTUNAXA, PIIKANI, AND KAINAI

Map 0.2 locates the four reserves of the Ktunaxa in southeastern British Columbia and the reserves of the Kainai and Piikani in southwestern Alberta in relation to the Crowsnest Pass and Elk Valley. David Thompson's journal entries from the early 1800s indicate that Ktunaxa regularly crossed the continental divide to hunt bison on the prairies, and Piikani were frequently encountered as far west as the Rocky Mountain Trench that separates the more westerly Purcell Mountains from the Rockies; hence, the traditional territories of both the Ktunaxa and Niitsitapi include the Crowsnest Pass and adjoining Elk Valley, one of the easier routes through the mountains.[69] The Ktunaxa never signed a treaty with Canadian authorities, explicitly refused to cede their traditional territory, and were coerced into moving onto the three reserves located in the Rocky Mountain Trench in the late 1880s under military threat by the Royal North West Mounted Police, D Division, headed by Sam Steele.[70] Kainai and Piikani leaders were among the signatories to Treaty 7 in 1877; based upon the testimony of Niitsitapi elders in the twentieth century, those leaders understood it to be a peace treaty rather than capitulation to the Canadian state.[71] In 1996, Walter Hildebrandt concluded that,

> by accommodating the newcomers, the Aboriginal people hoped to work out an arrangement to share the land so that both sides could benefit from living side by side. They could not have known that the newcomers expected more than a commitment to share the land, that in fact they wanted to take what they could, even if it meant disregarding the treaties.[72]

Hence, despite signing Treaty 7, the Kainai and Piikani, like the Ktunaxa, did not agree to being left out of decisions on future uses of their ancestral territories, but this is exactly what happened during development of the coal-mining industry in the Crowsnest Pass and Elk Valley. Their "right to benefit from their land[s] and decide how their lands should be used or not used" is enduring.[73]

Traditionally, the Ktunaxa, Piikani, and Kainai lived in kin-ordered societies involving subsistence production for use.[74] Over the eighteenth and nineteenth centuries, their lives were progressively disrupted as first mercantile capitalists and then industrial capitalists targeted the natural resources in their territories as sources of wealth, and the colonial settlement of the continent gained irresistible momentum. Beginning with smallpox epidemics in the latter half of the 1700s, recurring outbreaks of deadly infectious diseases resulted in distressing episodes of high mortality. Furthermore, securing the main sources of subsistence – bison on the prairies, fish and game in the mountains – became more difficult after the mid-1800s, culminating in the virtual disappearance of the bison in 1879 and the deaths by starvation of many Niitsitapi over the next few years.[75] In addition, after American merchants opened trading posts in southwestern Alberta, the alcohol that they bartered for bison hides profoundly disrupted the social cohesion of the Niitsitapi. "The early 1870s were years of alcohol, fear and bloodshed," noted Hugh Dempsey in his biography of Kainai Chief Red Crow.[76] On the other side of the Rockies, the Ktunaxa had to contend with a wave of 400 fortune seekers in 1864 after the discovery of gold in the Wild Horse River near present-day Cranbrook. "Ktunaxa people remember what happened when the first settlers came and what came after," Sean MacPherson wrote in his recent master's thesis. "They remember a people hungry for gold and land who fought, stole, burned homes and in some cases, murdered Ktunaxa people."[77] Matters came to a head in 1887 when twenty-five armed Ktunaxa led by Chief Isadore freed a Ktunaxa man from jail because they believed that he had been unjustly arrested for the murder of a settler. This precipitated intervention by the Royal North West Mounted Police, which in turn led to the Ktunaxa's pressured move to reserves.[78] Consequently, at the end of the nineteenth century, the Ktunaxa "were left with modest tracts of poor land that were insufficient to sustain the horses and cattle they had owned in 1884,"[79] whereas most of the land and resources in their traditional territory was controlled by the government, corporations, or new settlers. The same catastrophe had befallen the Piikani and Kainai.

As historian John Lutz has noted, prior to the influx of settler-colonists into British Columbia that followed completion of the first transcontinental railway in 1885, it was Indigenous labour "that allowed the rapid creation of an economic base, from the fur trade, to coal mining, saw-milling, and salmon canning." Thereafter, however, Indigenous people were "washed out of the capitalist economy"; indeed, "as the supply of white labour grew, 'white preference' pushed Aboriginal People out of the skilled and semi-skilled jobs, and they were increasingly confined by racialized European beliefs, which held that 'Indians' were barely suitable for menial work."[80] This racist logic of "white preference" ruled out Ktunaxa, Piikani, and Kainai from consideration for permanent jobs in the new coal mines in the Elk Valley and Crowsnest Pass at the turn of the century. Furthermore, even the two reserves on Map 0.2 closest to the coal seams in the Crowsnest Pass region are sufficiently distant that Piikani or Yaqit ʔaꞏknuqⱡiꞏit men could not be mobilized readily in the case of a temporary labour shortage at the mines.

During the decades that followed the devastating changes at the end of the nineteenth century, the Ktunaxa, Piikani, and Kainai struggled to preserve their cultures while developing what Lutz calls a "moditional" economy that combined available seasonal wage labour, business ventures such as cattle ranching and freighting, subsistence hunting and gathering, and government support.[81] The moditional economy of the Kainai in the late 1800s and early 1900s included a number of successful business ventures, as documented by historian Keith Regular.[82] However, bad faith by government officials hindered Kainai economic progress, and this was recognized in 2019 and 2021 when the Kainai secured two $150 million settlements for government mismanagement of their cattle and failure to supply the cattle promised in Treaty 7.[83]

Moving ahead to the middle of the twentieth century, a study of the Kootenay Indian Agency found that only thirty-three Ktunaxa held conventional full-time employment as farm operators, farm workers, loggers, or sawmill workers. Rather, most survived in a moditional economy that included small-scale agriculture, subsistence hunting and fishing ("game is particularly plentiful and easily available to Indians here, and they rely upon it for food far more than do Indians in most other agencies"), transfer payments from different levels of the Canadian state as well as Ktunaxa band councils, winter employment on reserve land harvesting Christmas trees or logging, handicraft production for commercial sale, and seasonal migration of entire families to the United States to harvest fruit. Harvesting fruit was "almost the sole source of employment and cash income" for most Ktunaxa. Furthermore, the band councils raised money by leasing reserve land to neighbouring agriculturalists for grazing.[84]

The ingenuity, adaptability, and diverse skills required to make this moditional economy function are admirable. The authors of the study emphasized the negative, however, stating that "unemployment, or underemployment, is proportionately more prevalent in Kootenay than in any other agency." They blamed Ktunaxa work habits and unwillingness to travel for work for this situation[85] instead of highlighting the significant constraints, including poor reserve land and persistent racist stereotyping, that blocked Ktunaxa from getting ahead in white-dominated markets (e.g., the labour market for coal workers in Elk Valley) and be full participants in white-dominated social settings. Ktunaxa elders interviewed by Sean MacPherson remembered the everyday racism that they experienced in Cranbrook in the mid-twentieth century. One recalled that the only place that her family could get served a meal was at a Chinese restaurant – and then only behind a curtain at the back of the establishment.[86] In sum, during the period 1945–68 investigated in this book, there were still impermeable colonial barriers to Ktunaxa, Piikani, and Kainai participation in the coal industry in the Crowsnest Pass and Elk Valley, either as wage labourers or as First Nations with abiding interests in the future of their traditional territories.

CHAPTER PREVIEWS

After the Second World War, the coal industry in the Crowsnest Pass and Elk Valley boomed for a few years, with production cresting in 1949. Chapter 1 sets the stage for the story of mine closures that begins in the early 1950s; it sketches changes in the coal industry between 1945 and 1949 and the push of workers and their organizations for economic advancement and a louder political voice.

The first wave of the crisis caused by the CPR decision to phase out coal-powered steam engines for locomotion hit in 1953 and 1954; in just two years, production at the Alberta coal mines in the Crowsnest Pass fell by 50 percent. Chapter 2 first describes the contours of life in the Crowsnest Pass and Elk Valley in the early 1950s and how the coal companies restructured their operations in anticipation of declining orders for railway steam coal. It then investigates how the operators, different levels of government, UMWA locals, and District 18 responded to the crisis in 1953–54. The central question addressed is why was the workers' fight against this wave of production cutbacks and mine closures not more energetic and militant?

The second wave of the crisis was more brutal than the first, and there was a widespread fear that the once vibrant communities in the region would become ghost towns. Chapter 3, covering events between 1957 and 1962, documents the economic devastation caused by the end of CPR purchases of steam coal and analyzes the logic and efficacy of the responses of various groups. It focuses on how the worker movement, weakened and divided, lost its sense of political mission and on how local business and political elites mobilized growth coalitions to see whether new industries and public institutions could be established to replace some of the lost economic activity.

By 1962, the deindustrialization crisis that had been ongoing for about a decade had resulted in a massive loss of jobs, economic output, and population in the Crowsnest Pass and Elk Valley. That year marked the end of the road for the Communist Party of Canada as a significant force in the region's political life after the two local labour/political leaders most closely associated with the party died: former MLA Thomas Uphill (a party sympathizer) and Michel Local 7292 secretary-treasurer Sam English (an election candidate in 1953). The bulk of Chapter 4 analyzes the three stages of the ruin of the party between 1946 and 1962 and how it was intertwined with struggles over deindustrialization.

Chapter 5 examines how various initiatives to rebuild the economic base of the region and avoid economic ruin panned out between 1963 and 1968. It concentrates on the most successful of these initiatives: a Phillips Cables factory just west of Coleman that began manufacturing wire and cable in 1966 and the push of Coleman Collieries and CNPC to develop new mines and lower production costs in order to convince their Japanese customers to commit to long-term contracts. The chapter analyzes the unequal distribution of harms and benefits resulting from expanding economic activity, concentrating on the workplace. One consequence of pell-mell growth in the mining industry was the coal dust explosion in the brand new Balmer North mine at Michel Collieries on 3 April 1967 that killed fifteen miners and seriously injured ten others.

The first part of Chapter 6 continues the story of the disparities in the costs of economic growth between 1963 and 1968, examining how the drive to increase the production of metallurgical coal created significant environmental hazards, particularly for people living close to coal production facilities. The problems of pollution were particularly dire in Natal and Michel because CNPC prioritized business expansion and diversification ahead of environmental stewardship and human well-being. Faced with an intolerable situation, the residents agreed to an urban renewal plan that promised to relocate everyone to Sparwood. A delay in implementing this plan and increased pollution, however, caused great suffering and anxiety. By 1967, a community environmental justice movement had taken shape and managed to reinstate the plan for a move to Sparwood, although the delay plus a reneging on promises by the BC government meant that half of the residents of Natal and Michel ended up moving elsewhere. The second part of Chapter 6 turns to political dimensions of the fight against economic ruin. It identifies political limitations in the Fernie Chamber of Commerce's efforts to promote economic growth and how workplace and community struggles centred on the costs of growth contributed to provincial NDP electoral wins on either side of the provincial boundary in 1966.

This case study of deindustrialization, covering a span of just over two decades in the middle of the twentieth century, is guided by the numerous sociological and political questions posed earlier in this introduction. I return to these questions in the conclusion, organizing my discussion under three headings: "The Worker Movement," "The State," and "Left Politics." I conclude the study by collating the lessons from this fight against mine closures and economic ruin with lessons from other struggles against deindustrialization and the inspiring campaign by the Haida Nation in recent decades to assert Aboriginal title to and significant control over its traditional territory on the Haida Gwaii archipelago. The Haida example could well become a template for efforts to build sustainable, rural, regional economies throughout Canada since First Nations such as the Ktunaxa, Piikani, and Kainai can be expected to likewise assert Aboriginal title and strive to fully participate in decisions on the futures of their traditional territories. Building reconciliation between Indigenous peoples and settlers in twenty-first-century Canada will entail complex and contentious decisions on the use of natural resources and the place of corporate capitalist resource companies in economies designed for long-term sustainability.

In a curious twist, the lessons from the fight against mine closures and economic ruin detailed in this book are likely to be relevant to the immediate future of the Crowsnest Pass and Elk Valley since another round of deindustrialization has appeared on the horizon. One source of the looming crisis will be the adoption of technologies such as self-driving trucks that will significantly reduce the number of jobs at the strip mines on mountain ridges. More importantly, the climate crisis and the drive to lower the emission of carbon dioxide from the manufacture of steel have inspired technological innovations that seem to be certain to render obsolete the traditional coal-dependent, integrated blast furnace/basic oxygen furnace method of producing steel from iron ore.[87] In just a few years, some steel plants, such as ArcelorMittal Dofasco in Hamilton, Ontario, will transition from coal and coke to natural gas and electricity as feedstocks.[88] Furthermore, over the next two to three decades, it is anticipated that many steel plants will adopt a nearly emission-free process of production: iron ore will be directly reduced using green hydrogen (manufactured using renewable energy to electrolyze water), and electric arc furnaces will be powered by green electricity. As decarbonized technologies for steelmaking spread, the demand for metallurgical coal will fade, and coal mines will close.[89]

"The lights on the tipple are going out" was the memorable warning issued by Alberta Cabinet Minister Gordon Taylor in 1960.[90] Tipples – the above-ground, multistorey structures where coal is sorted, cleaned, and loaded onto railway cars – are the visually striking, noisy, and dust-producing markers of an operating mine. A dark and quiet tipple is a sign of a mine in trouble. In 1960, Taylor, like his Social Credit colleagues in the government of Premier Ernest Manning, blamed the federal government for not doing more "to assure a larger market in Canada for Canadian coal" and thereby keeping the lights lit on at least a few tipples. This book shows that saving a coalfield society from economic ruin in the 1960s required a much more innovative mix of policies than that envisioned by a Manning government interested more in scoring political points than in nurturing regional economic opportunities. Even more inventive policies will be needed in the twenty-first century as the decarbonization of steel production in Asia shrinks the demand, little by little, for coal from the Elk Valley, and efforts to create a new, sustainable, regional economy must engage with the Ktunaxa, Piikani, and Kainai while charting a path of decolonization.

CHAPTER ONE

The Working Class on the Rise

Collective Struggles, Labour Improvements, and Larger Goals, 1945–49

The Second World War revived the coal industry in the Crowsnest Pass and Elk Valley, resulting in growth in yearly production of over 50 percent compared with 1939 (see Figure I.2). However, as the war was winding down, there was a degree of uncertainty about the prospects for coal mining in the region. In the same month that American President Franklin D. Roosevelt died of a brain hemorrhage and German Chancellor Adolf Hitler committed suicide, the Royal Commission on Coal headed by Justice W.F. Carroll held a week of hearings in Calgary before visiting the Crowsnest Pass and Elk Valley between 9 and 11 April 1945.[1]

Two things stand out when reflecting on the reports of this visit. First, Crow's Nest Pass Coal hosted a luncheon in Fernie on 10 April, and among the guests was the president of Fernie Local 7310, John William "Daze" Ashmore. Unlike company officials and local dignitaries, who constituted the vast majority of guests, Ashmore was a working coal miner in addition to his duties as president. The distinctive reality of his experience was proved just ten weeks later when he was killed by falling rocks and coal in the No. 1 East mine at Elk River Colliery. Ashmore was the sixth of seven workers who suffered fatal injuries in the region's coal mines that year; he would end up being one of the ninety-one workers to perish in mining accidents in the Crowsnest Pass and Elk Valley in the twenty years between 1945 and 1964 (see Table 1.1). The Royal Commission's report, completed in December 1946, neither commemorated Daze Ashmore nor included recommendations for improvements to safety

TABLE 1.1 Fatalities in Crowsnest Pass and Elk Valley coal mines, 1945–64

Mines/companies/provinces	1945–49	1950–54	1955–59	1960–64	Totals
Greenhill (closed 1960)	6	1	1	0	8
Bellevue (closed 1961)	2	2	0	1	5
Grassy Mountain strip	0	0	1	0	1
WCC[a] totals	8	3	2	1	14
Hillcrest-Mohawk (closed 1952)	5[b]	–	–	–	5
International (closed 1954, abandoned 1959; tipple operating)	3	2	1	0	6
McGillivray Creek (abandoned 1960)	6	13	0	0	19
Tent Mountain strip	0	1	0	0	1
Vicary Creek (opened 1957)	–	–	0	2[c]	2
CC[a] totals	14	16	1	2	33
Alberta Crowsnest	22	19	3	3	47
Elk River (closed 1958)	4	7	7	-	18
Michel	4	9	5	8	26
CNPC[a] totals	8	16	12	8	44
BC Elk Valley	8	16	12	8	44
Time period totals	30	35	15	11	91

NOTES: [a] WCC = West Canadian Collieries; CC = Coleman Collieries, formed through a merger of the Hillcrest-Mohawk, International, and McGillivray Creek coal companies in 1951; CNPC = Crow's Nest Pass Coal.

[b] This total includes one fatality at the Big Showing strip mine at Corbin, British Columbia (see Figure 1.1), in 1948, worked at the time by Hillcrest-Mohawk for Consolidated Mining and Smelting. See *Coleman Journal*, 22 July 1948.

[c] The CC mine where a miner died on 18 May 1960 was unspecified; assigned to Vicary Creek.

SOURCES: GWRC, M-2237, no file number, "List of Fatalities in Coal Mines in Alberta, 1904–1964 (updated to 1966)"; British Columbia, Minister of Mines, *Annual Reports*, 1945–59; British Columbia, Minister of Mines and Petroleum Resources, *Annual Reports*, 1960–64.

conditions in mines. Indeed, the topic of "Hazards of Coal Mines" consumed but 1 of the report's 663 pages.[2] Although it noted that the fatality rate per million man hours of labour worked in British coal mines was less than half the comparable fatality rate in Canadian coal mines, the report failed to address the reasons for the discrepancy and what could be done to narrow the gap.

Second, as the travelling party made its way through the region, there was no sense of urgency about the future of the railway steam coal industry. Yet just the previous week, the Royal Commission had been alerted to a disturbing trend in the United States: in its brief presented in Calgary, the Western Canada Bituminous Coal Operators' Association (WCBCOA) had noted that, between 1939 and 1943, Class 1 railways in the United States had purchased 3,184 diesel locomotives but only 1,424 steam locomotives. The brief observed that extension of this pattern of purchases to western Canada would dramatically reduce coal requirements since 70 percent of production was sold to railways.[3] However, the possible implications of this startling statistic never registered with the Royal Commission. Indeed, the majority recommendations, dated 14 December 1946, were premised on what seems at first to be a cavalier judgment: "Despite the importance of alternative sources of energy, coal is, and will probably continue to be, the most important source of energy for railway locomotives and for industrial and domestic heating."[4] In taking stock of this off-the-mark prognostication, we must remember that the Royal Commission's work concluded before the discovery of the massive Leduc oil field just south of Edmonton in early 1947.[5] Prior to that discovery, oil production in Canada had been falling; it seems that the commissioners had concluded that the shortage of domestic oil supply compared with the bounty of steam coal would discourage Canadian railways from following their American counterparts in aggressively switching to diesel.

The commissioners were not alone in thinking that the coal industry in western Canada had a healthy future going forward. For example, in 1946, Lethbridge's mayor told the inaugural meeting of the Coleman Board of Trade that, "one day, the Crowsnest Pass and Lethbridge coalfields will be the Ruhr of Canada."[6] In fairness to those who remained bullish on coal's future, this position was widely held. For instance, in his 1949 biography of UMWA International President John L. Lewis, Saul Alinsky wrongly guessed that coal would continue to be the main source of energy for centuries, thereby making it "not only our prime but our permanent mover. Coal is King."[7]

With the looming crisis in the railway steam coal industry obscured by such discourse as well as strong orders, the UMWA locals in the Crowsnest Pass and Elk Valley emerged from the Second World War with a head of steam and managed not only to orchestrate a number of significant gains between 1945 and 1949 for coal-mining families but also to further the general advancement of the labour movement and the drive for universal social welfare. The rise of the working class during these years was a welcome turnaround for all those families who had lived through the straitened economic conditions of the 1930s. It also coincided with the dramatic growth of private sector labour union density in Canada that began during the war and continued until the mid-1950s. Union membership as a percentage of the nonagricultural paid Canadian labour force steadily grew from 16.3 percent in 1940 to 33.7 percent in 1955.[8] However, what is distinctive about the postwar rise of the worker movement in the Crowsnest Pass and Elk Valley, compared with its general rise across Canada, is that it had been halted by the early 1950s because of the impending collapse in railway steam coal production.

In this chapter, I sketch the changes in the coal industry in the Crowsnest Pass and Elk Valley between 1945 and 1949 and document the rise in the power and influence of the working class. This sets the stage for understanding the roles of labour unions and kindred organizations in the fight against mine closures and economic ruin that began in earnest in the early 1950s.

CHANGES IN THE LABOUR FORCE AND COAL MINING AFTER THE SECOND WORLD WAR

Although coal production in the Crowsnest Pass and Elk Valley increased substantially during the Second World War, supply could not keep up with demand because of a shortage of labour. This was caused by the enlistment of many miners in the armed forces[9] and the near impossibility of recruiting skilled coal miners from other parts of Canada or other countries because of wartime conditions. The shortage of labour was partially met by recruiting "strangers, mostly from farming areas, to work in the mines."[10] However, these newcomers were inexperienced in underground coal mining and could not handle the most demanding jobs. The federal government responded to this labour crisis in May 1943 by declaring a state of national emergency that legally bound coal miners to employment in the mines. On at least two occasions, miners in the Crowsnest Pass were tried and convicted for not showing up to work, with the penalty for one of them being a ten-dollar fine or fourteen days in the Lethbridge jail.[11]

The order freezing existing employees to employment in Canadian coal mines was officially rescinded on 21 December 1945, but since the National Selective Service quickly became inoperative after the war in Europe ended on 8 May,[12] the order had been ignored long before it was rescinded. On 19 November, West Canadian Collieries reported that

> the labour situation is improving slowly at our mines, and some of the men are returning from the army and re-entering the mines, and our force is somewhat increased ... Control or freezing of min- ers has been removed, and they are free to move to other mines and to other work, and as they have been frozen for a considerable time, they are moving freely for the sake of doing so. The timbering industry and building trades are offering high wages, and we have lost some men to these branches of work.[13]

Therefore, the end of the war and the return of coal miners from military service did not immediately solve the shortage of labour in the region's mines. Indeed, high wages in booming postwar industries across Canada would be a significant "pull" factor for younger miners. A complement- ary "push" factor was the continuing danger of mine employment – there would be thirty mining fatalities between 1945 and 1949 (see Table 1.1).

Demand for steam coal from the Crowsnest Pass and Elk Valley ac- tually grew toward the end of the 1940s (see Figure 1.2), causing a 17 percent increase in the employment level in the region's mines (from 3,189 to 3,738) between 1945 and 1948.[14] Among the reliable sources of additional labour were male university students who returned home and worked in the mines during the summer break.[15] The mines in Alberta also worked out an arrangement with local high schools so that young men entering Grade 12 could work full time while completing their high school courses over two years. Bill Petrunik was among the students who took up this opportunity, going to school in the morning before working a steady afternoon shift in the McGillivray Creek mine between 3:30 and 11:30 p.m., five days a week, beginning in September 1948. Petrunik recalled that his daily pay of $10.07 exceeded what some of his high school teachers made.[16]

Migrants from nearby farming districts were a continuing source of new unskilled labour. However, in late 1947, West Canadian Collieries judged them to be "not very desirable" because they "seemingly float from one place to another." This suggests that labour turnover was a significant problem. Indeed, during 1946, the International and McGillivray Creek mines at Coleman hired 459 workers but experienced an astounding 443 separations.[17] Overall, the dearth of skilled underground coal miners was the biggest impediment to increased production at this time. One hopeful development in 1947 was the arrival of some coal miners from Nova Scotia. Late that year, however, West Canadian Collieries reported that these workers were "in the main ... not very satisfactory. Other mines have taken on some of these men and found them to be troublemakers." No definition of "troublemakers" was given, but perhaps the Nova Scotia miners had an aversion to the relatively unsafe working conditions in which they now found themselves.[18]

The arrival of migrants from Europe starting in the summer of 1948, in contrast, was welcomed by West Canadian Collieries, which immediately hired about a dozen of them and reported that "they appear to be good workmen and [are] fitting in nicely." These migrants had been displaced by the Second World War and then resettled in Canada.[19] An interesting political twist to this new source of mining labour was that many displaced persons had an anticommunist orientation. In Chapter 4, I discuss how their arrival caused considerable consternation in ethnocultural communities that had long been sympathetic to the work of the Communist Party.

As the coal companies struggled to find enough workers for their

FIGURE 1.1 Corbin, British Columbia, coal operation, 1945. | Photographer unknown. Courtesy of Royal BC Museum, Image I-27653.

underground mines in the immediate postwar years, they also pursued a production alternative, the development of strip and outcrop mines where coal seams were at or close to the surface. During the war, only one strip mine had operated in the region, at the Big Showing near the former underground mine at Corbin, British Columbia (see Figure 1.1).[20] After the war, however, all five of the companies with underground mines in the Crowsnest Pass and Elk Valley pursued surface-mining operations. The most important new strip mine was located on Tent Mountain, straddling the continental divide; it was opened by Hillcrest-Mohawk Collieries in 1946, would produce 69 percent of that company's 424,000 tons of coal in the first year for which separate strip-mining data are available (1951), and remained in operation until 1980.[21]

In the spring of 1946, West Canadian Collieries stated that the difficulty of finding workers for its underground mines made it necessary "to try and obtain as much tonnage as possible from surface working by stripping or similar methods." Two years later the company was surface

FIGURE 1.2 Strip mining, Crowsnest Pass, Alberta, circa 1950s. | By Thomas Gushul. Image NA-3381-8, held by Libraries and Cultural Resources Digital Collections, University of Calgary. Publication courtesy of Glenbow Archives.

mining in seven locations, six called "pits" (small outcrops often exhausted after a relatively short period of mining) and the seventh a strip mine on Grassy Mountain at about 2,100 metres of altitude (see Figure 1.2). The lower production costs of surface mines drove this expansion even as the shortage of labour eased in the late 1940s. By 1951, 38 percent of the total WCC production of 1.28 million tons came from surface mining.[22]

The coal companies would sometimes use their own equipment and employees to work a strip or outcrop mine and haul the coal to a tipple, but often they would hire a contractor to do this work. For example, CNPC contracted Fred Mannix Company in 1949 to develop two strip mines on a mountain ridge above Michel and Natal. In early 1949, the Blairmore unemployment office estimated that there were "hundreds" employed in the strip mines throughout the region, and there was virtually no unemployment of men, apart from "aged miners."[23]

When the underground mines were working steadily and employing as many miners as available, these strip and outcrop operations did not undermine the livelihood of the underground labour force. Nevertheless, activists in District 18 recognized the long-term danger of strip mines and unsuccessfully attempted to set limits on their operation in the negotiations for new collective agreements in both 1948 and 1949. (The union demand in both years was that strip mines operate only on days when the company's underground mines were also working.[24]) More ominously, in late 1947, the provincial LPP leader, Ben Swankey, "predicted that strip mining may yet make 'deserted villages' out of Alberta's mining camps and called upon the government to ensure that any miner who is displaced by strip mining will be adequately provided for."[25] If the demand for steam coal had held steady throughout the 1950s and into the 1960s, then Swankey's grim prediction might well have come to pass; indeed, it accords with what happened in southern Alabama in the 1950s (see the introduction). However, as I will detail in the next chapter, the crisis precipitated by the CPR decision to phase out coal-powered steam locomotives circumvented the crisis anticipated by Swankey.

Even with the development of new surface mines in the latter half of the 1940s, underground mining remained the heart of the railway steam coal business in the Crowsnest Pass and Elk Valley. Indeed, before the profitability of surface mining became apparent to the coal companies, three new underground operations (owned by CNPC, WCC, and Hillcrest-Mohawk, respectively) had commenced production. Furthermore, in 1948, International Coal and Coke reopened its York Creek underground mine, which had closed in 1935 because of a fire.[26] These new investments in underground operations are a further indication of the economic boom that swept this coalfield society during the Second World War and the immediate postwar years. It is little wonder, then, that miners were determined to make major improvements to their wages and benefits after the war.

ADVANCING MINERS' WAGES AND BENEFITS THROUGH COLLECTIVE BARGAINING

The successes that the bituminous miners in District 18 had in negotiating increased wages and improved benefits between 1945 and 1949 built upon the successes achieved in the very difficult labour relations environment of the Second World War. On 18 October 1939, just over a month after Canada had declared war on Nazi Germany, the federal government took on a directing role in the coal industry by appointing a coal administrator charged with tasks such as "maintaining and stimulating" the production of coal. Then, on 7 November, the government extended the jurisdiction of its Industrial Disputes Investigation Act to cover labour relations in any "concerns engaged in the production or distribution of munitions or supplies," where "supplies" were given a broad definition to include coal.[27] Therefore, for the duration of the war, the coal miners in District 18 were forced to fight labour relations battles on two fronts: the first involved the coal companies and encompassed day-to-day issues, and the second involved the federal government and encompassed wages, benefits, and the right to strike.

Table 1.2 shows that the real daily wage of company miners fell from $10.52 in 1939 (measured in 1954 dollars) to $10.02 in 1943 even though several government-approved cost-of-living increases were applied during these years. This was a source of considerable frustration for coal workers because in the winter of 1939–40 they had negotiated full cost-of-living protection for the duration of the war. However, the federal government nixed that deal for being too generous and inflationary and brokered the formula that saw miners' wages gradually lose purchasing power over the next three years.[28]

Astute negotiating by the District 18 leadership in combination with timely rank-and-file militancy resulted in two impressive victories in 1943 that would serve as an inspirational template for coal miners' struggles for improved wages and benefits after the war. The first victory came from pursuing a grievance through bureaucratic channels and resulted in miners being paid at time and a half whenever they worked Sundays, holidays, or a seventh consecutive day.[29] The second victory resulted from an audacious challenge to federal government authority led by miners in the Crowsnest Pass and Elk Valley. The strategy was to link the struggle in District 18 for better wages and benefits to the mass movement among UMWA members in the United States for an increase of "two dollars a day." That movement, sparked by a January 1943

TABLE 1.2 Wage rates and key benefits, Crowsnest Pass and Elk Valley miners, 1939–63[a]

Year	$ Nominal	$ 1954[b]	Key benefits added or subtracted
1939	5.78	10.52	—
1940	5.78	10.13	—
1941	6.24	10.19	—
1942	6.49	10.35	—
1943	6.49	10.02	Overtime pay for the seventh day of work in a week; overtime pay for Sundays and holidays
1944	7.55	11.78	Increase in vacation pay from one to two weeks; overtime pay for the sixth day of work in a week
1945	7.55	11.65	—
1946	8.95	13.10	Welfare Fund created and funded by three cents per ton assessment
1947	8.95	11.77	—
1948	10.95	12.85	Death benefit (January) and disability pension (October) introduced; Welfare Fund assessment increased to five cents per ton
1949	10.95	12.64	Welfare and Retirement Fund (WRF) assessment set at fifteen cents per ton
1950	10.95	12.05	Retirement pension payments begin
1951	11.75	11.75	Disability pensions and death benefits increase
1952	13.15	13.24	Retirement and disability pensions increase
1953	13.15	13.15	Disability to retirement transfers allowed; WRF assessment increased to twenty cents per ton
1954	13.15	13.15	—
1955	13.15	13.15	—
1956	13.65	13.37	One paid holiday (25 December); WRF assessment increased to twenty-two cents per ton
1957	14.35	13.58	WRF assessment increased to twenty-three cents per ton
1958	14.75	13.69	25 percent reduction in retirement and disability pensions; WRF assessment increased to twenty-seven cents per ton
1959	15.15	13.88	—
1960	15.55	14.06	Disability pension maximum increased to seventy-five dollars per month (same as retirement pension)

Year	$ Nominal	$ 1954[b]	Key benefits added or subtracted
1961	15.95	14.43	—
1962	15.95	14.16	Three paid holidays in total (two extra ones); death benefit increased from $400 to $600; retirement and disability pensions increased from $75 to $85 per month after a $10 increase in Old Age Security is clawed back from District 18 pensions
1963	16.15	14.16	Five paid holidays in total (two extra ones)

NOTES: [a] Miners working on contract rates (piecework) would usually make quite a bit more than miners working on the hourly rate (company miners). When company miners were making $10.95 per day in 1949, the secretary-treasurer of District 18, Angus Morrison, stated that most of the contract miners were making from $14 to $17 a day, a premium of between 28 and 55 percent over the company miner rate (*Coleman Journal*, 13 January 1949). Therefore, the company miner rate could be called the "miners minimum wage," a term used by coal operators in 1960 (GWRC, M-6000, file 198, COAWC submission to the Board of Conciliation, 1960, "Miners Minimum Wage and Consumer Price Index, 1950–1960"). [b] Nominal daily wage adjusted for inflation, 1954 as reference year.

SOURCES: (1) For nominal wage rates and key benefits between 1939 and 1952, see GWRC, M-1601, file 1144, K.A. Pugh, "Report of Conciliation," 20 February 1953. These rates include five cost-of-living adjustments awarded between 1941 and 1943 under wartime regulations plus the award of the O'Connor Royal Commission on 17 November 1943. Pugh's wage rates during the Second World War differ slightly from those found in the WCBCOA Brief to the Royal Commission on Coal (1945, 53), likely because the latter reported average wage rates in years when different nominal rates were in effect at different times. (2) On the new overtime pay won in 1943, see the text. (3) On overtime for the sixth day of work, see GWRC, M-6000, file 616, "Unauthorized Strikes in District 18, UMWA – During Last Three Years," 23 October 1945 (4) On the reduction in retirement and disability pensions in 1958, see DEB meeting minutes, 11 April 1958, and the collective agreement running between 3 July 1958 and 2 July 1960 (GWRC, M-6000, file 221).(5) For nominal wage rates and key benefits between 1953 and 1959, the sources of information include monthly "Labour Situation" reports produced by West Canadian Collieries (GWRC, M-1601, file 571), press reports, and copies of contracts and contract submissions found in the records of District 18. (6) A confirmation of company miner daily wage rates, 1950–60, is graphed in the COAWC submission to the Board of Conciliation, 1960. (7) For nominal wage rate and benefit increases in 1960–61, see Conciliation Board Chair Report (GWRC, M-6000, file 219) and letter to Hector Rae, Secretary-Treasurer of Blairmore Local 7295, from District 18 office, 29 November 1960 (GWRC, M-6000, file Blairmore 1955–61). (8) For changes to the contract in 1962 and 1963, see a signed copy of the agreement dated 4 June 1962 (GWRC, M-6000, file 454). (9) For a chronology of the Welfare and Retirement Fund, see GWRC, M-6000, file 392, "Summary of Operations from Inception to August 31, 1970." (10) On the rationale for increasing benefits from $75 to $85 per month, effective 1 February 1962, see letter from Edward Boyd to William C. Whittaker, 5 March 1962 (GWRC, M-6048, file 16). (11) Calculation of inflation-adjusted wage rates utilized the Bank of Canada inflation calculator available at https://www.bankofcanada.ca/rates/related/inflation-calculator/, on 23 November 2023.

wildcat strike by anthracite miners in Pennsylvania against wage controls and soaring prices, and effectively marshalled by UMWA President John L. Lewis starting in February, included unsuccessful strikes by over 500,000 miners in May and June 1943 and led to the American government's temporary seizure of the coal mines in May. After the War Labor Board rejected a negotiated settlement that camouflaged a substantial raise by paying miners at time and a half their normal rate of pay for one hour's travel time to and from the coal face, the stage was set for another coal strike in the United States, scheduled for 1 November.[30]

The demand for "two dollars a day" had great support from western Canadian coal miners. In addition, after having worked excessive hours during the war, miners wanted to increase paid vacations from one week to two weeks and to secure time and a half for the sixth working day in a week.[31] District 18 defied the federal government's authority to regulate the timing of strikes by scheduling a strike to coincide with the planned strike by American miners.[32] The cunning behind this coordinated labour action was that the Canadian government would not be able to purchase American steam coal to replace the production lost in western Canadian mines.

On 14 October 1943, the federal government constituted a Royal Commission "to investigate the demands of the coal miners of Western Canada." This was not enough to get miners in District 18 to back off, however, especially when the strike by their American brethren started as scheduled on 1 November. As miners across District 18 went on strike in what labour historian Allen Seager has called "a mighty demonstration of union power," almost the entire executive board of District 18 was in Ottawa at the behest of the government, which had not yet decided whether to negotiate or to declare a strike by coal miners a criminal act. After President Franklin D. Roosevelt moved on 3 November to negotiate an agreement with John L. Lewis in the United States, the government of William Lyon Mackenzie King followed suit in Canada. Seager maintains that District 18 President Livett negotiated a secret deal while in Ottawa, but the government insisted that the terms of the deal be released by the Royal Commission.[33] The union's official rationale for calling for the end of the strike on 6 November, however, was not that a secret deal had been reached but that the government had promised that wartime regulations would not constrain the recommendations of the Royal Commission.[34]

The call was ignored by coal workers on Vancouver Island and in the Crowsnest Pass and Elk Valley, who continued to strike to increase the pressure on the government to make contract concessions. In the Crowsnest Pass region, the strike did not end until 12 November,[35] and the Royal Commission issued its preliminary report a mere five days later. The timing alone suggests that the report merely transmitted a deal that President Livett had worked out with the King government: it included an extra week of paid vacation, time and a half pay for Saturday work, and an increase in pay per day of one dollar (not two dollars).[36] The real wage for company miners immediately jumped from $10.02 to $11.78 a day (see Table 1.2, comparing 1943 with 1944). The lesson that the miners of western Canada carried forward from their historic victory of 1943 was that astute strategy melded with irrepressible rank-and-file militancy was a winning combination when the demand for coal was strong.

After the war, there were three additional sets of contract negotiations between District 18 and the WCBCOA in the 1940s, with the first two (in 1946 and 1948) resulting in significant general advances for coal miners and the third (in 1949) winning a contribution level from the coal operators sufficient to initiate a retirement plan. The 1946 and 1948 collective agreements were negotiated in the spirit of the 1943 victory and are therefore consistent with the theme of this chapter, "the working class on the rise." I discuss them in the remainder of this section. The 1949 collective agreement, however, was concluded with the gloomy prospects for the steam coal industry evident to all parties. I therefore leave it to the conclusion of the chapter.

District 18 and the WCBCOA had signed a collective agreement in late 1938, and this agreement remained in place throughout the war (with adjustments to wages and benefits made in keeping with a "National Emergency" reopener clause).[37] However, the 1946 negotiations did not represent a full return to free collective bargaining since any agreement was subject to approval by the National War Labour Board, and the system of wartime price controls was still in place. Considering this, at the earliest point in negotiations, the WCBCOA insisted that any agreement reached by the two parties be conditional on "approval by the National War Labour Board and authorization given by the Wartime Prices and Trade Board for price increase or other means of recovery." District 18 accepted this condition, and the two parties were able to come to an agreement after less than five weeks of negotiations in the late summer of 1946. A few weeks later the National War Labour Board approved the agreement at the same time as the Wartime Prices and Trade Board announced an increase in the price of coal. The smoothness of this round of contract negotiations occurred because the coal companies did not have to worry about what the increase in labour costs would do to their bottom lines – a government decree shifted this increase to their customers.[38]

A second crucial factor in the 1946 negotiations in District 18 was a significant breakthrough by American coal miners earlier that year. After a hard-fought, fifty-nine-day strike that ended only after the American government seized the mines and came to an agreement with the union, the UMWA established the framework for a new health and welfare system for coal miners. The Welfare and Retirement Fund, part of the new system, came into existence on 29 May 1946 and was to be financed over time by per ton contributions from coal companies, with the initial levy set at five cents per ton.[39] Upon learning of this development, coal miners in District 18 were enthusiastic about initiating something similar.

That enthusiasm was heightened when International President John L. Lewis, who had been the main champion of the new health and welfare system, spoke at the District 18 meetings held just prior to the opening of contract negotiations in 1946. Lewis travelled to the meetings in Calgary by car from Spokane and hence spent a short time in the Elk Valley and Crowsnest Pass. With an appropriately poetic introduction, the *Fernie Free Press* recorded the mundane details of what would turn out to be Lewis's only visit to the region (see Text Box 1.1).

Lewis met with the District Executive Board just after it had settled on a list of seven contract proposals that it would recommend to the upcoming special convention; the establishment of the Welfare Fund was one of these proposals. The minutes note that Lewis was asked several

JOHN L. LEWIS: "LIKE A METEOR PASSING THROUGH THE SKY," 2 AUGUST 1946

The *Fernie Free Press* captured this fleeting moment of Elk Valley and Crowsnest Pass history.

> Like a meteor passing through the sky, driving all alone in a big Cadillac car, John L. Lewis, the stormy petrel of the American coal industry, passed through the district on Friday [2 August] going from Spokane to [a special convention of District 18 in] Calgary.
>
> The president of the United Mine Workers of America stayed all night at Wilfred Beaudry's tourist camp at Elko [a hamlet about thirty kilometres south of Fernie] and had breakfast at the White Spot in Fernie. He took in a local barber shop and was again on his way.

The reporter stated that Lewis was "in a great hurry" and did not try to meet with coal company or Local 7310 officials while in Fernie. However, he "stopped over at Michel for a little while and observed the outside operations at that camp." Lewis would then have crossed the continental divide by following the as-yet-unpaved Highway 3 traversing the Crowsnest Pass through the Rocky

questions "pertaining to the recent negotiations" in the United States. Two days later he spoke at the opening day of the convention. Avoiding mention of the long-standing, undemocratic, "provisional" status of District 18, he praised his hand-picked officers for their "unexcelled record of accomplishment." At the same time, he hinted at his tight autocratic control: "There are no stresses or strains in our organization, no factional warfare, no confusion." Notably, the most inspirational words quoted in a press report on the special convention came from Fernie Labour MLA Thomas Uphill; he used the familiar left-wing notion of a "vanguard" to situate the unionized coal miners in relation to the broader worker movement: "The United Mine Workers of America, doing the most hazardous and arduous work under the most obnoxious conditions,

Mountains. In Alberta, he would have wound his way through and past the coalfield communities of Coleman, Blairmore, Frank, Bellevue, and Hillcrest. It is hard to imagine that Lewis did not stop to observe one or more of the tipples within viewing distance of the highway before proceeding on his long automobile journey to Calgary (a journey that would have taken considerably longer than the two and a quarter hours that it takes on today's well-maintained highways).

At the time of his journey through the Elk Valley and Crowsnest Pass, Lewis was one of the most widely recognized public figures in North America, even though his power and influence had declined considerably since the latter half of the 1930s, when he was a close ally of Roosevelt and led the unionization of industrial workers as the president of the Congress of Industrial Organizations. The extent of his political importance at that time was recorded in Saul Alinsky's biography of Lewis: "In the year of 1937 John L. Lewis and his activities took in *The New York Times* 99,816 column inches or 4.2 per cent of the total news coverage for the year, foreign or domestic. This meant that about one-twentieth of *The New York Times* was devoted to Lewis and his operations" (194).

SOURCE: *Fernie Free Press*, 8 August 1946.

were in the vanguard of all legislative labour reforms in both Canada and the United States. They know what they want and how to get it."[40]

District 18 settled for a raise of $1.40 per day in 1946, after asking for an increase of $2.50 per day, and a contribution to the new Welfare Fund of just three cents per ton. In the Crowsnest Pass and Elk Valley, all five union locals voted to accept these terms, although opposition was considerable in the Bellevue (40 percent) and Blairmore (39 percent) locals.[41]

The 1946 agreement meant an immediate jump in coal miners' purchasing power, but during 1947 a relatively high rate of inflation (9.6 percent) resulted in wages significantly losing purchasing power month after month. In the summer that year, District 18 found a way to renegotiate this contract before its expiry date: since the 1946 agreement had been signed under the jurisdiction of the federal government's Wartime Labour Relations system, it was governed by the rule that either party to a collective agreement had the right, after one year, to cancel the agreement with proper notice. District 18 invoked this rule and later manufactured a breakdown in contract negotiations so that it had an excuse to immediately embark on a "No Contract, No Work" strike in early January 1948. Since it was the dead of winter, the demand for coal was high, and District 18's bargaining position was strong.[42]

The WCBCOA was outraged by District 18's seeming sleight of hand in terminating the collective agreement and disputed the legality of the manoeuvre right up to the Supreme Court of Canada. The court's ruling on 26 January 1948 dismissed with costs the operators' action and jump-started contract negotiations. A tentative one-year agreement concluded on 14 February included an increase in pay of two dollars per day as well as an increase in operator contributions to the Welfare Fund. Although in nominal terms the pay increase looked substantial (the company miner rate increased from $8.95 to $10.95 per day), the high rate of inflation at the time meant that, even with this increase, company miners' real daily wage in 1948 ($12.85 in 1954 dollars) was slightly lower than their real wage in 1946 ($13.10; see Table 1.2).[43]

Nonetheless, the tentative agreement met with workers' approval. The strike ended on 19 February after strong votes across District 18 in favour. In the Crowsnest Pass and Elk Valley, support ranged from a low of 65 percent at Bellevue to a high of 95 percent at Fernie, with an overall acceptance by 80 percent of the 2,202 workers who voted.[44] At this point, District 18 had perfected the art of combining shrewd negotiating with the mass strike (with 1948 having replicated the success of 1943). However, as I will document in the last section of this chapter and in the chapters covering the years between 1950 and 1962, the coal industry in western Canada was soon to fall on hard times, thereby greatly limiting the effectiveness of strike action and the propensity of coal workers to strike. Indeed, it would not be until 1965, seventeen years later, that Michel Local 7292 would again demonstrate how a strike could leverage significant contractual gains for coal miners.

Everyday Struggles in the Mines

Between 1945 and 1949, the pace of work in the mines in the Crowsnest Pass and Elk Valley was relentless because of the high production tonnages, and there continued to be many sources of friction between management and labour. Going back to the first decade of the twentieth century, the UMWA locals in the region had negotiated detailed collective agreements to cover a variety of issues in the employment relationship.[45] Many of what I call the "everyday struggles" of coal miners involved objecting when mine managers either ignored or (in workers' view) misinterpreted the terms of the collective agreement. Less frequently, everyday struggles involved a dispute over how the collective agreement should apply when there was a significant change in a mine's operation (e.g., the beginning of work on a new coal seam).

In the mid-1940s, coal miners in the Crowsnest Pass and Elk Valley had two routes of protest when they believed that their employer was guilty of an injustice: engaging in direct, collective action (usually in the form of a pithead or wildcat strike) or getting their union representatives (starting with the elected pit committee) to take up a grievance with mine management in accordance with the step-by-step procedure outlined in the collective agreement. At that time, pithead strikes were a useful weapon with very little downside since they were neither legally nor contractually prohibited. In 1943 and 1944, not including the district-wide strike that started on 1 November 1943, there were ten recorded pithead strikes by Crowsnest Pass and Elk Valley miners. They typically involved seemingly minor issues such as problems with the cost or quality of the bus transportation to the two new mines on the Alberta side of the Pass. Interestingly, because the federal government in effect was co-managing the coal industry during the war, wildcat strikes were also launched against government actions. For instance, after Bellevue's doctor was called up for military service in late 1943, leaving the community without a doctor, Bellevue Local 7294 struck for four days, resulting in a loss of about 2,500 man days of labour. The strike ended after the promise of federal government conciliation that in turn led to a victory for Bellevue.[46]

The largest wildcat strike by Crowsnest Pass and Elk Valley miners between 1945 and 1949 was likewise aimed at forcing a change in federal government policy. The source of grievance was the federal government's wartime meat-rationing policy, which gave miners the same allotment of meat as other workers across Canada; in contrast, the miners in District 18 believed that, because of their hard physical labour, they deserved extra meat on a daily basis. This was a cause dear to miners' hearts (and stomachs), as demonstrated by the fact that the wildcat strike, which began on 27 September 1945, generally lasted for eighteen to twenty working days (with about 131,000 man days of labour lost in total). This strike confirmed the power of rank-and-file miners and their local leaders at that point in District 18's history – most locals (including all five locals in the Crowsnest Pass region) continued to strike for an extra week in defiance of the District 18 executive officers who had "instructed" the miners to return to work after securing some minor concessions from an official of the Wartime Prices and Trade Board. The eventual outcome of the strike was a system by which miners could make an application for additional meat rations to a local committee (appointed by the board). On the Alberta side of the Pass, this local committee was a virtual rubber stamp for each application since two of the three members were the secretary-treasurers of the Blairmore and Coleman UMWA locals.[47]

There is no doubt about the effectiveness of a wildcat strike in forcing mine managers or government officials to address an issue that they might otherwise be tempted to ignore. Furthermore, the mere possibility of a wildcat strike often could have the same effect, as the following comment by a WCC manager in late 1946 revealed: "I believe for some time to come no strikes of a general nature will occur in the Coal Mining Industry but labour will have to be carefully handled in order to avoid petty troubles and Pit Head Strikes."[48]

The WCBCOA demonstrated its frustration with pithead strikes during the contract negotiations of 1946, proposing that the collective agreement be made "a binding instrument ... without unilateral interpretation or stoppages of work."[49] This frustration was shared by District 18's executive officers, whose opening salvo in an attack on pithead strikes came in late 1945 in the wake of most local unions ignoring the district leadership's instruction to return to work during the strike over meat rations. Their statement, circulated to the entire membership, condemned local UMWA leaders "who assume authority to direct and advise the membership in strike action, directly contrary to the provisions of our International Constitution." The letter concluded that "the time has arrived that disciplinary action will have to be taken if the interests of this Organization and its membership are to be preserved."[50]

This issue would not fully come to a head in District 18 until the mid-1950s and is therefore analyzed in Chapter 2. However, two further developments during the 1945–49 years bear noting. First, a new paragraph was inserted into the preamble to the collective agreement of 1946 that explicitly promised "no strike or lockout or local stoppages of work shall be called or maintained during the life of this agreement."[51] However, the penalty for a local stoppage was left to the discretion of the district organization (in accordance with the UMWA constitution), and over the next few years exercise of that discretion did not result in the imposition of any penalty even though wildcat strikes continued. Indeed, in early 1952, the coal operators pointed to an upsurge in pithead strikes and specifically complained that District 18's officers never fined such strikers, as was supposed to happen according to the collective agreement.[52]

Second, a battle occurred in the District Executive Board in November 1946 over whether the board itself or the executive officers of District 18 should have the authority to impose penalties after a wildcat strike. Michel Local 7292's Sim Weaver co-sponsored a motion that "District officers make an investigation of any local strike and report to a meeting of the District Executive Board." The motion was defeated; instead, the executive officers were given the authority to fine members participating in a wildcat strike at the rates of fifty cents per day for a first offence and one dollar per day for succeeding offences. This battle in the District Executive Board suggested that the imposition of fines for wildcatting would be closely scrutinized by rank-and-file leaders and most likely spark pushback. I suspect that the district officers' failure to levy any such fine over the next few years was because of a desire to avoid a debilitating internal union conflict.[53]

Although the wildcat strike remained an option for miners in the Crowsnest Pass and Elk Valley in the immediate postwar years, particularly when faced with a problem that required an immediate solution, most of the everyday problems that arose in the employment relationship could best be addressed through the grievance procedure outlined in the collective agreement. The institutionalized grievance system fell far short of creating a democratic workplace, but it did allow for a dialogue between managers and union representatives that promoted accountability for managers' decisions, workplace safety, and justice for workers.

Most grievances raised during the 1945–49 period were either settled to the union's satisfaction after discussions with mine management or withdrawn because union leaders decided that the case was not worth pursuing. Minutes of the joint conference at each mine record serious, thorough, and civil discussions – whether a grievance was settled successfully or not, the matter was almost always given a full airing. An example of a settled grievance was a claim for half an hour of overtime pay by a group of miners at the Hillcrest-Mohawk mine who had been delayed from exiting the mine at their scheduled quitting time because of a safety issue.[54] An example of a dropped grievance concerned the discharge "of two aged men ... who had given long service to the McGillivray Mine." In a joint conference, management maintained that it was obvious the two discharged men no longer had the ability to do their most recent jobs or any open jobs and therefore could be legitimately discharged. The matter was settled amicably since the union officials (including District 18 Vice-President John Stokaluk) agreed that the company was both "within its rights" and "quite justified" in discharging the two employees.[55]

Some grievances, however, could not be settled through negotiations between the two parties, and between 1945 and 1949 twenty-five grievances ended up in arbitration.[56] As might be expected, the majority (60 percent) involved disputes about how much workers should be paid for particular jobs. These sorts of disputes were endemic because of the complicated piecework system in which the rates for contract miners varied according to the geological conditions of each coal seam in each mine. An additional 28 percent concerned the "Holidays with Pay" clause in the collective agreement – union and management often had conflicting interpretations of when absent employees could qualify for a paid holiday day for a particular month.[57]

The most significant of the remaining arbitration cases disputed the discharge of two elderly miners at the WCC Greenhill mine in 1949. This case is noteworthy because it ended up in arbitration, unlike the parallel grievance at McGillivray Creek discussed above, which had been quickly abandoned. Local 7295's grievance was lost when the arbitrator upheld a manager's right to make an arbitrary (and ageist) decision about whether elderly workers could any longer do a particular job safely, even after the manager had conceded that the discharged workers were "faithful employees" with no complaints on record about their work.[58]

Therefore, the age structure of the workforce in the mines in the Crowsnest Pass and Elk Valley had clearly become an important issue by the end of the 1940s. Many of the employees who had started to work in the coal mines in the region prior to the First World War were now in their fifties, sixties, or even seventies, and their capacity for hard, back-breaking labour was understandably diminished. As I will discuss in the final section of this chapter and in Chapter 2, the wide scope of this problem was why the coal companies became reluctant converts to the idea of funding a retirement pension plan for miners in District 18.

THE LABOUR MOVEMENT'S PURSUIT OF BROADER ECONOMIC, SOCIAL, AND POLITICAL GOALS

The rise of the working class in the Crowsnest Pass and Elk Valley is also revealed in the wide range of economic, social, and political goals pursued by the five UMWA local unions and their activist members between 1945 and 1949, sometimes in conjunction with allied organizations and activists. One audacious campaign aimed to shift the decisions of the Workmen's Compensation Board (WCB) of Alberta in a pro-worker direction, and it culminated in a political strike by all 6,500 UMWA members in Alberta on 26 June 1946. Although this campaign was co-ordinated by the District 18 office, it was driven by the three UMWA locals in the Alberta section of the Crowsnest Pass.

The attempt to reform the Alberta WCB started during the Second

World War and included a November 1944 meeting between a large delegation from District 18 and members of the provincial cabinet, including Premier Ernest Manning. At that meeting, District 18 outlined seventeen recent compensation cases involving coal miners that it believed were improperly adjudicated by the board. (Nine of the cases were from the Crowsnest Pass.) One of the reported cases involved a Bellevue miner, Otto Haggland: "Serious skull fracture. Board awarded 50% disability May 21, 1943. Sent to Dr. Scarlett who reported that as far as earning a living was concerned, workman had 100% disability. March 14, 1944, Board increased pension to 75%." In light of the improper adjudication of so many compensation cases, District 18 asked for the removal of both the WCB chair, Dr. V.W. Wright, who had held this position since 1935, and the WCB labour representative, Alfred Farmilo, who had been first appointed in 1941.[59]

The cabinet did not immediately act on the UMWA demand. Consequently, at the DEB meeting in early February 1945, Locals 2633 and 7295 asked the district office to follow up. It turned out that Premier Manning had recently informed District 18 that his government would soon take action. That action was the resignation of the WCB chair, Dr. Victor Wright.[60] However, Farmilo remained in place, and the new temporary chair was the existing company appointee to the Workmen's Compensation Board, Carl C. Cook. In the eyes of District 18 officials, the switch from Wright to Cook as chair did nothing to change the biased WCB logic of decision making.[61]

The District Executive Board reconsidered this situation in the spring of 1946 after Cook had served as the temporary WCB chair for over a year. In order to pressure the provincial government to remove both Farmilo and Cook, it "decided that one day should be set for stoppages of work and holding of mass protest meetings in all mining camps in Alberta." The strike came off without a hitch,[62] but it was ineffective: although a permanent, new WCB chair was finally appointed in early 1947, both Cook and Farmilo remained as commissioners.[63] Premier Manning was clearly unmoved by the UMWA pressure tactic after having won fifty-one of fifty-seven seats in the provincial election on 8 August 1944.[64] Farmilo would hold on to the role of labour commissioner on the

Workmen's Compensation Board until he retired in 1955.[65] Nevertheless, this strike demonstrated that the coal miners of District 18, impelled by the union locals in the Crowsnest Pass, saw themselves as a powerful political force in 1946 and operated with a political vision that included workers having a say in how postwar institutions such as the Workmen's Compensation Board were run.

That political vision was also revealed in five types of outreach practised by the coal miners' movement in the Crowsnest Pass and Elk Valley in the 1945–49 period. First, rank-and-file leaders committed themselves to building the local labour movement during the Second World War, and these efforts continued after the war. In March 1946, Bill Arland (president) and Enoch Williams (secretary-treasurer) of Blairmore Local 7295 spoke at an initial meeting to unionize the lumber workers in the area.[66] In East Kootenay, Elk Valley miners were instrumental in founding a labour council in 1945. At that moment, labour activists in the region envisioned a fundamental reorganization of employment in Canadian society: "One of the council's initial purposes will be elimination of discrimination and blacklist in hiring methods, with agreement that a prime necessity is establishment of government-management-union hiring halls to replace this."[67]

Second, active labour participation in local governments and in provincial election campaigns continued to be a priority for the labour movement. There were four municipal governments in operation in the region between 1945 and 1949: the Village of Frank, the Towns of Blairmore and Coleman, and the City of Fernie (other communities were "unincorporated" and thus did not have local governments). Frank's electors returned a communist majority on the village council in 1945, the fifth municipal election result since 1930 that fit this pattern. Among the labour activists involved in Frank's government was Local 7295's Tony Patera, the LPP candidate in the Macleod riding in the 1953 federal election (see Chapter 4).[68] In Blairmore, labour control of local government began in 1933[69] and carried on without a break throughout the 1940s. Enoch Williams served as the town's mayor between 1937 and 1951 while working as secretary-treasurer of Local 7295. It is important to note that the union coalition controlling the town's government was broader than just the UMWA. For example, in the by-election in 1949 to fill a vacancy on the Blairmore town council, the labour group nominated Alrik Tiberg, a WCC safety fire boss. He went on to defeat "one of main street's leading businessmen" who had been "nominated by three of the town's most prominent mercantile and professional men."[70]

In Coleman, labour leaders had never tried to win all the seats on the town council, but they were committed to having a labour voice in the local government. This continued during the postwar years with Local 2633 leaders John Ramsay and George Jenkins serving as councillors on a council headed by Mayor Frank Aboussafy, a storekeeper.[71] The situation in Fernie can best be described as a cross between Blairmore and Coleman: labour activists ran a slate of candidates in local elections in the late 1940s, just as they did in Blairmore, but the result of the yearly elections invariably yielded a council that looked like the council in Coleman, with a mix of pro-labour and pro-business representatives. Labour politics in Fernie after the Second World War continued to revolve around Thomas Uphill, the former Fernie Local 7310 secretary, who had served continuously as the MLA for the Fernie District in the BC legislature since 1920. Uphill also served as Fernie's mayor for most of the decade following the Second World War. When he ran for mayor in a special election in the summer of 1946, just after Fernie had emerged from provincial trusteeship, Uphill demonstrated his power in local labour circles by insisting that the "miners' slate" of candidates be revised "to get a more popular team behind him." In that election, the labour group managed to elect only one councillor plus Mayor Uphill.[72]

UMWA leaders in the Crowsnest Pass and Elk Valley were also heavily involved in provincial politics in the immediate postwar years. This involvement was complicated, however, by the fierce rivalry between the Communist Party of Canada and the Cooperative Commonwealth Federation for the socialist vote. In the provincial election in Alberta in 1944, this rivalry resulted in the narrow defeat of Blairmore's mayor, Enoch Williams, long associated with the Communist Party of Canada, running as the Labour-Unity candidate in the riding of Pincher Creek–Crowsnest; his chances were ruined when, at the last minute, the Cooperative Commonwealth Federation ran a local United Church minister against Williams rather than going along with the Labour-Unity strategy.[73] The rivalry also almost ended Uphill's run as an MLA in the provincial election in 1949, which Uphill won by only nine votes against a prominent local businessman running as a joint Conservative-Liberal candidate. The only other candidate in that race represented the Cooperative Commonwealth Federation and thereby served to split the left-wing vote against a united right-wing candidate.[74] The main thing that secured the narrow victory for Uphill in 1949 was the unity of labour groups behind him, acting in the name of the Fernie District Labour Party.[75]

Third, in addition to engaging in electoral politics, the five UMWA union locals were community minded in many ways. For instance, "at Christmas 1946, Michel Local 7292 gave out $1,200 in gifts to the children of miners ($1.50 each), old-timers and widows ($2 each) and service personnel ($5 each)." The *Fernie Free Press* proclaimed that "Michel Union is Santa Claus."[76] At the same time in Coleman, Local 2633 allowed its union hall to be used as the town's community hall, with the municipal government and Local 2633 splitting the operating costs.[77]

By far the most important community project initiated and steered by the UMWA locals in the postwar years was the building of the first large (seventy-two-bed) hospital for the Alberta Crowsnest Pass communities. Prior to the opening of this hospital in 1949, about equidistant between the towns of Coleman and Blairmore, each community had only a small medical facility. The UMWA locals in Bellevue, Blairmore, and Coleman got the ball rolling on this project by setting up a committee in early 1944 "to gather information relating to the Central Hospital idea." By June, the three union locals had become proponents of the idea and had secured the support of the Coleman town council. It would take five years to bring this idea to fruition, with ratepayer plebiscites in late 1944 and early 1947 used to authorize construction costs. The guiding hand of the labour movement on this project is seen from the fact that Local 7295's Enoch Williams was the chair of the initial hospital board.[78] From a political perspective, the new central hospital was organized in a way that anticipated the universal hospital insurance scheme that became established across Canada in the late 1950s and early 1960s. Specifically, there were no user fees for residents of the municipalities in the Alberta section of the Crowsnest Pass since a general increase in property taxes was applied to cover the costs: "In 1949 when one was admitted to the old hospital, one received excellent care and treatment and on discharge no bill was given."[79] Residents of adjacent unincorporated areas (who were therefore not taxed by local governments) could also enjoy this "no charge" service by purchasing hospital insurance directly from the municipal hospital.[80] A new forty-seven-bed hospital was opened in Fernie in 1949, and it was likewise strongly supported by labour activists over the years.[81]

Fourth, the worker movement's broader labourist vision was also revealed in the support offered to struggling workers. A telling example involved the nondelivery strike by small farmers (mostly farming quarter- or half-section farms, where a quarter-section is 160 acres) organized into the Alberta Farmers' Union (see Figure 1.3).[82] On 17 September 1946, Sub-District 5 of the UMWA (which brought together the Bellevue, Blairmore, and Coleman locals) discussed a call for support of the nondelivery strike from the president of the Alberta Farmers' Union. Sub-District 5 not only decided to wire a message of support that could be read on a radio broadcast planned by the union but also came up with a plan for its own radio broadcast. It proposed asking District 18's officers to make a solidarity broadcast, but failing that it committed to producing and paying for its own broadcast.[83]

During these years of expansion of the union movement in Canada, there were many other examples of the UMWA locals in the Crowsnest Pass and Elk Valley expressing solidarity with striking workers, usually in the form of financial contributions. They included Coleman Local 2633, which voted to levy an assessment of one dollar per month against each member in order to financially support the strike in 1947 by coal miners in Nova Scotia's District 26 of the UMWA, and Fernie Local 7310, which organized a collection in 1946 to support twelve striking newspaper workers in Vancouver who had been arrested on a picket line and charged with "unlawful assembly."[84] Furthermore, the documentary record shows that UMWA leaders in the Crowsnest Pass and Elk Valley were keenly following developments in the broader labour movement and not shy about expressing displeasure with some of the positions

FIGURE 1.3 Farmers picket at Olds, Alberta, during the Alberta Farmers' Union delivery strike (blockading the Mountain View Livestock Co-op yard), 23 September 1946. | By Leonard D. Nesbitt. Image CU176598 held by Libraries and Cultural Resources Digital Collections, University of Calgary.

taken by the senior CCL leaders as the Cold War deepened in Canada. For instance, in late 1948, Blairmore Local 7295 condemned the United Steelworkers for raiding the Mine Mill local at Inco in Sudbury. In a letter to the CCL secretary-treasurer that called for an end to such tactics, Enoch Williams stated that "raiding actions that are becoming all too common in the ranks of organized labour should be viewed as, and treated as, downright scabbery."[85]

Fifth, the pursuit of broader political goals by the UMWA locals between 1945 and 1949 included agitating for a greater measure of democracy in District 18 itself. The five union locals in the region were highly democratic organizations that encouraged active membership participation and held regular elections for local positions.[86] However, democracy in District 18 was truncated. All of the executive officers in District 18 were appointed by the UMWA's international office rather than elected by members. Furthermore, although District 18 had a functioning executive board, all of the sub-district representatives on that board were appointed by the District 18 president rather than elected by their respective sub-district members. The contrast between a lively democratic culture in union locals and ultimate autocratic control at the district level was bound to cause considerable political dissonance for many UMWA activists.

The stifling of democracy at the district level of the UMWA was a conscious ploy by John L. Lewis to limit the possibility of districts taking oppositional political directions. During his forty years as the international president, Lewis frequently changed the status of a district from "autonomous" to "provisional" whenever he did not like some political development in that district. For example, District 7 in Pennsylvania was relegated to provisional status in 1941 after a wildcat strike, with provisionally appointed district officers replacing the elected officers. The term "provisional" was a misnomer, however, since Lewis, rather than finding a way to quickly restore a provisional district's autonomy, would let the district languish in provisional purgatory, content that it was being run by his hand-picked cronies. In the case of District 7, its provisional status continued without interruption from 1941 to 1969, when it was merged with two other Pennsylvania districts. Unsurprisingly, the amalgamated district was constituted as a provisional district.[87] The overall status of the UMWA's districts in 1963, three years after Lewis's retirement as president, reflects his years of autocratic abuse of district autonomy: nineteen of the union's twenty-seven districts "were controlled by the union president."[88]

In 1948, Michel Local 7292 initiated a grassroots movement calling for autonomy in District 18. It began with a letter circulated to all locals that presented a resolution in favour of democratic autonomy for District 18. Local 7292 requested that the other locals endorse the resolution and communicate that endorsement to the district office. Several local unions did just that, including Coleman Local 2633.[89] This matter was considered at the next meeting of the District Executive Board, at which discussion began one day and spilled over to a second day. In the end, the board did not take a definitive position on the question of autonomy and simply asked President Robert Livett to take up the issue with the International Executive Board.[90]

This initiative to secure autonomy for District 18 was unsuccessful. However, the demand for district autonomy did not die, as I will show in Chapter 2, with union locals in the Crowsnest Pass and Elk Valley and the Labor-Progressive Party leading the way in calling for greater internal democracy in the UMWA.

A CULTURE OF RESISTANCE AND COLLECTIVE STRUGGLE

The years between 1945 and 1949 were momentous in many ways for the Crowsnest Pass and Elk Valley. Joy and relief at the end of the Second World War were followed by determined struggles to improve the wages, benefits, dignity, and political power of coal miners and other working people. The five UMWA locals took the lead in these fights for working-class advancement, deploying the impressive repertoire of actions catalogued in this chapter. Such was the influence of the UMWA locals at this time that it was virtually inevitable that the miners' ethos of resistance and collective struggle would inform how other groups tackled their grievances with authorities.

An interesting development in the coal-mining industry in the mid-1940s was the unionization of fire bosses and other lower-tier mine supervisory staff. The UMWA constitution prohibited membership by mine officials,[91] so the unionization efforts came from the Trades and Labour Congress (which successfully organized the ninety-seven fire bosses working in Crowsnest Pass and Elk Valley mines in 1945) and the Canadian Congress of Labour (which successfully organized fire bosses in sixteen Drumheller Valley coal mines in the same year). A first contract was signed by fire bosses in the Crowsnest Pass and Elk Valley on 12 April 1945.[92] Their decision to unionize, as well as their subsequent demand for a Welfare and Retirement Fund, were stimulated by the successes of District 18. Furthermore, when the fire bosses went on strike in 1950 to back their demand for a Welfare and Retirement Fund, they mimicked the militancy of coal miners.[93]

Three other examples demonstrate how coal miners' culture of collective struggle had become the norm for life in the Crowsnest Pass and Elk Valley in the postwar years. First, on two occasions, high school students in Blairmore deployed strikes when faced with grievances. A strike in late 1948 "was to draw attention to the deplorable condition of the school and led to the forming of the first Home and School Association on the eastern slopes of the Pass."[94] Students voted to go back to their classes only after a large meeting of 300 ratepayers committed to basic improvements in the learning environment such as fluorescent lighting and improved heating. It is noteworthy that the students presented themselves as a "students' union" during this strike and that, even after the ratepayers' meeting committed to improvements, one-third voted against returning to classes.[95]

Second, the spread of the culture of resistance was evident in a strike for higher pay by the Town of Coleman's street and ash employees in the spring of 1948. The civic workers, unhappy with being paid only seven dollars per day, went on strike shortly after the successful conclusion of the District 18 strike that yielded an increase of two dollars per day and increased the rate of pay for company miners to $10.95 per day. One of the miners on the town council, George Jenkins, proposed that the street and ash employees should likewise receive an increase of two dollars per day, but none of the other councillors, including long-time Local 2633 official John Ramsay, agreed. The town council eventually settled on offering an increase of eighty-seven and a half cents per day.[96] This strike, like the one by the high school students, took the form of a wildcat strike and was successful in getting immediate action from the authorities in question.

Third, a wildcat strike at a Blairmore sawmill demonstrated that this culture of resistance was so much a part of the fabric of life that a union was unnecessary for either the initiation or the coordination of collective job action. The strike at the Sartoris Lumber Company in May 1949 involved thirty-five nonunion workers and lasted three days. The goal was an increase in the hourly rate of pay to recoup some of a 15 percent reduction in weekly pay packets caused by the company's move to reduce the daily hours of work from nine to eight, thereby eliminating an hour of work that had been classified as overtime and paid at time and a half. The majority of strikers voted to go back for an increase of five cents an hour, leaving ten of their workmates so unhappy that they quit their jobs.[97]

In early 1949, the strong labour market provided dissatisfied workers with options.

Unmistakable Signs of the Coal Industry in Trouble

Even though coal production in the Crowsnest Pass and Elk Valley hit a record high in 1949, there were a number of indications of impending trouble for the industry. At the beginning of the year, the president of the McGillivray Creek Coal and Coke Company warned that it was considering the closure of its mine at Coleman partly because of "the loss of markets brought about by the high cost of coal in relation to other fuels." At about the same time, the press reported that the Canadian Pacific Railway intended to convert 100 coal-burning steam locomotives to oil burners. In the spring of 1949, the *Calgary Herald* forecasted that "bituminous mines would lose about one-third of their market in the next three years through [the] decision of the Canadian Pacific and Canadian National Railways to switch from coal to oil-burning equipment in many sections of Western Canada."[98] For UMWA leaders, however, the clearest indication of an impending downturn in coal sales was the coal operators' demand for significant rollbacks during the contract negotiations that took place in January and February 1949.

In its opening negotiating salvo, the WCBCOA stated that "it is our view that the Bituminous Coal Industry of this district faces today the gravest situation in its history as regards the competition from other sources of energy ... Inroads on existing markets have already been made and will continue to be made at an ever-increasing rate until such time as the price of our coal is substantially reduced." A few days later the coal operators proposed several contract rollbacks, including "the immediate discontinuance of all further payments to the Welfare Fund" and reductions in wage rates of either one dollar or two dollars per day."[99]

Given this aggressive negotiating stance by the operators, it is somewhat surprising that an agreement on a new contract was reached without a strike or lockout. Indeed, District 18 managed to negotiate a significant increase in coal company contributions to the Welfare Fund (from five cents to fifteen cents per ton). One explanation of the settlement is that both sides recognized that any work stoppage could hasten some existing customers to switch from coal to oil or natural gas. Furthermore, given the operators' continuing efforts to shed elderly employees, District 18 was able to convince the WCBCOA that funding an expansion of the Welfare Fund to create a Welfare and Retirement Fund was an efficient and sure-fire way to remove elderly miners from the payroll.[100] Nonetheless, after the large wage increase that resulted from the district-wide strike in 1948, the absence of any wage increase in 1949 must have been galling to many workers. Approval of the contract signified that the rank-and-file miners had concluded that the coal industry was indeed facing a grave challenge.

Both the UMWA and individual workers soon modified their behaviours to align with this new reality. For example, in the spring of 1949, the District 18 office and the WCBCOA produced complementary briefs that protested a provincial government proposal to allow the export of natural gas from Alberta (on the understanding that such exports would undermine the markets for coal in any jurisdiction that received the gas). UMWA locals in the Alberta section of the Crowsnest Pass were drawn into this company-labour collaboration when they were asked to formally endorse the two briefs and then inform the Manning government of their endorsement.[101] At the individual level, the change in coal miners' behaviour was also distinctive. In July 1949, West Canadian Collieries reported that "there is no evidence of unrest among our men and absenteeism, so plentiful a year ago, is now almost a thing of the past."[102] Joint company-union collaborations to protect markets for coal therefore were matched by miners who voluntarily abandoned their truant ways – an adaptation to enhance incomes before potential production cuts resulted in decreased shifts worked every week and possibly even job cuts.

CHAPTER TWO

A Crisis Begins

Three Days a Week and Mine Closures, 1950–56

The first major plunge in coal production occurred in 1953 when Alberta mines produced half a million tons less than they had in 1952, a decrease of 23 percent (see Figure I.2). This downturn in orders continued into 1954, causing Coleman Collieries to suspend operations at its International underground mine at the end of March.[1] By the end of 1954, production in the Alberta mines in the Crowsnest Pass had dropped by 0.6 million tons compared with 1953. Therefore, in just two years, production in the mines on the Alberta side of the provincial boundary had been cut in half.

In contrast, the experience in the Elk Valley was less painful: the decrease in production between 1952 and 1954 was just 150,000 tons or 13 percent of the 1.2 million tons produced in 1952. Nevertheless, because of a general shortage of orders for coal between 1953 and early 1955, the underground coal mines that remained open were almost always working "short weeks." Even at Michel Collieries, where orders remained relatively strong, there were only two full ten-shift paycheques in 1953. It appears that the Michel miners usually worked four shifts a week during this span of retrenchment since a run of three consecutive weeks with only three shifts per week was newsworthy. In Alberta, however, the miners usually worked fewer than four shifts a week; indeed, an official of West Canadian Collieries opined in March 1954 that, "in the coal mining industry, and at our mines more particularly, the men seem to desire a steady four or five days a week work rather than increases and if we could accomplish a steady four day week all would, we think, be well."[2]

"Three Days a Week," a poem by Florence Del Rio of Coleman,

captured the mood of people during these straitened economic times and pointed to imported coal as the source of the problem. It was published in the Labor-Progressive Party's newsletter, *The Lamp*.[3] The first and eighth stanzas of the poem evoke key features of the natural environment in the Crowsnest Pass alongside the grim reality of short work weeks:

> *[1] Through the Crow's Nest Pass*
> *The mountain winds sweep*
> *Where the miners are working*
> *Three days a week.*
> *[8] High o'er the mountains*
> *Bright stars ever peak*
> *Down on towns where the miners*
> *Work three days a week.*

The refrain "three days a week" is featured in six of the eight stanzas, and in three stanzas blame for this sorry situation is levelled at Canada for importing American coal and at American coal companies for "dumping" coal into Canada (i.e., selling it for less than a reasonable market value).[4] The penultimate stanza best captures how this crisis had affected the mood of people in communities such as Coleman:

> *[7] Small business and miners*
> *All over the town*
> *Live in fear of the day*
> *When the mine might shut down.*

Although Florence Del Rio's poem was published in a communist newsletter, it was a passive reflection on the situation rather than a call to action or a celebration of collective resistance. This aligns with what transpired in the region in response to the 1953–54 downturn in the coal industry – the UMWA locals were slow to organize community resistance to the economic crisis, never pushed the struggle beyond mainstream channels into contentious political actions, and failed to take advantage of the 1955–56 lull in the economic crisis to regroup and plan how to respond to what everyone by then realized was inevitable: the end of steam coal purchases by the Canadian Pacific Railway. The central question addressed in this chapter is why was the fight against the first round of production cutbacks and mine closures in the 1950s not more energetic and militant, in pursuit of the goal of forcing both the wider public and senior levels of government to pay more than cursory attention to the crisis?

As reported in the introduction, when faced with calamitous mine closures and the impending depopulation of their communities, miners in other coalfields have sometimes responded with headline-grabbing political theatre, including underground mine occupations and hunger strikes. That nothing approaching this level of militancy occurred in the Crowsnest Pass is puzzling, especially given the history of labour radicalism in the region and the rise of the working class between 1945 and 1949, often fuelled by combative political protest.

The argument detailed in this chapter is that a complex of factors conspired against the organization of a broad fightback to the crisis in 1953–54. These factors fall into five categories. First, the union locals were internally weakened by the retirement of prominent leaders and long-time activists; by the failure to thoroughly rejuvenate union leadership ranks because many younger workers with leadership potential left the industry as the depth of the coal crisis became apparent; and by the challenges associated with trying to incorporate new segments of the workforce (e.g., recent immigrants from Europe) into the leftist union culture that had flourished over the first half of the twentieth century. Second, the uneven character of the production cutbacks in 1953–54 created divisions among the five UMWA locals, making it difficult to build region-wide unity. Third, the District 18 office, in step with the directives of President John L. Lewis's headquarters in Washington, promoted collaboration with the coal companies and centralization of union decision making. This undercut the power of the UMWA locals in the region and forced them to divert valuable time and energy away from fighting mine closures and cutbacks and toward the issues of local autonomy, union democracy, and whether wildcat strikes should be included in the locals' repertoire of actions. Fourth, as I will detail in Chapter 4, the socialist tendencies in the worker movement faltered at the end of the 1940s and into the 1950s; consequently, the UMWA locals were no longer being pushed and cajoled by a great many activists into taking militant initiatives. Fifth, the miners' commitment to electoral politics and community leadership limited their perspectives on the developing coal crisis. Many union leaders had to respond to the crisis not only while wearing their union hats but also as elected municipal representatives. Their years of service in municipal governments had trained them to try to solve problems through established political channels; consequently, it is hardly a surprise that this is the path chosen by UMWA local leaders during the crisis in 1953–54. I contend that this was a dead-end path, however, since the severity of the crisis demanded unconventional collective action if the miners were to have any chance of mobilizing broad public sympathy and significant intervention by senior levels of government.

THE CONTOURS OF LIFE IN THE CROWSNEST PASS
AND ELK VALLEY, CIRCA 1950

The 1951 census reported a population of 15,500 people in the region, with about 57 percent of them living on the Alberta side of the provincial boundary (see the bottom of the first columns of Tables 2.1 and 2.2). With the growth in coal-mining employment in the years between 1945 and 1949, the regional population was as much as 2,000 people more in 1951 than it had been during the Second World War.[5] Given this population growth, there was a strong demand for housing after the war, yet this did not result in a boom in housing construction. Writing in 1952, Jim Cousins reported that "the war period (1939 to 1945) and the period since have not seen any great spate of building such as the prairie towns experienced. The need was just as great but the people seemed to have lost faith in the future of their towns."[6] Certainly by 1949, when it had become clear that the Canadian Pacific Railway was moving away from using coal-powered steam engines, miners would have been loath to invest in major house renovations, let alone a new house, because of the worry that the housing market would collapse in tandem with coal

TABLE 2.1 Population change in Crowsnest Pass communities, Alberta, 1951–66

Locales	Pop. 1951	Pop. 1956	% change 1951–56	Pop. 1961	% change 1956–61	Pop. 1966	% change 1961–66	% change 1951–66
1. Blairmore								
(a) 1951–55 boundaries	1,933	1,526[b]	–21[b]					
(b) 1955–66 boundaries		1,973		1,980	0	1,779	–10	–31[f]
2. Coleman								
(a) 1951–61 boundaries	1,961	1,566	–20	1,713	+9	1,492[d]	–13[d]	–24
(b) Boundaries in 1966						1,507		
3. Bellevue[a]	n/a	n/a	n/a	1,323	–3[c]	1,174	–11	n/a
4. Frank	239	221	–8	223	0	178	–20	–26
5. Improvement District 10								
(a) 1951–55 boundaries	4,706	3,716[b]	–21[b]					
(b) Boundaries in 1956		3,269		3,168[c]	–3[c]			
(c) 1957–61 boundaries				1,844		1,599[d]	–13[d]	–37[f]
(d) Boundaries in 1966						1,584[e]		
Total: Alberta Crowsnest Pass	8,839	7,029	–20	7,083	+1	6,222[e]	–12	–30[e]

NOTES: [a] Incorporated in 1957; previously part of Improvement District 10. [b] Est. assuming equivalent population decline in Blairmore and Improvement District 10 (–21 percent). Part of Improvement District 10 was annexed to Blairmore in 1955. [c] Est. assuming equivalent population decline in Bellevue and Improvement District 10 (–3 percent). [d] Est. assuming equivalent population decline in Coleman and Improvement District 10 (–13 percent). Parts of Improvement District 10 were annexed to Coleman, 1961–64. [e] Excluding the est. eighty people added to Improvement District 10 in 1964 from the area of Improvement District 8 outside Waterton Park. [f] Est. by totalling % changes for time periods.

SOURCES: Census of Canada 1961, *Population Historical*, 6–80 and 6–123; Census of Canada 1966, *Population: Divisions and Subdivisions Western Provinces*, 9–19 and 9–68.

TABLE 2.2 Population change in Elk Valley Communities, British Columbia, 1951–66

Locales	Pop. 1951	Pop. 1956	% change 1951–56	Pop. 1961	% change 1956–61	Pop. 1966	% change 1961–66	% change 1951–66
1. Fernie								
(a) 1951–52 boundaries	2,551	2,580[c]	+1[c]					
(b) 1952–61 boundaries		2,808		2,661	−5	2,577[e]	−3[e]	−7[g]
(c) 1962–66 boundaries						2,715		
2. Natal[a]								
(a) 1960–64 boundaries	n/a	n/a	n/a	829	n/a	802[e]	−3[e]	n/a
3. Sparwood[b]	n/a	n/a	n/a	n/a	n/a	1,928		n/a
4. Unorganized Subdivision C								
(a) 1951–52 boundaries	4,088	4,134[c]	+1[c]					
(b) 1952–59 boundaries		3,906		3,506[d]	−10[d]			
(c) 1960–61 boundaries				2,677		2,593[e]	−3[e]	−12[g]
(d) Boundaries in 1966						1,329		
Total: Elk and Flathead Valleys	6,639[f]	6,714	+1	6,167[f]	−8	5,972[f]	−3	−10

NOTES: [a] Incorporated as a village in 1960. Prior to this, it was part of Unorganized Subdivision C. It was folded into the District of Sparwood in 1966. [b] Incorporated as a village in 1964; in 1965, it had a population of 356. Prior to 1964, it was part of Unorganized Subdivision C. It was folded into the District of Sparwood in 1966. [c] Estimated assuming that population increase in percent is equivalent in Fernie and Unorganized Subdivision C (+1 percent). [d] Estimated assuming that population decrease in percent is equivalent in Natal and Unorganized Subdivision C (−10 percent). [e] Estimated assuming that population decrease in percent is equivalent in Fernie, Natal, and the rest of the region (−3 percent). [f] Excludes those living on First Nations reserves. [g] Estimated by adding together percentage changes for each of the time periods.

SOURCES: Census of Canada 1961, *Population Historical*, 6–84 and 6–125; Census of Canada 1966, *Population: Divisions and Subdivisions Western Provinces*, 9–60 and 9–70; Regional Planning Division ... and Underwood McLellan and Associates, *Natal-Sparwood*, vi–8.

production. Therefore, while in early 1949 the federal employment office described the housing situation as "bad" since "there isn't a room or suite or house to rent" from one end of the region to the other, it seemed unlikely that this tight housing market would last much longer.[7]

By the late 1940s, a sizable percentage of the old houses in the region had been at least somewhat modernized. In his capacity as a high school teacher in Coleman, Jim Cousins got students to survey the condition of the housing stock along a street in West Coleman. Of the approximately fifty houses, 70 percent had furnaces, and 38 percent had indoor plumbing. Cousins estimated that the state of housing on this street approximated the region's average.[8] Across the Crowsnest Pass and Elk Valley, most houses were privately owned. The major exception was the village of Michel, where CNPC owned the housing stock (laid out in distinctive rows), renting accommodations to miners. The coal company also owned Michel Hospital (see Figure 2.1) before donating it to the Michel Hospital Society in 1964.[9]

The Crowsnest Pass and Elk Valley of 1950 were populated by two large language groups (Slavonic language speakers and English speakers), although several other language groups were also present, notably Italian speakers.[10] In the early decades of the twentieth century, there was strong residential segregation by ethnocultural group. For instance, West Coleman was known as "Slavtown," and East Coleman housed people with Polish or Ukrainian ancestry.[11] A similar residential pattern defined Coal Creek.[12] In 1952, however, Cousins observed, "this zoning is not nearly as distinct as it was twenty-five years ago as second and third generation couples move into better, less crowded residential areas."[13] There were two complementary reasons for the reduction in ethnocultural residential segregation: first, relations of solidarity sustained both by the labour process in the underground coal mines and by widespread union participation served to systematically erode ethnocultural stratification among workers; second, extensive intermarriage occurred among the second and third generations of families in the region. In reference to the effects of intermarriage, Cousins made the following observation after an attempt to trace the ethnic origins of schoolchildren by combining information from the father's and mother's sides of a family had "produced a

FIGURE 2.1 Michel, British Columbia, in winter, undated. Top: Michel Hospital. Bottom: Looking down a row of houses toward the hospital. | By Vern Decoux. Courtesy of Galt Museum and Archives/Akaisamitohkanao'pa, images 20151020602a and 20151020603b.

hopeless jumble": "It is becoming increasingly difficult to label anyone with any particular nationality – other than Canadian. In some cases there are four-way combinations of national origins."[14]

In the early decades of the twentieth century, there had been a distinctive ethnocultural hierarchy in the region. Pauline Griegel, who grew up in the 1920s and 1930s, reported that "there was a lot of bigotry. As a kid, we were called bohunks. Any nationality, unless you were English, Scottish or Irish – they were the elite. The rest of them, you're all bohunks." Reflecting on the same era, Liz and Steve Liska blamed "the Englishmen" for ethnic strife and pointed to intermarriage as the factor that dispelled the ethnic status hierarchy. "Before it was always square heads, bohunks, wops," noted Steve. "And then they started getting married to these square heads and bohunks. Then they changed their melody. They changed their tune completely."[15]

It is noteworthy that Cousins, writing about this subject in 1952, equated ethnic ancestry with "racial origin" and termed the sense of superiority expressed by Anglo residents vis-à-vis their Slavonic and Italian neighbours in the early decades of the twentieth century "white superiority."[16] Therefore, the change in the ethnocultural hierarchy by 1950 amounted to the reclassification of ethnocultural groups originating in Southern and Eastern Europe as "white." This means that ethnocultural stratification among the coal-mining working class in 1950 had lost the racialized edge observed in the early part of the twentieth century.

Nevertheless, racism was still an important dimension of life in the Crowsnest Pass and Elk Valley in 1950. For the reasons elaborated in the introduction, which include "white preference" in hiring, the neighbouring Ktunaxa and Niitsitapi had been excluded from possible employment in coal mining at the birth of the industry, a pattern that continued into the 1950s. A mid-1950s study of employment among the Ktunaxa living at Yaqit ʔaꞏknuqⱡi 'it (Tobacco Plains), just fifty-five kilometres south of Fernie (see Map 0.2), did not record anyone working in the coal industry.[17] Indeed, Indigenous peoples were virtually absent from the public record during these years except as part of the "pioneer" past.[18] Nevertheless, by this time, some Ktunaxa felt comfortable enough to journey to Fernie to take part in horse racing in early July and the city's Labour Day parade,[19] spectacles at which an Indigenous presence was a welcome addition of western authenticity.[20]

Japanese Canadians comprised another group who experienced racist exclusion and abuse. Some Japanese Canadian families living in the area in 1950 had spent from 1943 to 1945 in an internment camp in the Slocan Valley of British Columbia, and others had worked on sugar beet farms in southern Alberta. At the end of the war, they made their way to the Crowsnest Pass for the employment opportunities there (the ban on Japanese Canadians living on the West Coast was not lifted until 1949). Japanese Canadian men were apparently excluded from employment in the coal mines in the late 1940s and 1950s and thus forced to seek work at firms such as Knight's Lumber and Summit Lime Works. (The strong demand for labour from the coal industry made it difficult for employers who paid less than the mines to find workers.) Two daughters from one of these families found jobs at a café in Coleman. One of the daughters recalled being verbally abused by miners, who would gruffly complain to the proprietor "I don't want your bloody Jap to wait on me."[21] Bald-faced racism toward Japanese Canadian workers thus coexisted with the newly formed ethnocultural tolerance among the white working class.

Blacks were yet another group treated as a racialized "other" by the white working class in the 1950s. Educator Isabel Gill reported that a group of teenage boys adopted the persona of a Ku Klux Klan group in the 1950s, wearing white hoods, riding through Bellevue and Hillcrest on horseback, and causing mischief, to the irritation of residents.[22] These teenagers did not target African Canadians for abuse because there were very few if any people identifying as Black living in the area at the time.[23] However, the political insensitivity of their Ku Klux Klan costumes was indicative of the limitations of a white working-class culture that had not come to grips with the pernicious effects of racist thinking and practice.[24]

Life in 1950 in the Crowsnest Pass and Elk Valley was quite different from the rhythms and routines of life in the twenty-first century. For instance, married women, the vast majority of whom were not part of the paid labour force, often contributed to their family's well-being by tending a garden and keeping livestock (see Figure 2.2). In late 1947, a former dairy farmer near Coleman stated that "a large herd of cattle remained in East Coleman, as individuals retained one cow each for their own use."[25]

In 1950, TV reception was still a few years away in the Crowsnest Pass and Elk Valley. As a consequence, local cultural events still dominated residents' leisure activities. Hunting and fishing were very popular, particularly among men. There were "respectable" elements of working-class culture, notably avid musicianship[26] and the strong encouragement

FIGURE 2.2 Woman with milk bucket, cow, and chickens, Crowsnest Pass, Alberta. Although dated before 1950, this figure accurately represents the continuing importance of domestic food production in 1950. | By Gushul Studio. Courtesy of Glenbow Archives, Image NC-54-318.

that young people received to pursue postsecondary education. However, the male-dominated working-class culture was mainly "rough" in character. Jim Cousins noted that the Crowsnest Pass had "achieved a reputation as a rough, tough area with considerable drinking and brawling."[27] That reputation was demonstrated by an incident in Coleman in 1947 in which the town's police chief was beaten up; this caused the town council to increase police protection on Saturdays and "statement Fridays" (i.e., paydays). A conflict in Fernie in 1956 further demonstrated the sometimes testy relations between police and miners: Local 7310 of the UMWA authorized its secretary to "take [up] the matter of the Police picking up men for very little."[28]

One leisure activity that was simultaneously rough and respectable was ice hockey. The major communities in this coalfield society fielded competitive men's hockey teams in various leagues over the years, and the Coleman Grands won the Western Canada Intermediate Hockey

Championship in 1947. When the coal industry was in good shape, success in these leagues was not left to chance: each coal company would support the team in a particular community by employing "imported" hockey players during a particular season.[29] Despite the enthusiasm for competitive hockey, however, the infrastructure for the sport was somewhat lacking – the only artificial ice facility as of 1950 was in Bellevue.[30]

A momentous change to life resulted from the introduction of a retirement pension for coal miners beginning in 1950. District 18 had negotiated the financial basis for the retirement pension in 1949 (see Chapter 1), but in early 1950 the WCBCOA obdurately refused to agree to the payment of retirement pensions under the terms and conditions proposed by District 18 (miners were to be eligible for the pension at age sixty-two if they had a minimum of twenty years of service in the industry in a pertinent classification, with only six months of employment in a year needed to qualify for service in that year; only the last five years of service had to be with an employer contributing to the Welfare and Retirement Fund; and a pensioner would be paid the difference between seventy-five dollars per month and the value of any government benefits received). The WRF trustees, backed by both District 18 and the Domestic Coal Operators' Association of Western Canada, secured a court order on 23 June 1950 that allowed the payment of retirement pensions, backdated to the beginning of the year.[31]

This decision provided elderly coal miners with a newfound opportunity to retire from the industry with dignity. The qualifying age of sixty-two was particularly significant given that seventy years was the qualifying age for universal Old Age Security payments from the program's inception in 1952 to 1966 (although a means-tested benefit for Albertans aged sixty-five to sixty-nine also started in 1952[32]). Therefore, the District 18 plan was particularly advantageous to coal miners between the ages of sixty-two and sixty-nine who might otherwise have tried to continue working until age seventy.

Payments from the Welfare and Retirement Fund between 1948 and 1968 are recorded in Figure 2.3. These are figures for all of District 18. In 1950, $151,000 in retirement pensions was paid. The amount doubled in the next year (to $333,000) and almost doubled again in 1952 (to $616,000).

FIGURE 2.3 UMWA District 18, WRF benefits, 1948–68

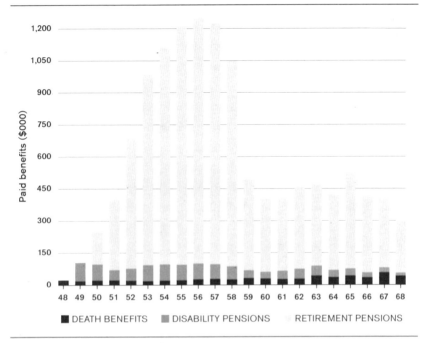

Paid benefits ($000)

■ DEATH BENEFITS   ■ DISABILITY PENSIONS   RETIREMENT PENSIONS

Data based on GWRC, M-6000, file 392, Welfare and Retirement Fund, "Summary of Operations from Inception to August 31, 1970."

By the end of the first major downturn in the steam coal industry in 1955, District 18 was paying out $1,117,000 per year in retirement pensions plus another $73,000 in disability pensions. A total of 1,400 UMWA members were in receipt of monthly pensions at the end of 1955, receiving an average payment of $71 per month. Starting on 1 June 1952, the maximum monthly retirement pension was increased to $100 per month (before any government benefits such as Old Age Security or War Veterans Allowance were deducted), and the maximum disability pension was increased to $80 month (before the deduction of Workmen's Compensation or other government benefits).[33] A reasonable estimate is that 560 miners from the Crowsnest Pass and Elk Valley (40 percent of the 1,400 total pensioners in District 18) were in receipt of monthly pensions from the fund in 1955.[34] Hence, close to 20 percent of the region's workforce of 3,000 miners at the end of the 1940s had shifted to District 18 pensions by 1955.

The immediate effect of the full implementation of the District 18 retirement pension was the opening up of employment opportunities in the
mines in the region, although this effect was offset to some extent by the
loss of jobs associated with the rapid contraction of production in the
Alberta mines in 1953–54 as well as the coal companies' decision to expand strip mining. Indeed, any new hires in 1953–54 had to be willing to
tolerate the small paycheques resulting from working "short weeks," so
the coal companies had difficulty filling skilled positions.[35]

Since the long-term prospects for the steam coal industry started to
look bleak in the late 1940s (see Chapter 1), some younger workers quit
working in the mines even before the regular occurrence of "short
weeks." Wilf Feller, the son of a miner, started to work at the Bellevue
mine in 1940 at the age of eighteen, and by 1947 he had earned his A-1
miner card. Married in 1946, he and his wife had been forced to live in a
renovated chicken coop for three months before finding more suitable
housing. In 1951, however, "seeing too many hints of the future," Feller
quit his job at the Bellevue mine for a position with a wholesale grocery
firm. That firm was unionized, and by 1957 Feller had become a business
agent for Local 987 of the International Union of Teamsters. He is an
example of a young miner who could have been part of the renewal of the
leadership of a UMWA local (in this case, Bellevue Local 7294) if only he
had kept working in the industry.[36]

Shortly after the introduction of the District 18 retirement pension,
Sub-District 5 recognized the need to cultivate and train new union leaders who could take the places of those long-time union leaders who chose
to retire.[37] (This decision did not come out of the blue – it was made only
a few weeks after the retirement of Enoch Williams, who had been Sub-
District 5's representative on the District Executive Board.) Although
well intentioned, this initiative could not overcome the departures of
young workers such as Wilf Feller from the coal industry.

As coal production declined sharply in 1953, more and more coal miners voluntarily left their jobs. In September, West Canadian Collieries
reported, "coal miners in the West are leaving the industry in increasing
numbers due entirely to short time work. Those that can are going on
Pension while the younger men are seeking and finding employment in

other fields of endeavour."[38] Another trend was for miners employed in the hard-hit Alberta mines to seek somewhat steadier employment in the BC mines. By the end of 1953, a bus was in service to transport miners from Coleman to Michel Collieries.[39]

RESTRUCTURING, RETRENCHMENT, AND TRYING
TO REINVENT THE COAL INDUSTRY, 1950–56

The decline of the railway steam coal industry was well under way by 1952. On 8 January, the coal operators informed District 18 that "the Railway Companies have converted nearly 500 [formerly coal-powered] locomotives in Western Canada to oil-burners. This represents a loss of coal tonnage of 1.5M tons annually ... The Diesel-powered railway locomotive is now a common sight in this area."[40] People living in the Crowsnest Pass and Elk Valley were among the first to learn how quickly the Canadian Pacific Railway would reduce its purchases of coal: "Perhaps the cruellest blow of all," asserted Jim Cousins, "was the fact that the railway through the Pass was one of the first lines to be converted to oil-burning."[41]

Behind the scenes, the Canadian Pacific Railway decided to "replace all its locomotives with diesels" in early 1951, according to information conveyed to the Alberta government by British Columbia's minister of mines.[42] Therefore, the inevitability of the looming economic crisis was known to provincial governments well before the first major drop in coal sales in 1953–54, and it is reasonable to assume that this information had been shared with coal operators. In this section, I detail the steps taken by the coal operators in the region to restructure and attempt to reinvent their businesses after they learned of the CPR plan to use diesel for locomotives.

The major restructuring strategy begun in the late 1940s – shifting production away from underground mines to surface mines – continued in the 1950s. Strip-mined coal as a percentage of the total coal produced by operators on the Alberta side of the region grew from 36 percent in 1951 to 49 percent in 1955.[43] Furthermore, in contract negotiations during the first half of the 1950s, the coal companies fought to limit improvements to, and sometimes to reduce, workers' wages and benefits. The rationale for this approach was that lower labour costs would help to keep the price of coal competitive with alternative fuels and thereby preserve jobs. In the next section, I will show that rank-and-file miners were not always willing to go along with such austerity. Even so, as shown in Table 1.2, the coal operators were largely successful in containing wage costs in the early 1950s since the average real wage of company miners in 1955 ($13.15 per day in 1954 dollars) was only marginally higher than the comparable wage in 1948 ($12.85 in 1954 dollars). Contributions to the Welfare and Retirement Fund were another matter, however, since they rose from five cents per ton in 1948 to twenty cents per ton in 1953. From the operators' perspective, this was the cost of efficiently moving less productive elderly workers off their payrolls.

One consequence of the operators' strategy of limiting wage increases was that it made retaining and recruiting workers that much more difficult, especially when wages were rising in other sectors of the Canadian economy. To meet their needs for new underground miners without having to compete for workers in the domestic labour market, the coal operators enlisted the federal government's help to recruit workers from Europe. However, this recruitment effort was temporarily side-tracked in the fall of 1951 when applications by CNPC and McGillivray Creek for immigrant workers were being "held up because of the opposition of local unions." Nonetheless, the federal government soon acceded to the applications, and the number of European miners subsequently recruited to work in the region in the early 1950s was substantial: a story in 1953 reported that, at Michel Collieries alone, "in the past two years 250 immigrants from Italy and Germany have been brought out to remedy the shortage of manpower."[44]

Because this large-scale recruitment of European miners substituted for the increased wages that would have been required to recruit domestic workers, union leaders in the area voiced opposition. Unfortunately, the language that they used was sometimes nativist and anti-immigrant. For instance, at a mass meeting in Blairmore on 14 March 1954, the president of Michel Local 7292, Sam English, offered the slogan "Put Canada First for Canadian People" and specifically questioned the continuing recruitment of immigrants from Europe at a time when 600,000 workers in Canada were unemployed. Happily, this anti-immigrant sentiment does not seem to have spilled over into how new immigrants were treated by the union locals. For example, the minutes for a Local 2633 meeting include this reassuring entry:

> The whole question of immigrants being brought into the mines and their protection was discussed. This matter was brought up as the result of the firing of an Italian immigrant. The Secretary was unable to secure him his job back in the mine. The committees at both mines were instructed to see that these men receive justice and protection from the Union.[45]

Furthermore, in opposition to the nativist narrative, Thomas Uphill later offered a pithy class analysis of the significance of the large-scale recruitment of immigrant miners: "The hand of the capitalist is stretched out to the newcomers to assist them in halting the progress of the union movement."[46]

Another restructuring strategy was company amalgamation to achieve economies of scale and make it possible to close duplicate production facilities. To this end, in late 1951, three of the four companies operating on the Alberta side of the Crowsnest Pass – McGillivray Creek Coal and Coke, International Coal and Coke, and Hillcrest-Mohawk Collieries – amalgamated into a new coal company, Coleman Collieries.[47] This move set the stage for several mine and tipple closures over the next three years (listed in Table 2.3). With these closures, and the short weeks worked by miners at Coleman Collieries' surviving operations, the new company's coal production decreased by 59 percent over its first three years of operation. Its production tonnage had been hurt not only by a decline in the CPR steam coal order but also by the end of its sales of coke to the CMS zinc smelter at Trail (see note c in Table 2.3 for details).

In addition to implementing various cost-cutting and productivity-enhancing strategies, the coal companies began to look for new customers for their coal. In the 1950s, extracting chemicals and manufacturing other by-products from coal was frequently posited as a saviour of the

TABLE 2.3 **Mine, by-product, and tipple closures, 1950–56**

1950 (by October)	Closure of the main underground mine of Hillcrest-Mohawk Collieries[a]
1952 (February)	Closure by Coleman Collieries of the Hillcrest-Mohawk tipple and No. 5 underground mine[b]
1952 (February)	Closure by Coleman Collieries of its beehive coke ovens[c]
1954 (29 March)	Closure by Coleman Collieries of the International underground mine and the McGillivray Creek tipple[d]
1956 (February)	Closure by West Canadian Collieries of the Adanac underground mine[e]

NOTES: [a] GWRC, M-1601, file 569, WCC, "Other Mines" report, 9 October 1950.

[b] LAC, RG 33/42, vol.2, file "Hearings Held at Calgary Alberta – Volume 9," submission by UMWA District 18 to the Rand Royal Commission on Coal, Calgary hearings transcript, 220.

[c] PAA, Serra, PR1972.0355/5, handwritten summary of interview with Joe Mayerchak. A note by Colin O'Brian of the Dominion Coal Board (DCB) dated 12 September 1951 stated that the loss of its coke outlet had been a serious blow to the International Coal and Coke Company; see LAC, RG 81, vol. 32, file 9-4-32. The sole customer for coke produced at Coleman had been the zinc smelter at Trail, British Columbia, operated by Consolidated Mining and Smelting (CMS). In the late 1940s and early 1950s, the company cut back its orders of coke from Coleman. "This was due in part," explained Jim Cousins, "to a surplus of coke built up by the smelter, but also to the poor quality of Coleman coke in the year or two preceding." Cousins, *Crow's Nest History*, 129n2).

[d] *Coleman Journal*, 24 and 31 March 1954.

[e] *Coleman Journal*, 29 February and 7 March 1956.

industry, including by the Industrial Federation of Labour (IFL) of Alberta.[48] A story in the *Star Weekly* in October 1953 envisioned a rosy future for mining at Michel because of coal by-products:

> At Michel, B.C., they've built a multi-million-dollar by-products plant [see Figure 2.4] to turn out the coal tar base for more than 2,000 manufactured items that bulk large on the Canadian market. Soon the entire output of the mine will go through that plant, and gone will be the worries about fluctuating sales, shortage of cars, dieselization of railways and new sources of competition.[49]

This prognostication was wildly off the mark. CNPC never invested in any of the technology that would have allowed for the manufacture of value-added products out of coal tar; instead, it simply shipped the car-

FIGURE 2.4 Construction of by-product ovens, Crow's Nest Pass Coal, Michel, British Columbia, 1952. Old beehive ovens are nearby, and housing is just across the tracks.
| Photographer unknown. Image GA, NA-3663-14, held by Libraries and Cultural Resources Digital Collections, University of Calgary. Publication courtesy Glenbow Archives.

cinogenic substance "to plants in the east" by tanker car. Twelve years after the *Star Weekly* article, the by-products plant remained a minor part of Michel Collieries' operations, employing just 60 of the company's 500 unionized workers.[50]

West Canadian Collieries was the operator most engaged in efforts to reinvent its business model during the first coal crisis of the 1950s. In 1952, the company diversified its holdings by purchasing a prairie strip mine located next to a CPR line near Halkirk, Alberta, about 120 kilometres east of Red Deer.[51] At the same time, the company worked to find a new market for the coal that it could produce at its mines in the Crowsnest Pass. West Canadian Collieries saw a steel plant as the best hope for a major new customer.[52] In March 1955, it secured a permit "to carry on surveys for iron ore on 38,268 acres of land surrounding Waterton Park." Later that year a press report titled "Enthusiasm Sweeps Pass" revealed that the company had found iron ore reserves at Burmis on the eastern boundary of the Crowsnest Pass (see Map 0.1) and invited "high ranking executives of the United States steel industry" to inspect the reserves. The story revealed that "what the inspection disclosed to the officials is not being divulged, but rumours are racing around the Pass region that 'something big is coming in the way of steel plants.'" However, residents' expectations were running far ahead of feasibility studies and planning. In contrast, a provincial civil servant was cautious in his assessment of the prospects for a steel smelter: "Several rumours regarding pending industrial development continue to spread throughout the Pass but confirmation could not be obtained anywhere."[53]

A newspaper report in early 1956 showed that the WCC objective was to convince a foreign steel manufacturer to build a steel plant. West Canadian Collieries was already mining small quantities of iron ore near Burmis: 100 tons of ore were to be shipped to Norway "for experiments and smelting," and iron ore had already "been sent to the United States Steel Corporation in Pittsburgh and to places in Canada for analysis." There was nothing in this report to indicate that investment in a steel plant was probable, let alone imminent, even though West Canadian Collieries was certainly diligent in trying to make such an investment happen. Nevertheless, many prominent Crowsnest Pass residents somehow came to believe that the establishment of a steel plant was all but guaranteed. In March 1956, the *Calgary Herald* reported that "at present the special committee [on unemployment] is carrying out a housing survey to cope with the expected boom when iron ore developments reach fruition and a surge of prosperity reaches the Crowsnest Pass area." Then in June 1956 the *Coleman Journal* reported that "well informed sources stated to the *Journal* that ... the erection of a smelter will be started in the near future." Tellingly, however, the paper ran the story without any comment by a WCC official or any details on who would be building the smelter.[54]

The steel plant "fever" of 1956 crested in mid-November. Pincher Creek–Crowsnest MLA William Kovach first told the *Calgary Albertan* that "drilling for the footings of the smelter would begin in a day or two" and then informed the *Coleman Journal* that "the construction of a $5,000,000 steel smelter at Burmis ... will get under way in the next few days." Kovach made the comments "after consultation in Calgary between a French banking and industrial group" and a WCC executive.

The MLA appears to have had inside information about these talks since he reported that a special technique had already been devised to smelt the iron ore found in southwestern Alberta, and the Canadian Pacific Railway would extend a spur line south from Pincher Creek to transport iron ore from various deposits to the planned smelter.[55]

Once again the story was run without any confirmation of the details from company or government officials. MLA Kovach ended up with egg on his face since the footings for the smelter were never drilled. The hopes of the eastern edge of the Crowsnest Pass for economic salvation were dashed. This episode shows that West Canadian Collieries was fully cognizant of the depth of the crisis and had invested a great deal of effort and resources in trying to reinvent its coal business at Blairmore and Bellevue as a supplier to a steel foundry. Because this effort had not been fruitful by the end of 1956, however, the company had no economic safety net in place on the verge of the Canadian Pacific Railway completely phasing out its purchases of steam coal.

By the mid-1950s, a confusing mix of pessimism and optimism pervaded discussions of the future of the coal industry in western Canada. The pessimism was based upon the recognition that the traditional markets for coal were fast disappearing. This was the context for a pessimistic comment by Wilbur Uren, chair of the Dominion Coal Board. "The next four or five years will be vital ones in the life of the coal industry," he stated in early 1954. "It is going to be difficult to keep the patient breathing."[56] Yet, at the same time, optimism was in the air, fuelled by efforts to identify new markets for the coal industry. In late September 1956, William Whittaker, the managing director of the Coal Operators' Association of Western Canada,[57] pointed to the development of a steel industry as one source of hope. "However," he added, "the coal industry expects power production to be the biggest factor in increased output in the years to come."[58] Whether coal from the Crowsnest Pass and Elk Valley would figure in the expected growth in coal-fired electricity generation was far from certain.

Power generation had long been a minor customer for coal mined in the region. Between 1927 and 1969, a small generation station operated at Crowsnest Lake (on the Alberta-BC boundary; see Map 0.1) to serve the regional market, powered by pulverized coal. For most of this time, it supplemented the power produced by East Kootenay Power Company at hydroelectricity generators on the Elk River.[59] However, if electricity generation was to revitalize the coal industry in the wake of the collapse of sales to the Canadian Pacific Railway, then that power would have to be produced in large quantities and transmitted to a market with fast-growing demand.

Between 1950 and 1956, there was public discussion of only one plan for extensive generation of electricity using the coal resources of the region. The California promoters envisioned a massive $2-billion invest-ment in a chain of 100 coal-fired power plants to be located "on a strip of land 35 miles wide and 125 miles long along the Alberta B.C. border" in southwestern Alberta, with the electricity to be exported to the United States.[60] But this grandiose plan disappeared without a trace after it was first announced.

POLITICAL STRATEGIES AND ALLIANCES

The campaign to oppose the export of natural gas from Alberta con-tinued into the 1950s. Several groups joined the coal operators and District 18 in supporting this cause, including Coleman's mayor and council, who sent a letter to Premier Manning in early 1951. The pre-mier's matter-of-fact reply reveals the principle that he would apply when coal production declined sharply in 1953–54: "There is no doubt but what the production of gas in the Province has adversely affected the coal industry, and that the export of gas may have even more far-reaching effect. However, in endeavouring to protect or assist one in-dustry we must not do so to the point which will discourage progress and development in other fields and progress generally." For Premier Manning, progress for Alberta was irrevocably tied to the exploitation of its oil and gas resources. In mid-November 1951, he proudly informed the annual convention of the Alberta Association of Municipal Districts that "[the provincial government's] revenue from oil royalties, leases and sale of development rights had passed the $110,750,000 mark," and he bragged that Alberta would likely soon be able to eliminate provincial income taxes.[61]

Coordinated action in opposition to the export of natural gas led to further company-union collaboration. In 1950, District 18 and the coal operators established an umbrella lobbying organization, the Western Coal Federation. The following year this new organization mounted a large delegation that travelled to Ottawa to lobby federal cabinet ministers, railway officials, and the Dominion Coal Board against the railways' proposal to increase the charge for moving coal.[62] Although the Western Coal Federation disappeared from the public record after this Ottawa trip, during the 1950s District 18 and the coal operators sometimes coordinated their lobbying efforts.

One of the important dimensions of the coal crisis of 1953–54 was that both the coal operators and District 18 focused their requests for assistance on the federal government, thereby implicitly absolving the province of any major responsibility. The Manning government encouraged this position by willingly supporting lobbying demands no matter how interventionist and contrary to its core conservative economic philosophy as long as those demands were addressed to the federal government. The result was that the provincial government was often misleadingly depicted as an ally of the Alberta coal industry. For instance, after a meeting in Edmonton in 1951, William Whittaker reported that "the meeting with the government officials was carried on in a most friendly and cooperative basis, both the premier and the minister of mines and minerals expressing the greatest interest in the future of the coal industry."[63]

Nevertheless, there were several voices challenging Premier Manning's right to stand above the fray and refuse any consideration of provincial aid for the coal industry, notably the leaders of three Alberta opposition parties: J. Harper Prowse of the Liberals, Elmer Roper of the Cooperative Commonwealth Federation, and Ben Swankey of the Labor-Progressive Party. Prowse, leader of the official opposition, intervened during a debate in the legislature shortly after the closure of the International mine in Coleman. He asked Premier Manning a pointed question demonstrating that he well understood the government's tactical manoeuvring:

"Has Alberta any plans for this serious coal situation without passing the buck to Ottawa?" The premier replied, predictably, that "Alberta never has and never will pass the buck to Ottawa."[64]

What the Manning government could reasonably have done to help the coal industry was spelled out in the conclusion to a series of articles on the coal crisis by Doug Collins, published in the fall of 1953.[65] Collins called on the Alberta government to match "federal transportation subventions dollar for dollar." He estimated that this would increase the market for Alberta coal in Ontario by 2 million tons. "The cost would at most be no more than $3,000,000. Such a sum would hardly bankrupt the provincial treasury, and in the light of the economic benefit to the province would be well worth it."[66] It is fascinating that the Manning government's hold on the province was so great that it was able to disregard this cogent argument without consequence.

The coal crisis of 1953–54 occurred while two long-established federal policies to assist the industry remained in place. Both policies were designed to improve western coal operators' ability to compete with American coal imports in the large Ontario and smaller Manitoba coal markets and therefore were the focus of intense political lobbying throughout this period. The first policy was a tariff on coal imports first introduced in 1928 that stood at a modest fifty cents per ton in the early 1950s. The second policy regarded transportation subventions for the shipping of western Canadian coal by rail to customers in Ontario and Manitoba. The modest levels of existing transportation subventions, in combination with the small tariff, garnered western Canadian coal a tiny portion of the large Ontario market, mainly served by imported American coal (to the tune of some 22 million tons in 1953). With the falling levels of railway purchases of steam coal in the early 1950s, the obvious short-term remedy was some combination of a federal tariff and subvention increases to allow coal from the Crowsnest Pass and Elk Valley to eat into the market share of imports. The federal Liberal government never warmed to this idea, however. C.D. Howe, the powerful minister of trade and commerce, had signalled his opposition to helping the coal industry in 1950 when he told the House of Commons that "the government did not see fit to extend capital assistance to modernize an industry

which was becoming economically unsound." In September 1954, federal Minister of Mines George Prudham rejected increasing either the
tariff or rail subventions, stating that "tariffs would be a real hardship on
the consumer."[67]

Despite these clear statements from the federal government, throughout the 1953–54 coal crisis, the District 18 executive never wavered in its
determination to secure tariff or subvention relief. In November 1954,
District 18 took the lead in organizing another union-company lobbying
trip to Ottawa. At this point, the coal operators and the district's executive
officers were singing from the same hymn book. Not only had the union
membership recently voted to renew the collective agreement for one
year without any wage or benefit increase, but also District 18's president
had lobbied for acceptance of that agreement using language positing a
commonality of interests between mining companies and workers: "We
are helping ourselves when we help the industry," avowed Robert Livett.
The *Lethbridge Herald* accurately opined that District 18 had swung "into
a friendly partnership for strengthening the industry."[68]

During the November 1954 lobbying trip, the joint delegation pre-
sented to the federal government a detailed, commissioned report, "The
Future of the Coal Industry in Western Canada," prepared by J.D.
Woods and Gordon. The Gordon in this firm's name was Walter L.
Gordon, who would go on to chair the Royal Commission on Canada's
Economic Prospects between 1955 and 1957 and serve as a Liberal MP
between 1962 and 1968, including a stint as the minister of finance.
Gordon was a nationalist who believed in active government intervention in the economy,[69] and this orientation informed the report in 1954. It
argued that Canada's future national interest (specifically in the case of
war or when the United States was no longer able to export oil to Canada)
would be served best by "using coal wherever possible and thereby con-
serving the country's oil resources." Specific recommendations included
creating an Energy Control Board that would have the power to artifi-
cially maintain coal markets in different sectors of the economy; replacing
2 million tons of coal imported into Ontario with western Canadian coal;
and requiring the railways to "maintain a minimum number of coal fired
locomotives."[70]

The more protectionist and interventionist of these recommendations did not have a chance of being accepted by the conservative, pro-business cabinet dominated by C.D. Howe and Prime Minister Louis St. Laurent. However, two recommendations found favour. First, the call for the federal government "to actively encourage ... the expansion of coal exports to Japan" was taken up by successive federal governments in the 1950s and 1960s. Second, the federal cabinet issued a directive on 18 March 1955 that partially implemented a recommendation to burn only Canadian coal in federal buildings: it stipulated that "Canadian coal must be used in all government coal burning installations" as long as the Canadian coal did not exceed the cost of imported American coal by more than 10 percent (a figure that would be increased to 20 percent by Prime Minister John Diefenbaker in 1958). This modest policy initiative has been estimated to cost the federal government $1.25 million between 1955 and 1960 – a small price to pay given the patriotic political optics.[71]

In the early 1950s, the UMWA locals in the Crowsnest Pass and Elk Valley followed the lead of District 18 and accepted the need to forge an alliance with the coal operators to improve the prospects of the industry. Besides joint lobbying efforts, the new collaborative relationship produced three consecutive, unproblematic sets of contract negotiations between early 1950 and 1952, with two of the negotiations yielding pay increases for miners (documented in Table 1.2). These increases were agreed to by the operators in recognition of how the high rates of inflation in 1947 (9.6 percent), 1948 (14.6 percent), and 1951 (10.4 percent) had eroded the purchasing power of miners' wages. This short run of labour peace ended in 1953 when the membership rejected a tentative agreement that would have reduced the vacation pay of most miners, with strong majorities opposing the agreement at the Michel, Bellevue, and Blairmore locals. A month later the two parties came to an agreement that maintained the existing formula for calculating holiday pay and increased operator contributions to the Welfare and Retirement Fund by five cents per ton, although wages were left unchanged; it was accepted by a solid three-to-one ratio across District 18.[72]

Although an agreement on a new contract in 1953 was reached without a strike, the sequence of events called into question the cozy relationship that the District 18 leaders had cultivated with the coal operators and reawakened oppositional currents. Indeed, in a surprising turn of events in the middle of the furor over the contract in 1953, the membership of Coleman Local 2633 rejected the incumbent secretary-treasurer's re-election bid. William J. White's loss to Norman Ash by a margin of 424 to 329 was particularly significant because White had been the Sub-District 5 representative on the District Executive Board for the previous two years and thus was closely identified with District 18's strategic emphasis on company-union collaboration.[73]

As the coal crisis on the Alberta side of the Crowsnest Pass deepened in late 1953 and early 1954, the UMWA locals in Sub-District 5 finally moved to organize a mass community response. A meeting on 14 March drew a crowd of 400. Among the speakers was Sim Weaver, of Michel

FIGURE 2.5 Miners coming off shift at the International mine, Coleman, Alberta, circa 1952. Included in this photo are Mike Tarcon, Hubert Haysom, Erwin Spievak, Nick Hleuka, Frank Gejdos, and Ed Churla. The International was the first large underground mine in the region to be shut down – in March 1954 – resulting in 322 layoffs. | By George Hunter. Courtesy of Crowsnest Museum and Archives, Image CC-05-01.

Local 7292, who had journeyed to Ottawa in late 1953 to join a CCL delegation that lobbied the federal government on its coal policy. Weaver stated that his experience in Ottawa revealed that the members of the House of Commons "did not know that such towns as Blairmore, Coleman and other Pass towns exist."[74] The mass meeting concluded with a commitment to organize a follow-up meeting "at which ... attempts will be made to have two or three members from every organization and business together with coal operators and union officials to form a central committee to draw up a brief to present to the government." However, this plan for a multi-community fightback soon took second place to efforts by Local 2633 leaders and Town of Coleman officials to focus attention on Coleman Collieries' closure of the International mine, announced 22 March.[75]

On 25 March 1954, Coleman Local 2633 held a special membership meeting at the Roxy Theatre to discuss the devastating layoffs. Three accounts of the meeting are available: a newspaper story, the official minutes of the meeting, and a confidential report provided to William Bird, general manager of West Canadian Collieries, by an unknown informant. The meeting attracted "the largest crowd to ever assemble in Coleman," with 200 people unable to get into the theatre. The mood of the many workers laid off from the International mine was soured by the fact that their mine's seniority list was separate from the McGillivray Creek mine's seniority list; this meant that long-serving employees at the International mine could not exercise seniority-bumping rights at the other underground mine operated by Coleman Collieries. Bird's informant called it a "rough meeting" that included "some remarks towards officials – Mr. Harquail mainly." F.J. (Frank) Harquail had been the general manager of Hillcrest-Mohawk Collieries prior to the creation of Coleman Collieries; in that earlier position, he had crafted the coal operators' strategy that successfully broke the strike in 1950 by fire bosses at the mines in the Alberta side of the Crowsnest Pass.[76] Two years later, when the International, McGillivray, and Mohawk companies merged to form Coleman Collieries, Harquail joined the new company's management team. He is pictured with family members and dogs in Figure 2.6.[77] He will reappear in this story in the 1960s when, as Coleman Collieries'

FIGURE 2.6 F.J. Harquail (mine manager) with family members and dogs, circa 1940s.
| By Gushul Studio. Courtesy of Glenbow Archives, Image NC-54-4010.

president, he schemed to limit workers' pay and, for a second time, crafted a successful strategy to beat a strike.

At the meeting at the Roxy, two potential responses to the closures were proposed, reflecting a split in the Local 2633 leadership. Vice-President Steve Penney advocated blaming the provincial government for the situation and demanded a provincial subvention for coal: "The coal industry is down yet they take royalties from the industry. The government at Edmonton is doing nothing, they are taking millions out of oil, being partly responsible for our being out of work. Why don't they quit taking the [coal] royalties and give us a subvention?" His confrontational strategy apparently had some support among Local 2633 members since there was mention of organizing a "mass parade to [the] Legislative Buildings." To be most effective, such a political action would have had to rely on support from miners and their families throughout the Crowsnest Pass and Elk Valley. The opposing proposal was for a "made in Coleman" approach that eschewed tapping into the potential power of the regional worker movement. It was based upon the idea that Premier Manning was more likely to respond favourably to a delegation of "respectable" citizens from Coleman than to a crowd of angry workers. John Ramsay, a former president of Local 2633 and Coleman's deputy mayor, moved "that we as union men and citizens of the town of Coleman send a delegation to interview Premier Manning, this to be comprised of two union delegates, two from the town council and two from the Board of Trade." His heartbreak at this economic tragedy was unmistakable: "I have been in two explosions," Ramsay stated, "and this is the greatest blow I have ever seen." But so was his fervent effort to exclude neighbouring, more militant UMWA locals from any role in trying to make things better. As Ramsay argued, "don't take this as district wide. We have done that all the time and that is where we have made our mistake."[78]

The delegation from Coleman secured prompt action from a government dealing with the layoffs of approximately 500 coal miners in other parts of Alberta in addition to the 322 at Coleman Collieries. However, there was no help for the coal industry. The Coal Miners' Rehabilitation Act authorized the spending of up to $100,000 "in the rehabilitation of coal miners who have become unemployed in [designated areas]." The definition of "rehabilitation" was initially restricted to covering the moving expenses of miners who found jobs elsewhere (anywhere from the Great Lakes to the Pacific Coast).[79]

Before the Coleman delegation had returned from Edmonton, a second mass meeting was held in Blairmore on 4 April. It resulted in the establishment of a large "Citizens' Committee" tasked with drawing up "a good brief on ways and means that the coal industry could be assisted." There was also further militant talk at this public forum: "Should the pleas of the 10,000 people living in the area be disregarded ... demonstrations by hundreds of Pass people will result in Edmonton." Furthermore, a powerful call to action was issued in a letter to the editor from "a Coleman coal miner's wife." It advocated a region-wide protest movement targeted at both senior levels of government (see Text Box 2.1).[80]

Even though the Rehabilitation Act was formulated and passed in a matter of days, the Manning government was conflicted that maybe it was being too generous in helping laid-off miners and could create new expectations for government welfare services. Premier Manning's personal files include a 15 April 1954 memo titled "CONFIDENTIAL – Directive to Miners' Rehabilitation Committee." The memo instructed committee members "not to imply any welfare or relief assistance in this project but ... to refer to the project as an effort by the government to *assist* in the rehabilitation of those men who wish to help themselves become relocated." The Miners' Rehabilitation Committee (MRC), composed of three civil servants, began its work by registering unemployed coal miners in Coleman on 21 and 22 April to determine how many were employable and therefore candidates for rehabilitation assistance.[81] Shortly thereafter, the clash of political viewpoints came to a head inside Coleman Local 2633.

On 17 April, the boards of Sub-Districts 5 and 8 decided that the May Day 1954 celebration should be held in Coleman. Their intention was to use the bleak situation in Coleman to catalyze a powerful demonstration of working-class solidarity and put pressure on senior levels of government to do more for the coal industry. However, this plan did not find favour with those Local 2633 members who believed that quietly cooperating with the Miners' Rehabilitation Committee would achieve the best outcomes for recently laid-off miners. These minutes from the next Local 2633 membership meeting sketch the contours of the debate and its outcome:

> Bro. Andros [union president] reported on a meeting of Sub-Districts 5 and 8 regarding May Day stating it was their decision to hold May Day in Coleman ... Bro. Binda was opposed to holding May Day in Coleman this year as we were expecting members of the government in Coleman to try and relieve the recent and existing condition here and the adverse publicity we would get from the press. The secretary pointed out that we could not participate due to the fact that [there is] a motion on the books [against Local 2633 participating in May Day, passed in 1951], stating this was never rescinded. A motion was passed that we take a vote on whether we should rent the hall to the Sub-Districts. The result: 17 for and 43 against.[82]

TEXT BOX 2.1

A CALL TO ACTION BY A COLEMAN COAL MINER'S WIFE, 7 APRIL 1954

PEOPLE OF COLEMAN, THE PASS

The question in Coleman is "What are you going to do now?" Yes, what are we going to do? Just sit back and wait for the next person to do something? This shutdown affects every single person in Coleman, so let's all stick together and get results. Let's voice our opinions. Let our "says" be heard, not just in our homes and with our friends, but let's get them into every newspaper possible and try to keep this news on the front page every day till something is done. Because if we just sit back we will end up like the other towns where they closed the mines down. Nothing was done because they gave up too easy ...

Don't we have a say? Doesn't our concern come first, or rather shouldn't they come first to our government in our province, and federal government of Canada[?] ...

Are we asking for too much? Out of 24 million tons of coal being imported can't they help us by giving us at least a million ton order a year? Is that too much? And what would it mean to us – just put the whole town back on its feet.

With this vote, Local 2633 members effectively blocked a May Day protest event in Coleman; Sub-Districts 5 and 8 were forced to move the May Day celebration in 1954 to Natal.[83]

The dominant faction in Local 2633 had an unrealistic view of just how much assistance would be provided to unemployed Coleman miners by the Miners' Rehabilitation Committee. Nonetheless, it accurately predicted that the Manning government would not take kindly to being the target of political criticism. This became apparent at a meeting that John Ferguson, the MRC chair, and Social Credit MLA William Kovach had with the secretary-treasurer of Local 2633, Norman Ash, in early July 1954. Ferguson outlined the result of his investigation of a Local 2633 complaint against the hiring practices of the local foreman of the Department

Coal mining is our only industry here and way of making a living. How many of us can just pack up and go? How many of us have invested all our money here in Coleman in our homes, provided education for our children, and with the intention of spending the rest of our lives here in the coal mine? Now what?

People of Coleman, we must do something, no matter who we are or what we are – miners, merchants, union, doctors, teachers, housewives etc. And not just the people of Coleman, but the people of Crows Nest Pass, cause even at present if you have a job, but for how long is it? So let's the whole Crows Nest Pass stick together and do something before it's too late. Let's keep after our government, provincial and federal, till something is done ...

Let's try to get the government to come to the Pass to see the situation for themselves (provincial and federal). To actually see how hard a miner's life is, and how that he has invested his life's hard earnings in Coleman to be wiped out ... We are not asking something for nothing. Our help is a coal order so we can keep working.

Come on people of Coleman and The Pass, our sitting days are over.

SOURCE: Letter to the editor of the *Coleman Journal*, 7 April 1954, shortly after the closing of the International mine.

of Highways. (The foreman, Social Credit insider Joseph Hanrahan, would play an important role in the provincial by-election in Pincher Creek–Crowsnest in 1966 – to be discussed in Chapter 6.) Ferguson insisted that the complaint was unfounded and then reminded Ash

that the Committee did not look very favourably upon the attitude of a group in Coleman which seemed to have no other purpose but to embarrass the Government in its efforts in re-establishing the unemployed in other areas. There is a small group in Coleman which appears to be influenced by propaganda agents [a.k.a. communists] in finding fault with every endeavour put forth by the Committee.

Ferguson went so far as to issue a threat: "If certain members of the community would do nothing towards their own rehabilitation then they may find at some not-too-distant date that it would be too late to receive any assistance from the Provincial Government."[84]

Clearly, the Manning government expected political subservience in exchange for modest help. To this end, the documentary record includes a few examples of ingratiating praise, such as a report to Coleman town council in which Mayor Aboussafy and Deputy Mayor Ramsay "signified their true belief that the government are doing all possible and are centring their attention towards aiding the coal industry." At this point, Local 2633 was charting its own, conservative political response to the devastating closure of the International mine. It included contacting the Coleman Board of Trade to complain about married women holding jobs when so many men were unemployed.[85] Local 2633's approach demobilized the mass, regional protest movement that had been taking shape in the early spring of 1954, and I have been unable to find evidence of any further activity by the "Citizens' Committee" constituted at Blairmore on 4 April.

In 1954, the Miners' Rehabilitation Committee registered 305 laid-off employees of Coleman Collieries as being eligible for assistance. By the end of the year, it had paid the moving expenses for thirty-seven mining families to leave the region and issued travel warrants to another twenty-seven single miners.[86] Mike Malanchuk was one of the married Coleman miners whose family's moving expenses were covered by the committee. Malanchuk had immigrated to Canada in 1921 from the Ukraine with his mother and three brothers to join his father, who had been working at the International mine since 1912. A talented guitar and mandolin player, Malanchuk spent the years between 1927 and 1940 away from the Crowsnest Pass in Vancouver, Winnipeg, and Edmonton, studying and teaching music. He returned to Coleman in 1940 to work at the International mine. The Miners' Rehabilitation Committee paid about $300 to move the Malanchuk family's belongings to Vancouver in August 1954.[87]

However, a much larger group of the laid-off Coleman Collieries workers secured employment at Michel Collieries with no assistance from the committee. CNPC was so eager to recruit these miners that it subsidized half of the cost of a bus that transported workers who lived in Coleman or nearby communities to Michel. In the spring of 1955, there were "110 reallocated miners from the Crows Nest Pass Alberta area" working at Michel. Getting laid-off Alberta miners to take jobs at Elk River Colliery near Fernie was a trickier proposition since the cost of a bus service to Fernie was more than twice the cost of that to Michel, and CNPC was unwilling to subsidize the run. The Miners' Rehabilitation Committee finally agreed to cover half the cost of a Fernie bus service, effective 30 May 1955, and at that time thirty-seven Alberta miners participated.[88]

At an early point in the work of the committee, its chair identified two significant impediments to getting the laid-off miners to pursue jobs outside the Crowsnest Pass. The first impediment was that almost two-thirds of the registered miners were homeowners "who must, on their transfer to other employment in other locations, sacrifice the savings which they have invested in homes and improvements." Savings would be sacrificed because the market for housing in Coleman had collapsed after the closings in 1954. Indeed, by 1955, "real estate values dropped to such an extent that $4,000 to $5,000 homes could be bought for $800 and it was possible to rent a home in the Coleman area free of charge if the tenant would pay taxes and maintain the property."[89] In light of this factor, it is understandable that many former employees of Coleman Collieries were reluctant to pick up and leave the area. Consequently, jobs within the region were in high demand among the laid-off miners: in August 1954, twenty-four of the registrants were working for the Department of Highways on a seasonal project, and another twenty-five were employed at nearby lumber camps. The following spring the Alberta government created additional temporary employment: in mid-June, "some 50 of the aged miners and amputees and cripples" were working on a road construction project on Highway 3, and in September another thirty-four former miners were working for the provincial forestry department. The idea behind such projects was to get the men enough weeks of work so that they would qualify for unemployment benefits during the coming winter.[90]

A second impediment to getting miners to consider moving away from the Crowsnest Pass was "the feeling or hope among the miners that the International mine may reopen through increased orders, subsidies or tariff barriers placed against the importation of American coal."[91] However, while the MRC chair presented this "feeling or hope" as something negative since it discouraged people from getting serious about moving away, those fighting against mine closures were doing everything in their power to nurture that "feeling or hope" and thereby get more citizens actively involved in the struggle. Without a belief that victory was possible, why would people respond positively to the exhortation by a Coleman coal miner's wife recorded in Text Box 2.1: "Let's keep after our government, provincial and federal, till something is done"? In this regard, the Miners' Rehabilitation Committee was working at cross-purposes to all those groups and individuals fighting to preserve the integrity of the regional economy, society, and way of life. Indeed, the committee's thrust served to disorganize and disperse the political movement against mine closures.

Nonetheless, there was an endearing aspect of the MRC work, particularly in 1955 when it showed compassion for elderly and often "burned-out" miners who needed to keep working because they did not qualify for a retirement pension. Joseph Robutka was one miner who found new employment through the government. He was sixty years old when the International mine closed but had worked in the coal industry for only ten years and therefore would not qualify for a District 18 retirement pension at age sixty-two. He secured employment with the "Alberta and B.C. Governments as a camp cook until his retirement."[92]

Despite the engaged efforts of the Miners' Rehabilitation Committee over its first year of existence, the unemployment situation in the Alberta section of the region was dismal in May 1955: the regional NES office had 398 people registered for employment, not including "another 100 or more unemployed who are not registered and 101 others who have just been laid off from the mine [McGillivray Creek] at Coleman Collieries."[93] The high level of unemployment that spring might well have led four Blairmore men to hatch an ill-fated plan to steal copper wire from a BC Hydro site west of Cranbrook. They made off with about 300 kilograms of wire, worth $200, but were caught and sentenced to two months in jail.[94]

The employment picture soon brightened, however, and the combination of seasonal work projects and a rebound in coal orders caused the number of men registered at the Blairmore NES office to fall from 370 to 91 between May and August 1955. This led John Ferguson to conclude that the MRC work was "virtually complete for the time being." That fall Coleman Collieries rehired thirty "for the most part aged miners" to work at the International tipple. The welcome stabilization of coal production in 1955 and 1956 (at about 1.2 million tons of production per year on each side of the provincial boundary – see Figure I.2) resulted in the Miners' Rehabilitation Committee going into abeyance; its final act in 1956 was to discontinue, effective 1 May, the partial subsidization of Alberta miners' bus fares to Fernie.[95]

The years 1955 and 1956 presented a window of opportunity for the five UMWA locals in the region, their allies in kindred organizations and municipal governments, and the District 18 leadership to take stock of the successes and failures of their political strategies leading up to and during the 1953–54 downturn and to come up with a revised game plan for the next stage of the struggle. However, an intractable assertion of centralized power by the District 18 executive officers, acting at the behest of the International UMWA office in Washington, not only preoccupied the union locals – wasting valuable time and resources – but also resulted in new limits on their scope for independent action. Furthermore, in refusing calls for fully fledged democracy in District 18, the Washington office blocked a pathway for greater mobilization of members.

New Attacks on Democracy and Local Autonomy in District 18

The democratic deficit in District 18 stemmed from its unjustifiable classification as a "provisional" district by the International UMWA (a classification imposed in the 1920s and left unchanged in the meantime). Michel Local 7292 had launched an unsuccessful campaign for an end to District 18's provisional status in 1948, and parallel efforts emerged between 1950 and 1956. Rather than being open to this campaign for democratic accountability in District 18, however, Washington embarked on a multi-pronged campaign to constrain the power and scope of action of union locals, thereby compromising the capacity of those locals to fight back against the downturn in the railway steam coal industry.

The context for the authoritarian turn in governance in District 18 was John L. Lewis's fateful decision to reposition the UMWA as a business partner of the American coal industry. Coal had lost its strategic importance in the American economy to oil by the early 1950s, and the combination of market losses and rapid mechanization resulted in a decline of the UMWA's membership in the United States from 400,000 in 1945 to 200,000 in 1955. Lewis "consented to use the union's resources to advance the industry's productivity, to find new markets for coal, and to eliminate non-union mines," and at the same time he cracked down on the wildcat strikes that interfered with the smooth business operation of mines. The new UMWA role as an investor in the coal industry is best seen in the partnership that the union formed with mine owners and coal-carrying railways in 1956 to create the American Coal Shipping Company, one-third owned by the UMWA.[96] The *Coleman Journal* recognized the pathbreaking character of this partnership, and it reprinted an analysis concluding that "it is extraordinarily interesting to see a powerful union moving powerfully to help its members by helping the industry."[97] Part of "helping the industry" was further stifling democracy in the UMWA and limiting rebellious actions by the rank and file.

Bellevue Local 7294 initiated a new campaign for the autonomy of District 18 in the summer of 1952. It convinced the Sub-District 5 board to undertake two actions. First, it sent a motion to the International Executive Board (IEB) that asked this group "to discuss district autonomy for District 18 UMWA as we feel that the time has now arrived that the District can look after its own affairs." Second, it sent a circular letter to all local unions in District 18 that read

> Sub-District #5 of District 18 UMWA, comprising Bellevue, Blairmore and Coleman Locals, would like to know the feeling of all the Locals in District 18 as to District Autonomy being discussed

at the next District Convention. Please put this question to your members at your next meeting and let the Secretary of the Bellevue Local and the District Office know the result.

By the middle of September, twelve local unions had responded to the circular letter, with nine favouring holding a discussion on district autonomy.[98]

This initiative in 1952 went nowhere. Nevertheless, the demand for autonomy in District 18 persisted through the coal crisis in 1953–54, as seen by the 1955 article "The Fight for Autonomy," reproduced in Text Box 2.2. In this article, the Labor-Progressive Party listed five basic rights denied to coal miners in District 18 and promoted the district's affiliation with the new, unified, labour central (Canadian Labour Congress) as a way to gain labour allies in the struggle for district autonomy.

Of all the authoritarian and centralizing measures initiated by the UMWA's leadership, the most important was the attack on the freedom of union locals to organize a wildcat strike when a grievance required immediate attention. At the beginning of the 1950s, pithead strikes continued to be an important component of workers' repertoire of actions in District 18, despite strong objections from both the UMWA headquarters and the coal companies. The international officers circulated a statement in 1951 that listed reasons why members should refrain from "unauthorized local strikes" (e.g., such strikes "endanger the stability of the coal industry"). During contract talks in early 1953, the COAWC reiterated its irritation at the failure of District 18 to fine union members for participating in wildcat strikes, despite the language allowing such fines inserted into the collective agreement in 1946 (see Chapter 1).[99]

Meanwhile, Canadian governments had taken steps to lessen the frequency of wildcat strikes across the entire economy. A new regime of industrial legality – known as industrial pluralism – was institutionalized in Canada in the late 1940s, based upon the template for labour relations laid out in the wartime Order-in-Council PC 1003, effective February 1944. Industrial pluralism legitimated unions and protected their right to engage in collective bargaining in exchange for legal restrictions on collective action.[100] However, District 18 was in a unique and enviable

TEXT BOX 2.2

"THE FIGHT FOR AUTONOMY"

(View of the Labor-Progressive Party in *The Lamp*, May 1955[a])

> By becoming part of a united trade union centre [the Canadian Labour Congress that would be founded on 23 April 1956], the coal miners will be strengthening the fight for the democratic rights that are denied to them today, the right of
>
> - autonomy
> - the election of district officers
> - the election of the international board member
> - the election of the district board members
> - annual wage scale convention
>
> These are the rights of all other trade unions in Canada, and the members of other unions will support the coal miners in their struggle for equal democratic rights.

NOTE: [a] GWRC, M-1601, file 1361, Wage Negotiations 1954–60; copy of *The Lamp* 5, no. 2 (May 1955), 4.

position at the dawn of industrial pluralism since it had already secured a large measure of legitimacy and security through the collective bargaining process (e.g., all mine employees in jobs covered by the bargaining unit were required to join the UMWA, and union dues were automatically checked off workers' pay and submitted directly to the union). Furthermore, the UMWA had strong support from workers at all the major coal mines in western Canada and hence was unconcerned about being raided by another union or having a coal company refuse to bargain when a labour contract expired.

The district officers formally considered District 18's relationship with the new regime of industrial pluralism in 1949: they asked a Calgary law firm for recommendations on whether the district should pursue certification under the Alberta or BC labour act. Helman, Mahaffy & Barren recommended against certification in Alberta since there was a possibility "that certification would make the Union as such liable in an action for damages for the breach of a collective agreement." The argument against certification in British Columbia was even stronger since the provincial government had amended the provincial labour act in 1948 to impose financial responsibility on unions for illegal strikes. Helman, Mahaffy & Barren believed that though "a certified agent could be successfully sued for damages resulting to an employer ... if the union is not certified it seems to us very doubtful whether that result would follow."[101] With these recommendations, the District 18 leadership did not pursue the certification of any of its local unions in the 1950s and therefore avoided judicial or quasi-judicial actions because of wildcat strikes. At the same time, the district office had three reasons to crack down on wildcat strikes in the mid-1950s: (1) to augment the collaborative bonds that it had been building with coal operators in western Canada; (2) to demonstrate allegiance to the International UMWA's wholesale rejection of wildcat strikes in current circumstances; and (3) to rein in the leaders of Michel Local 7292 unwilling to kowtow to orders from the district office.

The issue of a union local's right to engage in a wildcat strike came to a head in the fall of 1954. For over fifty years, the workers at the Michel Collieries had been working on shifts that began at 7 a.m., 3 p.m., and 11 p.m. Without consulting with the union and with only two weeks of notice, CNPC delayed the start of each shift by one hour to align with the beginnings of the shifts at other mines in the region. The new shift schedule was effective 18 October. At a well-attended local membership meeting on 17 October, Local 7292 voted 160 to 1 to maintain the old shift schedule. "All men were at work [on 18 October] on their shifts at old hours but were not allowed to start till one hour later so the men returned home." District 18 President Livett ordered the Local 7292 membership to return to work on 19 October, but another membership meeting decided to continue the strike.

Three days later Livett telegrammed Lewis, asking him to issue a return-to-work order, which Lewis did the next day: "The officers and members of Local Union 7292 are instructed forthwith to return to work ... Your complete co-operation is expected." Two days later the membership voted to return to work by a count of 370 to 230. An arbitrator later found in favour of the company's right to impose the new shift schedule.[102]

Local 7292's independence of action during this eight-day wildcat strike had a powerful impact on the thinking of District 18 President Livett. A few months later he would call Local 7292 a "rebel" local.[103] Furthermore, just one day after the end of the strike, he wrote to Lewis to express the belief "that the time has arrived when some disciplinary method should be applied to the Officers of Michel Local Union who opposed every effort of our representatives to have the men return to work." Livett got his wish, for Lewis struck an International Commission made up of two IEB members who not only journeyed to western Canada to investigate the matter but also strong-armed the executive officers of Local 7292 into signing a draconian undertaking. Threatened with disciplinary action as severe as expulsion from the UMWA, Local 7292's executive officers promised to never engage in wildcat strikes in the future and to "immediately carry out instructions from the District and International representatives of our Organization."[104]

The turmoil over the Michel Local 7292 wildcat strike occurred just a few months after the International UMWA had ordered the centralization of dues administration in District 18, breaking a long-standing tradition (going back to before the First World War) of coal companies submitting checked-off dues to each local's secretary-treasurer, who in turn would forward the appropriate portions to the district office and international headquarters. This order was part of a grand scheme to financially cripple locals that engaged in wildcat strikes, although it was not presented as such. Indeed, in late 1953, International Secretary-Treasurer John Owens justified the new system as a way to ensure accurate and consistent administration of records in the UMWA.[105]

The president and secretary-treasurer of District 18 were worried that unilaterally changing how checked-off dues were administered would add to the discontent already felt across the district "owing to the closing down of mines and the laying off of men in mines that are partially operating." On two occasions in early 1954, they appealed to Owens to leave the existing system in place, but eventually they bowed to his insistent request and informed the union locals and coal operators of the new system for handling miners' dues.[106] As expected, some locals were scathing in their criticisms of the change. Michel Local 7292 condemned "the Dictatorial Methods of the international executive on the question" and circulated a call to all local unions in the district to authorize their delegates to the upcoming wage scale convention "to strongly protest" the change. Coleman Local 2633 also objected. Therefore, it is probable that many, if not a majority, of the delegates to the convention held in Calgary in early April 1954 were authorized to oppose the centralization of dues administration. In keeping with the authoritarian turn in District 18, however, President Livett stifled democratic debate on the question. He explained how he did so in a letter to Lewis:

> The delegates attempted to raise the question of the International Executive Board instructing that all monies for union dues and assessments be turned over to the District Secretary for proper distribution; however, I ruled it out of order as it was not a matter for a Scale Convention, claiming that it was an order of the parent body and must be complied with.[107]

There is an interesting twist to this story. In attempting to implement the new system, the District 18 office received some pushback from coal operators who feared legal action by union locals if the operators unilaterally ended the practice of submitting checked-off dues to the local secretary-treasurer. In order to placate the coal companies, District 18 promised to reimburse each operator for any expenses incurred as the result of legal action by a union local and "to indemnify and save harmless your Company as against all claims that may be made at any time by any Local Union against you" because of the change in how checked-off dues were to be handled. This was a stupefying betrayal of the union membership.[108] Not surprisingly, it appears that the District 18 officers kept their legal undertaking to the coal operators a secret since there is no further mention of the matter in the archival record.

I surmise that the International UMWA had a long-term game plan when it wrested control over the administration of dues money away from local unions in 1954. In 1956, the International Executive Board issued a new policy on "local work stoppages" that built upon its statement of 1951. The most interesting feature of the policy in 1956 was the "ancillary instructions" to district officials across the United States and Canada. These instructions specified that any locals engaging in wildcat strikes would be cut off from receiving their portions of union dues until such time as the board determined whether monetary penalties should be deducted from the dues being withheld. Of course, this mechanism for imposing monetary penalties on a local could not have been implemented in District 18 if the secretary-treasurers of union locals still administered the distribution of dues rather than the district office.[109]

The attack on the autonomy of union locals in District 18 during this period even extended to the question of whether Coleman Local 2633 could continue its long-standing practice of maintaining a fund to pay for the funeral expenses of union members and their wives. When first informed by the District 18 office that the practice should be discontinued, the local issued a strong protest against "the ruling preventing us from either assessing the members for a funeral fund or paying [the] same out of our general account." The fact that the district officers quoted the UMWA's International Constitution to justify their position did not sway the Local 2633 members, whose defiant attitude comes through in the minutes of the 14 February 1954 membership meeting: "A letter from the District Office re. the funeral fund was read. It was M[oved] & S[econded] that the letter be ignored and placed on the files."[110]

The International mine's closure at the end of March 1954 put new strains on Local 2633's finances. In June, the local's secretary-treasurer "reported on the financial situation of the union, especially in regard to funerals, showing the local would be unable to carry on with this fund unless an assessment was placed on the membership." Rather than using this as an excuse to bow to the district office's instruction to close its funeral fund, the members passed a motion calling for an assessment of fifty cents per month to be placed on all working members, twenty-five cents for funeral purposes and twenty-five cents for general business. The desire to continue operating the funeral fund was confirmed at a membership meeting in early 1955, and later that year the members voted to keep the funeral fund solvent by drawing from general union funds. Yet another test of the membership's commitment to mutual aid and solidarity emerged in early 1956 when the Local 2633 executive recommended "eliminating all women from our local Funeral Benefit Fund due to the financial condition of our union." Those at the meeting rejected this idea and instead passed the following motion: "That a special 50 cent assessment be placed on all working members for women who come under our jurisdiction for funeral benefits, in the event that more than one case should occur in any one month, the assessment to carry on until such cases are taken care of."[111] On this single issue, then, rank-and-file democracy triumphed against the tide of bureaucratic and authoritarian rule. It is revealing that District 18 officers never moved to block Local 2633 from using general union dues and assessments to support its funeral fund: my guess is that they feared serious political backlash if they pushed the matter.

A long-standing democratic custom also came under attack in the mid-1950s. As discussed in the previous section, in 1953 the membership of District 18 had voted down a tentative agreement because of unhappiness with a new method for calculating holiday pay. Such a vote was not required by the UMWA constitution. However, as Livett explained to Lewis at the time, taking a membership vote on a tentative agreement "has been a custom ever since the District received a Charter." Union activists in District 18 realized that this democratic procedure was not guaranteed. Hence, at the next wage scale convention, held in April 1954, the following motion was proposed: "Resolved that all Agreements be negotiated by the Officers and Policy Committees and no Agreement be signed until ratified by all members in District 18 by vote." The motion passed 40–27 in a roll call vote.[112]

The tentative agreement reached in 1954 was submitted to a membership ratification vote as specified by this resolution. In the winter of 1955, however, the district officers decided that it would be best to ignore the resolution passed less than a year earlier and follow the practice of the International UMWA of renewing a collective agreement without any membership input. The rationale for doing so was the precarious state of the western Canadian coal industry. The matter was brought for decision to the District Executive Board on 16 March 1955. The representatives from Sub-Districts 8 and 5 (Sim Weaver and John Dugdale, respectively) pre-emptively moved a counter-resolution that called for a wage scale convention to be held in early April. That resolution was amended to state that a convention be called only if the executive officers were unable to renew the existing collective agreement. The board voted 10–3 in favour of the amendment, with Weaver and Dugdale among the dissenters.[113]

The district officers quickly got the COAWC to agree to renew the existing agreement for one year. The renewed contract was signed on 21 April 1955 by the district officers but only after Calgary law firm Mahaffy & Howard confirmed that Alberta labour law did not require membership ratification of negotiated contracts. Formal objections to this abandonment of membership participation in negotiations and control over contract ratification were raised by the Bellevue, Coleman, and Blairmore locals.[114]

The final major point of friction between the UMWA locals in the Crowsnest Pass and Elk Valley and the international headquarters involved District 18's formal participation in the Canadian labour movement. The UMWA had been a member of the Canadian Congress of Labour since its inception in 1940. The impending merger of the Canadian Congress of Labour and Trades and Labour Congress (effective 23 April 1956) promised to strengthen the lobbying power of organized labour and potentially be of considerable value to District 18 as it attempted to navigate the crisis in the coal industry. Without any consultation with the members of District 18, however, the Washington headquarters started the process of disengaging the UMWA from the Canadian labour movement by stopping the payment of its per capita tax to the Canadian Congress of Labour at the beginning of 1955. The issue prompting this move was the future of the UMWA's enigmatic District 50, which, since its formation in 1936, had acted increasingly like a general union, organizing workers in many jurisdictions, including those where other unions were also active.[115] John L. Lewis and other UMWA leaders had concluded that they would have to cede many District 50 members to unions with overlapping jurisdictions as a condition for joining the new Canadian Labour Congress (CLC); they were unwilling to do so. In the words of the *Financial Post*, "UMW does not want to give up at least one third of its 25,000 membership in Canada to other unions." There was likely a straightforward financial calculation behind this position: as the number of dues-paying coal miners was shrinking in the 1950s, District 50 was growing and providing financial stability to the UMWA.[116]

The matter came to a head in the middle of 1955 with the CCL annual convention just around the corner and the District 18 membership not yet knowing that the UMWA had stopped paying dues to the Canadian Congress of Labour. Some locals in District 18 were in the habit of sending delegates to CCL conventions, and District 18 Secretary-Treasurer Edward Boyd was concerned that they would send delegates to the convention in 1955 but then be denied the right to vote because the UMWA's dues payments were in arrears. In a letter to Owens, Boyd stated that "I am a little afraid that if such a thing happens local unions in District 18 would certainly blow their top." Owens replied with a letter that acknowledged the withholding of dues payments to the Canadian Congress of Labour and advised that no one in District 18 participate in the CCL convention.[117]

Boyd informed local unions of this situation by circulating his correspondence with Owens. In response, Michel Local 7292 staked out an oppositional position. "Our members do not agree with the International Executives' idea of stopping payment of per capita dues for their Canadian members to a Canadian organization," wrote Weaver in a letter to Owens. He added that "we hope this petty squabble is cut out at once." A couple of months later, Local 7292 asked for a special convention on the CCL membership issue as well as on "several other matters pertaining to the welfare of our Canadian members."[118] Although no such convention was ever organized, the matter of UMWA membership in the Canadian Congress of Labour was discussed at a DEB meeting in December 1955. By this time, with it now apparent that the UMWA had no intention of joining either the American Federation of Labour-Congress of Industrial Organizations or the soon-to-be-constituted

Canadian Labour Congress, other unions had launched numerous raids against District 50 bargaining units across the United States and Canada,[119] including in Medicine Hat, where District 50 had between 800 and 1,000 members. Coal miners' revulsion at such raiding might explain why no DEB members registered opposition to the International's isolationism.[120]

Still, there was considerable support across District 18 for the Canadian nationalism embedded within Michel Local 7292's opposition to the UMWA's withdrawal from the Canadian Congress of Labour and unwillingness to join the Canadian Labour Congress. That nationalism also informed a widespread critique of how Canadian coal miners' dues were distributed. Effective December 1951, the international office increased monthly union dues from three dollars to four dollars, with fully half that amount going to Washington, one dollar to the district office, and one dollar to the union local. At the large membership meeting held by Local 2633 after Coleman Collieries announced its intention to shut down the International mine, a miner questioned District Vice-President John Stokaluk on this division of the dues: "Why should the union send $2 to the International and $1 to the district when this money could be used to help the men here?" Stokaluk's officious reply would have been sure to stoke any Canadian nationalist sentiments in the crowd: "If you want to remain a member of the UMWA these must be paid. The constitution must be adhered to." Two months later, when protesting the centralization of dues administration in the district, Local 2633 likewise advocated trying "to obtain a larger portion of per capita tax for Local Union purposes." To this end, it endorsed a proposal from Mercoal Local 5453 sent to the International Executive Board in 1955; it suggested that the monthly dues of four dollars be reapportioned, with one dollar to the international union, one dollar to the district office, and two dollars to the local union. The proposal was summarily rejected.[121]

The events discussed in this section demonstrate that union locals in District 18 were increasingly hamstrung in the 1950s as the district office and International UMWA asserted greater authority, overrode established democratic conventions, worked to eliminate wildcat strikes from miners' repertoire of actions, and ignored calls for creating the autono-mous governance of District 18, re-establishing the district's member-ship in the Canadian house of labour, and reapportioning union dues so that the Washington headquarters got a smaller portion. My argument is that the development of an effective response to the downturn in the steam coal industry was impeded by these regressive changes inside the UMWA.

Although all five UMWA locals in the Crowsnest Pass and Elk Valley opposed the International UMWA's autocratic, business-unionist turn in the 1950s, Michel Local 7292 was the biggest "rebel" by far. The mem-bers of this local benefited from Michel Collieries having the strongest coal orders of all the mines in the region; consequently, the workers did not live in perpetual fear of their mine being shut down. Furthermore, the humiliating discipline meted out to the Local 7292 officers by an International Commission in 1955 would have intensified oppositional sentiments in the local. Given all of this, it is not entirely a surprise that the "Town Chatter" column in the 19 September 1956 issue of the *Coleman Journal* reported the "hot rumour of the week – Michel and Natal UMWA union to break away and join the C.I.O."

The paper meant, of course, the Canadian Labour Congress, which had recently incorporated the Canadian Congress of Labour, Canada's version of the CIO (Congress of Industrial Organizations). I have been unable to determine how close Local 7292 came to pursuing the break-away option in 1956. Robert Livett and Edward Boyd were in Cincinnati in early October attending the International UMWA convention and re-ceived two telegrams from Vice-President John Stokaluk on this matter while there. Before leaving Cincinnati, they met with John Owens to give him a report on what they knew at that point. In the middle of October, Stokaluk was tasked with investigating the possibility of Local 7292 breaking away. A copy of his report was forwarded to Owens on 25 October, but the report does not appear to have survived in the archival records of either District 18 or the International UMWA. However, Boyd offered a comment in his letter to Owens suggesting that there was something to the rumour: "The situation in the British Columbia side of the Crow's Nest Pass is at the moment somewhat critical." At the same time, to keep up appearances, District 18 disingenuously informed the *Coleman Journal* that the rumour was "unfounded"; the newspaper apologized for publishing the rumour.[122]

A RESILIENT WORKER MOVEMENT

In this chapter, I have concentrated on the economic, social, and political processes that weakened the capacity of the UMWA locals in the Crowsnest Pass and Elk Valley to effectively organize against the sharp downturn in the steam coal industry in 1953–54. But this story of failure and limitation in fighting capacity must be tempered by an acknowledgment that the worker movement retained considerable fortitude in 1956.

Underpinning this resilience was a strong trade union identification. Indeed, the UMWA locals had a quasi-religious centrality in many people's lives. This was apparent at the burial service held for Phillip Mallock, who died in the Michel Hospital in the early spring of 1954. No minister or priest was in attendance. Rather, "final graveside services were conducted by Simeon Weaver, secretary of the Michel Local No. 7292, UMWA, on behalf of the union members."[123]

As noted in Chapter 1, labour union density in Canada grew steadily between 1940 and 1955, at which time one-third of the nonagricultural paid labour force belonged to a union. There are numerous indications of a vibrant union movement in the Crowsnest Pass and Elk Valley in the early 1950s, quite apart from the durable presence of the five UMWA locals. First, in 1955, the International Woodworkers of America successfully unionized the employees of three small sawmills (two at Blairmore and one at Burmis).[124] Second, in 1953, employees at nine bars and hotels on the Alberta side of the Crowsnest Pass, members of the Hotel and Restaurant Employees and Bartenders International Union (TLC), Local 308, waged a successful strike for the equalization of pay and hours for all employees and a small increase in pay (three dollars per week). During this strike, "hotelmen were soliciting business with promises of free beer," and three executive members of the Blairmore branch of the

Canadian Legion were enticed to cross a picket line. The pervasive pro-union mentality in Blairmore was demonstrated when twenty Legion members then signed a petition demanding an emergency branch meeting to discipline their executive officers for this transgression.[125] Third, after the head nurse at the new Crowsnest Pass Hospital was "dismissed without written notice or given reason," the members of the local chapter of the Alberta Association of Registered Nurses demonstrated a capacity for labour solidarity equivalent to their coal-mining counterparts: they took out a front-page advertisement in the *Coleman Journal* that proclaimed their "full confidence" in the head nurse. In turn, the hospital's Ladies Auxiliary joined the protest by "suspending all meetings for the time being."[126]

In the first half of the 1950s, labour representatives continued to be actively involved on the municipal councils and school boards in the region. In Blairmore, the tradition of running a slate of labour candidates endured. For example, in 1951, the labour slate won the mayoralty and a majority of seats on the town council and school board. "One of the first things the Blairmore Council did when it took office," *The Lamp* reported, "was to increase the wages of the town employees. It has also passed a bylaw making May 1st, May Day, an official town holiday."[127] The worker movement's successes at the polls in the first part of the 1950s included provincial electoral contests in British Columbia; Thomas Uphill overcame the hostile Cold War environment to win his bids for re-election to the legislature in Victoria in 1952, 1953, and 1956, backed by Elk Valley labour unions.[128]

As mentioned at the beginning of this chapter, the Japanese Canadian families who moved to the region around the end of the Second World War experienced racist abuse as well as exclusion from employment in the mines. One of the employers that hired Japanese Canadian men was Summit Lime Works. The growing everyday acceptance of Japanese Canadian families by the 1950s was demonstrated in a story on the history of baseball in Coleman in a newspaper supplement that celebrated the town's fiftieth anniversary: "During recent years Coleman teams have been strengthened by the Japanese Canadians at the Summit Lime

Works, these boys are adding zest to the club." The election of one of these Summit Lime Works employees to the Coleman School Board in 1956 was a testament to the political growth of the worker movement.[129]

Tets Kitaguchi had worked at the Summit Lime Works since moving to the Crowsnest Pass in the fall of 1945. He was "one of the main cogs" in organizing the workers at the company into the Canadian Union of Lime Product Workers in 1954. The spark for unionization had been the death of Sadajiro Nishikawa, crushed in a rock slide at the lime quarry. The coroner's inquest into his death suggested how racism continued to affect Japanese Canadians' everyday experiences in the workplace in 1954. A number of employees testified that, on the day of the fatal accident, the work site appeared to be unsafe. A mines inspector asked the employees why they did not report the unsafe work conditions to the company or him. Kitaguchi replied that "our background is well known in B.C. Anytime we have complained we were fired. Now we know enough to keep our mouth shut." In a similar vein, "Charlie Kitaguchi stated that if we complain that we don't want to go into the quarry they send us home, then they can't find work for us ... then what? ... We are not working steady now and need our jobs." Tets Kitaguchi added the interesting observation that "we haven't complained for so long [because of the fear of being sent home or fired] we have forgotten how." The union drive at Summit Lime Works, therefore, was an important step in Tets Kitaguchi and other Japanese Canadian workers asserting their voices in their workplaces after so many years of being expected to keep their mouths shut if they wanted to keep their jobs. A story in 1956 noted that, "since the inauguration of the union, working conditions and wages have become comparable with other similar industries."[130]

The school board election of 1956 was hotly contested, with four candidates for two open positions. Two of the candidates represented conservative interests: a Coleman merchant and a well-known member of the Social Credit League, Joseph Hanrahan, the foreman for the Department of Highways who had attracted the ire of members of Local 2633 in 1954. The other two candidates were affiliated with the labour movement: Norman Ash of Local 2633 and Tets Kitaguchi. The fact that Kitaguchi was a candidate in this election indicates that, by 1956, the worker movement in the Crowsnest Pass had come to recognize him as one of its own. In an interview in 2005, he recalled that "I never went door to door or anything. The people who wanted me in were the teachers union. They did all the work and I got in by a big majority." His victory indicates that, by 1956, a majority of the electors of Coleman were able to set aside negative stereotypes of Japanese Canadians and assess Kitaguchi's record of service to the labour movement and community as the salient factors when judging his candidacy.[131]

As can be seen in Figure I.2, in 1955 and 1956, there was a discernible uptick in coal production in the Crowsnest Pass and Elk Valley from the trough of 1954. Returning to the medical metaphor advanced by the DCB chair in 1954 ("it is going to be difficult to keep the patient breathing"), "the patient" not only continued to breathe in 1955–56 but also appeared to be recovering somewhat. Indeed, it was hard for anyone to forecast the impending collapse of railway steam coal sales because a number of coal-burning steam engines continued to operate on tracks in western Canada (707 in 1955, compared with 642 oil-burning steam engines and 440 diesels).[132] In addition, there were definite signs of the improved health of the coal industry in the region in 1956. For instance, operations at Coleman Collieries were described as going at "full blast" in April, and that summer the local NES office reported that "there is a heavy demand for certified miners in both B.C. and Alberta mines and also for labourers for inside mine work."[133]

Consequently, in the middle of 1956, it looked like the region was entering a new period of economic and population stability after the devastating collapse in coal production in 1953–54 that resulted in the Alberta Crowsnest Pass communities losing fully 20 percent of their population between 1951 and 1956 (see Table 2.1). Many rumours were afoot. On 22 August 1956, the *Coleman Journal* reported "International Mine to reopen in near future a great possibility so we hear." A few weeks later William Whittaker of the COAWC predicted that "[coal] production would remain steady for the next few years with demand beginning to increase in five years."[134] In Chapter 3, I will show just how wrong that forecast was. However, the widespread optimism about the future of the coal industry in 1956 would have an important immediate effect – it sparked coal miners in District 18 to wage a successful struggle for a significant wage increase. Miners in the Elk Valley were integral to this victory.

District 18's wage scale convention in 1956 was another impressive demonstration of active democratic participation, with the resolutions committee tasked with processing 232 resolutions submitted prior to the convention and the delegates spending four and a half days discussing and voting on resolutions. Three decisions stand out. First, delegates voted to seek an increase of two dollars per day. Second, they supported a motion from Michel Local 7292 to attempt to negotiate equivalency between the disability pension (then $80 per month) and retirement pension (then $100 per month). In doing so, the delegates overruled the resolutions committee's recommended nonconcurrence with this change. Third, several resolutions demonstrated a commitment to broader left-wing political goals. For example, the delegates voted in favour of building a coalition "to press for a national health plan."[135]

Despite the convention's call for a two-dollar per day increase in pay, District 18's negotiating committee came back to the membership with a tentative agreement including an increase of only twenty-four cents per day. Of the twenty-two locals participating in the referendum ballot on the agreement, eighteen voted in favour, including Coleman Local 2633. Yet, because the votes against the agreement were so overwhelming in the Elk Valley (217 against to 55 for at Fernie and 493 against to 72 for at Michel), the agreement was rejected by a margin of 53 percent to 47 per cent.[136]

This led to a process of nonbinding arbitration, sanctioned by both provincial governments, that recommended an increase of fifty cents per day but fell short of the tentative agreement on statutory holidays and payments into the Welfare and Retirement Fund. The arbitration award was rejected by 72 percent of voters from the Crowsnest Pass and Elk Valley and by 54 percent overall. West Canadian Collieries had anticipated this result: "The mines in British Columbia are working steadily hence their men are in good mood to demand more in the way of increases or fringe benefits."[137]

The next step in this elongated process involved government-supervised strike votes among District 18 members. In Alberta, only 57 percent favoured strike action: the noticeable recovery in the coal industry in the Crowsnest Pass in 1955–56 had not been matched in other coalfields, such as the Coal Branch, where a strip mine at Luscar had just closed, thereby creating the fourth "ghost town" on the branch since 1954 (and the sixth since 1950). The vote in the Elk Valley was more definitive: 78 percent of the miners favoured going on strike.[138]

The matter was then brought to a head by the 900 miners in the Drumheller region who, in open defiance of the UMWA's recently strengthened stricture against wildcat strikes, "almost immediately" launched such a strike after the result of the strike vote was announced. According to a WCC report, "at the same time all other mines in Alberta and British Columbia were threatening similar action." This militancy spurred the COAWC into agreeing to an increase in pay of $1.20 per day over two years (with fifty cents of this amount retroactive to 3 July 1956), an increase that topped inflation (see Table 1.2), as well as the first paid statutory holiday in District 18's history and an increase of three cents per ton in operator contributions to the Welfare and Retirement Fund. This deal was approved by a margin of 5–1, with even Michel Local 7292 voting in favour.[139]

Rank-and-file miners capitalized on what would turn out to be a very temporary respite in the western Canadian coal crisis to secure significant improvements in wages and benefits at the end of 1956. Coal miners in the Crowsnest Pass and Elk Valley thus ended 1956 on a high note. Within a few years, however, three of the UMWA locals in the region would have no more than a handful of working members because of mine closures, and the worker movement would no longer be central to the economic and political life of the region.

CHAPTER THREE

Ghost Town Future?

Searching for Economic Revitalization, 1957–62

They'll never make another Nordegg out of this town – I'll starve here first.
— *Veteran coal miner on the occasion of the suspension of operations at the Greenhill mine, Blairmore, Alberta, 30 April 1957*[1]

The stabilization of coal production in 1955 and 1956 proved to be a temporary respite in the crisis. In the winter of 1957, there was a "complete deterioration of markets for coal" as the Canadian Pacific Railway continued its shift to diesel engines. Then, at the beginning of October of that year, "the CPR placed an order bringing to 944 the number of its dieselized locomotives and completing the changeover in Alberta and British Columbia."[2] The end of the railway steam coal business in the Crowsnest Pass and Elk Valley was at hand. Four questions loomed. Could sufficient new markets for coal be secured so as to breathe life into the industry? Could new businesses and public institutions be established to replace some of the economic activity lost with the decline of coal? What would happen to all those residents (including miners, service workers, professionals and local business owners, and their families) who had depended on a healthy coal industry for their livelihoods? And would the communities in the region survive or join the long list of former coal-mining centres that were now ghost towns?

The collapse in 1957–61 of coal production was different from the collapse in 1953–54 discussed in Chapter 2 in three main ways. First, because it reduced coal production to such low levels (see Figure I.2), it caused more of the big underground mines to close and even one of the three large coal operators, West Canadian Collieries, to wind down. Second, this crisis seriously affected both the BC and the Alberta sections of the region; this brought the BC government into public policy debates and activated an important new political actor – the Fernie Chamber of Commerce – with its membership of about sixty local businesspeople.[3] Third, mine closures led to the rapid demobilization of three of the five UMWA locals in the region.

This chapter is divided into five sections. The first section details the devastating mine closures between 1957 and 1961, including the reactions of governments, miners' union locals, District 18, and community organizations. An important dimension of the federal government's response was the establishment of yet another Royal Commission to study and make recommendations on what the federal government should do to help Canadian coal operators and the many citizens who relied on a healthy coal-mining industry.

The second section details the perspective of Commissioner Ivan Rand, who recommended ending the federal transportation subvention for coal exported to Japan, and explains why this recommendation was rejected. The section concludes by describing a "new normal" in the coal industry of 1962, with levels of production and employment at about one-third and one-quarter, respectively, of those of the early 1950s.

The "new normal" yielded a weakened and divided worker movement, the focus of the third section. Whereas Coleman Local 2633 and the District 18 office became parochial and timid during this economic crisis, Michel Local 7292 kept alive the tradition of union militancy. At the same time, a second line of cleavage intensified – between unionized workers in the resource and government sectors and the growing proportion of workers employed in low-wage and usually nonunion workplaces, employed seasonally or sporadically, or lacking employment altogether.

The collapse in coal production in 1957–58 was a severe blow to the owners of small businesses since it reduced consumer purchasing power and thus deflated both sales and the value of their businesses. In response, business groups looked for ways to regenerate economic demand. The Fernie Chamber of Commerce was particularly active in the search for economic alternatives after the surprise closing of Elk River Colliery in 1958.

The fourth section analyzes the significance of this group's failed attempt between 1958 and 1962 to secure a federal penitentiary for Fernie and its quixotic effort in 1960–61 to see Fernie selected as the Canadian Olympic Committee's choice to bid for the 1968 Winter Olympic Games.

By 1962, the shock of the closures of major coal mines had passed, but the future of the Crowsnest Pass and Elk Valley was still highly uncertain. The fifth section outlines the main elements of that uncertainty and analyzes the negative reactions on the Alberta side of the provincial boundary to a nationally televised CBC program based upon the premise that coal mining in the Crowsnest Pass was "virtually a dead business."[4] This controversy demonstrated that local elites expected citizens to parrot a growth-at-all-costs ideology, no questions asked.

FOUR MINE CLOSURES, 1957–61, THE END OF AN ERA

As described in Chapter 2, West Canadian Collieries had staked the future of its coal business in the Crowsnest Pass to the establishment of a new steel plant that would require coking coal. The company remained committed to this strategy at the end of the 1950s. For instance, in 1958, it applied to the province for an extension to when it would have to complete the required abandonment work at the Adanac mine, giving the reason as "inasmuch as our steel plant venture is tied up to the possible operation of this mine." Furthermore, West Canadian Collieries expanded its search for iron ore to Montana, where a large discovery of magnetic ore was reported in late 1958.[5]

Continuing WCC efforts to catalyze the development of a steel industry led to yet another newspaper story that made a new steel plant seem to be a foregone conclusion. In a front-page story in the summer of 1959, the *Calgary Herald* reported that "the British firm of Stewarts and Lloyds and the French steel company of Schneider are expected to announce soon plans for the building of a $20,000,000 to $30,000,000 steel plant in the Crowsnest Pass area of Alberta," with the plant expected to produce rolled strip steel that could be used to manufacture pipelines.[6] In the end, the hopes of residents on the eastern edge of the region were again dashed when this latest plan for a steel plant fizzled.

West Canadian Collieries was hit hard by diminished CPR orders in the winter of 1957. The Greenhill mine at Blairmore was working only one shift per week in mid-March 1957, and the *Coleman Journal* commented that "the seriousness of the situation is registered by the consistent rumour that a mine closing in one of the neighbouring towns will take place in the very near future."[7] District 18 responded by sending two of its executive officers to Ottawa to lobby federal government officials for aid. On their return, the officers reported pessimistically in a letter to local unions that "there did not seem to be much hope for the industry."[8]

The failed effort in Ottawa was soon followed by a trip to Edmonton to meet with Premier Ernest Manning, four cabinet ministers, and MLA William Kovach; a delegation presented a brief that had been endorsed not only by District 18 but also by the town councils of Coleman and Blairmore, the boards of trade of the respective towns, and the Alberta-based coal companies.

The brief's initial point was that the provincial government could well afford to subsidize the Alberta coal industry: "Since the inception of oil and gas development [Alberta has] benefited to the extent of a figure now approaching one billion dollars, from the sale of oil and gas rights and leases, plus considerable other revenues from royalties etc." It went on to identify "a market for suitable Alberta coals ... in Manitoba and in Northern and Western Ontario" of 500,000 tons that could be secured if a provincial production subsidy of no more than two dollars per ton was provided on this tonnage. Accordingly, the brief proposed a subsidy of $1 million to capture those 500,000 tons; this would serve to maintain "a nucleus of a coal industry which could be expanded in case of market improvement, or in the event of a national emergency."[9]

A few weeks later it fell to MLA Kovach to convey a reason for refusing the request: "If the provincial government provides assistance to the Pass, then others will want assistance also – it will snowball and there will be no end." This simplistic statement failed to acknowledge that, though there was a stable industrial market in Ontario and Manitoba for bituminous coal like that mined in the Crowsnest Pass, the market for Alberta's domestic heating coal was quickly disappearing; hence, the logic of subsidizing the former did not apply to the latter. The reality was that Premier Manning's aversion to moderating the market forces buffeting the coal industry had once again ruled the day. In response to the suspension of all operations at the Greenhill mine on 30 April 1957, the premier said that this was a "regrettable thing, but it is one of the consequences in general in the coal industry as a result of progress of other types of fuel."[10]

West Canadian Collieries was operating two underground mines, two tipples, and a strip mine in early 1957 when the second coal crisis hit. It closed the Greenhill mine and tipple at the end of April but kept open the Bellevue mine and tipple and Grassy Mountain strip mine. Only a few of the approximately 250 UMWA members at the Greenhill mine and tipple were transferred to another location, meaning that there was suddenly very high unemployment in Blairmore. At this time, the unionized workforces at both WCC underground mines were dominated by men between fifty and fifty-nine years of age, with hardly anyone under thirty years of age (see Figure 3.1). Many younger miners had either left the coal industry altogether or sought work at Michel, where employment was much more reliable.[11]

The unusual age distribution of the Greenhill mine workforce meant

FIGURE 3.1 Age distribution of Blairmore and Bellevue mine workers (%), 5 April 1957

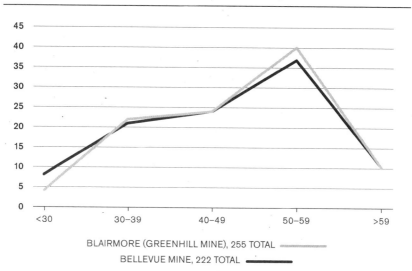

BLAIRMORE (GREENHILL MINE), 255 TOTAL

BELLEVUE MINE, 222 TOTAL

Data based on GWRC, M-1601, file 1244, table produced by WCC, "Age Groups of all Employees as at April 5th, 1957."

that a large proportion were homeowners who had little inclination to walk away from the life savings built up in their homes or little motivation to move away to start a new career that would not last long. Indeed, in the days immediately after the closure, only two of the Greenhill mine workers "applied for movement out of the town through the miners' rehabilitation program." In a report on the unemployment situation in the Crowsnest Pass at the end of May 1957, the chair of the Miners' Rehabilitation Committee highlighted his concern about the employment prospects of 108 Greenhill miners aged fifty or older since there were very limited "opportunities for older unskilled men many of whom have minor disabilities." Given this problem, the focus of the committee and the Alberta government quickly shifted to creating temporary jobs. In the fall of 1957, West Canadian Collieries reported that many of its laid-off Greenhill mine employees had been "working in the woods and on government projects." Furthermore, its Bellevue mine workforce was "quite happy" with the mine operating three days a week.[12]

Still, there was further decline in the WCC railway steam coal business in the first part of 1958. "Labour conditions in our particular area are getting bad," the company noted, "with many of the men and families showing signs of losing heart. With the [Bellevue] mine working only six days a month and with unemployment insurance benefits being nearly all used up, such is not too difficult to understand." Things got worse on 21 May 1958 when West Canadian Collieries laid off 135 of the remaining unionized workers at the Bellevue mine, leaving a skeletal workforce of 60. Mining continued that year on Grassy Mountain, where one of the truck drivers working for a contractor was killed in a landslide in mid-December; adverse weather delayed the recovery of Phillip Malanchuk's body for eight days. The following March underground mining at the Bellevue mine was suspended altogether, although several surface workers were kept on the job. At the beginning of 1960, West Canadian Collieries even laid off these surface workers "on account of costs."[13]

Therefore, West Canadian Collieries was mining only small quantities of coal in late 1957 and early 1958 and even less in the second half of 1958 and into 1959. As a result, the communities at the eastern end of the Crowsnest Pass were economically depressed. During the earlier contraction in 1953–54, approximately 20 percent of the population had left Blairmore and neighbouring communities (see the first panel of Table 2.1). A few more moved away after the Greenhill mine closure. The area was therefore somewhat depopulated. An article published in the fall of 1957 pointed out that "houses are a liability – they can neither be rented nor sold. Sportsmen going into the area to fish or hunt can rent a five-room furnished house for $10 a month."[14]

Yet, with so many of the miners who had recently lost their jobs choosing to remain in the area rather than relocating, there was a continuing need for temporary employment at the end of the 1950s. The Alberta government was consistently willing to create short-term employment for ex-miners. For example, in late 1958, a group of Social Credit members from the Crowsnest Pass convinced the government to immediately issue a special winter works grant of $70,000 for widening rock cuts on Highway 3. The following winter, not only did the province help municipalities to cover their share of the federal government's winter works program, but it also funded fully three temporary employment projects of its own.[15]

The local economy also received a boost when West Canadian Collieries reopened both of its underground mines. The Greenhill mine was reopened in the middle of 1959 in order to produce a small (10,000 long tons) test shipment of coking coal for Japanese steelmakers. After the test order was shipped, the company continued to prepare the Greenhill mine for larger production tonnages. Several months of pumping were required to dewater the mine, and railway tracks were relaid. The mine was therefore ready when, in March 1960, West Canadian Collieries secured an order from Japan for 100,000 long tons of coal.[16]

The mining of coal at Greenhill for export to Japan resumed on 21 April and continued until 16 November. Just under 100,000 tons were shipped to Japan. The average UMWA membership at the mine during these seven months was 163, and the "payrolls for all day wages and contract men" came to $438,000, a definite boost to the local economy. After completing that year's export contract, West Canadian Collieries continued to produce coal at the Greenhill mine for several weeks before laying off the entire workforce on 22 December.[17] The company blamed the layoff on uncertainty about whether it would be able to sign "satisfactory export coal contracts" for 1961. Behind the amorphous term "satisfactory" was profitability. West Canadian Collieries had been unhappy with the economics of mining at Greenhill in 1960. A memo on 30 July 1960 pointed to two problems at the mine: low recovery rate (55 percent compared with a projected 70 percent) because the coal was high in ash and low production per miner (seven tons per day compared with a projection of ten tons). These problems resulted in a labour cost of $2.42 per ton, 80 percent higher than the anticipated $1.34 per ton. One reason offered for the low production per miner was "poor miners." The company characterized its workforce, hired as required by the collective agreement by following the mine's seniority list, as "an army of old men" unable "to do the amount of work they previously could do." The WCC experience operating the Greenhill mine in 1960 led the company to conclude that neither the quality of the coal nor the productive capacity of an aged labour force in an unmechanized mine would allow it to make any profit on future sales to Japan.[18]

When the Greenhill mine was back in production in 1960, West Canadian Collieries decided to reopen the Bellevue mine on a small scale "to protect our future and the future of [the] Bellevue mine." However, with the company unable to make any headway with its steel plant promotion or any profit from selling coal to Japanese steelmakers, it decided early in the new year that it no longer had any future to protect; the Bellevue mine closed for good on 20 January 1961.[19]

Therefore, two more of the historic underground mines in the Crowsnest Pass – the Bellevue mine opened in 1903 and the Greenhill mine opened in 1913 – had fallen victim to the end of steam coal purchases by the Canadian Pacific Railway, as had the only company that had ever operated the mines, the French-owned West Canadian Collieries. The company could not help but recognize how devastating these closures were to neighbouring communities. Nevertheless, true to its capitalist ethos, its parting shot to the Village of Bellevue in early 1961 was a request "for relief wholly or in part of taxes for the coming year." The WCC tax bill from Bellevue in 1960 had been $19,000 (or $192,000 in 2023 dollars).[20] This amount pales beside the profits earned by the company over the years. For instance, in 1952, just prior to the first sharp drop in orders, it recorded a profit after taxes of $877,000 (or $9.9 million in 2023 dollars).[21]

The final closings of the Greenhill and Bellevue mines occurred just prior to a temporary construction boom in the region sparked by the federal government's approval of the export of natural gas to the United States. Starting in late 1960 and continuing into 1961, crews built new gas plants and laid two gas transmission pipelines, including the main export pipeline that ran from Alberta through the Crowsnest Pass and then across southeastern British Columbia to Kingsport, Idaho. Although the federal government stepped in to help unemployed miners by convincing contractors and subcontractors to do their hiring through the Unemployment Commission office in Blairmore, this did not guarantee employment. A meeting attended by 350 people in Blairmore on 25 March 1961 learned that "in some cases men who had been hired were discharged the following day for reasons not compatible with the facts, and it was the consensus of the meeting that these practices were for the sole reason of re-hiring former pipeline employees." This mass meeting was a powerful demonstration of the continuing capacity of the worker movement to mobilize. However, the unemployed workers' organization that it spawned had a very narrow aim: to ensure "preference to be given to Pass unemployed" whenever they were qualified for jobs.[22]

During the crisis years in the 1950s, WCC officials were generally contemptuous of the quality of the mining operations of their Alberta rival, Coleman Collieries. In early 1957, a WCC official wrote that "Coleman Collieries continue to operate on a semi-salvage basis and it is difficult to forecast what the future for this company will be." Indeed, the collapse in steam coal sales to the Canadian Pacific Railway in 1957–58 caused a decline at Coleman Collieries' McGillivray Creek mine that paralleled the declines at the Greenhill and Bellevue mines of West Canadian Collieries. During the three weeks ending on 9 March 1957, there were only four days of work at McGillivray Creek, and by the summer of 1957 Coleman Collieries employed just 150 workers, a far cry from the 1,200 employed in the year of the company's formation, 1952. Despite this grim situation, however, Coleman Collieries survived the end of steam coal purchases by the Canadian Pacific Railway, unlike West Canadian Collieries. Why?[23]

Coleman Collieries survived initially during the throes of the downturn of 1957–58 by successfully redeploying idle strip-mining equipment into an expanding general construction business. For example, for the twelve months ended 30 June 1957, the company lost $185,000 on its coal-mining operations but realized a profit of $315,000 on construction.[24] The long-term explanation for the company's survival, however, goes back to 1951, when the McGillivray Creek Coal and Coke Company started to open up a new mining area about twenty kilometres north of Coleman at Vicary Creek. The coal at Vicary Creek turned out to have excellent metallurgical properties. This put Coleman Collieries in a good position to respond when the federal government initiated discussions on the possible sale of Canadian coal to Japan in 1956, and Japanese officials visited Canada in the spring of 1957 to collect small samples of coal for testing in Japan. The initial tests on the Vicary Creek coal proved to be "highly satisfactory," and as a consequence a larger test order of 1,000 tons was placed. It was shipped on 1 November 1957, and a large delegation "representing over 80 per cent of Japan's pig iron industry and various Japanese steel companies" visited the Vicary Creek mine later that month. At that time, the new mine employed but fourteen miners. Nevertheless, everything was in place for rapid expansion if larger sales to Japan could be secured.[25] The Vicary Creek mine filled another test order for export to Japan in 1958. Although the federal government undertook a trade mission to Japan in the winter of that year, and despite a hefty increase in the transportation subvention from $2.50 to $4.00 per ton, only a measly 3,561 tons were shipped from the region to Japan in 1958–59.[26] There was still no definitive sign that coal exports to Japan would keep Coleman Collieries alive.

In the meantime, the historic underground mines run by Coleman Collieries met the same fate as the WCC Greenhill and Bellevue mines. The International mine, closed in 1954, was formally abandoned in 1959. The same fate befell the McGillivray Creek mine in 1960.[27] By then, the prospects for substantial sales of Vicary Creek metallurgical coal to Japan were improving. Coleman Collieries had filled an order for 35,000 long tons in the spring of 1959. A small interim order at the beginning of 1960 was followed by orders for 100,000 long tons in 1960–61, 150,000 long tons in 1961–62, and a somewhat larger amount in 1962–63. To accommodate this rising tonnage, the tipples at both the International and McGillivray Creek mine sites operated. Given that Coleman Collieries had produced 1.1 million tons of coal in 1952, the tonnage that it sold to Japan in the early 1960s was decidedly anemic. Nevertheless, compared with the alternative on display in Blairmore and Bellevue in 1962 – abandoned WCC mining facilities – steady production at the Vicary Creek mine was a lifeline for the town of Coleman.[28] Coleman Collieries' survival was the result of the geological good fortune of accessing a superior seam of coal at Vicary Creek. Furthermore, the company managed to avoid the "army of old men" problem that had confronted West Canadian Collieries at the Greenhill mine – of the 130 workers at Vicary Creek in the summer of 1959, about 80 percent were "from the outside."[29]

The only other underground operation closed in this period was Elk River Colliery at Coal Creek (see Table 3.1). Unlike Coleman Collieries and West Canadian Collieries, CNPC had a diversified customer base in 1957 that allowed it to strategically realign its business in response to the end of CPR purchases. Part of that realignment was the closure of Elk River Colliery and the consolidation of all production at the company's mines at Michel Collieries, starting in February 1958. Although CNPC's net coal production fell by 278,000 tons between 1957 and 1959, the com-

TABLE 3.1 Underground mine closures, 1957–61

1957 (30 April)	First closure by WCC of the Greenhill mine
1958 (31 January)	Closure by CNPC of Elk River Colliery
1959 (March)	First closure by WCC of the Bellevue mine
1959	Abandonment by Coleman Colliers of the International mine
1960	Abandonment by Coleman Collieries of the McGillivray Creek mine
1960 (22 December)	Final closure by WCC of the Greenhill mine
1961 (20 January)	Final closure by WCC of the Bellevue mine

SOURCES: Based upon sources cited in the text.

TABLE 3.2 Customers for CNPC coal production, 1957–62
(in thousands of short tons[a])

	1957	1958	1959	1960	1961	1962
Gross (net) coal production	884 (795)	660 (607)	569 (517)	731 (673)	878 (792)	824 (733)
coal sold to Canadian customers	487	305	231	168	186	198
coal sold to American customers	92	68	40	20	9	4
coal sold to Japanese customers	0	0	62	273	375	331
Total coke production	149	161	129	139	161	153
coke sold to Canadian customers	77	88	70	72	89	80
coke sold to American customers	72	74	59	67	72	73

NOTES: Gross production = net production plus washery refuse. Net production includes coal used to make coke.

[a] Short ton = 2,000 pounds; tonne (1,000 kilograms) = 2,205 pounds; long ton = 2,240 pounds.

SOURCES: British Columbia Department of Mines, *Annual Report*; British Columbia Minister of Mines and Petroleum Resources, *Annual Report*.

pany still produced 517,000 net tons in the latter year. Furthermore, by 1959, the loss of coal sales to North American customers began to be compensated by export sales to Japan (see the first three columns of Table 3.2).

The diversified base of customers for CNPC in 1959 meant that, unlike Coleman Collieries, it would have survived for some time even if Japanese steel companies had not increased their purchases in the 1960s. Nevertheless, CNPC eagerly pursued Japanese export sales, and by 1961 sales to Japan exhausted 47 percent of net production. The purchase option agreement with the United States Steel Corporation signed in 1960 (discussed in the introduction) revealed that the controlling shareholders of CNPC (St. Paul, Minnesota, and Seattle investors with strong ties to the Great Northern Railway[30]) were not all that keen to remain in the coal industry. However, they were committed to a strategy of building up sales to Japan in order to make a sale more likely.

Although the closure of Elk River Colliery in 1958 might have been a relatively routine business decision for CNPC, it was a jolt to the residents of Fernie because the city had been minimally affected by the coal crisis up to that point. Indeed, Fernie had actually experienced a 1 percent increase in population between 1951 and 1956 (see Table 2.2). When Elk River Colliery closed, however, the unemployment situation in the city suddenly became grim. The NES office in Blairmore pegged the number of unemployed in Fernie on 31 January 1958 at 441, including 278 mine workers, 132 other male workers, and 31 female workers. The *Fernie Free Press* reported that "most of the non-miners find themselves out of work due to layoffs as many business places cut down their staffs in anticipation of a decline in purchasing power." Compounding residents' concerns about the economic future of the city was the knowledge that Interior Breweries planned to close the Fernie Brewery (as well as three other small breweries) and to centralize beer production in southeastern British Columbia at a new plant in Creston. This closure happened in May 1959 and resulted in the further loss of fifty jobs.[31]

The day after CNPC announced the impending closure of Elk River Colliery, four groups met to organize an initial political response. Representatives from city council, the chamber of commerce, UMWA Local 7310, and District 18 decided to send a six-person delegation to Victoria to seek assistance from the provincial government; the delegation included two members of the Local 7310 executive (Fred Dawson and Mike Nee, who doubled as a city alderman) and District 18 representative William Ure. At a meeting with Premier W.A.C. Bennett and the entire provincial cabinet, Mayor James White argued that government intervention to give Elk River Colliery a temporary reprieve was justified so that new markets could be pursued. To the delegation's disappointment, the BC government proved to be as unwilling as the Alberta government to challenge market logic and the property rights of coal company owners. Ure reported that, at the delegation's initial meeting with cabinet ministers, "we were definitely informed that the government could not force a company to operate if [it] had decided to close down due to lack of markets and loss of money." He added that "we pointed out ... that as [CNPC] owned all lands and minerals and they had in the past been able to retard business, was the Government willing to take away land and coal rights if the company closed down. The answer was 'No.'"[32]

The delegation left Victoria disappointed. Ure believed that "the Cabinet did not consider the closing of Fernie to be of any importance." Immediately after returning to Fernie, Mayor White told a mass meeting attended by 300–400 residents that, "while the delegation was received with courtesy, the proposals were regarded with evident coolness and the Premier would make no definite promise of assistance to Fernie." Back at the legislature in Victoria, MLA Thomas Uphill's remarks on the government's speech from the throne highlighted how worker and community rights and well-being were ignored in this unilateral shut-down decision; "the greatest indictment of the capitalist system in North America exists in Fernie, B.C., today" is how a reporter paraphrased Uphill's central message.[33]

The delegation to Victoria made three further requests of the provincial cabinet premised on the mine closure going ahead as planned. One was for public works projects, and a second was for help with the anticipated increase in welfare payments. The government was particularly willing to fund public works projects. The third request asked the government to somehow arrange for laid-off Elk River Colliery workers to bump 147 Alberta residents out of their jobs at Michel Collieries (see Figure 3.2). As noted in the introduction, District 18 unequivocally opposed this request. MLA Uphill, however, "requested that the Cabinet contact Mr. Manning, Premier of Alberta, and have him agree to take Coleman men off jobs in Michel and find them work." Needless to say, no action was taken on this unorthodox appeal since there has never been any question in law that Canadians living in one province have the right to hold employment in any other province.[34]

The initial lobbying mission to Victoria was significant for two other reasons. First, it was dominated by the labour representatives and elected city officials. In this regard, it was an aberration in Fernie's fight against economic ruin since the Fernie Chamber of Commerce would soon take the lead. Second, it revealed a split in labour's ranks: whereas Fernie Local 7310's representatives were eager to discuss all possibilities for

FIGURE 3.2 Overhead view of the Michel Collieries tipple, undated. Crow's Nest Pass Coal consolidated production at Michel Collieries after closing Elk River Colliery in 1958.
| Photographer unknown. Courtesy of Fernie Museum and Archives, Image 0755 1.

keeping the mine open (including a reduction in wages),[35] District 18 offered a play-by-the-rules response that condoned neither unconventional ideas nor even a hint of contentious political protest. Whether the members of Local 7310 ever came to rue following District 18's leadership during this crisis I do not know. However, after an arbitrator ruled that CNPC did not have to give Local 7310 members priority for positions at Michel, let alone do so following a seniority list (see the introduction), it would be surprising if Robert Lilley was the only Fernie miner who became angry or disconsolate at how District 18 acceded to CNPC's plan to sever ties with many in the Elk River Colliery's labour force.

Other than Thomas Uphill's pointed anticapitalist speech in the legislature, oppositional working-class voices were at the margins of subsequent political discussions of this mine closure. Yet the following three
examples demonstrate their persistence. First, in early February, "a former citizen of Fernie," then living in Winnipeg, suggested that "the spirit
of cooperation" be mobilized to develop new industry in Fernie. The
proposal was for a cooperative society to organize this initiative so that
"Fernie will have an industry owned and operated by its citizens." This
idea directly challenged the approach to economic revitalization that
would be promoted by the Fernie Chamber of Commerce. Second, at a
Fernie Local 7310 membership meeting in mid-February, "Bro. Albert
Smith ... spoke about his enforced idleness, which was well received by
the meeting." His reflection was immediately followed by evidence of
workers' continuing defiance and militancy. Since the laid-off miners
would no longer be able to buy coal at the subsidized "miner's rate" after
1 July 1958, "President Dawson [said] ... that if the worst came to pass,
we, the unemployed miners, could and would dig out our own house
coal. The men were in hearty accord with this statement." Third, at a
subsequent membership meeting, Local 7310 voted "to sponsor a public
meeting regarding a doctors' contract for everyone in town." The idea
was that, since Local 7310 could no longer hire doctors to serve its membership, the system of group coverage by doctors should be expanded to
include all citizens of Fernie.[36]

In the meantime, the District 18 office was stultified by its subservience to the UMWA's international headquarters and its failure to understand the nature of this coal crisis. District 18's memorable actions at this
time included overruling the democratic decision of Local 7310's membership to use the local's funds to ensure that no member fell behind in
dues payments. This was a significant issue because, if unemployed
workers stopped paying their monthly union dues of $1.25, then they be-
came ineligible for a retirement benefit at age sixty-two even if they
otherwise met all other criteria for eligibility. In addition, in an indication
of the inability of the District 18 leadership to appreciate how some markets for coal had been irrevocably lost, President Edward Boyd travelled

to Vancouver in February 1958 "in an endeavour to persuade authorities there not to switch from coal to gas for heating purposes in the Vancouver General Hospital."[37]

In its initial response to the closure of Elk River Colliery, it appeared that the BC government might follow the lead of the Alberta government and do nothing to help the coal industry to survive. However, Premier Bennett soon charted a distinctive path. For one thing, British Columbia never promoted the depopulation of Fernie by copying Alberta's provision of moving expenses to miners who found jobs elsewhere. More importantly, the BC government was behind the CMS decision to produce pig iron, steel ingots, and rolled steel products at a new manufacturing facility in Kimberley. In fact, the decision to begin construction "on a $20,000,000 iron and steel smelter" was announced by Bennett rather than CMS, and he claimed that "this is one of the most important developments in the industrial history of our province." A contract for CNPC to provide the coke for iron and steel production at Kimberley was signed in August 1959, showing that buttressing the coal industry in the Elk Valley was very much part of the raison d'être for the new Kimberley facility.[38] A $7.5-million plant capable of producing 36,500 tons of pig iron per year was operational by early 1961. Within a year, CMS had begun construction on an expansion that would triple production of pig iron.[39]

To the chagrin of the *Fernie Free Press*, the only other initiative taken by the BC government to prop up Fernie's economy in the years following the closure of Elk River Colliery was funding for a modest number of temporary works projects aimed to give unemployed workers enough weeks of employment to requalify for unemployment insurance benefits. The newspaper unfavourably compared the BC government's relative inaction at Fernie with how the Ontario government had responded to the threat of the closure of uranium mines at Elliot Lake.[40]

Fortunately, other factors worked together to ameliorate Fernie's unemployment crisis. Looking just at men, the unemployment count in the year following the closure of Elk River Colliery dropped from 410 to 180. "A study of the figures," reported the *Fernie Free Press*, "reveals that a large number of those thrown out of work a year ago have since been absorbed in the mines at Michel while lesser numbers have either found other employment or left the city."[41] When Fernie residents were hired at Michel, and chose to commute to work each day, their wages provided a helpful boost to the city's economy. In contrast, when residents left the city in search of new employment, the local economy shrank. In the first year following the closure of Elk River Colliery, about 200 people moved away. Comparing school enrolments in September 1959 and September 1957 reveals that Fernie suffered a net loss of only fifteen to twenty families with school-aged children in the twenty months after the closing of the mine. More ominous, however, was the loss of those just starting out in their working lives. The *Fernie Free Press* commented in 1959 that "one of the more noticeable things about Fernie is the shortage of younger people between 18 and 35 ... Most of our boys and girls, on graduating from high school, leave here never to return."[42]

The census data in Table 2.2 indicate that Fernie experienced a population decline of only about 150 people (5 percent) between 1956 and 1961. Nevertheless, the shrinkage in the city's economy was much larger than 5 percent since neither Elk River Colliery nor Fernie Brewery any longer purchased goods and services from local businesses, and many residents were surviving on considerably less income than before the closures. Deindustrialization therefore created hardship for the local business community and prompted the Fernie Chamber of Commerce to organize a local growth coalition that searched for ways to attract new industries or institutions to help rebuild the city's economic base. I will analyze their initiatives later in this chapter and in Chapter 5. Nevertheless, I should note here that some local business owners and service workers decided that the best course of action was to pull up stakes and pursue opportunities elsewhere. For example, by the middle of 1959, the owner of the Fernie Insurance Agency (and a former member of the board of directors of the Chamber of Commerce) had managed to sell his business and move to Victoria, the owner of a clothing store had left Fernie to establish a new store in Ponoka, Alberta, and a car salesman had moved with his family to California.[43]

NEITHER SYMPATHY NOR HELP FROM THE ROYAL
COMMISSION ON COAL, 1960

I see no reason for pessimism here; your situation is relatively first class.

> — *Royal Commissioner Ivan Rand at a meeting with*
> *Fernie's mayor and council, 8 April 1960*[44]

Appointed on 6 October 1959, just six months after retiring from the
Supreme Court, Ivan Rand was asked to investigate the future prospects
for the use of coal in Canada and to make recommendations on what coal
producers and governments could do "to secure as large a market as possible for Canadian coal." Rand and his support staff had already visited
other parts of the country when they journeyed to Alberta and British
Columbia in late March and April 1960.[45] By this time, Rand had already
reached conclusions about the problems facing the coal industry in western Canada and what sort of support the federal government should offer
that industry going forward. Those conclusions were on display during
two days of hearings in Calgary at which Rand and his staff pursued information that accorded with his own priorities and sometimes challenged or even dismissed opinions with which he disagreed. Given his
performance in the Calgary hearings, and his comment a few days later
in Fernie quoted at the beginning of this section, it is of little surprise that
his final report portrayed the coal problems in western Canada as insig-
nificant compared with those confronting eastern Canada; as Rand would
write, "a minimum of difficulty attends the reaching of conclusions on
the Western coal situation."[46]

   At the outset of the report, Rand posed the question that he faced as
"when, in spite of all efforts, competing commodities destroy a coal market, if that ruthlessness, a relatively easy solution, is not to be followed,
what measures are legitimately available?" In answering this question as
it applied to western Canada, Rand invoked three guiding principles.
First, he was adamant in his support for cross-border economic competition rather than protectionism since worldwide competition yielded
greater economic efficiencies. Hence, the commissioner concurred with
the 1946 Royal Commission's judgment that the idea of protecting

Canadian coal markets for coal mined in Canada "is too impractical to merit further attention."[47]

Second, Rand posited the primacy of provincial responsibility: "Each province must bring its capabilities into action and restrict national action to measures which it is not itself able alone to undertake."[48] His uncompromising view was that the federal government should pay a continuing transportation subvention on metallurgical coal exported to Japan only after western Canadian provinces stepped up with their own financial subsidies.[49] Third, Rand argued that not all provinces should be treated the same and recommended considerably more government support for coal operators in New Brunswick and Nova Scotia than for those in the western provinces, where vibrant economies could absorb displaced coal miners.[50]

His principles and priorities were evident in how Rand and his staff responded to two of the submissions at the public hearings in Calgary. The first submission was from District 18. Its central recommendations – for a higher tariff and a quota on coal imported from the United States – were ignored in the discussion period following the reading of the submission. Instead, the Royal Commission's chief counsel asked President Edward Boyd whether District 18 had ever asked the Alberta government to assist the coal-mining industry and, after Boyd responded in the affirmative, how much had been asked for.[51]

The second submission was from the Joint Crow's Nest Pass Towns' Committee, read by Mayor of Coleman Frank Aboussafy, after which Rand questioned him confrontationally. This submission supported maintaining or increasing federal transportation subventions on coal produced in western Canada. It also proposed building a thermal power plant in the Crowsnest Pass while recognizing that burning coal from underground mines would produce relatively expensive electricity; it argued that the greater employment in underground mines justified the higher cost.[52]

Rand began his questioning by challenging the mayor's support for protectionism. When Aboussafy dodged addressing a question on subsidizing the use of coal in a pulp mill, Rand reprimanded him: "Now just let's hold ourselves to that simple question, because we are listening today to a great many statements that have never been analyzed and people are not carrying out the logical implications of them."[53] Later the commissioner asked for the distance between Fernie and Toronto. Mayor Aboussafy replied that "it is quite a distance" and then started to make a point about the limited amount of Nova Scotia coal sold in Ontario. Rand petulantly interjected: "Nova Scotia. Really, that is a province that can speak for itself. It has some eloquent advocates to speak for it. I am talking of Fernie."[54]

The exchange ended on a more courteous note after further consideration of the advisability of subsidizing the cost of coal from the Crowsnest Pass region so that it could find a larger market in Ontario. Rand pointed out that shutting out American coal would drive up the cost of production and ultimately make it more difficult for Canadian manufacturers to compete for contracts with international buyers. Aboussafy proposed to solve this problem with government subsidies, for the government subsidizes "a lot of things." Rand wryly retorted that "we are going to be prosperous by taking in each other's washing," and on that note he adjourned the hearing.[55]

Rand and his staff spent three days in the Crowsnest Pass and Elk Valley after concluding the hearings in Calgary. At a banquet at the Turtle Mountain Hotel in Frank, Alberta, Rand made no attempt in a speech to hide his views on the coal crisis in western Canada. Among his key points was that "it is the wealth of Alberta that has caused this trouble."[56] The advantage of his candour was that no informed observer could harbour the illusion that Rand would be coming to the rescue of the coal industry in western Canada. Indeed, minutes of a May meeting of the COAWC noted that coal subventions were "increasingly under fire" in the community, and "it seems likely the Rand Commission Report may also be strongly critical of subvention policy." The COAWC was thus prepared for Rand to issue some unfavourable recommendations and, in the course of contract negotiations with District 18 in the spring of 1960, attempted to use that intelligence to "put the Union on the defensive."[57] Nevertheless, nothing in the archival record indicates that the COAWC knew in advance that Rand would recommend the complete end to subventions for the export of metallurgical coal, a policy that, if implemented, would have destroyed this promising new export business.

Beyond the arguments already enumerated, was there a hidden factor that explains the commissioner's dismissive attitude toward the future of coal mining in the Crowsnest Pass and Elk Valley? In early 1961, the COAWC learned from no less an authority than the chair of the Dominion Coal Board that Rand believed that the coal operators were no longer committed to keeping their mines in operation. Specifically, he believed that Coleman Collieries was "convinced that the coal business is finished" and saw the company's future in construction work and cattle and that West Canadian Collieries saw no problem with shutting down its underground mines and letting them fill with water since they could "be re-opened years later with little or no loss."[58]

The Royal Commission report was publicly released on 26 September. In response, the COAWC did a masterful job of convincing the federal government to set aside Rand's main recommendations for the coal industry in western Canada and instead pursue a modified program of transportation subventions for the export of metallurgical coal to Japan.[59]

In disputing Rand's recommendations, coal company officials emphasized the social and economic devastation that an end to transportation subventions would cause in the Crowsnest Pass and Elk Valley, including "the almost complete elimination of home values built up over many years by coal mine employees, and the community as a whole."[60] The COAWC issued a press release critical of Rand's recommendations on 28 September 1960, warning that without subventions for export coal to Japan "at least three large mines would be forced to cease operations, and the output of a fourth [Michel Collieries] would be seriously curtailed." It followed up this statement with a detailed memo sent to the federal minister of mines, "many informal representations to various federal cabinet ministers and private members," and a brief submitted to Prime Minister John Diefenbaker on 10 November. Although these lobbying efforts secured the renewal of the $4.50 transportation subvention on coal exported to Japan for the 1961–62 fiscal year, there was a catch: the minister of finance, Donald Fleming, had argued for a smaller subvention and warned that "the coal operators would be wasting their time to come back one year from now at the $4.50 figure." This led William Whittaker to offer the following advice to COAWC members: "We have about nine months from now to set our house in order ... We must attempt now to reduce the subvention level as an evidence of good faith."[61]

Lobbying in the fall of 1960 took Whittaker to Edmonton as well as Ottawa. His conversations in both places established that there was absolutely no chance that the Alberta government would change course and contemplate subsidizing Alberta coal producers. At one point in his confidential memo, Whittaker noted that the Alberta government had "sold" the federal Department of Labour "on the idea that it would not be too great a problem to place unemployed coal miners in other industries." He added that, "apropos of this thought, when I was in Edmonton several weeks ago, Jack Oberholtzer, Deputy Minister of Trade and Industry, asked me point blank if I did not think the best solution for the underground coal industry would be to close the mines and move the employees elsewhere." Whittaker also discussed the possibility of subsidization of the western Canadian coal industry with a senior federal civil servant. This bureaucrat asked him "what the reaction of the provincial governments would be if a request were made by the Dominion government that they should pay part of the subvention cost. I replied that they would likely be unreceptive." The civil servant "then mentioned that the Alberta government had shown no particular concern as to the fate of the industry and that the Dominion Labour Department seemed unconcerned as well."[62]

Therefore, the COAWC expected no assistance from the Alberta government even in the face of the impending permanent closures of WCC mines. Indeed, at no time during the coal crisis that began in 1953 did the Manning government deviate from its position that the trouble of the coal industry was the result of market forces that should just be left to run their course.

After the winding down of the WCC coal business in early 1961, the only coal mines remaining in operation in the region were at Michel Collieries (owned by CNPC) in British Columbia and at Tent Mountain and Vicary Creek (owned by Coleman Collieries) in Alberta. The dramatic changes in the coal-mining industry between 1952 and 1962 are recorded in Table 3.3. Whereas 2,791 miners had been employed in the region in 1952, the number of production workers employed by Coleman Collieries and CNPC in 1962 was only 677. During the same time period, coal production fell by two-thirds – from 3.3 million tons to 1.1 million tons. Equally significant was the shift in the major customer for coal: in 1952, the Canadian Pacific Railway purchased approximately 70 percent of the production, and no coal was sold to Japanese steel producers; in 1962, the Canadian Pacific Railway no longer purchased coal, and slightly more than half of the production was exported to Japan for use in the manufacture of steel.

TABLE 3.3 The "new normal" in coal mining, 1962 versus 1952

	1962[a]	1952[c]
Number of production workers	248 Coleman 429 CNPC **677 total**	1,019 Coleman 991 CNPC 781 WCC **2,791 total**
Coal sales to Japan	205,000 tons Coleman 340,000 tons CNPC **545,000 tons total**	None
Total coal sales	325,000 tons Coleman 734,500 tons CNPC[b] **1.1 million tons total**	1.1 million tons Coleman 1.2 million tons CNPC 1.0 million tons WCC **3.3 million tons total**

NOTES: [a] Data for 1962 are from LAC, RG 81, vol. 153, file 4-2-41-1, memorandum to file, 6 November 1963, attached to a submission of the COAWC to the Honourable William M. Benidickson, Minister of Mines and Technical Surveys, Re: The Export of Canadian Metallurgical Coal to Japan, 26 November 1963. The data for CNPC are for the calendar year 1962. The data for Coleman Collieries are for the fiscal year ended 30 July 1962. Employment at the coal mines in the region (including a few maintenance workers at closed mines) fluctuated in 1962, with 771 wage earners in December 1962 compared with 682 wage earners in July 1962; LAC, RG 81, vol. 134, file 4-2-42-1.

[b] This figure for total coal sales in 1962 (734,500 tons) comes close to matching CNPC's net coal production as recorded in Table 3.2 (733,000 tons).

[c] Coal sales data for 1952 are from the sources cited in Figure I.2. The employment figures for 1952 are for September; GWRC, M-6000, file 229, "Average Membership for the Three Months upon Which Payment Has Been Made, Previous to Month of Convention," 15 November 1952.

Therefore, in both 1952 and 1962, the coal industry faced the unenviable situation of being dependent on a single customer. However, there was an important complication in 1962: sales to Japan would be uneconomical without the rail transportation subvention provided by the federal government, which had unambiguously signalled a desire to decrease the size of the subvention. Consequently, collective agreement negotiations between District 18 and the COAWC were just one of the rings of a three-ring circus of negotiations involving the coal operators, the other two being negotiations with Japanese steelmakers over the commodity price and negotiations with the federal government over the size of the transportation subvention. This was an especially complicated negotiating environment for Coleman Local 2633 since Coleman Collieries' sales, aside from exports to Japan, were so low (120,000 tons) that the company would not be viable without the Japanese contract. In contrast, Local 7292 was in a better position since Michel Collieries had sales of more than 400,000 tons on top of its exports to Japan.

A Weakened and Divided Worker Movement

The traditional economic power of the UMWA locals in the Crowsnest Pass and Elk Valley had been amplified by their influential and often leading role in the struggles of almost 10,000 unionized coal miners across western Canada. Dramatic changes in District 18 in the later part of the 1950s and early 1960s, therefore, had important consequences for the worker movement in the region. District 18 grappled with both organizational and financial crises as its working membership plummeted from 9,500 in the early 1950s, to 2,700 in 1958, and to only 1,625 in April 1961.[63] Although there were nine union locals with a working membership of at least 250 in 1958, by 1962 only the Coleman and Michel locals had at least 250 members. Therefore, in 1962, District 18 was not only tiny in absolute size but also unbalanced with two larger union locals in the Crowsnest Pass and Elk Valley and nine smaller locals elsewhere.[64]

The primary financial crisis faced by District 18 centred on the sharp decline in assessments paid by unionized coal companies to the Welfare and Retirement Fund as the quantity of coal mined across western Canada nosedived in the 1950s. This drop occurred at the same time as many long-time coal miners (those born in the 1890s) hit the age of sixty-two and qualified for retirement benefits. In 1952, companies remitted fifteen cents per ton to the fund. As documented in Table 1.2, District 18 secured increases to the contribution rate to the fund to twenty-seven cents per ton in successive rounds of contract negotiations between 1953 and 1958. Although the rising contribution rate almost offset the decline in production until 1956 (the fund's revenue was $962,000 in 1956 compared with $1,080,000 in 1952), additional cuts in production in 1957 and 1958 left the fund with only $633,000 in revenue in the latter year. Most ominously, the fund's aggregate deficit for 1954 to 1958 was $1,679,000, causing its accumulated surplus to decline from $3.6 million to $1.9 million.[65]

Local 7292's Sam English had highlighted the sustainability of the fund as an issue as early as 1953, but it was not until the spring of 1957 that the District Executive Board instructed the district officers "to hold meetings at each Local Union with a view to advising the membership of the serious and precarious financial situation of the Welfare and Retirement Fund" as a prelude to proposing corrective changes at the next District 18 convention. The same DEB meeting considered a grassroots motion on retirement pensions that had been drafted by Michel Local 7292 and endorsed by a number of other locals. Given that universal Old Age Security (paid at that time to those aged seventy or older) was set to increase by six dollars on 1 July 1957, the motion called for the increase to "be considered as a cost-of-living bonus and therefore should not be deducted from the benefit that Old Age Pensioners are receiving from the Welfare and Retirement Fund." The motion occasioned a "lengthy discussion." In the end, the District Executive Board voted against passing on the six-dollar monthly increase to retirees because of "the precarious financial position" of the fund.[66]

At the wage scale convention in 1958, delegates voted in favour of the District 18 leadership's proposal to cut the maximum retirement benefit from $100 to $75 per month and the maximum disability benefit from $80 to $60 per month. They also agreed to a new protocol that required a member in receipt of a District 18 retirement benefit to apply for any means-tested government pension or benefit for which the member was eligible; failure to do so would result in loss of the WRF benefit. The new collective agreement, effective 3 July 1958, mirrored District 18's recommendations for rollbacks to miners' retirement and disability benefits.[67]

Just before the maximum monthly retirement and disability benefits available through the Welfare and Retirement Fund were cut, the universal Old Age Security was increased in two stages from $40 to $55 per month.[68] In combination, the WRF benefit decrease and the OAS increases meant that, whereas a retired miner aged seventy or older and ineligible for any government financial assistance beyond Old Age Security would have collected $60 per month from the District 18 fund in early 1957 ($100 maximum retirement benefit reduced to $60 by the OAS $40), the same miner would have collected only $20 per month from the District 18 fund starting in August 1958 ($75 maximum retirement benefit reduced to $20 by the OAS $55). Indeed, many retired coal miners were cut off District 18 benefits altogether at this time since their combined monthly income from government assistance programs was $75 or more. This explains why, although 1,272 individuals had been in receipt of retirement benefits from the Welfare and Retirement Fund in December 1955, by December 1959 this number was only 961. Furthermore, of the miners approved for retirement benefits as of 31 December 1959, fully 50 percent qualified for a mere $5 per month.[69]

Benefit reductions largely account for the massive decrease of $726,000 in payments from the Welfare and Retirement Fund between 1957 and 1959 (see Figure 2.3); the decrease in retirement benefit payments was 62 percent, and disability benefit payments fell by 46 percent. The fund was thereby put on a sustainable financial footing, although the organizational cost was high – the alienation of many retired miners or miners living with disabilities forced to survive on a reduced pension after enduring 7 percent inflation between 1956 and 1958.

The financial crisis also negatively affected the day-to-day work of District 18. Union education and esprit de corps suffered when the District Executive Board decided to save money by ceasing publication of the *Canadian Mineworker* as of 1 July 1957; the monthly magazine had run a deficit that averaged almost $4,000 per year between 1954 and 1956. There was no rank-and-file opposition to this decision because by this point the severity of District 18's financial trouble was incontrovertible. In contrast, back in 1954, the majority of delegates to the wage scale convention had rejected a DEB recommendation to change the publication frequency of the *Canadian Mineworker* to bimonthly in order to save money.[70] An additional consequence of the financial crisis was less staffing in the District 18 office: between 1957 and 1961, the complement of executive officers and union representatives shrank from six to three.[71]

A partial salvation for District 18 at this time of organizational crisis would have been to successfully unionize the workers at nonunion strip mines. The district leaders had recognized this imperative as early as 1952–53 when they launched a unionization drive at Forestburg Collieries, about 150 kilometres east of Red Deer and served by a CNR branch line. The drive "succeeded in having the matter go to a vote of the men," but the majority voted to stay nonunionized. At this juncture, most of the nonunion strip mines were seasonal in operation and, like underground mines, struggling to stay afloat as their traditional markets shrank. Their precarious economic footings and seasonal operations made them difficult to unionize.[72]

However, in 1956, the first coal-fired thermal generating station opened in Alberta on the Battle River near Halkirk; it was fed by nearby strip mines, including the aforementioned Forestburg Collieries.[73] Six years later Calgary Power (known since 1981 as TransAlta) switched the power source for its initial thermal generating station on Lake Wabamun, Alberta, from natural gas to coal from a nearby strip mine.[74] Because of the large capital investment involved in such stations, neighbouring strip mines promised to have long lives and provide decades of steady employment. District 18's officers were well aware of the importance of trying to unionize this new sector of the coal industry in order to partially compensate for the loss of members at all of the mines that had closed across western Canada in the 1950s. For three main reasons, however, they failed to make any headway.

First, District 18's efforts were sabotaged by the imperiousness of the International UMWA that had forbidden its Canadian districts from joining the Canadian Labour Congress when it was formed in 1956 (the ins and outs of which I laid out in Chapter 2). This put District 18 into a relationship of direct competition with the Canadian Labour Congress and its affiliates when attempting to organize workers at strip mines. It is noteworthy that District 18 took preliminary steps toward launching an organizing drive at the Wabamun strip mine between 1959 and 1961 but then was caught unawares the next year when it learned that the Alberta Strip Miners Union, a direct CLC affiliate, had gained collective bargaining rights at that mine. Had District 18 been part of the congress, it would have had sole jurisdiction over coal miners and could have drawn support from the congress in unionizing strip mines.[75]

Second, District 18 failed to come to terms with the reality that organizing workers at the new strip mines was nearly impossible as long as the mine operators were "mortally scared" that their production costs would jump if they had to pay a hefty WRF assessment. What is puzzling about this situation is that District 18 had already given two unionized strip mines in Saskatchewan a special deal – they were assessed four cents per ton instead of twenty-seven cents. Why a similar deal was not promised for prairie strip mines in Alberta is unknown.[76]

Third, despite the enormous difficulties associated with unionizing the workers at strip mines, District 18 never came up with an organizing strategy beyond showing up at a mine site and attempting to chat with anyone who would stop to talk.

Although District 18's leadership failed to rise up to the challenge of organizing the workers at strip mines in Alberta, it successfully negotiated new two-year collective agreements in 1958, 1960, and 1962: in total, it secured a 3 percent increase in miners' real wages and four new paid holidays. These are notable improvements at a time when District 18's bargaining power had been decimated. Nonetheless, the successive ratification processes between 1958 and 1962 revealed a growing fissure between workers at Michel Collieries and other coal workers.

As recorded in Table 3.2, production at Michel Collieries reached its nadir in 1959. The contract negotiation process in 1958, therefore, occurred when the economic prospects at Michel Collieries were only marginally better than the prospects at other coal mines across District 18. This explains why the members of Local 7292, in step with the membership at other locals, voted to accept the recommendations of the conciliation board that formed the basis for the 1958 collective agreement (see Table 1.2). At the same time, opposition to the conciliation board recommendations was stronger in Local 7292 (48 percent) than elsewhere (25 percent).[77]

In both the 1958 and the 1960 contract negotiations, District 18 followed the same successful script for resisting the coal operators' demands for no increases. First, they pushed matters to a conciliation board, where they made cogent arguments for substantial increases and got the boards to recommend modest increases. Second, they successfully pressured the COAWC to accept the recommendations of each conciliation board.

The prelude and sequel to the strike vote in 1960 illustrate how the District 18 leadership still had a firm grip on the dynamics of its relationship with the COAWC. The bituminous operators unanimously rejected the conciliation board's recommendations in 1960.[78] The operators had no interest in provoking a strike, however, since they were soon to engage in delicate negotiations with the federal government over the subvention level for coal exported to Japan in 1961–62; therefore, they came to an understanding among themselves that they would reverse course and accept the conciliation board award should District 18 vote to strike.[79]

Prior to the strike vote, however, the operators endeavoured to convince/threaten the coal workers to vote against striking. To this end, each of the companies sent a letter to employees. Whereas CNPC matter-of-factly presented "the reasons for our position in the present wage dispute,"[80] West Canadian Collieries and Coleman Collieries threatened mine closures. The key sentence in the WCC letter read thus: "IF WE WERE TO LOSE THIS BUSINESS THROUGH AN INCREASE IN PRICE OF [sic] LOSS OF SUBVENTION, WE WOULD BE FORCED TO CEASE OPERATIONS." The Coleman Collieries message was similar though less belligerent.[81]

Facing this onslaught of propaganda, the primary job of District 18 leaders was to convince workers to stand together. Before the vote, William Bird of West Canadian Collieries downplayed the commitment of miners to job action, saying that they "probably wouldn't be willing to 'risk working less time.'"[82] Bird was wrong. In the Crowsnest Pass and Elk Valley, the vote in favour of a strike ranged from a high of 83 percent at Michel to a low of 63 percent at Bellevue. Across the entire district, 77 percent of the membership supported strike action. The next day the COAWC activated the plan that it had laid out in advance – it called for a resumption of talks that yielded on 29 November a new agreement based upon the conciliation award.[83]

The events of 1960 demonstrated District 18's continuing proficiency in contract negotiations. At the same time, the political division between Michel Local 7292 and the rest of District 18 had grown: whereas 59 percent of Local 7292 voters rejected the terms of the conciliation board award, 71 percent of the other voters in District 18 supported the award.[84]

The COAWC took an aggressive approach in bargaining in 1962, proposing contract changes that would be sure to anger coal miners; they included a new contract clause titled "Accident Prone Employees" with the stipulation that "any employee experiencing more than two lost-time accidents in any twelve-month period to be considered accident prone" and thereby subject to discharge. The two parties quickly came to a tentative agreement that specified very modest improvements in workers' wages and benefits (including no wage increase in the first year of the agreement and a paltry increase of twenty cents per day in the second year) but did not include any of the COAWC's unpalatable proposals. Although at this time the coal sales of CNPC were much higher than during either of the two previous sets of contract negotiations (see Table 3.2), District 18 as a whole was in desperate straits given the recent closures of the WCC mines in the Crowsnest Pass as well as the Hy Grade and Nacmine mines in the Drumheller Valley and its failure to unionize new strip mines. The tentative agreement was barely accepted by the membership by a margin of 51 to 49 percent. By this point, the bifurcation of District 18 was fully formed: only 23 percent of the 573 votes at Michel Local 7292 favoured the agreement compared with 71 percent of the 737 votes at other locals. This latter figure included Coleman Local 2633, where 68 percent of the 260 votes were in favour.[85]

At the regional level, the second phase of the coal crisis correspondingly had important effects on the worker movement. First, there was some migration into the Crowsnest Pass and Elk Valley as skilled underground miners were recruited to replace those who had left. For example, in the first couple of months of 1957, CNPC hired twenty "fully qualified miners" who had fled Hungary after the Soviet Union repressed the revolution in 1956. Among the other categories of miners who migrated into the area between 1957 and 1962 were former employees of Alberta mines that had closed, miners who were recruited from Springhill or Glace Bay, Nova Scotia, and even former residents who had left the area in the 1950s because of a lack of work but returned in the early 1960s.[86] The upsurge in enmity toward Alberta residents working at Michel Collieries after the closure of Elk River Colliery in early 1958 suggests that new migrants could have been scapegoated by long-term residents during this crisis if they had been portrayed as usurping jobs that rightfully belonged to the long-term residents. However, this sort of finger-pointing did not develop. For one thing, a majority of young people were more than happy to leave the region rather than try to secure a job in a coal mine; consequently, opportunities for outsiders were increasing. Furthermore, there was a gradual trickle of migrants that was much easier to absorb into the labour market than a rush.

Second, the social scope of the worker movement was diminished because of the economic crisis. Indeed, many ethnocultural organizations with significant working-class memberships simply disappeared as members were forced to leave the region in search of work. For example, a Ukrainian Greek Catholic Church was constructed in Coleman in 1949–50 and served a vibrant religious community of thirty-two families. However, thirty of those families left the Crowsnest Pass as a result of the downturn in the coal industry in the 1950s, and the congregation became inactive. In subsequent years, the church building was vandalized before being demolished in 1971.[87] Even large ethnocultural organizations experienced significant declines. An example is the Association of United Ukrainian Canadians, formerly known as the Ukrainian Labor-Farmer Temple Association. It was an integral cog in the leftist current of the worker movement, with a history stretching back to the First World War. (I will detail its connection to the work of the Communist Party in the next chapter.) The Coleman chapter of the association celebrated its fortieth anniversary on 9 November 1958 at an event attended by sixty people, including five charter members. The waning of the local chapter was evident from the fact that the long-standing choral group and dancing classes run by the chapter were no longer in operation. Overall, the decline of the Association of United Ukrainian Canadians was a significant blow to the worker movement since, as founding member Andrew Halluk commented, "the menfolk have worked in the mines, forests and railroads as honest workers and have been and continue to be good union members."[88]

Third, although UMWA involvement in local governments persisted across the region, there were some notable changes. The worker movement ceded its position of dominance on the Blairmore town council, played a supportive but behind-the-scenes role in the new village council in Natal,[89] and maintained something close to traditional levels of minority representation in Coleman[90] and Fernie[91] despite evidence of flagging enthusiasm for mine workers' participation in the local political process. In a general sense, the worker movement had lost its sense of political mission even though it maintained a number of long-standing commitments to participating in local governments.

The most significant change occurred in Blairmore, where a labour slate headed by coal miners had won a majority on the town council in 1933[92] and maintained control into the 1950s. This arrangement ended in 1959 when William Gray, who had taken over as Local 7295's secretary-treasurer and Blairmore's mayor when Enoch Williams retired from both positions in 1951, stepped down as mayor in 1959; he was replaced by a high school principal, William Jallep, who in turn was replaced by a former Greenhill mine fire boss, Alrik Tiberg, in 1963. Still, since both Jallep and Tiberg had first been elected to town council as part of labour slates in the 1940s, a pro-worker orientation continued to inform council's decisions into the 1960s.[93]

Fourth, workers' connections to provincial and federal politics were put on new paths by the coal crisis. In the Elk Valley, the Fernie District Labour Party disappeared after Thomas Uphill announced, just a month prior to the provincial election of 12 September 1960, that he did not plan to run for re-election. Furthermore, the Cooperative Commonwealth Federation nominated a local farmer rather than a member of the mining community. Both developments suggest that the worker movement had

taken a step back in provincial Elk Valley politics, as did the election results, which saw the Liberal Party's Harry McKay returned, with the
CCF candidate finishing third.[94] Meanwhile, on the Alberta side of the
continental divide, the worker movement had not been a strong force in
provincial or federal election campaigns since the early years of the
Cold War (see Chapter 1). It is therefore interesting that the collapse
of the coal industry on the eastern edge of the Crowsnest Pass rekindled
the broader political interests of a number of working-class activists.
This was shown in the formation of a Crowsnest Pass New Party Club
(part of the transition from CCF to NDP). The club held a meeting in
Blairmore on 22 June 1961 addressed by the CCF leader in the House of
Commons, Hazen Argue. Attended by sixty, the meeting was chaired by
President of Local 7295 Albert Mark.[95] This re-engagement with federal
and provincial politics would prove to be a harbinger of the unexpected
election of the NDP's Garth Turcott to the provincial legislature in a
1966 by-election (to be discussed in Chapter 6).

Despite the evident signs of organizational shrinkage and a narrowing
political vision, in a number of crucial areas, workers and their unions
still did what they had always done. Local 7292 remained a cultural force,
as shown by the picnic that it sponsored in August 1959 attended by close
to 1,000 people and the continuing role of union executives in conducting
graveside services for deceased members.[96] Workers still engaged in
wildcat strikes in order to address immediate issues of concern. Examples
included the truckers hauling coal from the Tent Mountain strip mine
who refused in 1957 to undertake any new runs until the mountain road
was repaired and miners at Vicary Creek wildcatting in 1961 because of
a number of grievances, including being regularly scheduled to work on
Saturdays, after which the mine was closed for lack of work on Mondays.[97]

Furthermore, the UMWA locals still fought with the coal companies
on issues small and large. For instance, Local 7292 engaged in a prolonged fight in 1959 that resulted in a worker gaining an extra hour of pay
for time spent hobbling out of a mine after injuring his leg. A more important issue that preoccupied Local 7292 was an unprecedented run of
six workplace fatalities at Michel Collieries in 1961. After four fatalities
in less than a month, the union and CNPC held a contentious meeting on

mine safety on 14 June 1961. After this meeting, District 18's William Ure reported that "places reported unsafe in Sept. 60 had not been attended to. These cases had been reported every month until now. I charged Mine Manager and Mine Inspector especially with being lax in their duties and advised them if no improvement is shown I would notify [BC Deputy] Chief Inspector of Mines Bonar to make [an] investigation."[98]

In addition, during this period, there were still unmistakable signs of the working-class solidarity and sharp class consciousness that had long been the regional worker movement's defining features. For example, after the massive underground earthquake (bump) at the coal mine at Springhill, Nova Scotia, in the fall of 1958 that not only killed seventy-five miners but also saw the rescue of nineteen men who spent many days trapped underground,[99] a wide cross-section of community organizations and individuals in Coleman contributed to a disaster relief fund that raised $791.50 "even though the Town of Coleman is itself suffering serious economic problems."[100] Meanwhile both within the UMWA and in public forums, Sam English of Local 7292 continued to challenge not only CNPC management but also segments of the local power elite that rallied around the coal company's perspective. English's style combined humour with sharp critique, as demonstrated in a letter to the editor of the *Fernie Free Press* published on 22 February 1962 (see Text Box 3.1).

Nevertheless, neither Sam English nor any other District 18 leader tackled the thorny issue of how the export of metallurgical coal from Canada intersected with the struggles of Japanese coal miners. It was far from a coincidence that the major uptick in sales of metallurgical coal to Japanese steelmakers by CNPC and Coleman Collieries overlapped with a wave of strikes by Japanese coal miners. In the middle of 1960, the *Lethbridge Herald* reported that "[Japanese coal] mines have been plagued by strikes for the past 18 months, disrupting the flow of coal to the steel mills. Consequently, a heavier demand is put on exporting coal companies." At that moment, Coleman Collieries was being pressured by its Japanese customers to fulfill its current order three months or more ahead of schedule.[101] It seems unlikely that UMWA leaders in the Crowsnest Pass and Elk Valley were oblivious of the troubles then facing tens of thousands of coal miners in Japan and in particular the fact that

TEXT BOX 3.1

"YOURS FOR A SHORTER DAY," BY SAM ENGLISH

My blood pressure is extremely high, but on Thursday, Feb. 15, it zoomed and nearly blew my head off on reading your editorial on shorter hours.

With over half a million unemployed I wondered how anyone could be that way. Shorter hours would do much to solve that question, or would you like to have a war?

You state that anything below 40 hours a week would be dangerous. Well, I can tell you lots of miners would like that danger, and I can also suggest lots of things they could do and not find, as you say, boredom. And I do not mean moonlighting – that should be cut out altogether.

The C.N.P. Coal Co. have a notice posted on the office door "No Men Needed." They do not need them now because the new mining machine can produce up to 500 tons of coal in eight hours with seven or eight men. This same work used to employ at least 50 men. Similar conditions exist throughout [the] industry.

I am reminded of what the late Robert Livett, then president of District 18 U.M.W.A., said some years ago, "The *Fernie Free Press* is the voice of the Crow's Nest Pass Coal Company." The management of the Free Press may change but the policy is still the same, "My master, it is for thee."

Yours for a shorter day,
Sam English, Secretary-Treasurer, Michel Local Union, District 18.

SOURCE: Letter to the editor of the *Fernie Free Press*, 22 February 1962.

the substitution of imported coal for domestic coal in the steel industry was costing many Japanese miners their jobs.[102] What we do not know is whether these leaders refrained from expressing even token support for the strikers because of the parochialism that David Harvey posits as inevitable when workers' jobs are under threat[103] or whether, in this case, parochialism was mixed with a racist "othering" of Japanese miners.

Besides the rise in parochialism and bifurcation in economic and political outlooks between the memberships of Michel Local 7292 and Coleman Local 2633, the coal crisis had a third telling impact on the regional worker movement: an intensification of the division between the stably employed segment of the working class on the one hand and the precariously employed or unemployed segment on the other. This division grew in importance because the stably employed segment was reduced by the substantial decline in mine employment.

Unionized workers in the Crowsnest Pass and Elk Valley enjoyed decent wages, benefits, and protections in the early 1960s, things that the precariously employed and unemployed desired. Accordingly, the latter could readily be mobilized to support proposals for new job-creating businesses. An example is a meeting held at the Coleman high school auditorium on 9 January 1961 organized by local governments. The purpose of the meeting was to demonstrate to the provincial government that there was complete public support for the construction of a sour gas processing plant about five kilometres upwind of Coleman at Sentinel, and therefore the province could approve the plant without fearing any sort of public backlash. A crowd of "well over 100 persons" attended the meeting. "Many aspects of the benefits of such a plant were discussed," reported the *Coleman Journal*, "and it was unanimously felt that construction of the plant would be definitely beneficial." The only mention of health in the newspaper story was that "it being understood that matters of public health have been investigated." At this meeting, workers dutifully fulfilled the role of a cheering section for the proposed sour gas plant. No one asked the simple question that would be expected in a genuine public consultation: what are the options for locating the plant at a greater distance from the town in order to minimize potential health risks? Economic desperation – not only of precariously employed and unemployed workers but also of the struggling owners of small businesses – ruled the day.[104] In the end, the public meeting fulfilled its scripted purpose – the sour gas plant and its companion sulphur plant were operational by the end of 1961.

I have shown in this section that by 1962 the worker movement in the Crowsnest Pass and Elk Valley was much changed from the movement that had existed prior to the loss of railway steam coal sales. Nevertheless, the accomplishments of the historic worker movement were indirectly honoured on the afternoon of 22 February 1962 when the people of Fernie paused for the funeral of Thomas Uphill, who had died on 17 February of a heart attack at the age of eighty-seven.

Uphill had come to Fernie from Britain in 1906, just thirty years old. He quickly secured work as a miner at Coal Creek. Six years later he was elected as the secretary of the Fernie local of the UMWA, having already filled a similar role in a union of coal miners in Wales before he emigrated. His union involvement paved the way for his election as a Fernie alderman in 1913, as Fernie's mayor in 1915, and as the representative for Fernie District in the BC legislature in 1920.[105] Over his long career as an elected politician, Uphill (pictured in Figure 3.3 about halfway through his forty years of service in the legislature) exemplified the major characteristics of the traditional worker movement in the region: a deep respect for the labour of coal miners and other working people; an egalitarian drive to help the disadvantaged in society; a thoroughgoing commitment to working-class solidarity and labour unions; and a socialist political inclination that led him to cultivate political friendships and alliances with a number of prominent members of the Communist Party of Canada and the Cooperative Commonwealth Federation.

The city office, local schools, and local businesses were closed on the afternoon of Uphill's funeral. Attendance at the service at the Anglican church was so large that, "in spite of the fact that arrangements were taken to accommodate an expected overflow of persons in the church basement, quite a number had to wait outside until the service was over."[106] Despite this public outpouring of respect, however, Uphill's passing marked the end of an era for the Crowsnest Pass and Elk Valley and more specifically for Fernie, which, as I argued in the introduction, was no longer a trade union city where the worker movement and socialist politics held the pride of place. The unexpected death of Local 7292's Sam English in April 1962 accelerated the development of a new type of worker movement in the region that, in addition to being divided in important ways and no longer as central to the affairs of each community, lacked a strong socialist voice. I investigate this latter phenomenon in Chapter 4.

FIGURE 3.3 Thomas Uphill in a mine cart, high above the tipple and railway tracks in the Coal Creek Valley, circa 1940. (Compare this downhill perspective with the uphill perspective of Figure I.1.) MLA Uphill's purpose in visiting the mine that day was unspecified, and the members of his travelling party were unidentified.
| Photographer unknown. Courtesy of Fernie Museum and Archives, Image 0441-a.

EARLY ATTEMPTS TO DIVERSIFY ECONOMICALLY

With the closing of Elk River Colliery in early 1958, Fernie joined Alberta's Crowsnest Pass communities in actively seeking new industries or institutions that would replace some of the jobs and income lost because of mine closures and layoffs. In both provinces, there were a number of small initiatives to increase summer tourism, including new roadside tourist information booths established separately by the Coleman Board of Trade and Fernie Chamber of Commerce in the spring of 1959.[107] Furthermore, the economic desperation of the situation was reflected by the wide spectrum of unusual and often unrealistic ideas for new business ventures floated in 1958, including fly-tying, potato chip production, filling a new gas pipeline from a coal gasification plant once sour gas wells ran dry, and producing knock-off totem poles and "other novelties" by members of the Fernie Fine Arts Club.[108]

Starting in the spring of 1958, a local growth coalition in Fernie was led by its Chamber of Commerce. This was partially because of the group's large membership of sixty but mainly because the business climate in Fernie had remained relatively healthy until 1958. Fernie business owners were therefore shocked into action by the closure of Elk River Colliery, whereas business owners across the provincial boundary had already been worn down by years of diminished sales. Consequently, in Alberta, the main initiative to revitalize the economy was taken by local governments. Indeed, the Coleman Board of Trade, which had initiated an annual Crow View Rodeo in 1946 in order to boost retail trade in the summer, could not even keep this project going as the years of hard times lengthened. The Coleman group first threatened to cancel the rodeo in 1960 "due to lack of interest." The rodeo was cancelled for good in 1961.[109]

During these years, there was only sporadic coordination of revitalization efforts across the continental divide. One example of a region-wide initiative occurred in April 1958 when representatives of local industrial committees from Fernie to Lundbreck (see Map 0.1) met in Coleman to initiate a new Industrial Board. Before this board faded from the historical record, it endorsed "a brief drafted by Coleman's mayor F[rank] Aboussafy that supports the export of natural gas." By this time, Aboussafy had concluded "that if the Crows Nest Pass area is to flourish economically the only thing within its grasp is the construction of the sulphur plant at Sentinel." When completed in 1961, the plant was the companion to a sour gas processing plant that had first been proposed by Westcoast Transmission in early 1957; the plant removed hydrogen

sulfide from the sour gas, thereby readying it for export to the western
United States. Before construction of these side-by-side plants could
begin, however, the Canadian government had to approve the export of
natural gas to the United States, which finally occurred in early 1960.[110]

In 1958, the communities in the Alberta Pass lined up behind Frank
Abousaffy's judgment that a sulphur plant was the single thing worth
pursuing. They therefore made no attempt to join the competition to be
selected as the site for a new federal prison, instead supporting Fernie's
bid in exchange for Fernie's support for the export of natural gas.[111]

A new federal prison as an economic saviour had been promoted as
early as 1955.[112] By 1958, federal-provincial penal reform that would
transfer a number of prisoners in provincial jails to federal prisons appeared to be imminent, and, in the wake of the closing of Elk River
Colliery, the Fernie Chamber of Commerce identified bidding for a new
prison as the best hope for rebuilding the city's economic foundation. As
the *Fernie Free Press* put it, the chamber "staked the entire future of the
community on one great big play to obtain a federal prison for this area."
During 1958, the chamber secured declarations of support from a wide
range of groups, including the BC Chamber of Commerce and a meeting
of 100 delegates, representing twenty-five union locals in West and
East Kootenay, that had been convened by Bert Herridge, the CCF MP
for Kootenay West. After the delegates unanimously backed Fernie's
bid for a new prison, the decision was conveyed to the federal justice
minister.[113]

The *Fernie Free Press* might have topped the Chamber of Commerce
in over-the-top boosterism for the prison bid. At an early date, the paper
went so far as to make the unfounded claim that there was complete
unanimity in the city behind the endeavour: "In view of the present situation and probable future developments, the federal authorities could
rest assured that resentment of such an institution would never develop
in this city. Local citizens in all walks of life realize and appreciate that a
substantial and permanent payroll is now, and will always be, of paramount importance." A few weeks later the paper's editor, Joe Weber,
launched a highly charged attack on Fernie residents who, contrary to his

earlier prediction, were organizing against the prison bid. Forsaking any balanced coverage of this issue, Weber wrote that

> any and all objections to a prison would appear to be trivial, to say the least ... We do not believe that any person with even the semblance of a conscience would knowingly subscribe to a movement that could do irreparable harm to his own neighbours and friends. It is therefore only sensible that the opinions of crackpots be treated with the contempt they deserve.[114]

A sharp split in citizens' responses to a proposal to establish a new prison was likewise seen in Youngstown, Ohio, in the wake of the massive loss of jobs from the closure of steel mills in the late 1970s and early 1980s. Public hearings in the mid-1990s on whether a for-profit prison should be approved pitted "those who were desperate for work" against more prosperous residents "who worried about how a prison built in their neighborhood would affect safety and property values."[115] In Fernie, and undoubtedly in Youngstown, prison boosters included not only job seekers but also business owners desperate to rebuild the local economy and the value of their businesses. Because their capital was immobile, these business owners were hamstrung by "locality dependence"[116] and hence were single-mindedly committed to growth.

Yet, in the midst of an avalanche of boosterism for Fernie's prison bid, there was some sobering news. In 1958, the competition for the site of a new prison was fierce, with over 100 municipalities in western Canada alone expressing an interest in hosting a prison.[117] Over the next several years, the plan to expand the federal prison system went ahead but not with the alacrity displayed in the first part of 1958. A federal-provincial conference on penal reform in October 1958 decided against assigning all prisoners with sentences longer than six months to federal institutions, consequently reducing the number of prisoners who would have to be transferred from provincial correctional centres. Furthermore, the federal government decided to first expand the capacity of its prison system by establishing satellite prison work camps before building new prisons.[118]

In response to a question in the summer of 1960, Minister of Justice Davie Fulton remarked that "I know the situation in Fernie and there are at least a dozen, if not more, similar communities in British Columbia, all of whom have been pressing me for a penitentiary to be located in their community." Fulton's statement suggested that Fernie was nowhere close to being the leading candidate for a prison in 1960. It therefore came as little surprise when the minister announced, while visiting the area during the federal election campaign in 1962, that Drumheller rather than Fernie would be the site of a new federal prison.[119]

Although the Fernie Chamber of Commerce failed to land a new prison, the organization was correct in thinking that such an institution would have made a significant difference to the local economy. During the past half-century (and counting), the economies of Springhill, Nova Scotia, and Drumheller, Alberta, both former centres for coal mining, have been stabilized by the federal prison opened in each community in 1967. Furthermore, prisons are one of the replacement industries (the other being waste disposal) that has demonstrated staying power during the long decline in the anthracite region of Pennsylvania; these industries have come to look good to persevering residents when no other alternatives take hold despite decades of attempts at economic renewal.[120] However, this model for economic survival need not be the fate of the Crowsnest Pass and Elk Valley when coal mining starts to wind down in the coming decades – as I will discuss in the concluding chapter, the region has a unique array of opportunities that Indigenous and settler groups could pursue to forge a path of long-term sustainable development.

By the time Fernie learned that it had lost in the federal prison competition, the new sour gas processing and sulphur plants near Coleman were up and running. Yet they did not turn out to be the "godsend" anticipated by residents and officials in 1960. Although the plants would provide steady employment for local residents for over fifty years,[121] jobs were relatively few – for example, in 2000, the employee list numbered just twenty-four.[122] The proponents of the project had anticipated that the sulphur produced at the facility would attract important new industries to the region[123] – another vision of the region's future as a Pittsburgh or Ruhr Valley – but this did not happen. In the end, the sulphur plant's contribution to the economy of Coleman and neighbouring communities was small.

The energy that the Fernie Chamber of Commerce first invested in the bid for a federal prison was soon transferred to other projects. A primary underlying concern was moral reform of the community. May 1959 was designated by the city as "clean up month." After noting the city's "beautiful surroundings," the *Fernie Free Press* implored that "what remains to be done is a general tidying up of streets, alleys and particularly the vacant lots, many of which appear to be used chiefly as a dumping ground for wrecked equipment, cars, and junk which the owners found it easier to abandon than dispose of." The Chamber of Commerce supported clean-up month with a newspaper advertisement that called for "a concerted drive to clean up and paint up by individual householders." The unrealistic aim of the initiative was to remake Fernie so that it would appear to the visitor (especially the potential investor) as a tidy, middle-class community rather than a down-on-its-luck, blue-collar community with numerous low-income residents.[124]

Kenny Stewart, the owner and managing director of the Trites-Wood department store, was a leading member of the Chamber of Commerce. He added an intellectual voice to the call for moral reform with a series of five newspaper articles on "community development and study." The first article contrasted the histories of two coal-mining towns in Illinois after the mines shut down. According to Stewart, the reason that one town had shrunk to a population of twelve whereas the other was "a busy town of 1,200" was because of "the interest of the people and the use of community development and study." This article concluded with a question and warning: "Are you prepared to devote part of your time to thoroughly study this community with a view to its Improvement? It could mean the difference between becoming a ghost town or continuing as a happy, prosperous community."

Kenny Stewart's second article described examples of revitalization in five American towns that had first undertaken a community study approach. He argued that the foundation for solving most of Fernie's problems was "a fully developed sense of citizen achievement and a moral climate for progress." The concluding article emphasized that what was needed was a new community consensus that transcended the class divisions and struggles that had dominated Fernie's decades as a trade union city. Stewart maintained that "a community much 'divided unto itself' wastes much creative effort on unnecessary conflict and aimless activity."

Kenny Stewart's articles failed to generate widespread enthusiasm for his vision of a "moral climate for progress." His one prominent public endorsement, by the general manager of Interior Breweries, was counterproductive since that company was in disrepute after just shutting down the Fernie Brewery. Furthermore, some owners of retail real estate were unable or unwilling to renovate their "run-down" storefronts.[125]

Despite the failed attempts by the Fernie Chamber of Commerce to land a federal prison and initiate a process of community development, the group was indefatigable. In March 1960, shortly after the conclusion of the Winter Olympics in California, it launched an unlikely and audacious bid to host the 1968 Winter Olympics. The Chamber of Commerce first invited a prominent BC ski official, Sam Wormington, to undertake a "ski reconnaissance" of the slopes of the Lizard Range of the Rocky Mountains bordering Fernie. Wormington, who had recently worked as an official for cross-country ski events at the Olympics, concluded that the nearby mountains were suitable for hosting the Olympics. Yet there was no ski development or even an access road into the area.[126]

To disinterested observers, Fernie's interest in hosting the Olympics seemed impractical because of the city's geographic isolation and dearth of infrastructure. A story published by the *Calgary Herald* in April 1960 raised these issues but was labelled "anti-Fernie propaganda" by the *Fernie Free Press*. The Fernie Chamber of Commerce was undaunted by the opposition. In the summer of 1960, it hired the director of ski events at the just-concluded Olympics to conduct a technical assessment of the suitability of the Lizard Range mountains. After a three-day visit, Willy Schaefller came to the same conclusion as Sam Wormington. Yet he noted diplomatically that he "was not prepared to give an opinion on what could be offered here for ice competitions and facilities for press, radio and television. These should be considered by more competent and experienced persons."[127]

Using this positive technical assessment as legitimation for proceeding, the Chamber of Commerce quickly informed the Canadian Olympic Committee that it intended to bid to be the committee's choice to enter the international competition to host the 1968 Winter Olympics and struck a local committee to manage the bid. The next few months involved a great deal of rushed activity since the Canadian Olympic Committee expected to make its decision in the spring of 1961. In the late fall of 1960, the Fernie Olympics Committee completed an access road into the Lizard Range area (known as Snow Valley) and installed both a rope tow and a chalet at a skiable slope. The committee also lobbied the provincial cabinet and tried to secure expressions of support from Chambers of Commerce throughout southeastern British Columbia. It is notable that the bid met resistance from the latter group. Because of a lack of accommodations in Fernie and concerns about cost, the executive of the Association of Chambers of Commerce of South-Eastern British Columbia refused to endorse the bid. Furthermore, a member of the Castlegar Chamber of Commerce spoke forcefully against his organization backing the bid, saying that he did not want "to be a party to Fernie's publicity stunt."[128]

Skepticism about the viability of Fernie's bid was reinforced "when a representative of the engineering firm hired to survey all the sites paid a 'courtesy call'" to Fernie and did not even bother to venture out to the newly installed rope tow, instead doing "his viewing of the Snow Valley hills from a downtown window." Nevertheless, the movers and shakers behind the bid remained committed to the process because, as noted by the *Fernie Free Press* in early 1961, "even failure in the main objective would probably result in private development of the site."[129]

Sam Wormington formally presented Fernie's bid to the Canadian Olympic Committee in April 1961. There were five other bidders. A few days later the committee chose Banff, in line with the recommendation of the engineering firm that had investigated each bid site.[130] On learning of the decision, the chair of the Fernie Olympics Committee, Telfer

Dicks, commented that "Fernie has not lost completely. Much benefit should come from the publicity received during the campaign and in the near future we may see a development on our skiing site that could mean a much-needed secondary industry in this area." Ever optimistic, the *Fernie Free Press* claimed that a "Calgary group of promoters" had reached the final stages of financial arrangements for a major skiing development.[131]

By the end of the summer of 1961, however, the Calgary promoters were out of the picture. Furthermore, a spring flood had washed out a bridge and some of the access road leading to the ski chalet and rope tow. Nonetheless, there was still local interest in developing the ski potential of the Lizard Range at Fernie's doorstep. Two competing proposals were floated. First, some members of the Chamber of Commerce saw the development of a ski hill as a potentially lucrative investment. Second, a Fernie physician, George Leroux, proposed developing the ski hill on a not-for-profit basis, an approach that would guarantee "local control in perpetuity." Fernie's path forward on ski hill development was decided on 31 October 1961 at a small gathering of twenty people, most of whom were Chamber of Commerce members. Leroux proposed raising money to develop the ski facility through donations. He further proposed that any profits from the venture either be reinvested in the ski facility or used to develop other recreational and sports facilities in Fernie. A *Fernie Free Press* report indicated that Leroux's community-centred idea did not attract any supporters. Less than a month later, Snow Valley Ski Development (renamed Fernie Snow Valley Ski in 1964) was incorporated, and by the summer of 1962 the company had raised enough capital from local investors to purchase a T-bar lift; it was installed that fall, along with a new ski chalet.[132]

The meeting that rejected George Leroux's proposal was another indication that Fernie no longer could be classified as a trade union city. The Fernie Chamber of Commerce had replaced Fernie Local 7310 as the most important organization in the city, and the worker movement was so disengaged that it did not mobilize to get behind Leroux's not-for-profit vision for the development of ski and other recreational facilities. An irony of the episode is that Leroux's proposal was in keeping with the spirit of the community development project promoted by business leader Kenny Stewart in 1959. However, community development was conveniently forgotten as the owners of small businesses in Fernie dreamed of making a pile of money from ski hill development.

An Uncertain Future

All was not "gloom and doom" in the Crowsnest Pass and Elk Valley in 1962. From its nadir in 1959, coal production had modestly rebounded by 1961 on the strength of substantial increases in sales of metallurgical coal to Japanese steelmakers. Furthermore, in 1961, there was an uptick in CNPC's production of coke after the new CMS pig iron plant in Kimberley became a regular customer. Nevertheless, the future of coal mining in the region was precarious. Although the coal operators had managed to convince the federal government to disregard Royal Commissioner Rand's recommendation in 1960 to end the transportation subvention for coal exported to Japan, government ministers had made it clear that the subvention would be decreased starting in 1962–63. In October 1961, a company-union delegation journeyed to Ottawa to negotiate the fate of the subvention that had been set at $4.50 per ton for the past three years. The best that they could do was to get the coal committee of the federal cabinet to agree to a $3.50 per ton subvention for 1962–63. To partially offset the upcoming $1.00 per ton loss in the subvention for rail transport to the coast, the coal operators flew to Japan in late 1961 and managed "to negotiate a price increase ... of 30 cents per long ton and a decrease in loading charges of 20 cents per ton." In a communication with District 18 the following spring, William Whittaker of the COAWC claimed that

> these items, together with the more favourable rate of exchange, will enable us to offset to some degree the decrease in subvention of $1.00 per ton and last July's wage increase of 40 cents per day. The fact remains, however, that our realization on the 1962–63 Japanese business will be 40 cents per ton less than it has been over the past few months.

Hence, the coal companies faced a cost-price squeeze in 1962–63.[133] To make matters worse, in the absence of a long-term commitment on subvention levels from the federal government, the operators faced cost uncertainty for 1963–64 and subsequent years, and hence they were in no position to negotiate a long-term sales contract with Japanese steelmakers.

It is important to acknowledge that the economy of the Crowsnest Pass and Elk Valley in 1962 was not entirely dependent on coal production. The lumber/forest industry was on the rise in the early 1960s and particularly strong "in the immediate area of Fernie," with five lumber mills and a total employment of 500 people.[134] Furthermore, in recent years, there had been several successes in efforts to revitalize the economy and improve infrastructure, including the installation of residential natural gas lines.[135] It is therefore understandable that many living in the region in 1962 could be at least somewhat optimistic about the economic future, even if they recognized the tenuous state of coal contracts with Japanese steelmakers.

In early 1962, a CBC TV program created an uproar in the Crowsnest Pass when it offhandedly rejected the possibility that coal exports to Japan could substantially grow and argued, in no uncertain terms, that "coal was virtually a dead business." The half-hour episode, titled "The Pass," aired on 4 February as part of a series on *Industry and the Way People Live*. The writer and host of the episode, Gordon Hawkins, presented a set of interviews with Alberta Crowsnest Pass residents that showed them to be very knowledgeable and reflective about the economic uncertainties of the coal industry. Hawkins noted, with approval, that many young people had come to recognize that "the future is bright because the future is elsewhere" and were moving away from the Crowsnest Pass for educational and job opportunities. Indeed, they were "being urged by their parents to do so." In a memorable exchange, John Squarek, a coal miner with two sons aged twenty and seventeen, was asked whether he viewed education as a "luxury." Squarek replied that, "well no, I don't ... As far as I'm concerned, education is a must. Right now I figure a fellow without an education is like a fellow without a right hand."[136]

Despite the thoughtful ideas in this episode, it raised the hackles of many residents of the region because it presented visuals of abandoned and dilapidated storefronts in Hillcrest, Alberta, without explaining that its business district had been suffering economic malaise since the village's coal mine had closed in 1939. TV viewers across Canada saw old, weathered buildings with wood siding and nary a human being in sight. The effect was to portray Hillcrest as a frontier ghost town. Since no visuals of more prosperous sections of Alberta Crowsnest Pass communities were presented to counterbalance the shots of desolation in Hillcrest, the program conveyed a false impression of the state of the economy and society in the Crowsnest Pass in 1962. The presumption that "coal was virtually a dead business" led Hawkins to conclude that the rough shape of Hillcrest's business district prefigured the entire region's future.

In early March, MLA William Kovach complained about the CBC program in a speech in the Alberta legislature, terming it "a stab in the back" that would hinder the development of tourism.[137] A few days before, the *Lethbridge Herald* had published a set of eight photos of well-appointed homes, businesses, and public buildings under the prominent title "No 'Ghost Towns' in Crowsnest Pass Region." It also published a lengthy story meant to correct the record but unwittingly made the same fundamental error as the CBC TV episode – it failed to accurately depict how the Crowsnest Pass in 1962 was simultaneously decrepit and showing signs of new economic life. Whereas Hawkins accepted as inevitable the worst-case scenario of the coal industry dying and accordingly featured visuals of Hillcrest's boarded-up stores, the *Lethbridge Herald* story was Pollyannaish, even going so far as to claim that "the general feeling is that conditions and business now are better than they ever were."[138] The story made it seem as if the previous decade's numerous mine closures and significant depopulation had not left their marks.

A second troubling feature of the *Lethbridge Herald* story is that many of the residents interviewed for their reactions to "The Pass" used similar language in criticizing the CBC TV program, therefore leaving the impression that they had been coached. The contrived response to the program demonstrates that local growth coalitions expected residents to "grin and bear it" when it came to new economic schemes: a growth-at-all-costs assumption underpinned elites' economic boosterism. In Chapters 5 and 6, I will show that this assumption was consistently rejected later in the decade as new growth initiatives threatened the health and safety of both workers and residents living close to coal production facilities and that struggles to defend workers' and community rights became crucial components of the fight against economic ruin. Before turning to this story, however, I step back in Chapter 4 to consider how the Communist Party of Canada went from being the most influential political party in the Crowsnest Pass and Elk Valley in 1945 to being inconsequential by 1962 and the significance of its ruin for working-class politics in the region.

CHAPTER FOUR

We Were Continually Losing Membership and Losing Public Support

Tracing the Ruin of the Communist Party, 1945–62

At the end of the Second World War, the Communist Party of Canada, forced to operate at that time as the Labor-Progressive Party, enjoyed more support in the Crowsnest Pass and Elk Valley than any other political party. In the federal election of 1945, the LPP candidate on the Alberta side of the Crowsnest Pass finished well ahead of the second-place Social Credit candidate (37 percent to 29 percent) in a five-party contest and won a clear majority of votes cast in a number of polls. On the BC side of the provincial boundary, again in a five-party contest, the LPP candidate, well-known labour organizer Harvey Murphy (pictured from afar in Figure 4.1) was victorious in Natal and Michel but edged out overall 33 percent to 29 percent by the CCF candidate.[1]

Over the course of the next generation, however, the Labor-Progressive Party (once again called the Communist Party of Canada starting in 1959) lost most of its members and much of its electoral following in the region. I date its end as a distinctive voice in Elk Valley and Crowsnest Pass political life to early 1962, when, within the space of nine weeks, the two prominent public figures most closely aligned with the party died. As noted in the previous chapter, the first to pass was the elderly Thomas Uphill, who had maintained friendly relations with the Communist Party of Canada over his forty consecutive years (1920–60) as the elected member of the provincial legislature for the Fernie District. Uphill's election campaigns had been sponsored by the local labour movement in the guise of the Fernie District Labour Party, but Uphill

FIGURE 4.1 Karl Marx Park, west of Natal, almost certainly 1935. Communist Party labour organizer Harvey Murphy (on the left) and Mayor of Blairmore Bill Knight address an outdoor rally. | By Gushul Studio. Courtesy of Glenbow Archives, Image NC-54-2009.

counted on strong backing from CPC supporters since, in a number of elections prior to 1953, the provincial Cooperative Commonwealth Federation would run a candidate against him (despite objections from some local CCF members). His victories in successive provincial elections after the Second World War, and his willingness to be a "fellow traveller" of the communist movement (e.g., attending the Congress of the Peoples for Peace in Vienna, Austria, in late 1952), gave the Communist Party of Canada a political boost during the early years of the Cold War.[2]

The second public figure to die in 1962 was Sam English, secretary-treasurer of Michel Local 7292 (see Figure 4.2). English, only fifty-six when he passed away, was a highly respected union leader who took an active role in public debates (see Text Box 3.1) and single-handedly had kept alive the tradition of holding a yearly May Day celebration in the late 1950s and into the 1960s. In 1961, Local 7292 sponsored a parade and rally in Natal to mark May Day, with English serving as the chair and Uphill as a featured speaker. Also speaking was none other than Murphy, at that time a senior official with the Mine Mill and Smelter Workers Union of Canada. Uphill likely had Murphy in mind when he "told the

FIGURE 4.2 Sam English and family at their home in Natal, British Columbia, 29 September 1947. By Dorothy Beierbach (née Sailer), who along with Mabel Cranmer (née Degg) stayed at the English home during a trip to the Crowsnest Pass and Elk Valley to seek support for a strike by Medalta Potteries workers in Medicine Hat (Loch-Drake, "Medalta Potteries"). | Courtesy of Dorothy Beierbach.

meeting he always enjoyed meeting old friends especially on occasions such as May Day."[3] The premature death of English the following year not only brought an end to the long-standing tradition of celebrating May Day but also meant that there was no opportunity for him to pass the communist organizing torch on to any of the new members of Local 7292 who would be hired in the 1960s as larger coal sales to Japanese steel mills sparked a revival in the industry.

The remainder of this chapter is broken into three sections. In order to understand the ruin of the Communist Party in the Crowsnest Pass and Elk Valley after the Second World War, it is first necessary to understand the history of the communist political current, particularly in relation to the broader socialist movement. If communist strength throughout the region in 1945 had been a temporary blip, then explaining the virtual disintegration of the CPC/LPP influence in the ensuing years would amount to no more than showing how "things returned to normal." This was not the case, however, and I will show how CPC/LPP support had been deeply embedded in the fabric of life in the years leading up to the federal election in 1945.

My explanation of the ruin of the Communist Party of Canada, outlined in the second section, therefore must trace how the party's real advantages and strengths in the region in 1945 somehow dissipated in a short time, thereby creating a new political scenario for the worker movement just as the railway market for steam coal entered a death spiral. My main finding is that the Cold War took its toll on CPC membership and activism far more quickly and deeply than on its electoral support. The communist current in the region had built its positive reputation and following because of its energetic and militant leadership of miners' struggles, but the capacity to provide such leadership was greatly diminished as activists fell by the wayside. It was inevitable that electoral support would decline over time as working people came to realize that the Communist Party of Canada no longer had the fighting capacity of the past.

The party might have been able to revive its fortunes in the 1950s and 1960s had it faced up to how its blind worship of the Soviet Union had caused it to divert its eyes and stay silent in the face of mounting evidence of Joseph Stalin's dictatorial methods, political crimes, and imperialist policies. However, the party that had been created in the early 1920s in a burst of enthusiasm for the Russian revolution, and had religiously followed the twists and turns in Soviet foreign policy thereafter, proved to be incapable of recasting its history at this decisive moment.

In the third section, I briefly consider whether the ruin of the Communist Party of Canada in the Crowsnest Pass and Elk Valley between 1945 and 1962 had any deleterious effects on working-class life. If the

withering and eventual demise of the party had few negative consequences for workers in the region, then the entire communist period can
be treated as a historical curiosity and judged only on its entertainment
value. However, this is far from the case. The anticapitalist/militantly
pro-worker political project abandoned by the communist current was
never re-engaged. Therefore, the demise of the Communist Party of
Canada as a leading political force narrowed the range of political debates and options and handicapped the worker movement going forward
into the era of a globalized metallurgical coal industry controlled by
giant transnational corporations.

Communism's Roots and Appeal, 1921–45

Communist parties were a new tendency within socialist movements
around the world in the early 1920s, established to build upon enchant-
ment with the Soviet revolutionary experiment and apply the lessons
of the Soviet revolution in other countries. The Communist Party of
Canada was founded in 1921. The Crowsnest Pass and Elk Valley were
fertile ground for this new party since there was a well-entrenched history of allegiance to the socialist movement,[4] labour unions were well
established and strongly supported,[5] and notions of class exploitation
and struggle made immediate sense to workers and their families given
that coal miners laboured in dangerous underground environments and
were paid wages that often fell short of subsistence (they had to be supplemented by tending a vegetable garden, raising chickens and milk
cows, and hunting and fishing). In terms of the socio-political context for
the establishment of the Communist Party of Canada, the situation in the
South Wales coalfield applied in equal measure to the Crowsnest Pass
and Elk Valley: "Communism emerged ... in the inter-war period as an
extension of the pre-war radicalism, and it co-existed with the existing
labour movement."[6]

In analyzing the support for communism in the Crowsnest Pass and
Elk Valley between the 1920s and the Second World War, it is necessary
to consider the responses of four separate groups: veterans of the socialist movement; workers with transnational ties to a part of the Soviet

Union or nearby countries; young people politicized by the mass un-employment of the 1930s and the rise of fascism in Europe; and the gen-eral population of coal miners and their families, struggling to survive in hard times.

Among the veterans of the early socialist movement, support for the new communist tendency would have come from a small group of true believers in Lenin's version of Marxism (the ideologues), a larger group who saw the Soviet experiment as creating something akin to a Kingdom of God on Earth (the utopians), and a much larger group who offered conditional support to the Communist Party of Canada because of its relative strength (the pragmatists).

The existential importance of the Soviet experiment to the communist tendency in the Crowsnest Pass and Elk Valley can be seen in a talk that prominent communist (and former Methodist minister) A.E. Smith gave at the Ukrainian Labor Temple in 1933 on the subject "Russia: How I Saw It"[7] and the tag day held in downtown Blairmore in the spring of 1939 to raise money for Yasinovataya, a coal-mining city in southeastern Ukraine (see Figure 4.3).[8] The attractive promotional banner for the tag day depicted a Yasinovatayan coal miner, framed by the hammer and sickle, shaking hands with a Crowsnest Pass miner, framed by a maple leaf.

An indication of the tone of Smith's remarks in 1933 on Russia is found in a newspaper column that Smith wrote concerning a train trip in 1946 that he and a delegation of fellow Canadian communists took between Germany and the Soviet Union.

> As we approached the border of the Soviet [Union], over which we would pass from the world of capitalism into the new world of Socialism, I kept warning the comrades to stay awake. I did not want to pass the border line with any of our delegation fast asleep. I felt that on such a momentous occasion in our lives, we should all be aware of the thing we were doing.

Then, upon being informed that the train had crossed the border, "tears of joy, which I could not repress, streamed down my face." Smith con-

FIGURE 4.3 Tag day (fundraiser) for the miners of Yasinovataya, held at Blairmore, Alberta, 22 April 1939. | By Gushul Studio. Courtesy of Crowsnest Museum and Archives, Image BL-12-11.

cluded his column with this assertion: "The Soviet Union is a different world to ... and superior in every way to that which is described as the capitalist Christian world."[9]

This depiction of the Soviet Union as a socialist paradise appealed not only to the utopians among the veterans of the socialist movement but also to the ethnocultural communities with transnational ties to the Soviet Union or neighbouring parts of Europe alongside leftist political traditions and convictions. Their interest in and support for the Soviet Union was simultaneously utopian and intensely personal because of family and biographical connections. The strong presence of these ethnocultural communities in the Crowsnest Pass and Elk Valley during the interwar years accounts for much of the solid support for the Communist Party of Canada. Two RCMP reports sustain this interpretation. The first, filed in 1929, noted that "the Ukrainian Labor Temple [see Figure 4.4] is a bad nest for the Communists at Coleman." The second, filed in 1931, revealed the importance of the Soviet experiment in

FIGURE 4.4 Ukrainian Labor Temple, in "Bushtown," near Coleman, Alberta. | By Gushul Studio. Courtesy of Glenbow Archives, Image NC-54-1974.

the worldview of many Ukrainian Canadians in the region (as well as the RCMP inspector's unmistakable sense of Anglo superiority vis-à-vis the "foreigners"):

> I learned that the C.P. is very active throughout these mining camps, especially the foreigners, members of the [Ukrainian Labor and Farmer Temple Association]. These are the people who are the troublemakers. They don't want to work and have the idea in their heads that in a short time they are going to have Canada under Soviet rule. In fact they all talk saying that capitalism is as good as dead ...
>
> Most of these foreigners are not educated, can't even read or write ... When an agitator takes the platform the foreigners listen to every word and believe all that is said. When the speaker starts telling what a wonderful country Russia is for the working man the audience goes crazy with enthusiasm and applause. Every conversation by this class on street corners is about the Communists and

how much better off the workers will be when capitalism is over-thrown ...

I find that these foreigners are led as easily as sheep by the C.P. agitators. They are ignorant and their imaginations are easily in-flamed by the speakers.[10]

By the 1930s, many of the young people coming of age had been born and raised in the region and generally had higher levels of education than their parents. The second-generation youth whose parents had immi-grated to Canada from continental Europe were ready to integrate into Canadian society in a way beyond the reach of their parents. However, the deprivations of the Depression, and the belief that the world had en-tered a decisive phase of struggle (between a seeming workers' paradise on the one hand and capitalist reaction in the form of European fascist movements on the other) frequently steered that integration in a unique direction. With mobility through mainstream channels largely unavail-able, some youth became active Canadian citizens through participation in a communist movement that preached the need for fundamental change. Scholars have termed this "negative integration" since what seemed like a total rejection of Canada in fact integrated the youth by way of civic engagement.[11]

According to Ben Swankey, who served as the Alberta leader of the Young Communist League (YCL) between 1934 and 1939, there was a "very active branch of the YCL in Blairmore" in the 1930s.[12] One indica-tion of the extent of involvement of young men in the region's commun-ist movement at that time was the high number of volunteers who joined the international fight to defend the Spanish republic against fascism. At first glance, the number of volunteers – seven confirmed, with four of them killed in action – seems to be modest.[13] Coal-mining employment was down in the 1930s; however, in order to include the full complement of unemployed miners and would-be miners in the following calculation for the volunteer rate, I have set the coal-mining labour force between Hillcrest and Coal Creek at 5,000 men in the mid-1930s. Therefore, the rate of volunteers for the international brigades from the Crowsnest Pass and Elk Valley was approximately 1 volunteer for every 700 miners. This rate was considerably higher than that for the South Wales coalfield (1 volunteer for every 1,050 employed miners in 1937, or 1 volunteer for every 1,300 miners, if we assume that the unemployed miners living in South Wales represented half of the mining jobs lost between 1926 and 1937).[14] Perhaps a better comparison is with the Rhondda region of South Wales, renowned, like the Crowsnest Pass and Elk Valley, for the strength of the socialist movement and pockets of communist political dominance during the interwar years. Historian Chris Williams has noted that "Spain was not simply another international issue to Rhondda – reaction to it was urgent, inspired and sustained. Rhondda supplied the International Brigade with thirty-two volunteers, the largest valley contingent from within the ranks of the Welsh miners, and a larger contingent than all those volunteering from English coalfields."[15] Expressed as a rate, how did this compare with the Crowsnest Pass and Elk Valley? Setting the coal-mining labour force at 25,000 in the Rhondda region in 1936 (5,000 higher than actual employment),[16] the volunteer rate to fight fascism in Spain was 1 volunteer for every 780 miners. Hence, judged against the gold standard of the Rhondda coalfield in South Wales, the volunteer rate in the Crowsnest Pass and Elk Valley – 1 volunteer for every 700 miners – was robust. It confirmed the popularity of the communist cause and worldview in this region in the 1930s.

In the interwar years, support for the Communist Party of Canada, though certainly far from universal, extended into all corners of the broader community of miners and their families. What caused such widespread sympathy? The reflections of local residents provide some answers. One such resident was Jim Cousins, whose 1952 MA thesis is an invaluable source of information on life in the region just after the Second World War. As a teacher in Coleman between 1928 and 1950, Cousins arrived at unsympathetic judgments on the labour movement and communism. In reference to the labour movement, he wrote that "union leadership has often been unreasonable and far too radical" but then partially balanced this judgment by stating that "the operators themselves have not always been above reproach."[17] His view of the communist movement was even more critical and deployed stereotypical anti-communist imagery to make his points. Cousins attributed the spread of support for the Communist Party of Canada during the Depression to the expert work of organizers such as Harvey Murphy (termed "the chief agent of communism") who took advantage of the chronic unemployment of youth "which made many of them easy prey to radicalism."[18] This is the one-sided "communist agitator" explanation for the growing support for the communist movement. Rather than appreciating the creative organizing work coordinated by Murphy during the strike in 1932 (e.g., mobilizing women to picket and parade in support of the strikers),[19] all that Cousins could do was offer a summary dismissal: "Every tactic known to the communists was used."[20] To top it off, Cousins questioned the character of Murphy in a way that exploited prevalent ethnic prejudices of the time. He revealed in an aside to the reader that Murphy was not of the ethnic ancestry suggested by his name: "His real name is not immediately available, but it is a name of central European origin."[21] (See Text Box 4.1 for more information on Murphy's origins.) In the end, Cousins overinflated the agency of Murphy and treated the working class that supported the communist cause as at best innocent dupes. There is little to choose between his condescending perspective and that found in RCMP Inspector W.W. Watson's 27 September 1931 report, quoted above.

Gustaf Eriksson also lived and worked in the Crowsnest Pass during the interwar years. He came to the region in 1928 and worked in the mines until 1945, starting as a timber packer and ending up as a pit boss. He later became a part owner and manager of a lumber business. Thinking about the strike in 1932, Eriksson indicated that the union leaders were "pink to red" and that "half of the people in [the] Crow's Nest Pass [were] pink and a few red." If we treat "pink" as socialists and "red" as vocal communists and join the two groups, then this is not an unreasonable assessment of the socialist voting bloc in the region. In addition, Eriksson offered a "hardship and strife" explanation for why so many of the pink socialists came around to supporting the Communist Party of Canada in the 1930s: "I do not believe many of the population actually were communists, but without money, very little work, and with their children hungry and with poor clothes – you may draw your own conclusions."[22]

TEXT BOX 4.1

HARVEY MURPHY: "THE CHIEF AGENT OF COMMUNISM" IN THE CROWSNEST PASS AND ELK VALLEY

Maryann Murphy, Harvey's daughter, told Rolf Knight in an interview in 1977 that Harvey came to Canada in 1914 from Poland, along with his mother and two younger siblings, to join his father, who had migrated to Canada a number of years before that. He was eight years old. His family was Jewish. The parents had six additional children in Canada.

The family first lived in Kitchener, where Harvey got a taste of working in industry and was attracted to socialist ideas after hearing speeches by organizers for the One Big Union. They then moved to Toronto, where his father ran a kosher butcher shop in Kensington Market. As a teenager, Harvey was militantly irreligious and attracted to communist ideas. He spent a great deal of time at the home of Tim and Alice Buck, who lived nearby.

Around this time, his father kicked Harvey out of the house "for hanging around with the communists, but probably more because of Harvey's irreligious behaviour." Maryann continued

> what kind of anti-religious behavior? Well, Harvey and the others from his background who he got to know in the movement, they were very offensive in what they did and said. Free love, atheism, any vehicle to incense traditional Jewish views. They would have picnics on Sabbath or parties where there'd be a big thing about eating pork ... Rebelling not only against the capitalist system but also against the kind of traditions they came from.

One of Harvey's first assignments as a labour organizer was in southern Illinois in 1928, attempting to organize coal miners into a communist-initiated union that challenged the UMWA. Therefore, Harvey was familiar with labour relations in the coal industry before beginning his organizing work in western Canada in 1930. While working in Blairmore in the early 1930s, he got to know the Rae family, whom he remembered as one of the few Anglo-Saxon families who supported the strike in 1932. When he started dating one of the daughters in the Rae family, Isobel, "he mentioned [to the parents] that he wasn't Irish but Jewish. That he's just picked up the name Murphy." Harvey's eldest child, Rae

Murphy, told Ron Verzuh that his father jokingly said the Murphy name was chosen to "keep him out of trouble with the anti-immigrant authorities." The original family name was spelled Chernikovski or Chernikovsky.[a]

Harvey Murphy and Isobel Rae were married in 1934. After Harvey ran unsuccessfully as the CPC candidate in Rocky Mountain in the Alberta provincial election of 1935, the family relocated to Toronto. He never worked again as a labour/political organizer in the region. However, he was not easily forgotten, in part because the Murphy family regularly returned to Blairmore to see Isobel's family. In 1942, Isobel and her children had a longer visit with her parents while Harvey served a stretch in an internment camp in Hull, Quebec. (The Communist Party of Canada was outlawed at the time because it had opposed Canada's declaration of war against Nazi Germany. The party had a change of heart after Hitler invaded the Soviet Union.) Released from internment in late September 1942, Harvey journeyed to Blairmore to join his family. On 11 October, Blairmore Local 7295 sponsored a meeting to discuss the progress of the war and honour Murphy's release. The RCMP noted that "approximately 300 miners attended this meeting and Communists and ex-Communists were there in large numbers. They seem to feel now that they can come into the open with their activities after the release of a number of communist leaders from internment."[b]

The RCMP was watching Murphy closely during this period, and another intelligence report recorded a prime example of his wry sense of humour (even though the humour was lost on the writer): "Murphy has also been noticed talking to small groups of miners and has been overheard to remark that he has done plenty for the citizens of Blairmore and the least they can do for him is elect him as Mayor of the Town." (The job of Blairmore mayor was then held by a prominent CPC member, Enoch Williams. Historian Allen Seager noted at the time of Harvey's death that "it can never be said that Harvey Murphy lacked a sense of humour."[c])

His time in Blairmore in 1942 did not last long. "The company wouldn't give me a job," Harvey told Rolf Knight. "So the boys loaned me enough money to get to Vancouver where I got a job at the shipyards ... We were a great labor movement in B.C. at the time," he noted in 1976. "Workers were becoming organized en masse." His time as a manual labourer ended the next year when District 7 of the International Union of Mine Mill and Smelter Workers hired him as an organizer. Harvey spent most of the rest of his career as a leader of the union, based first in British Columbia and then, after the Canadian section of the union became an autonomous union in 1955, in Toronto (although he returned periodically to western Canada). After the merger of the International Union of Mine Mill and Smelter Workers with the United Steelworkers in 1967, Harvey finished his career as a United Steelworkers official.

After 1942, he would make many visits to the Crowsnest Pass and Elk Valley for family and political reasons. No doubt the ruin of the Communist Party in the region caused him consternation, but there was nothing even "the chief agent of communism" could do to stop the party's slide into oblivion between 1945 and 1962. Harvey Murphy died in Toronto in 1977, but his ashes are interred in Blairmore[d] – a fitting, proletarian resting place for "this street-taught, street-tough Marxist trade unionist."[e]

NOTES: [a] Speisman, "Antisemitism in Ontario," 124; Verzuh, "Trade Unionist Harvey Murphy."

[b] CSIS AIR, 96-A-00189, CPC Blairmore, 315, report by RCMP Sgt. T.E. Mudiman, 14 October 1942.

[c] Ibid., 317; Seager, "Memorial," 10.

[d] Crowsnest Pass Historical Society, *Crowsnest and Its People*, 736.

[e] Verzuh, "Trade Unionist Harvey Murphy."

SOURCE: Knight, "Harvey Murphy," 5–8, 14, 21–22, 24, 44, 72–74, 77.

This explanation for why citizens supported communism was likewise espoused by Steve Liska, who began his mine employment in the early 1930s. Interviewed in 2005, Liska treated the explanation for communist support in the interwar years as obvious: "What do you expect?" he asked. "When people got nothing, they turned to communism." He also clarified what being a communist was all about: "Sure you're going to be communist. You got nothing to eat, what are you going to be? Fight."[23] Liska's "hardship and strife" explanation focused on the conditions of miners and their families, whereas his complementary "fight" explanation focused on what the Communist Party of Canada offered the working class: a way to fight. This insight echoed a local Labour councillor's analysis of the appeal of communism in Britain during the general strike in 1926: "As far as the Communist Party was concerned, I think it was just a spirit of fighting the boss, you see that was the idea, fighting the boss."[24]

Applying this idea to the appeal of the Communist Party of Canada in the Crowsnest Pass and Elk Valley in the interwar years, it was neither its Marxist philosophy nor its dutiful promotion of Soviet state socialism that won it a mass following among the working class but its willingness and capacity to lead workers' fights. Therefore, pragmatic support for the party from many of the veterans of the socialist movement was matched by pragmatic support from the broader community of miners and their families, who came to believe that an organized, militant struggle led by the Communist Party of Canada was an effective way to advance working-class well-being.

As a political organization, however, the Communist Party of Canada in the region was often in a state of flux in the 1930s and early 1940s, with participation in local clubs rising and falling and considerable in-fighting. This generalization applied in particular to the party stronghold of Blairmore, which elected a communist mayor and council in 1933 and gained national notoriety in the early autumn of 1934 for renaming its main street Tim Buck Boulevard (see Figure 4.5) in honour of the CPC leader, held as a political prisoner in the Kingston Penitentiary since 1932.[25] An RCMP intelligence report stated that party membership had fallen to only nine in Blairmore after Murphy left the area but had risen to seventy in early 1938, with branch meetings being held twice a week at the miners' hall. Furthermore, CPC support far exceeded the membership figure: "There is a large number of radicals in the Crow's Nest Pass sympathetic to the Party but who are not paying dues and therefore cannot attend meetings."[26]

Some of the CPC in-fighting was public, with the original communist mayor of Blairmore, Bill Knight, not only splitting from the party in 1936 and declining to run in the next election but also "at the last moment [throwing] his support to the Independents and against the Communist

FIGURE 4.5 Original Tim Buck Boulevard sign, Blairmore, Alberta. This artifact is part of the collection of the Crowsnest Museum. | Courtesy of Crowsnest Museum and Archives.

Party and their candidates."[27] Other in-fighting, despite roiling the party in the late 1930s, is known to us only through a statement recorded in an RCMP intelligence report. The speaker was a former CPC member of Blairmore (name redacted) who had been the editor of the party's local newspaper, *The Spotlight*: "The alliance in the Crow's Nest Pass broke up as a result of disputes with [redacted] of Calgary who came down here and stated he was going to run the show. Anyway we decided that we were not going to have any dictators around here." This reveals a confident, antidictatorial spirit inside the socialist movement at the end of the 1930s. It is noteworthy that, although the former editor of *The Spotlight* had been expelled from the Communist Party of Canada "some years ago," in 1942 he maintained a strong commitment to the socialist project. "It is inevitable that this country will turn to communism after the war," he stated, "or socialism as some call it, perhaps not all at once of course."[28] This sort of faith in socialism during the latter part of the Second World War would have bolstered pragmatic support for the Communist Party of Canada/Labor-Progressive Party in the region, simply because the party was still seen by many as the most effective and trustworthy vehicle to advance the socialist project. Nevertheless, party leaders' dictatorial tendencies would have planted seeds of doubt about long-term CPC prospects in the minds of many in the socialist movement, both inside and outside the party.

THREE STAGES OF THE CPC RUIN

The Cold War had an early start in Canada with the Gouzenko spy scandal hitting the press in early 1946 and the only LPP MP, Fred Rose, arrested in March and convicted in June for espionage.[29] Despite this cataclysmic blow to the party's national reputation, and the encouragement that it gave to its many opponents, the Labor-Progressive Party managed to carry on with a very ambitious program of organizing in the Crowsnest Pass and Elk Valley in 1946 and 1947. In this regard, the local party's fortunes mirrored those of the national party, which, in wishful defiance of the rising, virulent wave of Cold War anticommunism, began publishing the *Canadian Tribune* as a daily on May Day 1947, only to be forced to revert to a weekly schedule after six months.[30] The first stage of the ruin of the Communist Party of Canada in the region, therefore, was an upsurge in activism that only hinted at the dark days ahead.

In the Crowsnest Pass and Elk Valley, LPP members took on three major new tasks in the sunny days at the end of the Second World War. First, they worked to extend the influence of the labour movement, both by helping with union organizing drives and by supporting the establishment of the East Kootenay Labour Council.[31] Second, they organized a large Slavonic cultural festival (one of a number of such festivals organized across the country under the auspices of the Association of United Ukrainian Canadians) that a press report described as "the biggest event to take place in the history of the Crowsnest Pass" (see Figure 4.6). Among the dignitaries in attendance was a representative of the Soviet embassy.[32] Third, they initiated a local branch of the Housewives Consumers Association, which advocated tight price controls on food and was the LPP means of involving local women in a political campaign.[33] Ben Swankey, who headed the Alberta Labor-Progressive Party at this time, remarked that "the policy of the Communist Party was always to involve the women in the struggle, not to leave it just to the men." As a result, a number of

FIGURE 4.6 Slavonic festival – two singers, Crowsnest Pass, August 1947. | By Thomas Gushul. Courtesy of Crowsnest Museum and Archives, Image CP-35-38.

women joined the party in the Crowsnest Pass but not as many as men.[34]

The communist tendency in the region had contended with police surveillance and anticommunist countermobilization throughout its existence. For instance, an RCMP intelligence report on the municipal election in Blairmore in 1937 indicated that the Catholic Church had come out against the "Progressives" slate made up of CPC members and allies.[35] However the anticommunism of the Cold War proved to be more intense and multidimensional than previous versions.

It is impossible to gauge which element of the anticommunist assault made the greatest contribution to this demobilization of activists. During the preparations for the Slavonic cultural festival in the summer of 1947, three ethnocultural organizations publicly refused to participate in the festival, thereby revealing organized anticommunism in the local Italian and Slovakian communities.[36] Anticommunism was bolstered when Europeans displaced by the war were recruited to work in the mines. An RCMP intelligence report from 1948 suggested some political turmoil in the communist ranks caused by these new arrivals: "There have been house gatherings and general discussion of the Labor-Progressive Party in Maple Leaf, a community adjoining Bellevue. The population here is largely Ukrainian, Hungarian and Polish. The arrival of some displaced persons from Europe has been the cause of much discussion as the D.P.'s are said to be anti-communist."[37] With a growing population of anti-communist immigrants from Eastern Europe in the region, and a hardening of the anticommunism in some local ethnic organizations, it is understandable that some LPP members and supporters scaled back their party activism in the late 1940s: either they started to doubt their previous view of the Soviet Union as a workers' paradise and accordingly soured on the Labor-Progressive Party, or they simply wanted to avoid confrontation and finger pointing in their ethnocultural communities.

A big part of the politics of the Cold War in Canada was the expulsion of communist-linked unions such as the International Union of Mine Mill and Smelter Workers from the Canadian Congress of Labour and the removal of LPP members from leadership positions in other unions.[38] At the same time, there were a few Canadian unions that both were independent of the Labor-Progressive Party and chose not to purge communists from their leadership ranks. One was the International Brotherhood of Pulp-Sulphite and Paper Mill Workers' Union,[39] and another was District 18 of the UMWA. Consequently, LPP members who held leadership positions in the UMWA locals in the Crowsnest Pass and Elk Valley did not face censure from their own organizations. Indeed, after CNPC refused Sam English employment in 1949, the matter was brought before the District Executive Board and then turned over to the district officers, who got English rehired.[40] In the federal election of 1953, two local UMWA leaders carried the LPP banner in Kootenay East (Sam English) and Macleod (Anthony Patera), demonstrating that open communist political involvement remained viable.

Nevertheless, in the late 1940s and early 1950s, there was some political countermobilization inside the UMWA locals that aimed to weaken the ties between those locals and the Labor-Progressive Party. In 1947, John Lloyd was elected as president of Blairmore Local 7295. The next year he agreed to run for the Cooperative Commonwealth Federation in the provincial election rather than support the LPP call for a "united labour candidate."[41] Lloyd deepened his anticommunist work after the election. In early 1949, an RCMP officer reported "that John Lloyd ... had recently joined the Catholic Faith and in cooperation with [redacted] was organizing an anti-communist drive in the Blairmore Local of the UMWA. Their first objective, which apparently has failed, was to stop the Blairmore Local ... from paying for 25 copies of the communist publication *Canadian Tribune*."[42] Although Lloyd could not convince Local 7295's members to discontinue the bulk subscription, he eventually succeeded in winning this anticommunist battle by undercutting local union autonomy. When the matter was referred to the DEB meeting in May 1949, the board ordered a discontinuation of the practice because using local union funds to purchase "any political organ" contravened one of "the laws of our Organization."[43] A cartoon in an issue of *The Lamp* in 1951 was one way that the Labor-Progressive Party combatted the anticommunism of union officials such as Lloyd (see Figure 4.7) – those officials' red-baiting was depicted as lining up with the interests of coal operators.

The withdrawal of Coleman Local 2633's support for May Day celebrations was another example of the successful disengagement of part of the labour movement from the communist current. The first hint of this move came when the local's secretary-treasurer, William J. White, reserved the right to refuse to serve as the secretary for May Day celebrations when he assumed the post of secretary of Sub-District 5 in 1948.[44] A motion to withdraw Local 2633 from participating in May Day events was narrowly defeated in 1949, but in 1951 the Coleman local officially withdrew from the May Day celebration, citing poor weather conditions as the reason, and proposed holding a new midsummer celebration. This reasoning provoked an acerbic rejoinder from a "Crow's Nest Miner": "Our best answer to the boss and his stooges (the July May Day men) is to tell them to go to hell and it will be plenty warm enough for them there."[45] The next year Local 2633 confirmed its decision to turn its back on the May Day tradition when a motion to rescind the 1951 decision was defeated.[46] As reported in Chapter 2, this position proved to be consequential in 1954 when Local 2633 used it as an excuse to block the organization of a region-wide May Day meeting in Coleman meant to protest the closing of the International mine.

It is important to note that the internal anticommunism seen in the preceding examples coexisted with strong opposition to the anticommunist purges tearing apart the broader labour movement. On this issue, there was unity among the UMWA locals in the Crowsnest Pass and Elk Valley. For instance, in 1950, both the Coleman and the Blairmore locals sent letters to the Canadian Congress of Labour protesting its

FIGURE 4.7 "Red-Baiting Union Official" cartoon in *The Lamp*, June 1951, 8.
| CSIS AIR, 96-A-00189, CPC Blairmore, 148–55, copy of *The Lamp* 1, no. 7 (June 1951).

raiding campaigns against the International Union of Mine Mill and Smelter Workers.[47] The principles of labour solidarity and unity remained paramount.

Despite communist miners having a sanctuary for activism inside their UMWA locals, however, LPP membership and activism fell precipitously in the region between 1948 and 1953, the end of the Korean War. These years cover the second stage of the ruin of the Communist Party of Canada. In July 1949, the RCMP estimated LPP membership between Hillcrest and Coleman at eighty-four. This was a respectable number even if greatly reduced from the mid-1940s when the Blairmore branch alone had "a paid up membership of 104."[48] Over the next three years, LPP membership in the region collapsed, leading the party leadership to assert that "the once numerically strong Party organization in this proletarian centre ... had practically withered away." The RCMP confirmed this decline when it noted that there was no LPP branch activity in Coleman or Blairmore in 1952 and 1953 despite a visit from a party organizer in 1951 that tried to rekindle involvement.[49] Meanwhile, the Fernie and Michel/Natal clubs continued to function, with the Fernie club's membership estimated to be ten to twelve in 1952–53.[50] It thus appears that the decline in LPP membership in the Crowsnest Pass and Elk Valley well exceeded the party's nationwide loss of one-third of its members between 1948 and 1956.[51]

My explanation for this sudden decline in membership and activism incorporates two intertwined factors: first, the poisonous, Cold War anticommunism so severely stigmatized LPP involvement in the broader community that only the most committed and battle-hardened communists could resist it; second, there was a falling away of the pragmatists among the party's membership who could see that the Labor-Progressive Party had lost the capacity to lead workers' struggles.

The concentrated anticommunism in Eastern European ethnocultural communities (discussed above) is an important part of the explanation for the rapid decline in LPP membership and activism because this is where the party had considerable strength until 1948. In addition, during the Korean War, there was general panic about "what communists might be up to" that understandably caused LPP members and supporters to fear for their security and liberty. The Canadian government actually had plans in place by 1948 for the large-scale internment of communists,[52] and this possibility must have been a worry to many party members as anticommunism grew in intensity in the early 1950s. The extent of the panic was illustrated in the commercial relationship between the Labor-Progressive Party and the *Pass Herald*, a mimeographed news advertiser based in Blairmore. In the summer of 1948, the party had placed a number of articles in the *Pass Herald* in the lead up to the provincial election, apparently without any public outrage. Then in 1953 the party hired the *Pass Herald* to deliver one of its leaflets along with the newspaper. "Subscribers took exception to having communist literature distributed with their weekly paper," stated an RCMP report, "and as a result many cancelled their subscriptions and advertisers withdrew their advertisements." My contention is that many LPP members, aware of the development of this anticommunist panic, would have cut back their involvement in the party to limit stigmatization and abuse. For instance, the teacher who declared to her class in 1945 that she was a communist and proud of it would likely have thought better of doing so in 1953.[53]

Even as the Labor-Progressive Party became dormant in Blairmore in the early 1950s, the RCMP's over-the-top Cold War suspicions dogged those who had been associated with the communist movement in the past. An RCMP report in 1951 recorded, as if this was a matter of national security, that "observations ... reveal that communists have taken over key positions in the Blairmore branch of the Canadian Legion." After a report in 1952 noted that Blairmore's civil defence was "almost entirely under the control of known communists," a senior RCMP officer asked for more details, terming it a case of a civil defence organization being "infiltrated by Communists." Fortunately, S. Bullard, an assistant commissioner of the Emergency Planning Branch, was able to answer this request with a measure of common sense:

> I do not attach much significance to civil defence positions being filled in Blairmore by people described as "Communists" ... It would certainly look bad if Blairmore decided to have no civil defence preparations but the fact that the town is interested in

self-preservation is, in my opinion, a sign of good citizenship. There are no secrets in civil defence, it is simply the citizen helping himself when everything else fails. I think we should be more realistic about these things and not keep on reporting them for the sake of reporting.

The assistant commissioner added this provocative thought: "I would like to ask the question, Who else is there in Blairmore who could operate the civil defence if these people called Communists did not do it? Let the investigator tell us this."[54]

The RCMP's scrutiny of the volunteers for the Legion and civil defence demonstrates the "chilly climate" for LPP members and supporters in the early 1950s. This was bound to suppress many people's willingness to be openly associated with anything that the party was doing. When asked in 1997 how the Cold War affected left-wing miners, Ben Swankey, the Alberta leader of the Labor-Progressive Party from 1945 to 1956, asserted that

> I don't think they were [affected] in the sense that their ideologies changed, but I think they were in the sense that many of them were from ... Eastern Europe, and there was always the fear of more persecution or some kind of discrimination against them. And I think that would have caused many of them to sort of back off a bit in their public association even if their hearts were in the same place.[55]

The Cold War attacks on the Communist Party of Canada/Labor-Progressive Party made it a far more polarizing force than it had been and concomitantly thinned its ranks of active members. Both developments diminished the party's capacities to build broad support for socialism and to lead a united worker movement. Without these capacities in play, the many pragmatists among LPP members in the region (including new members who had joined "not because they were convinced communists or anything [but because] they just thought it was a good party, one that fought for them"[56]) had lost their main motivation for staying involved. The unpleasantness of Cold War anticommunism would only have hastened their withdrawal. Once set in motion, there was no stopping the exit of the pragmatists from the Labor-Progressive Party: each member who dropped out was another reason for the next pragmatist to leave. In looking back at this time, Swankey remarked that "we were continually losing membership and losing public support."[57]

For pragmatic supporters of the Labor-Progressive Party, the results of the Alberta provincial election of 1948 would have confirmed that the party was on a serious downward slide. Rather than sitting out the election to increase the likelihood of a labour victory over the Social Credit, the Labor-Progressive Party chose to run a candidate in Pincher Creek–Crowsnest against Blairmore Local 7295's John Lloyd, the CCF nominee. Furthermore, rather than nominating a well-known local candidate, the Labor-Progressive Party chose its Edmonton-based provincial leader, Ben Swankey. That this was a losing strategy was apparent to local communists. An RCMP intelligence brief from three months prior to the election reported "that leading LPP members in the Pass towns hold out very little expectation that [redacted] LPP candidate ... can poll more than 800 votes in the next provincial election." That estimate was not far off the mark: Swankey won 856 of the 5,377 first-count votes (16 percent) despite a campaign that included visits by LPP dignitaries Tim Buck, A.A. Macleod (a sitting member of the Ontario legislature), and Annie Buller (a prominent CPC organizer who spent the last three weeks of the campaign in the constituency) and the active involvement of Mayor of Blairmore Enoch Williams.[58] Swankey finished third behind the Social Credit and Liberal candidates and only narrowly edged out Lloyd, the CCF candidate. Significantly, the pro-labour/socialist voting bloc was only about one-third of the electorate in 1948, sharply down from the 57 percent won by leftist candidates in 1944.[59]

The results of the 1948 election demonstrated that the Labor-Progressive Party still had some electoral support in the region but was no longer a serious challenger for victory. Local communists had accurately predicted this result, but senior party leader Buller was caught off guard on election night and clearly had not asked her local comrades for an honest appraisal of what was likely to happen. According to an RCMP informant at the LPP election headquarters, on learning the results,

Buller "flew into a rage ... and insisted that court action be taken by the party to have the Pincher Creek–Crowsnest election declared invalid." Among those also in attendance at the headquarters were Swankey and Williams. The informant continued that

> a lengthy argument followed in which Annie Buller insisted on such action and the others led by [redacted] insisted that it was useless and that the party could not stand any further expense when it was apparent that they could get nowhere ... The argument finally terminated when it was agreed to take the matter up with the Provincial Committee. Everyone present left the committee room in a huff.[60]

Although Buller could not believe it on election night in 1948, the Communist Party's days as the most popular political party in the Crowsnest Pass had come to an end, as had the pragmatic case for joining and getting involved with the party.

By 1953, the end of what I term the "second stage" of the Communist Party's ruin, there was virtually no membership activity on the Alberta side of the region and only small groups of members in clubs in Michel/Natal and Fernie. Nevertheless, as if to provide a concrete measure of how far the Labor-Progressive Party had fallen since the end of the Second World War, that year the party repeated its election strategy of 1945 of running candidates in both the Kootenay East and the Macleod federal ridings. In Kootenay East, LPP candidate Sam English secured 14 percent of the votes cast in coal-mining communities, about half the percentage won by Harvey Murphy in 1945. In Macleod, LPP candidate Anthony Patera secured 15 percent of the Crowsnest Pass votes, down from the 37 percent attained by the LPP candidate in 1945.[61]

The third and final stage of CPC ruin in the Crowsnest Pass and Elk Valley extends from 1954 to the deaths of Thomas Uphill and Sam English in 1962. Between 1945 and 1953, the Communist Party of Canada/Labor-Progressive Party had lost most of its active members and more than half of its electoral support. It had fallen from being the most popular political party in the region to being a party with a small group of loyal supporters but no hope of electoral victory. In many ways, the party was already in ruin by 1953. However, the period between 1954 and 1962 is important because of key developments that explain why the Communist Party of Canada/Labor-Progressive Party was unable to reverse the decline in its fortunes and consequently disappeared as a political voice after 1962.

The third stage began with a slight uptick in the party's fortunes as the end of the Korean War coincided with a lessening of the "chilly climate" around anything to do with communism. In 1954, the RCMP reported that LPP clubs in Bellevue and Coleman now existed and that the clubs in Michel and Natal had held a social, chaired by Sam English, in support of the party's West Coast newspaper, the *Pacific Tribune*.[62] An Alberta LPP leader captured the shift in political climate in a June 1956 report: "Each of us is beginning to notice how much easier it is to do party work in that we are finding it easier to talk to people."[63]

In 1955, the Labor-Progressive Party continued to publish and distribute *The Lamp*, a newsletter for coal miners in District 18 that had first appeared in 1950. Yet the May 1955 issue was only half the size of issues in 1951 and contained no submissions attributed to miners, unlike the September 1951 issue, which had five such submissions, including ones from "Michel Miner" and "A Crow Miner Who Wants Action."[64] Nevertheless, with the easing of Cold War anticommunism and the continuing legitimacy of LPP activism inside District 18, it seemed to be possible that the party would be able to rejuvenate the newsletter and use it to rebuild its support among coal miners in the Crowsnest Pass and Elk Valley (and anywhere else in District 18 where the coal industry survived) over the coming years. However, two calamitous international events in 1956, and the failure of the Communist Party of Canada to end its subservience to the Soviet Union because of those events, greatly reduced any chance that the party had to mount such a comeback.

The first international event was the publication in the *New York Times* on 5 June 1956 of Nikita Khrushchev's report on the depravities of the Joseph Stalin era (a report first presented earlier that year at the Twentieth Congress of the Communist Party of the Soviet Union). It documented "the cult of the person of Stalin" that had developed in the Soviet Union and how the Soviet government apparatus had been marshalled under Stalin's command in campaigns of mass repression, terror, and killing. This astounding information caused an understandable crisis of faith for many of the remaining CPC/LPP members and supporters since, as Karen Levine writes, "the mystique and magic of the Soviet Union – a force that in the past had provided unity, comfort, and confirmation in adversity – were now gone." Yet some party leaders refused to let the information in the *New York Times* shake their settled views: they concluded that this incongruous report must be a fraud. Hence, after the national LPP leadership decided to circulate Khrushchev's report as a supplement to the *Canadian Tribune*, and copies of the supplement arrived in British Columbia, the provincial committee chose to burn rather than distribute those copies.[65]

Even before the content of Khrushchev's report became publicly known, the Labor-Progressive Party in Alberta was in the process of reducing the staff in its provincial office from "three comrades down to one comrade" because of a shortage of funds, with Swankey voluntarily stepping down as provincial leader and moving to Vancouver.[66] His last electoral campaign as LPP leader was as a candidate in Pincher Creek–Crowsnest in the June 1955 provincial election. He garnered just 362 votes (7 percent) even though there was no CCF candidate in the contest.[67]

The second calamitous international event was the Soviet Union's military invasion of Hungary on 4 November 1956 to suppress a popular uprising with widespread working-class participation.[68] At that point, LPP leaders were split and involved in an acrimonious debate about whether or not the party should step away from the shadow of the Communist Party of the Soviet Union. The debate was soon settled in favour of subservience, however, and in January 1957 the LPP National Executive Committee proclaimed its support for the invasion.[69] The logic behind such support is often termed "Stalinist" (in reference to a way of thinking that outlasted Stalin's death in 1953) and has a two-step argument: first, because the Eastern Bloc countries were "socialist" by definition, their preservation was tantamount to defending the interests of the entire international working class; second, given this perspective, a workers' rebellion in a state socialist country (e.g., the Hungarian uprising of 1956) was objectively anti–working class and antisocialist.[70] There is no evidence that the Communist Party of Canada/Labor-Progressive Party ever promoted its position on the events in Hungary in the Crowsnest Pass and Elk Valley.[71] However, the party's unwavering support for the Soviet Union would have been enough to hasten the exodus of members and supporters with personal ties to Eastern Europe.

After the two calamitous events of 1956, the Soviet Union could no longer credibly be portrayed as a model for the development of socialism in Canada. However, for the remainder of this third stage of the party's ruin, the Communist Party of Canada/Labor-Progressive Party in the Crowsnest Pass and Elk Valley continued with a discordant combination of pro-worker analysis of and agitation on coal industry issues and advocacy of a host of foreign policy positions in line with Soviet foreign policy. In consistently defending such policy stances, the Communist Party of Canada revealed its fidelity to the Stalinist equation of the Soviet state with socialism.

Going back to 1948, the Labor-Progressive Party had sponsored many educational events to advance an understanding of the Cold War that challenged conventional interpretations promoted by the United States and its allies. Most of these events advocated for peace – a position that appealed to more than a few citizens during the uncertain early years of the nuclear age and served to undermine the rationale for any military action against the Soviet Union. Among the events organized in the late 1940s and early 1950s was a talk in Fernie by the first president of the Canadian Peace Congress, Reverend James Endicott.[72] Mass advocacy for peace continued in the region in the period 1954–62. What disappeared from the party's educational curriculum in this last stage of the Communist Party's ruin were attempts to convince the workers of the Crowsnest Pass and Elk Valley that Soviet workers were much better off than they were. Articles on this theme had appeared with regularity in issues of *The Lamp* in 1951, and the same theme was a focus of a talk in 1951 in Natal by Drumheller checkweighman Arthur Roberts, who had joined a trip to the Soviet Union organized by the Canadian Soviet Friendship Society. In announcing his trip, *The Lamp* proclaimed breathlessly that, "while there, Brother Roberts will be able to see with his own eyes what Socialism has done for Soviet workers."[73] This sort of naive discourse became impossible after 1956.

Nevertheless, as LPP political support and influence in the region continued to diminish, it is telling that the party hierarchy prioritized agitation on international issues that aligned with Soviet foreign policy positions. For instance, on 12 January 1955, Ben Swankey led a parade of automobiles from Pincher Creek to Fernie to demonstrate "against the rearmament of Germany." The RCMP reported that only five cars took part. Six years later the Communist Party of Canada publicized its opposition to a possible war over Berlin through an advertisement in the *Fernie Free Press*.[74] In focusing on pro-Soviet foreign policy issues at a time when the coal industry was in crisis, and many working families were struggling to survive, the CPC leadership demonstrated that it had lost sight of what had won the party support in the area in the past – its commitment to improving workers' well-being through militant struggles against the coal company bosses and their allies in government and the trade union movement.

Khrushchev's revelations in 1956 had immediately sparked a number of calls for significant reforms in the Labor-Progressive Party. For example, in June, the Quebec Provincial Executive issued a devastating critique of the party's political practice, calling for a "sharp struggle" against a number of problems, including "an entrenched dogmatism and intolerance," "the stifling of criticism," and "the idea that divergence from accepted Party policy automatically flows from alien ideology." Shortly after a meeting in October 1956 at which Tim Buck "was not conciliatory in his response to the questions and challenges of the Montréal membership," the provincial leader, five other major Quebec organizers, and several hundred members left the Labor-Progressive Party.[75] At this time, there were two groups of dissidents in the party's National Executive Committee; the first group called for "the dissolution of the LPP and a 'socialist realignment' of progressive forces," and the second group opposed dissolution but believed that the party needed to "alter its whole approach to politics" in order to overcome "left-sectarianism."[76] A major problem for the dissidents was that, as the inner-party debates on the future of the party worked toward a resolution in 1957, many members sympathetic to the dissidents' critiques simply gave up on the party, thereby tilting the balance of forces toward the Stalinist old guard. Karen Levine estimates that "hundreds, perhaps thousands, of rank-and-file party members and sympathizers" as well as a few major leaders "had already voted with their feet" prior to the LPP National Convention in April 1957, leaving the dissidents bereft of supporters. The convention, therefore, was "anticlimactic."[77]

By 1958, the composition of the Labor-Progressive Party was much different from what it had been prior to the events of 1956. All of the prominent reform leaders had left the party. Furthermore, party membership had been reduced by more than half. Particularly hard hit were Montreal and Toronto, where Jewish membership had collapsed because of revelations about anti-Semitism in the Soviet Union. In addition, so many young people had left the party that "the Communist youth organization was not revived until several years later."[78] With the loss of so many activists, supporters, and leaders, opportunities for mass LPP political work dwindled, and party leaders retreated inside a Stalinist political cocoon. This approach had no hope of rebuilding the influence of the Communist Party of Canada in the Crowsnest Pass and Elk Valley; its adoption, therefore, accounts for why the party died as a political force in the region after Thomas Uphill and Sam English passed away in 1962.

The political successes of English over the period 1954–62 suggest that there remained enough goodwill toward the Communist Party of Canada in the regional worker movement that some sort of long-term, if modest, comeback for the party was possible. Besides continuing to hold leadership positions in Michel Local 7292, taking on special assignments for District 18, and ensuring that May Day was celebrated in the region every year, English took a leadership role in public discussions on what could be done about the deepening crisis in the coal industry. Importantly, he did not simply repeat CPC/LPP policy proposals on the coal crisis year after year but independently rethought his views over time. Indeed, by the end of the 1950s, English had come around to rejecting protectionism as the way to save the western Canadian coal industry.[79]

Although the CPC/LPP voice remained notable in the Crowsnest

Pass and Elk Valley during the mine closures of the 1950s, by the early 1960s its capacity to exercise this voice relied far too heavily on the solitary figure of English. His premature death was very unfortunate for the communist cause in the Elk Valley and Crowsnest Pass, especially after so many of the older generation of communist miners had retired in the 1950s and many of the younger generation of miners had left the area in search of more stable and better-paying work. But the fact that there were absolutely no activists in the wings ready to take on some of Comrade English's responsibilities suggests that the Communist Party of Canada also contributed to its own bad luck – its insular Stalinist focus had blocked it from renewing the left-labourist leadership cohort inside the UMWA across the region.

When Tim Buck went on a speaking tour of western Canada in early 1962 after stepping down as the CPC general secretary, a position that he had held since 1929, one of his stops was Local 7295's union hall in Blairmore. At seventy-one years old, Buck could still draw a crowd in the Crowsnest Pass to hear him reminisce about Tim Buck Boulevard and Karl Marx Park and regale with a story about the time that he gave Mao Zedong advice on building socialism in China. Nevertheless, the party was a shell of the fighting force that it once was, and it no longer had the capacity to lead the struggle for dignity and justice of the working class in this coalfield society. Buck's visit was a reminder of how much times had changed and how far the Communist Party of Canada had fallen.[80]

Living in the Shadow of the Communist Party's Ruin

I have shown in this chapter that the ruin of the Communist Party between 1945 and 1962 was so deep and thorough that the party was in no position to mount a political comeback in the late 1960s when long-term contracts to supply coal to Japanese steel companies would result in a new coal boom. However, the problem for leftist politics in the Crowsnest Pass and Elk Valley went deeper than the ruin of the Communist Party of Canada since the anticapitalist/militantly pro-worker political space squandered by the communist current was never adequately filled by the

New Democratic Party. This was the case even though communist miners such as Coleman's Bob Sallant chose to become involved in the party – as much as these onetime communists would have liked to have shifted the moderate NDP policies toward socialism, they were forced instead to adapt to that moderation.[81]

The connection between the fortunes of the Labor-Progressive Party and Cooperative Commonwealth Federation during the Cold War is an important issue. In the Elk Valley, the overall socialist voting bloc decreased by 17 percent between the federal elections in 1945 and 1953; however, though the CCF share of the vote declined by only 2 percent, the LPP share fell by 15 percent. In interpreting this decrease, it is important to recognize that, if the Cooperative Commonwealth Federation had been largely unaffected by the Cold War processes that ruined the Communist Party of Canada, then it should have increased its share of the vote as numerous socialist voters shifted from the Labor-Progressive Party to the Cooperative Commonwealth Federation. As it stands, however, any shift of votes from the former party to the latter party between 1945 and 1953 was more than cancelled by the loss of CCF votes to other parties. The situation on the Alberta side of the region, where the Cooperative Commonwealth Federation never had much electoral success prior to the Cold War, was different: the collapse in the socialist voting bloc was an unambiguous 31 percent between 1945 and 1953, with the CCF decline (from 13 percent to 4 percent) every bit as consequential as the LPP decline (from 37 percent to 15 percent).[82] Each of the two distinctive patterns of vote shifting indicates that, despite the often open opposition between the two socialist parties, Cold War processes linked their fortunes.

Reg Whitaker and Gary Marcuse have partially blamed the Communist Party for the problems that the Cooperative Commonwealth Federation ran into during the Cold War: "With their slavish loyalty to Moscow, the Communists not only shot themselves in the foot as a party; they also harmed the entire Canadian left, non-Communist as well as Communist." The Communist Party of Canada inflicted such harm by "poison[ing] the atmosphere of debate and thought on the left" since its obsequious loyalty to the Soviet Union prevented it from critically assessing many public policy issues. However, the Cooperative Commonwealth Federation, in turn, poisoned leftist intellectual culture by joining the red-baiting chorus. Indeed, the more the Cooperative Commonwealth Federation tried to distance itself from the Communist Party of Canada through anticommunism, the more it contributed to the Cold War narrative that linked all socialist ideas to subversion and treason and thereby limited its own ability to pursue a more leftist path going forward. Taking stock of the damage suffered by each of the parties during the Cold War, Whitaker and Marcuse declared that "the Cold War was waged against the Left. Anti-communism was used not only to repress Communism but also to domesticate the social democrats."[83]

Therefore, the Cold War produced not only the ruin of the Communist Party of Canada in the Crowsnest Pass and Elk Valley but also the moderation of the social democratic alternative. The New Democratic Party that succeeded the Cooperative Commonwealth Federation in the early 1960s was neither unambiguously anticapitalist nor a strong advocate for the rank-and-file worker, two defining characteristics of the historical communist movement. Indeed, the New Democratic Party was temperamentally unsuited to filling the leftist political space vacated by the ruin of the Communist Party of Canada, and therefore that space would lack an organizational proponent in the years after 1962. This, in turn, would restrict the political scope of subsequent worker movements in the region. In particular, rank-and-file struggles would lack the coherence that they might otherwise have had under the guidance of a politically focused, socialist leadership.[84] Nevertheless, as I will detail in Chapter 6, leftist traditions and sentiments survived the deaths of Thomas Uphill and his Fernie District Labour Party and the ruin of the Communist Party of Canada – in 1966, NDP provincial candidates won elections on either side of the continental divide. This coincided with the mounting strength of movements asserting worker and community rights in opposition to a growth-at-all-costs orthodoxy.

CHAPTER FIVE

Pursuing Alternatives for Growing the Economy

Dead Ends, a Tragic Underground Explosion,
and a New Beginning for Coal, 1963–68

The economic uncertainty of 1962, described at the end of Chapter 3, persisted into the first half of 1963. At Michel Collieries, a layoff of 95 miners in early April reduced the unionized workforce to just 500. A spokesman for Crow's Nest Pass Coal attributed this layoff to a decline in orders from Japanese steelmakers and the replacement of workers by machines. During the winter of 1963, CNPC deployed three labour-saving continuous mining machines that accounted for 60 percent of coal production. At the same time, CNPC sales to Japanese customers had decreased by 12 percent between 1961 and 1962 (see Table 3.2) and, in the early months of 1963, were on pace to decline even further. Meanwhile, at Coleman Collieries, almost entirely dependent on the Japanese export business and not yet mechanized, there were only four days of work in March, prompting a temporary layoff of 120 union members and leaving a skeleton crew of just 60 on duty. The company also had many idle days during other months in the first half of 1963.[1] The idle days were entirely the result of a slowdown in orders from Japanese steel companies.

To make matters worse, the regional economy was hit by three other reversals. First, CNPC and British-American Oil abandoned a joint exploratory venture after spending in 1962 over $1 million (close to $10 million when adjusted for inflation to 2022) drilling an exploratory well on a mountain ridge near Fernie that yielded no fossil fuels down to 8,531 feet.[2] Second, completion of the Rogers Pass section of the Trans-Canada

Highway in 1962 diverted traffic from the southern route (Highway 3), which adversely affected the hospitality industry. Third, later in 1963, the controversial decision to end passenger rail service through the Crowsnest Pass added to the sense that the region was increasingly on the periphery of Canada's economy and society.[3]

Over the last half of 1963, however, five positive developments suggested that the region's economy and labour force would expand going forward. Nonetheless, these developments were modest rather than transformative in scope, uneven in effect across the region, and, in one case, promised new jobs that could only be realized after several years. Consequently, it is understandable that economic frustration persisted.

The first positive development was the announcement on 13 June 1963 by the new federal Liberal government of Lester Pearson (elected to a minority position on 8 April) that it would provide tax and depreciation incentives to encourage investments in new businesses in "designated areas of slower growth." In September, the Crowsnest Pass and Elk Valley area was designated as one of the thirty-five slow-growth areas in Canada. In the first section of this chapter, I investigate the quantity and quality of the jobs created by this program and assess how it unfolded compared with what transpired in the Panther Valley, Pennsylvania, which also attempted to replace lost coal-mining employment with jobs in manufacturing.[4]

The impetus for diversified economic growth that started in the late 1950s with the unsuccessful drive to locate a new federal penitentiary in Fernie continued into the mid-1960s. In the second section, I detail the fate of prominent efforts at diversification that did not originate in the federal government's incentives for slow-growth areas, including competing proposals near Fernie that raised the question of whether additional heavy industrial development would be compatible with a major expansion of tourism.

The other four positive developments in the second half of 1963 all pertained to the coal industry, which remained the most probable source of new jobs and income. First, the new federal government committed to granting transportation subventions for coal sold to Japan on a five-year basis rather than year to year. This pledge gave Coleman Collieries and CNPC the opportunity to negotiate longer-term sales contracts with Japanese steelmakers. Second, representatives of the two coal companies journeyed to Japan in the early summer of 1963 to successfully lobby their customers to immediately increase purchases of coal from the Crowsnest Pass and Elk Valley, thereby providing relief from the layoffs and short-time conditions described above. As a result, Coleman Collieries increased its unionized labour force to 293 by December 1963, up 51 percent since May. Third, CMS committed to opening a second pig iron furnace at Kimberley, British Columbia, as well as a $2-million steel plant, thereby increasing the demand for coke from CNPC.[5] Fourth, the most important development, the first multiyear contract with Japanese steelmakers was signed; it was for 800,000 long tons per year, from April 1964 to March 1967, split equally between CNPC and Coleman Collieries. The federal government was persuaded to provide transportation subventions for the entire tonnage, although the amount was $2.73 per short ton, down from the $3.50 provided in 1963–64.[6] At the time of its signing, CNPC claimed that the contract "will bring a bright future for the area for the next three years in that it will mean full employment and an increase in manpower."[7] Beyond the obvious benefit of stability with a three-year contract, however, the future turned out to be not so bright. Growth of metallurgical coal production in the mid-1960s did not create as many new jobs as promised, was organized in tandem with new attacks on workers' rights, generated significant health and safety problems inside the mines, and prompted heightened struggles over the extent to which miners, as opposed to company owners, should benefit from the growing prosperity of the industry. I explore these issues in the third and final section of the chapter.

At the end of 1963, the hopeful signs of an economic turnaround fell far short of compensating for the loss of jobs and income caused by the collapse of the railway steam coal business. A controversy in early 1964 demonstrated that many of Fernie's working-class families continued to experience economic hard times. In this case, married working women, and by extension the dual-income family, were scapegoated for those hard times. On 6 February, the *Fernie Free Press* published a letter from twelve women who complained about working wives:

The young people of this city are being looked down on because they are walking the streets, supposedly making a public nuisance of themselves. Why? We can tell you. Quite a few married men holding positions in this city also have their wives holding positions, meaning there are two healthy pay cheques going into one home every month, while a good percentage of the citizens have to live on unemployment insurance and welfare.

In its next issue, the newspaper published a letter from an anonymous young person who supported this point of view:

It becomes disappointing when we apply for jobs and hear the old familiar lines: "Sorry, no vacancies" ... "We'll let you know ..." I believe the reason is that many of the jobs we apply for are filled with married women. Don't they realize they are destroying opportunities for young, single men and women? Why do they work? In many cases it's due to boredom and a desire for luxuries, not financial problems.[8]

These letters show that some of Fernie's unemployed could be mobilized by an exclusionary argument denying married women the same right to employment as single people and married men. One reason that this scapegoating could gain traction was that countervailing, leftist explanations of unemployment were no longer in widespread circulation after the demise of Fernie Local 7310, the deaths of Thomas Uphill and Sam English, and the ruin of the Communist Party of Canada.

The scapegoating of married, working women reveals one of the ways that women in the Crowsnest Pass and Elk Valley faced gender inequalities in the mid-1960s. A second way was violence against women. Most of this violence was hidden from public view, so it is impossible to estimate accurately its prevalence. However, an extreme example did come to light: a sixty-two-year-old Natal man shot and killed his wife in their living room in July 1964 before turning the gun on himself. This tragedy took place two decades after a coal miner had murdered his estranged partner with an axe in his home outside Coleman, a crime for which he was hung at the Lethbridge Jail in 1944.[9]

Overall, the contours of growth during this period can be compared fruitfully with a pattern identified by urban sociologist Harvey Molotch: "Under many circumstances growth is a liability financially and in quality of life for the majority of local residents. Under such circumstances, local growth is a transfer of quality of life and wealth from the local general public to a certain segment of the local elite."[10] Using Molotch's insight, throughout this chapter and the next, I assess the extent to which working people gained or lost in terms of economic advancement and quality of life from each elite-driven scheme to rebuild the economy of the Crowsnest Pass and Elk Valley. I also detail instances when working people struggled to make growth schemes better serve their interests. In this chapter, I focus on struggles at work, whereas in Chapter 6 I examine how working people's struggles spilled over into the community and were integral to successful NDP campaigns in provincial elections in Alberta and British Columbia.

Of Dubious Benefit: Jobs Resulting from the Slow-Growth Area Incentives

In response to the mine closures of the 1950s, local growth coalitions had taken shape on either side of the provincial boundary. Each coalition's objective was to convince new industries and public institutions to set up shop nearby, thereby replacing some of the economic output and jobs that had been lost with the collapse of the railway steam coal business. Up to the end of 1962, however, only the sour gas and sulphur plants just west of Coleman and Fernie's fledgling ski hill could be counted as successes.

The long distance between the Crowsnest Pass–Elk Valley region and major urban markets was one reason for the recruitment difficulties. In contrast, the Panther Valley was only 135 kilometres from Philadelphia. A second difficulty, at least until 1963, was that senior levels of government did not assist by offering incentives to entice firms to set up in the

Crowsnest Pass and Elk Valley. In contrast, in 1956, Pennsylvania established an industrial development authority that offered low-interest second mortgages to firms that invested "in economically depressed regions of the state." The importance of subsidies for attracting new employers to Pennsylvania's anthracite region is demonstrated by this statistic: between 1940 and 1970, 103 firms relocated to the region, with 72 percent of them receiving financial assistance.[11]

When Lester Pearson's government decided to assist depressed regions immediately after winning the election in 1963, it introduced financial incentives that far exceeded what American governments had been offering. Specifically, it offered companies that set up a new firm or expanded an existing business in a designated slow-growth area (1) freedom from corporate income tax for the first three years of operation; (2) accelerated depreciation of equipment and machinery (two years versus the usual five years); and (3) accelerated capital cost allowances for new buildings.[12] When introducing this initiative, Minister of Finance Walter Gordon commented that, "if these proposals do not stimulate marked activity in the Atlantic provinces and in other areas of slowed economic progress, I do not know what will."[13] At the heart of this federal program was a gamble: significant taxpayer dollars would be spent to get new firms established in a slow-growth area on the hope that they would stick around after the incentives had expired.

Designation as a slow-growth area soon gave the Crowsnest Pass and Elk Valley consideration for two major enterprises connected to power generation: a coal-fired thermal power plant, proposed for Blairmore, with its electrical output destined for export to the United States, and a plant to produce heavy water (deuterium oxide) for use in CANDU (CANada Deuterium Uranium) nuclear reactors. The possibility of a coal-fired power plant at Blairmore was announced on the front page of the *Lethbridge Herald* on 9 May 1964. In that year, West Canadian Mineral Holdings owned the assets of the closed Greenhill mine at Blairmore, and the new proposal was to generate electricity by burning the more than 1 million tons of coal slack (small pieces of coal) piled around the old mine site. Although the story noted that survey crews and a drilling rig were doing exploratory work at Blairmore and acknowledged the region's designation as a slow-growth area as an impetus for the project, nothing more came of the initiative – it met the same fate as the steel plant that West Canadian Collieries had fervently sought in the 1950s.

In the early 1960s, the Canadian government invited submissions for the construction of a plant that would produce heavy water to supply the CANDU reactors that it expected would be built in coming years. The first heavy water plant built in the 1960s was located at Glace Bay, a Cape Breton coal-mining community.[14] In 1964, the federal government invited submissions for a second heavy water plant, and an official from the area development agency in Ottawa suggested that one or both of the coal companies in the Crowsnest Pass and Elk Valley join up with a nuclear engineering firm to submit a joint proposal for the plant; the official estimated that up to $10 million in rebates would be available through the slow-growth incentive program. The coal companies were uninterested in this idea, however, since they "did not have access to the large sums of money required to build a plant of this kind."[15]

After the plan to build the second heavy water plant at Estevan, Saskatchewan, fell through, new tenders were invited. One of the bidders this time, Canadian General Electric (CGE), left CNPC executives and local government officials with the impression that it was giving serious consideration to building the $65-million plant in the Elk Valley. Although the CGE bid was successful, it chose instead to build the plant at Port Hawkesbury on Cape Breton Island, another area that qualified for slow-growth area incentives. The main technical advantage of Port Hawkesbury over Fernie was that it had "high isotopic feed water," but lower labour costs in Cape Breton likely factored into the decision.[16]

Had that heavy water plant been built in the Elk Valley, it would have generated a construction boom in the late 1960s and thereafter several hundred permanent, well-paid jobs. The Port Hawkesbury plant began producing heavy water in 1970, was sold by Canadian General Electric to Atomic Energy of Canada Limited in 1976, and was shut down in 1985 because by then Canada had a surplus of heavy water productive capacity since not as many CANDU reactors had been commissioned as expected.[17] Therefore, although the heavy water plant initially looked like it would have added long-term diversification to the economy of the

Elk Valley, much like a federal prison, the good times would have lasted for two decades only.

In two other cases – Phillips Cables and Becker Drills – the slow-growth area incentives proved to be large enough to overcome the region's geographical isolation. Both firms settled on the Alberta side of the slow-growth area, with the absence of a provincial sales tax in Alberta a key reason for this choice. The failure of the federal government to take the sales-tax differential into account, argued the *Fernie Free Press*, made "the federal incentive plan unfair."[18]

To take advantage of the slow-growth area incentives, Phillips Cables established a new subsidiary and built a medium-sized factory to manufacture telephone and communication wires and cables.[19] Located at Sentinel, near the sour gas and sulphur plants opened in 1961, the plant operated between early 1966 and 1985. During the initial years of operation, the factory's hourly paid workforce ranged from 110 to 140.[20] Although the jobs created at this Phillips Cables plant offset only a small proportion of the more than 1,500 coal-mining jobs that had disappeared in the Alberta Crowsnest Pass between 1952 and 1962, the plant was a significant addition to the struggling local economy. In the spring of 1968, the 150 jobs at Phillips Cables made up almost 20 percent of all jobs in the resources and manufacturing sectors of the Alberta Crowsnest Pass economy.[21] Furthermore, in this instance, the federal government's gamble in offering generous start-up incentives with no strings attached paid off in a long stretch of continuous operation – the first major layoff at Phillips Cables was not until 1980, and the plant lasted almost twenty years. As a bonus, a secondary manufacturer was spawned by the Phillips Cables plant, a local company, ultimately called Universal Reel and Recycling, that initially produced wooden cable spools for Phillips Cables but expanded in the 1990s "to become a leading manufacturer of cable reels in North America and overseas."[22] Nonetheless, the economic growth and jobs produced by the Phillips Cables plant were accompanied by a number of costs and a decidedly unequal distribution of benefits. Consideration of four additional factors helps to flesh out a critical perspective on the slow-growth area initiative.

First, when Phillips Cables built its new manufacturing plant in the Crowsnest Pass, it had existing production capacity at its Vancouver plant that could have been deployed to produce the wire and cable that eventually came out of the Alberta plant. Hence, the slow-growth area incentives caused a duplication of capital investment as well as job losses in Vancouver.[23]

Second, the initial collective agreement covering the workers at the Sentinel plant (signed with the International Brotherhood of Electrical Workers in 1966) revealed that from the outset Phillips Cables squeezed additional profits out of the plant's operations by underpaying the workers relative to workers at its plants in Brockville, Ontario, and Vancouver. Table 5.1 compares the wage rates for four of the jobs in the functionally similar plants. The final column reports the wage penalty experienced by workers at the Sentinel plant relative to workers at the other two plants. The wage penalty is "super wage exploitation" since it is the part of the average wages paid to workers at other Phillips Cables plants denied to Crowsnest Pass workers.

TABLE 5.1 Hourly wage rates at three Phillips Cables plants, 1966 and 1969

Job classification	Year	Crowsnest Pass	Brockville	Vancouver	Crowsnest Pass Penalty[a]
(Female) spooler	1966	$1.25	$1.86	$1.90	−34%
machine operator	1969	$1.55	$2.45	$2.42	−36%
(Male) labourer	1966	$1.65	$2.01	$2.42	−26%
	1969	$1.95	$2.62	$3.00	−31%
(Male) stranding	1966	$1.85	Avg.	Avg.	
machine operator	1969	$2.15	$2.10	$2.53	−20%
			$2.68	$3.17	−26%
(Male) tradesmen	1966	$2.52	$2.67	$2.95	−10%
	1969	$2.82	$3.50	$3.75	−22%

NOTE: [a] The penalty is calculated relative to the average of the hourly rates at the other two plants.

SOURCE: The hourly wage data were collected by the Canadian Electrical Workers Union during its successful attempt to win a union representation vote at the Crowsnest Pass plant in February 1969; LAC, RG 124, vol. 68, file 718-1-0, part 1-1, Jess Succamore to Jean Marchand, 9 June 1969.

The Canadian Electrical Workers Union was very critical of the wages paid by Phillips Cables at Sentinel between 1966 and 1969. In a letter to Jean Marchand, the federal minister of regional economic expansion, the union's Jess Succamore focused on the $1.95 per hour paid to a (male) labourer in 1969. He pointed out that the yearly wages of such a worker would be insufficient to give a family of four a "decent standard of life" according to the Economic Council of Canada. "So much for the contribution that the Phillips Co. has made in utilizing the Federal Grant for the purpose of improving the economic well-being of the Crowsnest," Succamore disdainfully remarked. His point applied doubly to the female workers who operated a spooling machine at the Sentinel plant. Not only was the 1969 wage rate for this job classification further below the "decent standard of life" line than the wage rate of the labourer, but also, in both 1966 and 1969, its "Crowsnest Pass penalty" exceeded that of the male job classifications. Perhaps Phillips Cables targeted female workers for additional wage exploitation based upon its knowledge that their exclusion from coal production jobs limited their employment options in the area.

Third, there was a turnover of 500 employees over the factory's first four years of operation.[24] The plant's original manager acknowledged that turnover in the early years was "higher than we would like to see it" and blamed employees' cavalier attitude toward absenteeism.[25] Perhaps a few of the people hired by Phillips Cables were clueless about managing absences from work, yet a yearly turnover rate in excess of 75 percent, particularly in a locale where jobs were scarce, suggests an unpalatable work environment. Therefore, it is little wonder that the workforce voted in early 1969 to have a militant, Canadian-based union (the Canadian Electrical Workers Union) take over as their collective bargaining agent.[26]

Fourth, I contend that workers did not gain as much from the creation of more than 150 jobs at the Phillips Cables plant as one might suppose since so many of the jobs were poorly paid and low quality. The flip side of this coin is that the company enjoyed record profits in 1967 and 1968. In the year prior to the Sentinel plant beginning production, Phillips Cables in Canada reported an after-tax profit of $2.2 million. The following year after-tax profit jumped by 77 percent to $3.7 million. It remained high in 1967 at $3.5 million ($29.5 million in 2022 dollars). In commenting on its profit in 1967, the company stated that "these earnings reflect reduced income taxes due to the tax exemptions of our wholly owned subsidiary, Phillips Cables (Western) Ltd." To take full advantage of the exemption from paying corporate income tax that would expire in early 1969, Phillips Cables, after only four months of operation, had increased the size of the Sentinel plant by one-quarter to allow for a 60 percent increase in productive capacity. Furthermore, no later than 1968, it moved to a round-the-clock operation.[27]

Taking the preceding factors into account, Jess Succamore argued in 1969 that the Phillips Cables factory at Sentinel served the interests of corporate shareholders more than the "economic enhancement of the region."[28] At the same time, though, three positives stemmed from this experiment in government-stimulated economic growth: Phillips Cables stayed in business a relatively long time, supported local employees who desired to go into skilled trades, and established an industrial management club "to aid interested employees to develop management techniques and to prepare them for future promotion."[29] Nevertheless, after the plant was shuttered in 1985, some residents felt resentful toward Phillips Cables since its years in the Crowsnest Pass amounted to a stop gap measure rather than a transformative economic initiative. Twenty-five years later a letter published in a local newspaper dismissively summed up the legacy of the Phillips Cables plant as "providing, for a time, minimum-wage employment for some residents." In interviews in the 1990s, Thomas Dublin and Walter Licht found a similar resentment in the Panther Valley because of decades of reindustrialization initiatives "that did little to stop economic decline."[30]

Becker Drills was the second company that set up shop in the mid-1960s to take advantage of the slow-growth program's incentives. The company's Blairmore factory manufactured the Becker Hammer drilling rig, which bored a hole in the earth and cased the hole in one operation. The key difference between the operating histories of Becker Drills and Phillips Cables is that, whereas the latter plant stayed in operation long past the expiration of its tax incentives, the former plant was shuttered just eighteen months after the company started paying corporate income tax. In the absence of the tax break, two drawbacks to Becker Drills remaining in Blairmore came to the fore: difficulty in recruiting and retaining skilled workers and difficulty in marketing drilling rigs to Calgary-based drilling companies when the rigs were not readily available for inspection.[31] There was no easy fix to the marketing drawback. However, the problem of skilled labour could have been surmounted. Manufacturing the drilling rig required a high number of skilled workers. Since skilled tradespeople were in short supply in the Crowsnest Pass in the mid-1960s, Becker Drills recruited skilled workers from outside the region. The company's reliance on out-of-town workers was demonstrated by the fact that, after more than four years of operation, in August 1970, "there were only ten Pass residents on the Becker payroll of twenty-eight employees." To recruit skilled workers from afar, the company not only had to pay wages competitive with those for skilled workers in Calgary but also, when there was a production crunch, sometimes had to pay a premium to ensure that workers would stay put. A second problem with this recruitment strategy was a high turnover rate since workers would jump at any reasonable opportunity to work at jobs closer to home.[32]

Becker Drills could have addressed its skilled labour problem proactively by following the lead of Phillips Cables and offering incentives to local employees to enter skilled trades. Over several years, such a program would have reduced the need to recruit out-of-town tradespeople and lowered the turnover rate. Furthermore, when skilled labour from afar was needed, Becker Drills could have covered moving expenses and subsidized housing costs, thereby encouraging workers to make a permanent move to the Crowsnest Pass.[33]

In the anthracite region in Pennsylvania in the decades after the Second World War, assisted firms that relocated to the region remained in business for an average of almost twenty-two years. Phillips Cables, which stayed in business in the Crowsnest Pass for nineteen years, fit this typical pattern. Yet some of the assisted firms in Pennsylvania "failed to meet expectations or moved out of the region almost as quickly as they came." Becker Drills fit this second typical pattern.[34] The slow-growth area program of the mid-1960s therefore produced one winner and one loser for the Crowsnest Pass (although classifying Phillips Cables as a "winner" must be qualified by the low wages and high employee turnover observed right at the start of the Sentinel factory and evidence that the company prioritized corporate profits ahead of community enhancement).

The tax and depreciation incentives that attracted Phillips Cables to the Crowsnest Pass in the 1960s simply would not work in today's globalized, neo-liberal world, where so much manufacturing takes place in lower-wage countries. Hence, as the metallurgical coal industry in the Elk Valley winds down later this century, the development of a new, sustainable economy will require more thoughtful and strategic government investments, a democratic planning process that fully involves First Nations and settler communities, and mechanisms to ensure that more of the wealth generated in the region is reinvested in the people and their future prospects there. I discuss these recommendations in the concluding chapter.

"A Permanent Second-Class Industrial Backwater"? Industry or Tourism as Fernie's Future?

In the mid-1960s, three proposals were floated for significant new businesses in the Fernie area apart from the federal government's slow-growth area incentive program. Considerable controversy swirled around each proposal, and in the end all three were abandoned. Consequently, the Fernie Snow Valley ski hill would remain the city's only success at economic diversification in the wake of the closure of Elk River Colliery in 1958.

The first abandoned proposal was more interesting for what it revealed about the political fault lines in Fernie than its economic implications. In 1963, two Fernie residents began promoting the idea of establishing a new brewery in the city. This idea resonated with many in the community because of the heritage of local beer production that had ended in 1959. The conduct of the promoters, however, did not impress members of Fernie's business elite. For instance, after a lobbying trip to Victoria in June 1964 by a delegation of city officials and brewery promoters, Alderman Jack Minton, a past president of the Fernie Chamber of Commerce, stated that "he was surprised the delegation wasn't 'thrown out in the first five minutes,' because of holes in the presentation." At the same meeting of council, a brewery promoter berated the councillors for failing to convince the BC attorney general to grant a brewery licence and argued that the failure proved that council members "don't want industry here."[35]

In August 1964, the provincial Liquor Control Board informed the promoters "that a license is not available and they consider the matter 'closed.'" Nevertheless, the brewery remained a contentious political issue. Alderman Mike Nee claimed that provincial cabinet minister Wesley Black, the MLA for Creston, where Interior Breweries' modern plant was located, had blocked approval because a new Fernie brewery would compete with the Creston plant. Another supporter of the brewery proposal came to prominence in the fall of 1964 during a by-election to fill the post of mayor. Vernon Uphill, one of Thomas Uphill's sons, was a maintenance foreman at East Kootenay Power Company and president of Fernie's minor hockey association. At an election forum, Uphill complained that "local hotels are denied supplies of draught beer except from one company" and "criticized the 'stooges of the brewery syndicates' for blocking the provincial licence for the proposed Fernie Spring Brewery." His category of "stooges" would have included members of Fernie's business elite who had soured on the brewery proposal over the course of working with the promoters. Alderman Minton, Uphill's opponent in the mayoralty by-election, was one such "stooge." On election day, Uphill won 62 percent of the 1,018 votes cast.[36]

That by-election revealed an interesting fault line in the city. The *Fernie Free Press* assessed the contest as pitting "two factions" against one another — "those for the businessmen and those against."[37] Members of the Chamber of Commerce had not had much success in turning around the city's economic fortunes. As a result, public disappointment with the business-led local growth coalition contributed to Uphill's election as mayor. Although in 1964 Fernie was no longer a trade union city, neither was it uniformly in step with the worldview of its small-business class.

Meanwhile, though Snow Valley was attracting a modest number of skiers (e.g., 373 on the weekend of 11–12 January 1964), it was far from a financial success, operating at a loss of around $5,000 in 1962–63 and just breaking even in 1963–64. Local investors had bought shares in 1962 because they saw it as an investment that would yield a significant financial return, but the project was caught in a financial squeeze in 1964, not generating the profit needed to pay down an existing loan, let alone finance ski hill improvements.

To try to get out of this bind, the shareholders came up with a creative share offering in June 1964 that aimed to raise new capital while richly rewarding the original investors. The specifics were 12,000 new shares offered at ten dollars each, with the proceeds to be allocated to paying down a bank loan and financing new development, and the original shares appreciated by 300 percent in value. If the share offering had come off as planned, then the original shareholders who had invested $125,000 would have ended up holding 50,000 shares valued at $500,000, whereas the new shareholders who would have invested just $5,000 less would have ended up holding 12,000 shares valued at $120,000. Unsurprisingly, this offering fell flat.[38]

Two years later the ski hill venture faced a crisis when the federal government's Industrial Development Bank called in its $86,000 loan. The company avoided collapse only when Crows Nest Industries (CNI)[39] guaranteed $20,000 of Snow Valley's bank loan.[40]

Therefore, in the 1960s, Snow Valley was undercapitalized and losing money. It would begin to realize its promise only after Heiko Socher, who started to operate the ski school in 1967, began buying up the shares in Snow Valley in 1972. He would build up the ski hill for a quarter-century before selling it to a larger operator. The reasons for Socher's success,[41] as well as the twists and turns in the property's history since 1997, lie beyond the scope of this book. Today the ski hill, renamed Fernie Alpine Resort, is a pillar of Fernie's economy.

For a short time in early 1965, the two remaining proposals that eventually would be abandoned were in direct conflict with each other. The proposals envisioned dramatically different economic futures for the Fernie area. One came out of CNPC's drive to diversify economically. Late in 1964, the company bought four area lumber companies. Then in early 1965, it announced that it was interested in building a pulp mill and intended to compete with other firms for the pulp-harvesting rights on crown land in East Kootenay. The pulp mill was slated for development at Morrissey, just fifteen kilometres south of Fernie (see Map 0.1).[42]

News of CNPC's intention to build a pulp mill in such close proximity to Fernie was greeted with strong negative language from an American company, Third Equity Corporation, that had been working quietly behind the scenes to develop a luxury mountain resort near Island Lake, located just ten kilometres west of Fernie in the shadow of the Lizard Range of the Rocky Mountains. Third Equity held an option on an eleven-square-mile parcel of land. According to the company's executive vice-president, Philip Ray, who had grown up in Fernie, "the first stage of development would include a $5,000,000 expenditure eventually aimed at providing a large chateau-type hotel, golf course, ski development, swimming pools and year-round lodges for U.S. company executives." In late January, Third Equity indicated that the pollution from a pulp mill would scuttle its development plan. "A pulp mill, in our opinion, would seal the doom of the Fernie area as a recreational centre." Ray pointed to Fernie as "the finest area still undeveloped in the Rockies. Properly handled, recreation could transform the area to an extent no heavy industry could hope to equal, besides spreading the benefits over a much wider base in the community." He continued by painting a grim picture of Fernie's future should a pulp mill so close to the city get the go ahead: "A pulp mill ... with its smells, smoke and wanton stripping of wood lots is certain to discourage whatever tourism there is already ... The results of such installation will certainly be to render the Kootenay district a permanent second-class industrial backwater, ever more at the mercy of an industrial octopus which has never been noted for its public mindedness." His critical depiction of CNPC demonstrated his insider knowledge of the reputation of the American-owned coal company among Elk Valley residents.[43]

Despite Ray's tough talk, Third Equity allowed its option on the Island Lake property to lapse. At the beginning of the following year, the "industrial octopus," now known as Crows Nest Industries, applied to the provincial government to discharge, every day, up to 27 million gallons of partially treated effluent into the Elk River from its yet-to-be-built pulp mill. The local rod and gun club wrote to the provincial pollution control board to express concerns that such a large volume of effluent could pollute the river.[44] The story took a surprising turn in the summer of 1966 when Crows Nest Industries stated that Morrissey was "out" as the site of its planned sawmill/pulp mill complex. The company would subsequently drop its plan for a pulp mill altogether but opened in 1968–69 a new sawmill at Elko, about thirty kilometres downriver from Fernie (see Map 0.1).[45]

In an ironic twist, it was the coal company that took charge of the Island Lake property when Third Equity Corporation let its option lapse. Crows Nest Industries never pursued the recreational potential of the property, however, and it would be twenty-three years before back-country cat-skiing (in which skiers and boarders are transported up a mountain in a snowcat) would start at Island Lake.[46]

The conflict between industrial and recreational development at Fernie in the mid-1960s was never settled definitively. Neither was the more fundamental conflict between environmental preservation and any sort of major development (whether recreational or industrial). Fernie had the good fortune not to become a "second-class industrial back-water" when Crows Nest Industries abandoned its plan to build a pulp mill at Morrissey. This opened up an opportunity for the city to plot an economic future without having to kowtow to Crows Nest Industries. However, Kaiser Steel's massive investment in a mountaintop strip mine beginning in 1968 pulled Fernie back into the orbit of resource indus-trialization, for it provided many well-paid jobs for Fernie residents and encouraged allegiance to the coal industry. Jumping ahead to the twenty-first century, the question of what sort of economic development would best secure an environmentally sustainable long-term future for the Elk Valley and Crowsnest Pass is again front and centre. Importantly, al-though First Nations were ignored during the debate in the 1960s, they now have a legal basis for insisting on being at the table for planning decisions. I analyze this new dynamic in the concluding chapter.

FIGHTING FOR WORKERS' RIGHTS AS THE METALLURGICAL
COAL INDUSTRY GROWS

In this section, I investigate the growth of the coal industry in the Elk
Valley and Crowsnest Pass from 1964 to 1968. By the middle of 1967,
coal's recovery had so improved the regional economy that the federal
government removed the region from the list of designated slow-growth
areas.[47] However, the growth in coal production – fuelled by sales of
metallurgical coal to Japanese steelmakers – was not without significant
harms. In the mines, it had negative impacts on miners' job autonomy,
health, and safety. It also sparked struggles by the two surviving UMWA
locals for improvements in workers' pay and benefits.

Growth was far from smooth during these years as CNPC and
Coleman Collieries faced a serious cost-price squeeze and therefore prioritized productivity gains. On the price-of-coal side of the squeeze, the
two coal companies had to deal with a buying cartel of Japanese steel
companies that already had dependable supplies of metallurgical coal
from both the Appalachian region of the United States and Australia.[48]
This was a situation of "vertical quasi-integration" in the relationship
between coal producers and customers, created because the market
power of the customers was so great relative to the two Canadian producers that lacked a diversified customer base.[49] The cartel's willingness to
exploit its position of market dominance was shown in the terms of the
contracts signed with producers in the Crowsnest Pass and Elk Valley in
the mid-1960s: in 1963, the cartel forced CNPC and Coleman Collieries
to accept a decrease of eighty cents per ton compared with the previous
year's price, and it insisted on a price decrease of twenty cents per ton in
the second year of the three-year contract that began on 1 April 1964.
This tactic pressured the coal operators to create cost savings to offset
looming price decreases; it also pressured the federal government to consider providing additional subsidies to the industry.[50]

In the late 1950s, underground mines in Appalachia supplied 80 percent of Japan's coal imports and charged a high price because of a "near
monopoly of supply."[51] By the mid-1960s, the Japanese cartel had significantly deflated the market power of Appalachian producers since, of the

approximately 15 million tons of metallurgical coal that it was importing, "one-half of this comes from Australia and about one-third from the United States," with the balance "supplied by other countries such as Russia, Communist China and Canada." Australian coal could be produced for a much lower cost than coal from the Crowsnest Pass and Elk Valley. Nevertheless, the Japanese cartel continued to import metallurgical coal from Canada in the mid-1960s and to encourage further expansion of the mining industry there. The Dominion Coal Board believed that the cartel was interested in Canadian coal because of the "undependable nature of the labour element at Australian mines" that contrasted with the "stable political climate" in Canada.[52]

Australian historian Bradley Bowden notes that "both academics and industry observers" uncritically accepted this explanation for the cartel's willingness to overpay for Canadian metallurgical coal. He dismisses the explanation, however, arguing that it would have been far cheaper to accumulate stockpiles of coal to guard against strike action by Australian coal miners. His alternative explanation is that the cartel wanted to block Australian producers from developing a near monopoly of supply and to this end sponsored "the Western Canadian producers as a foil to the potential dominance of the market by Australia's miners."[53] Therefore, the renaissance of coal mining in the Crowsnest Pass and Elk Valley was the result of an international power play by Japanese steel companies against Australian coal producers.

The cost-of-coal side of the cost-price squeeze was difficult for the two coal companies to manage because it involved four separate sets of negotiations. By 1964, the first set of negotiations had been settled, with the subvention from the federal government for the next five years set at $2.73 per ton up to a maximum of 800,000 tons. CNPC and Coleman Collieries were responsible for the costs of inland transit by rail and storage/loading of coal at a deep-sea dock. Consequently, two additional sets of negotiations focused on rail-shipping and dockage costs. In March 1964, the Canadian Pacific Railway was charging Coleman Collieries $5.13 per ton, and the dockage charge in Vancouver was an additional 83 cents per ton. The extreme sensitivity of the coal companies to even minimal increases in costs was shown after the Canadian Pacific

Railway indicated that it planned to increase its charge by 25 cents per ton on 1 April 1965. This prompted the COAWC to send a delegation of executives to Montreal to lobby a CPR official and then to Ottawa to lobby cabinet ministers for relief from the planned increase. In the end, the railway company mandated an increase of 15 cents per ton effective 1 October 1965. This prompted a pointed letter to the company's president from Progressive Conservative MP Lawrence Kindt. He asked that the increase of 15 cents be rolled back and called for the railway to find ways to decrease shipping costs. "The obsolete methods now used by the CPR are appalling," the MP stated.[54] One modern method adopted in the United States at that time but not yet by the Canadian Pacific Railway was dedicated coal trains.

Collective bargaining was the fourth set of negotiations that affected the cost of coal in the mid-1960s. The cost-price squeeze forced the two coal companies to look for ways to increase the average amount of coal produced per eight-hour shift while simultaneously striving to limit the size of negotiated increases in wages and benefits. The operators deployed two strategies to increase coal production per shift: mechanization of mining (which eliminated jobs) and tighter control of workers (e.g., on absenteeism) to extract more labour.

Of the two mining companies, Crows Nest Industries made the greatest commitment to mechanization. In 1967, Michel Collieries had four operations where seams outcropped at the surface and deployed seven continuous mining machines inside its three underground mines; it also deployed a fast-moving belt to transport coal out of one mine.[55] Gross production at Michel Collieries increased by 24 percent between 1963 and 1968. Yet average monthly employment decreased by sixty-four people (11 percent) in the same period (Table 5.2) because of mechanization. Therefore, the "bright future" ushered in by the first long-term contract with the Japanese steel cartel involved job losses rather than gains at Michel Collieries. The benefits of growth did not spread to the broader working-class and small-business communities in the Elk Valley.

In contrast to Crows Nest Industries, Coleman Collieries was much slower to invest in mechanized underground production. Because of this delay, the only way for Coleman Collieries to fulfill its contract with

TABLE 5.2 Michel Collieries production and sales[a] (in thousands of short tons), employment, and fatalities, 1963–68

	1963	1964	1965	1966	1967	1968
Net coal production	757	834	767	837	704	890
Coal usage						
coal sold to Canadian customers	188	183	172	230	252	238
coal sold to American customers	2	2	1	1	10	1
coal sold to Japanese customers	367	394	403	376	407	450
coal used to make coke	192	189	206	227	212	236
Coke production	146	144	157	172	159	150
coke sold to Canadian customers	77	76	96	94	n/a	n/a
coke sold to American customers	78	74	71	79	n/a	n/a
Average monthly employment[b]	606	597	552	552	563[c]	542[d]
Fatalities	1	1	2	2	16	0

NOTES: [a] Sales of coal or coke could exceed production in any year because of a stockpile carried over from previous years. [b] Total of hourly and salaried employees. Approximately 90 percent were hourly UMWA members. [c] The average monthly employment reported by the government for 1967 was 446. This number was affected by the temporary loss of employment because of a strike in February and then the Balmer North mine explosion in April. Therefore, I have substituted the number 563. This is based upon an exact figure: there were 507 eligible voters in the Michel Local 7292 strike vote of 15 February 1967 (GWRC, M-6000, file 582, notice of strike vote results) and an estimate that these 507 union members made up 90 percent of a total workforce of 563. [d] This does not include the 650 workers employed at the end of 1968 in developing Kaiser's new mountaintop strip mine (British Columbia Minister of Mines and Petroleum Resources, *Annual Report*, 1968, 466).

SOURCE: British Columbia Minister of Mines and Petroleum Resources, *Annual Report*, 1963–68.

Japanese steelmakers in the mid-1960s was to expand its workforce engaged in the manual mining of coal. As recorded in Table 5.3, the company's overall increase in yearly coal production, from 1963 to 1968, was 301,000 tons (an increase of 84 percent). To realize this increase, Coleman Collieries expanded its labour force from 284 in 1963 to 488 in 1968 (an

TABLE 5.3 Coleman Collieries production and sales[a] (in thousands of short tons), employment, and fatalities, 1963–68

	1963	1964	1965	1966	1967	1968
Net coal production	360	555	609	633	621	661
Coal usage						
coal sold to Canadian customers	119	120	150	110	88	84
coal sold to American customers	1	4	5	1	0.5	0
coal sold to Japanese customers	260	447	459	520	552	582
Average monthly employment[b]	284[b]	364	437	459	483	488
Fatalities	1	0	3	0	0	0

NOTES: [a] Sales of coal could exceed production in any year because of a stockpile carried over from previous years. [b] Total of hourly and salaried employees. Approximately 85 percent were hourly UMWA members.

SOURCE: Alberta, Department of Mines and Minerals, *Annual Report of the Mines Division*, 1963–68.

increase of 72 percent). For the first time in over a decade, young men in the Crowsnest Pass had decent job prospects since the company "was taking on any local boy who had the education to be trained as a welder or machinist, was treating them as apprentices and was sending them to Technical School in Calgary."[56]

The two mining companies were in much different financial positions in the mid-1960s. Because Coleman Collieries was so dependent on sales to the Japanese cartel (e.g., 86 percent of its sales in 1967 were to Japanese customers; see Table 5.3), and because it relied on manual mining, it felt the pressure of the cost-price squeeze to a much greater extent than Crows Nest Industries. The shaky financial situation of Coleman Collieries was revealed by its arrears of over $100,000 in required payments to the District 18 Welfare and Retirement Fund accumulated during 1965.[57]

In contrast, CNPC/CNI could better manage the cost-price squeeze. Not only was its mechanized operation less dependent on labour, but also it had a long track record of profitability, so it could raise capital by selling additional shares or borrowing money as need be.[58] Furthermore, in

1967, only 46 percent of CNI coal sales went to Japan (see Table 5.2); hence, a small profit margin on sales to the steel cartel could be augmented by larger profit margins on sales to other customers. The competitive advantages of Crows Nest Industries, however, did not translate into a gentler treatment of its workforce, and the company was committed to squeezing as much profit from Michel Collieries as possible to fund new investments in forest products and oil and gas "in a multi-million-dollar program of diversification."[59] Therefore, workers at the two coal companies faced similar attacks on their rights and well-being.

Class struggles in the workplace in the mid-1960s were propelled by the coal companies' search for ways to mine more coal (to meet the shipping commitments of the long-term contract) and to lower the labour cost of mining a ton of coal. I present four examples of such struggles. The first example is that, toward the end of 1962, Coleman Collieries announced its intention henceforth to pay the miners the minimum wage rate (company miners) for pillar recovery mining (in which the pillars of coal supporting the rock ceiling in a room of a mine are removed, causing the ceiling to collapse); until then, pillar recovery had been paid at the higher piecework rate (contract miners). At a contentious union-company meeting, F.J. Harquail, now the president of Coleman Collieries, backed down when told that the Local 2633 pit committee would lead a wildcat strike if the piecework rate was not maintained. District 18's William Ure included the following comment in his report on the meeting: "We had the same lecture on co-operation as we got from Whittaker [of the COAWC]. Advised Harquail he was lucky as he had received too much one-sided co-operation from the union in the past."[60]

The second example is that the coal companies pursued punitive measures to control absenteeism. At Michel Collieries, new procedures for how to return to work after having been absent for two or more days had the miners "really raising hell" in the spring of 1964.[61] At about the same time, Coleman Collieries complained to Local 2633 that approximately 10 percent of all shifts had been lost to absenteeism in a single week and threatened "drastic action ... against habitual offenders."[62]

The third example of class struggle stems from a push by the two coal companies for workers to be more flexible about their hours of work. This led to controversies at Coleman Collieries over work on Saturdays[63] and at Michel Collieries over scheduling workers for two shifts in a twenty-four-hour period.[64] The union locals were prepared to pursue these struggles because they had strong contractual language to protect workers from being at the beck and call of their employers.

Safety and health are the foci of the fourth example. The increase in production, introduction of continuous mining machines and conveyor belt transport, and availability of overtime increased the risks of accidents and occupational diseases. The provincial governments had an important role to play in protecting workers, both through mine inspections and through analyses of fatalities and "dangerous occurrences"; so did the union.

Excessive coal dust in underground mines was both a significant safety problem (because it could explode if methane caught fire and flared in a mine) and a danger to workers' long-term respiratory health. Mechanical mining machines spewed a great deal of dust into the air, creating a respiratory hazard for "the extremely vulnerable operators."[65] Since this technology had been widely adopted in American mines in the 1940s and 1950s, the excessive dust associated with it was widely known. Unfortunately, the problem of black lung disease (coal workers' pneumoconiosis, a preventable but incurable disease) had been downplayed by the UMWA after the Second World War while the union prioritized production growth through mechanization instead of protection of workers' health.[66] District 18 made the same tragic mistake after the deployment of continuous mining machines in the Crowsnest Pass and Elk Valley. In this case, the long-term cost of the growth in coal production in the 1960s would become apparent in pneumoconiosis statistics only fifteen to thirty years later.

The last row of Tables 5.2 and 5.3 records the fatalities at each mine between 1963 and 1968: just four fatalities at Coleman Collieries but twenty-two fatalities at Michel Collieries, a figure that includes the fifteen miners who died in a massive coal-dust explosion in 1967. The workplace deaths between 1963 and 1966 did not hint at the possibility of an impending major disaster at either operation: there were three deaths because of roof falls at Michel Collieries and two at Coleman Collieries; there were two haulage deaths at Michel and one at Coleman; a worker was asphyxiated in a surface coal bin at Michel; and a worker drowned while underground at Coleman. However, yearly government reports on "dangerous occurrences" at Michel Collieries for the same years suggest that there were major safety hazards inherent in CNPC/CNI's underground operations. For instance, the company was forced to abandon, in 1963 and 1965, respectively, two of the mines working the "A" coal seam; this was because of readings of carbon monoxide produced by an underground fire in an area where the coal had already been mined and the overlying roof of shale had collapsed (known as a gob). In addition, on two occasions, a spark produced by a continuous mining machine contacting rock ignited a build-up of methane at the coal face. Fortunately, workers were able to extinguish these fires.[67]

In 1967, Balmer North was the newest underground mine at Michel Collieries, with mining of the northward thrust of the No. 10 seam (some forty feet thick) beginning in February 1966. This was a highly mechanized mine that deployed continuous mining machines and conveyor belts. Nevertheless, the mine was not without safety issues. In 1966, three underground fires were recorded as "dangerous occurrences." One of these fires occurred when a build-up of coal dust caused a conveyor belt to jam, leading to frictional heating of the belt.[68]

Balmer North's rapid development was predicated on the desire of Japanese steel companies to access its high-quality coal, the drive by Crows Nest Industries to lower production costs through mechanization, and the recent abandonment of some of the older mines at Michel Collieries. The devastating coal dust explosion that killed fifteen workers and seriously injured ten others on 3 April 1967 occurred in a mine where the push to increase production contributed to the chain of events that resulted in the explosion. An investigation by R.B. Bonar, British Columbia's deputy chief inspector of mines, concluded that (1) an initial fire started in a gob area of the mine where a very high concentration of methane had built up after ventilation air that should have passed through the gob was redirected to a part of the mine where production was under way; (2) the spark that caused the methane to catch fire most likely resulted from "a fall of rock in the gob area, possibly striking a roof bolt"; and (3) the methane fire flared and in turn ignited the excess of coal dust in the mine created by the conveyor transport system.[69] Local historian John Kinnear compared the sequence of events in the Balmer North mine that day to the firing of a shotgun: "With one spark (the hammer strikes the bullet), the gas ignites (the bullet's primer explodes), the gas flares and causes the coal dust to explode (the gunpowder goes off) and a horrendous flash rips through the mine carrying all sorts of debris with it (the bullet charges down the barrel)."[70] All but two of the dead and most of the injured were afternoon shift workers who had started to walk into the mine through a rock tunnel at the start of their shift. The coal dust explosion hit them travelling at close to 1,000 miles per hour; this explains why "the killed and injured men were just about unrecognizable due to being heavily plastered with coal-dust mud,"[71] and almost all had suffered head injuries.[72]

By allowing such an enormous build-up of coal dust in Balmer North, both Crows Nest Industries and the provincial government's mine inspectors were culpable for this tragedy. This was the view of John Desjardins when interviewed in 1992, twenty-five years after the explosion. Desjardins, who started to work at Michel Collieries in 1944 and served as the president of Michel Local 7292 at various times in the 1960s and 1970s, believed that, over the years, safety was "pretty good" in the underground mines run by his employer. At the same time, he offered an important qualification to the generalization: "That explosion – there should never have been that much coal dust, it should have been looked after." Desjardins was one of the volunteers who cleaned the mud off the bodies of the miners who had been hit by the full force of the blast. "After a while you become numb you know," he said, "but a lot of head injuries. You know it was terrible" (see Figure 5.1).[73]

The government's requirements for the rehabilitation of the Balmer North mine after the explosion acknowledged the lax attitude toward coal dust that had characterized the mine's first year of operation. The requirements included that "the abnormal amounts of visible coal-dust and debris must be loaded up and taken out of the mine" and that "to reduce the make of coal-dust from spillage and at transfer points a system

FIGURE 5.1 Mine rescue after Balmer North explosion, Michel Collieries, April 1967.
| By Vern Decoux. Courtesy of Galt Museum and Archives/Akaisamitohkanao'pa, Image 19861119016.

of water-sprays on all belts must be introduced as far as practical." The
rehabilitation requirements also included sealing off the gob areas from
the active sections of the mine and revamping the ventilation system so
that eventually there would be a separate stream of circulating air for
each continuous mining machine.[74] Among the miners who refused to
work underground again after the explosion was Larion Savilow, one of
the injured, and his son Bill, a worker in another of the mines at Michel
Collieries. Explaining his decision, Bill Savilow said that "I've had my
fill of it all: the gas, the coal dust, the rock falls, the close calls, the
complacent management, the whole damn unpredictability of a life in
the mines."[75]

Another worker who decided to give up underground mining after the
Balmer North blast was Jack Newton, who stated that "I saw this coming. I said it and said it and it happened." His reservations about the
safety of the Balmer North mine prior to the disaster had been shared by

many of his co-workers. When Frank Travis finished the guiding season (for hunters) in 1966, he was rehired at Michel Collieries to work at Balmer North. He remembered "all the miners" telling him "boy, you're foolish. I wouldn't come in this mine." When Travis asked why, they told him "because it's going to blow up some day. This is a dangerous mine." Furthermore, the wife of one of the dead miners reported that, just the night before the blast, Bill Cytko had told her "it'll blow up one day." Still, there is no indication that union officials had lobbied for greater attention to safety issues in Balmer North prior to the explosion.[76] My hypothesis is that the union had bought in to the "growth-at-all-costs" strategy of the company and, as a result, did not advocate for immediate fixes to the design flaws of the mine that became apparent during its first year of operation. The harsh lesson from this tragedy was identified in real time by the *Fernie Free Press*: "Tragedies such as that at Balmer North Mine ... emphasize that no safety practices can be too rigid, no regulation too strict, if they help prevent a loss of life."[77]

The cost of pell-mell growth at Balmer North was devastating and touched all parts of the region. Three of the dead miners had lived in Coleman, five in Fernie, and the remaining seven in Sparwood, Natal, or Michel; the latter miners were buried in a mass grave at the Michel cemetery on 7 April after a funeral service attended by 1,300. All but one of the deceased was married, and a total of twenty-four children lost their fathers in the blast.[78]

The immediate aftermath of the disaster demonstrated the ruthlessness of Crows Nest Industries. Faced with the resignations of a number of miners after the explosion, the company blocked former employees from holding alternative jobs in the local area. In a grievance pursued shortly after the explosion, Local 7292 reported that the coal company's management had asked subcontractors (e.g., a coal-hauling company) not to hire former mine employees and even had forced its lumber division to lay off a recently hired electrician who had worked at Michel Collieries. In response to this hounding, Local 7292 asked the District 18 office to pursue a complaint "with the [BC] Labour Department, under the Fair Working Practices Act."[79]

Overlapping with these ongoing class struggles in the workplace were two sets of contentious negotiations over the collective agreement, the first in 1964–65 and the second in 1966–67. The two-year contract signed in 1962 had included a wage increase of merely twenty cents a day, causing real wages to decline (see Table 1.2). Therefore, many workers saw the contract negotiations in 1964–65 as an opportunity to make up for lost ground.

District 18 held a wage scale convention prior to the start of bargaining in 1964. That year the UMWA locals at Lethbridge and Canmore joined with Michel Local 7292 and Coleman Local 2633 in sectoral bargaining with the COAWC. Convention delegates elected a militant four-person policy committee to be responsible for negotiations. A rift between this policy committee and District 18's not-so-militant executive officers would prove to be decisive in how the negotiations unfolded.[80]

At first, contract negotiations in 1964 proceeded with a predictable rhythm and logic. In response to District 18's demand for a wage increase of two dollars per day, the COAWC called for "a halt to general wage increases over the next two years." A conciliator recommended an increase of forty cents per day in each year of a two-year agreement, and a subsequent board of conciliation increased this to fifty-five cents per day. In a vote conducted on 25 November 1964, the board of conciliation award was soundly rejected by the workers at all four mines.

The COAWC then reconvened to craft a new strategy that built upon insights into internal union dynamics. President of District 18 William Ure had told William Whittaker that the negative sentiment toward the conciliation board award was because "the Michel representatives led the way and influenced others to their point of view." Furthermore, Ure indicated that the two District 18 executive officers were at odds with the elected policy committee: "There is a fight in the organization and we had to fight for what we thought best." Ure added that "I know one thing, so far as Coleman and Canmore are concerned, the officers of the local union who are not members of the policy committee do not wish a strike or trouble of any kind."[81]

Crucially, District 18's executive officers accepted the financial claims of the operators at face value. This left them vulnerable to manipulation. For example, in 1964 and early 1965, Coleman Collieries repeatedly asserted that it was losing money on its coal operations. Behind closed doors, however, the company's president, F.J. Harquail, reported a profit of forty cents per ton before depreciation.[82] Moreover, in December 1964, after the COAWC convinced the Japanese cartel to forgo a scheduled price decrease of twenty cents per ton starting on 1 April 1965 and instead increase the price that it paid by twenty-four cents per ton,[83] not a word of this price adjustment was breathed during the continuing contract negotiations. By abrogating their responsibility to challenge the coal companies' financial claims, District 18's executive officers fell into the role of adjunct to rather than adversary of the operators.

Whittaker had also surveyed the mood of workers. His report on Coleman Collieries indicated that "they do not want trouble ... and are not a bit concerned about what Michel may do." This accurately captured the dissonance between the Coleman and Michel miners and a lack of enthusiasm at Coleman for "trouble" (i.e., a strike). The COAWC's new strategy was two-pronged. First, as suggested by CNPC, it journeyed to Japan and pleaded successfully for price relief. Second, it approved of Harquail's strategy to threaten the closure of Coleman Collieries if faced with a strike and to use this threat as leverage to negotiate "a local agreement separate and apart from anything the Michel local union or district office decided."[84]

After securing the price relief of forty-four cents per ton in Japan, the COAWC came up with a new contract offer that marginally improved on the conciliation board award: a three-year agreement with an increase of sixty-four cents per day in each year and other advances such as two new statutory holidays. In the meantime, 80 percent of union members voted to authorize a strike. The stage was thus set for more negotiations. COAWC's offer on 21 December was rejected by the policy committee, whose counteroffer was rejected in turn.[85]

On 24 December, the COAWC sent a letter to District 18 emphasizing that its latest offer remained available to workers. When the COAWC next met on 5 January 1965, the three companies that remained in the negotiations (Lethbridge Collieries had quit the association on 31 December) compared notes and learned that workers had not yet been apprised of the operators' latest offer. A strike date had been set for

12 January, so quick action was necessary if the UMWA locals were to be driven apart. Coleman Collieries and Canmore Mines indicated that they would do an end run around the District 18 policy committee and try to negotiate separate deals with their respective UMWA locals.[86]

The next day Harquail of Coleman Collieries wrote a letter to Local 2633. It outlined the terms of the latest contract offer and explained why the companies had rejected the policy committee's counterproposal. The letter concluded by repeating the claim that Coleman Collieries had lost money on its coal operations the previous year and hinted that closing the mine was a real possibility: "With this offer Coleman Collieries Limited has reached the extreme limits of its capabilities."[87]

Harquail's gambit created a rift in Local 2633's leadership. On the one side was the local's president, George Jenkins, a member of the militant policy committee. On the other side was Local 2633's secretary-treasurer, John Ramsay, and, according to Whittaker, other members of the Local 2633 executive. What is known about the process of negotiation in Coleman is that it did not move fast enough for the company, so it locked out the afternoon shift on 12 January. That evening the union met and decided to organize a membership vote the next day, which saw the company's offer accepted by 75 percent of 311 voters, thereby confirming Whittaker's conclusion that the workers at this mine did not want "trouble." The miners at Canmore voted narrowly to accept the same offer.[88] Harquail's bold move ended up sabotaging the looming district-wide strike and splitting Coleman Local 2633 away from its more militant neighbour at Michel. Most importantly, it suppressed Coleman Collieries' labour costs at a time when the company's profit margin on coal was razor thin and counts as Harquail's most notable victory over the worker movement in the Crowsnest Pass and Elk Valley.[89]

Meanwhile, Michel Local 7292 went on strike as scheduled on 12 January 1965. "An unnatural silence prevailed the scene," reported the *Fernie Free Press*, "as the tipple machinery which ordinarily screams and groans for 16 hours five days a week, came to a stop." Right from the beginning of the strike, the newspaper questioned its wisdom: "There are many other countries which would be more than happy to take over the coal contracts with Japan."[90] The newspaper was correct in asserting that multiple sources of metallurgical coal were available to steel producers in the mid-1960s, but it failed to appreciate two factors that somewhat protected Michel Collieries from international competition: the Japanese cartel's commitment to the development of a Canadian alternative to coal from Australia and the high quality of the metallurgical coal in No. 10 seam.

Negotiations resumed in late January, and a tentative agreement was reached a few days later. It specified significant wage increases above those included in the contract signed by the Coleman and Canmore locals in January and was accepted by a healthy four-to-one ratio on 6 February. The membership of Local 7292 benefited from larger wage increases in 1965 and 1966 compared with the membership of Local 2633 and from the fact that those wage increases kicked in at the beginning rather than in the middle of each year. Consequently, the average miners' minimum wage at Michel Collieries in 1966 ($18.80 per day in 1954 dollars) was 4.5 percent higher than the comparable average miners' minimum wage at Coleman Collieries.[91]

The splitting apart of the UMWA local unions during contract negotiations in early 1965 had a deleterious effect on subsequent governance in District 18. Notably, the District Executive Board failed to meet even once during 1965. Furthermore, the threads of labour solidarity that linked coal miners from the Elk Valley across the Crowsnest Pass were frayed. This disunity was a boon to the coal companies committed to keeping labour costs in check and quickly expanding productive capacities as they strove to sell more metallurgical coal to Japan.

By 1966, the combined net production of coal at Michel Collieries and Coleman Collieries was still a modest 1.5 million tons (see Tables 5.2 and 5.3), far below the region's peak production of 3.7 million tons in 1949. In the mid-1960s, however, there were many signs that a surge in coal investment was just around the corner because of geological good luck. Since 1960, CNPC had been mining higher-quality metallurgical coal from the No. 10 seam (later renamed the Balmer seam) on the south side of the Michel Creek valley; indeed, in late 1964, the Japanese cartel was paying a premium price of more than fifty cents per ton for coal from the Balmer South mine.[92] The company's fortunes turned for the better when

its geologists "discovered an extension of the Balmer coal seam northward of Natal."[93] Extensive exploration in 1965 identified more than 50
million tons of accessible "premium grade, low volatile coking coal
which [was] in short supply throughout the world and [was] essential to
the blends used in Japanese steel mills."[94] On the heels of this discovery,
Crows Nest Industries rushed to develop the Balmer North mine (the
negative consequences of which I discussed above) and renewed negotiations for a "huge new coal contract." Despite the Japanese cartel's keen
interest in this new coal discovery, getting a signed contract proved to
be elusive.[95]

The next year CNI executives returned to Japan for more negotiations
but had their proposed price in the $12.50–$13.00 per ton range not merely
rejected but also ridiculed. The main impasse in the negotiations was that
the CPR charge for transporting coal from the region to Vancouver was
far too high (then at $5.28 per ton) to make a contract possible when the
federal government was unwilling to extend its existing subvention of
$2.73 per ton to higher volumes of coal exports. Also problematic were
CNI demands to have the sale price cover all of its mine development
costs and to be "safeguard[ed] against any unforeseen cancellation of the
deal." Not only did the cartel balk at these demands, but also it kept
Crows Nest Industries guessing by negotiating with two other companies that proposed supplying coal from mines that would be developed
from scratch – McIntyre-Porcupine in the mountains west of Edmonton
and Pacific Coal on land south of Fernie.[96]

With monopoly control over rail transport across southern Alberta
and British Columbia, the Canadian Pacific Railway was very slow in
looking at ways to move coal more efficiently and therefore slowed the
CNI push for a big coal contract. Indeed, it resisted introducing unit coal
trains until August 1967.[97] However, Crows Nest Industries had a unique
opportunity to pressure the railway company: not only did it have corporate interlocks with the Great Northern Railway, which operated an
east-west rail line just south of the Canadian border, but also it already
held a rail licence to operate a spur line south from Natal and into
Montana. To leverage concessions from the Canadian Pacific Railway,
in the fall of 1965, Crows Nest Industries publicized that its back-up

transportation plan was to build the spur line so that it could get its coal to the West Coast over the Great Northern Railway.[98] After the BC government's initial refusal to approve the CNI application to build the spur line, however, the company concluded that it would be impossible to sort out the transportation issue in time to sign a long-term coal deal. It therefore negotiated an extension to 31 March 1969; again it was for 400,000 long tons of coal per year, all of which was eligible for the $2.73 per ton subvention.[99]

The CNI failure in 1965–66 to land the holy grail of a high-volume, multiyear contract with the Japanese cartel was an important factor in the next round of collective bargaining. Although it had big plans, Crows Nest Industries was having trouble producing enough coal even to meet its existing Japanese contract, as demonstrated by the mere 376,000 short tons shipped to Japan in 1966 (see Table 5.2). The company's ability to ramp up its production of export coal was limited by its plant for washing coal that needed replacement. In late 1966, therefore, Local 7292 was negotiating with a firm that, although it looked like it might be on the cusp of a business breakthrough, could legitimately claim that it was just hanging on to its existing export trade.[100]

Another contextual factor in the negotiations, which began in early October 1966 for a contract that would begin on 1 January 1967, was a wave of new investments in coal exploration in the Crowsnest Pass and Elk Valley. In June 1966, Scurry-Rainbow Oil purchased the abandoned WCC mines and 20,000 acres of mineral leases and announced that it would work with C. Itoh and Company of Japan "to develop an export operation of at least 1,000,000 tons a year." Although this ambitious plan never came to fruition, it made it seem that competition for a long-term contract with the Japanese cartel was stiffening. So did continuing coal exploration work south of Fernie and applications by two major companies – McIntyre-Porcupine and Canadian Pacific Gas and Oil – for coal-mining permits on huge swaths of land north of Michel and Natal.[101]

In preparation for negotiations, District 18 held a wage scale convention in September 1966. It approved Local 7292's desire to negotiate separately from other locals. The complete list of demands presented to Crows Nest Industries on 3 October included special pay increases for skilled workers, two more paid holidays, and an across-the-board increase of \$3.20 a day.[102]

The CNI response pointed to the high productivity of the American and Australian coal mines against which it was competing and the need for labour moderation to convince the Japanese steel companies to agree to a big coal contract. "To obtain long term large tonnage contracts we must demonstrate to the Japanese that our labour force is a stable and moderate one," the company reasoned.[103] Thus, Michel Local 7292 was introduced to a line of argumentation that later would become common in the neo-liberal world of globalized production systems: labour should accommodate global competitive pressures in order to preserve or expand employment while setting aside the class struggle between owners and workers.

Although the negotiations that began in October 1966 were meant to concern just the collective agreement at Michel Collieries, District 18 and the COAWC took the opportunity to strike a new deal on the Welfare and Retirement Fund. This was necessary because of the federal government's newfound commitment to the income security of elderly Canadians, as shown by the start of the Canada Pension Plan at the beginning of 1966; the planned introduction of the Guaranteed Income Supplement (GIS) for low-income seniors at the beginning of 1967, and the scheme, already in motion, to lower the qualifying age for universal Old Age Security by one year every year between 1966 (sixty-nine years qualifying) and 1970 (sixty-five years qualifying).

Between 1958 and 1967, there were only two increases in monthly OAS rates – from \$55 to \$65 in 1962 and from \$65 to \$75 in 1963. In response, the WRF retirement and disability rates were increased in kind, thereby keeping the monthly WRF pension \$20 higher than Old Age Security.[104] In practical terms, this meant that retired miners who collected Old Age Security but no other government support received \$20 per month from the Welfare and Retirement Fund during these years; retired miners who collected Old Age Security plus a means-tested supplementary allowance of \$15 per month received a token \$5 per month from the Welfare and Retirement Fund. In 1964, approximately 500 pensioners fell into one of these two groups. Another 150 miners aged from sixty-five to sixty-nine similarly collected monthly pensions of $20 or $5 from the Welfare and Retirement Fund since they were in receipt of $75 per month from the income-tested Old Age Pension plus, in some cases, a supplementary allowance of $15 per month. That left just 375 pensioners in position to collect the full pension of $95 from the Welfare and Retirement Fund: 200 retirees aged from sixty-two to sixty-four who were too young for the Old Age Pension or Old Age Security, and 175 retirees aged from sixty-five to sixty-nine who were too well off to get the Old Age Pension.[105]

Michel Local 7292's contract negotiations with Crows Nest Industries in October 1966 occurred with a Guaranteed Income Supplement valued at a maximum of $30 per month set to be introduced on 1 January 1967. Local 7292 proposed setting the WRF retirement benefit at $125 per month; had this amount been implemented, retired miners in receipt of both Old Age Security ($75) and the maximum Guaranteed Income Supplement ($30) would also have received $20 per month from the Welfare and Retirement Fund. However, District 18 and the COAWC increased maximum benefits to just $105 per month. This reduced the WRF pension for most retired miners to zero (calculated as $105 WRF minus $75 OAS minus $30 GIS). The growth-at-all-costs mentality of the budding metallurgical coal industry had a new victim – retired, low-income miners for whom an extra $20 or even $5 a month made a significant difference in their lives.[106]

The impact of this change was profound. In 1966, the average number of miners who received a retirement pension from the Welfare and Retirement Fund was 832. In May 1967, however, only 372 miners were paid a retirement pension.[107] Instead of providing a pension payment to most retirees, the main function of the Welfare and Retirement Fund now was to provide a bridge pension to workers aged from sixty-two to sixty-four until they qualified for Old Age Security and the Guaranteed Income Supplement. Consequently, in 1968, the Welfare and Retirement Fund paid out less in retirement pensions than in any year since 1950 (see Figure 2.3). Notably, at the same time as most District 18 retirees were disqualified from receiving a pension, the Welfare and Retirement Fund was restructured to provide a tangible benefit to every working miner. At the beginning of 1967, the coal operators started to pay employees' premiums for the new Canada Pension Plan. Furthermore, the operators were allowed to deduct all premiums paid to the plan from the assessments owing to the Welfare and Retirement Fund, thereby reducing by 25 percent the assessment revenue submitted to the fund.[108]

Whereas this agreement on changes to the Welfare and Retirement Fund was in place at the beginning of 1967, other bargaining issues particular to Michel Local 7292 and Crows Nest Industries were not so easily resolved. Meetings with a conciliator in November were followed by two sessions (spreading over five days) with a board of conciliation in December 1966 and January 1967. During the final session of meetings with the conciliation board, union negotiators made a major concession by proposing to spread an increase in pay of $3.20 per day over two years. Yet Crows Nest Industries refused to settle for that amount. The majority report from the conciliation board recommended wage increases of $1.28 per day (or sixteen cents per hour) in each year of a two-year contract.[109]

On 15 February, the members of Local 7292 voted 426 to 26 in favour of strike action. This almost immediately brought the two sides together for further negotiations in which Crows Nest Industries not only upped its across-the-board wage offer to twenty cents per hour in each year of the contract but outdid the conciliation board's recommendations in most other areas. The company estimated that its latest offer amounted to an average increase in wages and benefits of four dollars per day over two years. The union's negotiators signed a tentative agreement eventually accepted by the membership but only after an original rejection, short strike, and intense advocacy by the coal company. These events demonstrated that many rank-and-file members resoundingly rejected their negotiators' willingness to settle for so much less than originally demanded, believing that they were well positioned to achieve a significant gain in real wages. At the final vote on the tentative agreement, when the choice was between acceptance and more winter days on the picket line, 148 of 413 (36 percent) still voted "No."[110] As I will discuss below, subsequent developments in the coal industry in western Canada in 1967 suggest that Crows Nest Industries easily could have improved its contract offer with no adverse effects on its coal business.

Shortly after Michel Local 7292 finalized its new collective agreement, the prospects for the coal industry took a dramatic turn for the better. First, in late March, the giant American corporation Kaiser Steel was publicly identified as a potential "co-partner" of Crows Nest Industries. Kaiser Steel, which could be a major source of capital for the development of coal mining in the Elk Valley, also had a history of "supplying the resource needs of the Japanese steel industry" because of its co-ownership of an iron ore mine in Australia.[111] The relationship of trust that Kaiser Steel had built with the Japanese cartel could help in negotiating the long-term contract that so far had eluded Crows Nest Industries.[112] Second, in the middle of April, Coleman Collieries signed a fifteen-year contract to supply 13.3 million long tons of metallurgical coal to Japanese steelmakers. News of this contract, according to the mayor of Coleman, was "better than a shot of LSD." The town's postmaster "indicated that the contract would put Coleman back on its feet after a long period of deterioration since the International mine closed."[113] Third, Kaiser had a momentous change of heart. In early May, after a quick visit of company executives to the Elk Valley, the company ditched the partnership idea and instead entered into a conditional agreement to purchase outright Michel Collieries and the coal rights on 65,000 acres of neighbouring land; Kaiser Steel had until 31 January 1968 to determine whether the coal reserves on the land included in the sale matched "what Crows Nest claims they do."[114]

Local 2633 sat down with Coleman Collieries in early May to begin negotiating a collective agreement to replace the contract that would expire on 2 July. Recognizing that the newly signed sales contract with the Japanese cartel had put Coleman Collieries in a much better financial situation, Local 2633's initial wage demand of an increase of fifty cents per hour in a one-year contract surpassed the initial demand made by Michel Local 7292 in October 1967. In the end, the two sides came to an agreement without a strike or lockout; it involved the same two-year term, the same wage increases, and the same addition of two paid holidays as found in the contract at Michel Collieries. Local 7292's gains were superior only in a few areas, such as the medical services agreement.[115]

After the collective agreements were renegotiated in 1967, the workers at Michel Collieries were still better compensated than the workers at Coleman Collieries because of the larger increases negotiated in early 1965 and the fact that the Michel Local 7292 contract increases continued to kick in six months prior to the Coleman Local 2633 increases. The miners' minimum wage at Michel Collieries in 1968 averaged 6.3 percent higher than the comparable rate at Coleman Collieries. Nevertheless, given the superior coking properties of the coal from the Balmer seam, the big plans and financial power of Kaiser Steel, and the recent financial struggles of Coleman Collieries, the failure of Michel Local 7292 to outpace Coleman Local 2633's wage increases in 1967–68 would have frustrated many members. When the coal industry in the Elk Valley flipped from a pattern of modest growth to major expansion in 1967, Michel Local 7292 was not able to take advantage of its newfound power because it was locked into a just-signed collective agreement. This might just have been a case of the union's bad luck with timing, although Crows Nest Industries and Kaiser Steel might well have created such "luck" by deliberately keeping their courtship quiet until the contract negotiations had concluded. In a strategic sense, the error that Local 7292 made was to think that going alone in negotiations would always yield a superior contract such as was achieved in 1965. The uneven growth in the coal industry in the region in the mid-1960s had made it seem that sectoral bargaining and coordinated labour action were passé. Two years later, however, the market position of Coleman Collieries had dramatically improved, and coordinated negotiations by the Michel and Coleman locals likely would have been advantageous.

As long ago as 1960, CNPC had indicated its desire to get out of the coal business when it signed a conditional sales agreement with the United States Steel Corporation. That deal fell through, but the company's rebranding of itself as Crows Nest Industries in 1965, as well as its diversified investment strategy, suggested that the company was far from committed to a future of mining coal. The tens of millions of dollars in investment that would be needed to properly mine the northward extension of the Balmer seam, clean the coal, and then efficiently transport it to a deep-sea port would have been one factor that Crows Nest Industries weighed in deciding whether to sell to Kaiser Steel. A second factor was the environmental liabilities accumulated by Crows Nest Industries over almost seven decades of mining in the Elk Valley. Accordingly, the sale of Michel Collieries not only put money in CNI shareholders' pockets and eliminated the need to raise capital for major investments in new coal facilities but also turned accumulated environmental liabilities over to Kaiser Steel. I detail the scope of those liabilities, and the negligence of Crows Nest Industries in addressing them, in the first part of Chapter 6.

CHAPTER SIX

Growth at What Cost?

Community and Political Struggles, 1963–68

The whole thing makes me sick. They're doing nothing but complaining out here about the dust and dirt ... Everywhere you have heavy industry you've got to expect a certain amount of dirt. Other communities are crying out for industry. Here you'd think they want to drive away what we've got.

    – An unidentified Natal man, spring 1965[1]

When industry hampers a community, it is time for the community to take a stand ... We have been toyed and played with for years in this community.

    – Orlando Ungaro, reeve of the District of Sparwood, May 1967[2]

In the middle years of the 1960s, several different schemes for economic growth were in play in the Crowsnest Pass and Elk Valley. Some of these schemes failed, whereas others had modest economic impacts. In the end, only growth in the export of metallurgical coal to Japanese steelmakers offered hope of an immediate and substantial economic revival.

The expansion of metallurgical coal production was far from a smooth process. For one thing, it was geographically uneven, with communities other than Coleman and Sparwood-Natal-Michel having to be content with trickle-down effects. Furthermore, both surviving coal companies faced an intractable cost-price squeeze during these years. In this context, growth in coal production often came with harm. The harms for mine workers were highlighted in Chapter 5. In addition, because the tipples of Coleman Collieries and Michel Collieries abutted residential neighbourhoods, the residents there experienced harms as the production of metallurgical coal increased. The initial harms were the extreme pollution of air, soil, and water that made everyday life barely tolerable and often unhealthy. This development aligns with Harvey Molotch's insight that economic growth can be "a liability financially and in quality of life for the majority of local residents."[3] In this instance, the growing prosperity of the two coal companies depended on a significant reduction in the quality of life of local residents as well as a drop in the value of their houses and business properties.

In the first section of this chapter, I focus on the environmental protests that arose in Coleman and Natal-Michel to demand a reduction in pollution. The fight against environmental pollution was most complex at Natal and Michel. CNPC wanted to get rid of these communities so that it could expand its production facilities on their lands, and to this end it joined with the federal and provincial governments in a project of "urban renewal." When this scheme was first unveiled in 1964, the promise to residents was that they would be relocated to nearby Sparwood so that they could get away from smothering coal dust and smoke, continue to live in an area that they loved, and reconstitute strong community ties. Yet the plan did not unfold as promised, and the coal company took only token steps to address complaints about pollution in 1965–67.

The first quotation at the beginning of this chapter justified the pollution of Natal and Michel as economically necessary. The anonymous speaker was sickened not by the dust and dirt permeating the communities but by all the complaining about the dust and dirt. My research indicates that this was a minority view in 1965. The persistent pollution problems, as well as delays in organizing the relocation of residents to Sparwood, pushed elected local officials from a conciliatory to an adversarial posture and stimulated grassroots protests by large groups of local women. These protests in turn strengthened the adversarial resolve of the local government (as demonstrated by the quotation from Reeve Orlando Ungaro at the beginning of the chapter) and helped to draw Michel Local 7292 into the community struggle.

Beginning with grievances against pollution, the movement in Natal and Michel grew into something much more, a defence of the community and its way of life, threatened not only by the negligence of Crows Nest Industries but also by the provincial government, which failed to exercise a duty of care after it had initiated the relocation process.

Significantly, working-class women played a prominent role in the fight – a development that ran counter to the typical male domination of the public sphere in coal-mining communities at that time. Because of the focus on defending a way of life, and the important role of "activist mothers" in protecting and mobilizing the community, the protest movement in Sparwood-Natal-Michel in 1967–68 fits the profile of an environmental justice movement. Indeed, it is an early example of the locally focused movements that became prevalent throughout North America in the late 1970s and 1980s, including the movement focused on the toxic waste underlying Love Canal, New York.[4]

Community struggles over the environmental harms of increasing coal production had ramifications for the course of electoral politics in the region. So did the strikes by Michel Local 7292 in 1965 and 1967 that contested whether below-average increases in pay and benefits were costs that workers should have to bear in order to keep the Canadian metallurgical coal industry on an upward trajectory. On balance, there were new opportunities for leftist political organizing, but at the same time coal companies, senior levels of government, and local growth coalitions continued to push a growth-at-all-costs orthodoxy. In the second section of this chapter, I assess the extent of political realignment of the Crowsnest Pass and Elk Valley in the mid-1960s, concentrating on how different communities voted in three provincial election campaigns in 1966 and 1967 and explaining how some of the leftist political spirit, smarts, and energy of the past was rekindled.

FIGHTING FOR ENVIRONMENTAL JUSTICE AS THE
METALLURGICAL COAL INDUSTRY GREW

This section details the environmental costs of the growing coal industry in the mid-1960s as well as community mobilizations aimed at reducing the contamination of air, soil, and water. The coal dust and smoke were so thick and noxious in Michel and Natal that a proposal to relocate all residents to a new housing development in Sparwood (located about five kilometres away, just past the confluence of Michel Creek and Elk River; see Map 0.1) was supported by 95.6 percent of Natal voters in an

April 1966 plebiscite. In addition, almost all residents of nearby unincorporated areas signed a petition in favour of relocation.[5] The relocation scheme was obstructed by Crows Nest Industries and mismanaged by the provincial government, however, and in the end the damage wrought by coal-mining pollution included not just the demolition of Michel and Natal but also the dispersal of the residents, with only about half ending up in Sparwood.[6]

Complicating the crisis caused by coal dust and smoke in the mid-1960s was a legacy of environmental problems stemming from over six decades of mining. The years after the Second World War had seen the rapid expansion of strip mining (see Chapters 1 and 2). The largest strip mine was at Tent Mountain near the continental divide. The environmental problems associated with this mine were far off the beaten path, although fish and game enthusiasts monitored the situation and began informing the provincial government in the mid-1950s that overburden from the strip mine was being dumped into "one of the most beautiful lakes in Alberta." In a speech in the Alberta legislature in 1960, MLA William Kovach reported that erosion had caused acres of mountainside to slide into the lake and that, when he and a group of sanitary engineers had attempted to hike to the headwaters of a stream to see if it had been affected by the Tent Mountain strip mine, they had discovered that Coleman Collieries had blocked the access trail.[7]

In the mid-1960s, both coal companies continued to operate strip mines, although their primary focus had turned to the development of new underground mines. A recurring environmental problem stemming from strip mines was the blockage or pollution of streams and rivers. For instance, on 24 May 1966, Mrs. Emma Gris "complain[ed] about CNI mining operations on the mountainside where they are pushing debris into the river which may cause a flood hazard." Later that year the water in Michel Creek ran discoloured for several days, a problem attributed to the collapse of a slack pile into the creek.[8] These incidents were harbingers of the major environmental problems that would emerge starting in 1968, the beginning of the era of massive mountaintop strip mining.[9] In the mid-1960s, however, coal dust and smoke associated with the transportation, cleaning, and drying of coal, and the processing of coal into

FIGURE 6.1 Old and new tipples, Coleman Collieries, circa 1969. The Coleman
to Port Moody, British Columbia, unit coal train is in the foreground as well as a
sliver of housing. | By Vern Decoux. Image NA-3903-152, held by Libraries and Cultural
Resources Digital Collections, University of Calgary. Publication courtesy of Galt Museum and
Archives/Akaisamitohkanao'pa.

coke at Michel Collieries, created the gravest environmental damage.
This was because the residential areas of Coleman, Michel, and Natal
were located cheek by jowl with tipples. Figure 6.1 shows this proximity.
The wooden structures on the left made up the old International mine
tipple that Coleman Collieries continued to utilize until 1969. The metal
structure on the right was the new tipple, constructed in 1968–69.[10]

A legacy environmental issue caused considerable damage, inconvenience, and health threats in West Coleman in 1963. This part of the town
was above the workings of the International mine that had been allowed
to flood after being abandoned in 1959. Prior to abandonment of the
mine, water would seep into the basements in West Coleman every
spring for four to six weeks while the water table was high during spring
runoff. The problem worsened after abandonment, however, for the
water seeping into basements was now rusty in colour and foul smelling,
contaminated with oil, and would linger for up to six months. Furthermore, the oily water pooled in various locations on the surface, filled
outhouses, and disrupted the operation of septic systems. Fifty West
Coleman residents came together on 29 May 1963 to try to get action on

this problem. They charged "that Coleman Council would do nothing for them and that a Chinook Health Unit Officer had been told to 'Lay Off' his investigations on the water situation." At the end of 1963, the provincial government considered dredging the Crowsnest River where it flowed through West Coleman to lower the water table. I do not have data on the efficacy of this mitigation, although residents must have thought that it worked since in 1968 the MLA for Pincher Creek–Crowsnest, Charlie Drain, told the legislature that, based upon requests from his constituents, dredging the Crowsnest River was a priority.[11]

In 1963, the residents of West Coleman faced a double pollution whammy: the oily water from below was accompanied by thick coal dust in the air. The latter problem was the direct result of increasing sales of coal to Japanese steelmakers that required "crushed, fine coal, washed," unlike. the major customer of bygone decades, the Canadian Pacific Railway, which had mainly burned lump coal to power its steam engines. To create coal to the liking of the Japanese cartel, Coleman Collieries had installed dryers in 1962 at the wooden tipple pictured in Figure 6.1. A consequence of this new technology was the emission of a greasy coal dust that wafted over West Coleman. At the 29 May 1963 protest meeting, residents reported that the dust was so thick that windows in the school could not be opened, and as a result "heat is terrific in the building." Furthermore, "children it is said come home from school looking like miners after a day in the pits."[12]

To get action on the coal dust problem, the residents "threatened to take their children out of school and to picket the Coleman plant." This prompted the provincial health board to appoint an investigation committee headed by the deputy minister of health. At a hearing on 9 August 1963, a spokesperson for the residents, John Jenkins, provided further details on the severity of the dust problem: "You can't see across the alley to your neighbour's home," "motorists have to stop cars because they can't see to drive," and "you have to clean windows and floors about every half hour." Jenkins emphasized that the residents were not out to cause trouble or shut Coleman Collieries down. However, "with just one promise after the other and nothing being done, we had to take our own action." The severity of the problem was further demonstrated by dust measurements reported by the provincial health department. At 1,190 tons per square mile over thirty days in May 1963, the dust fall in West Coleman far exceeded the typical range of the dust fall in Calgary and Edmonton over thirty days (from 30 to 50 tons per square mile). The combination of determined action by residents and investigations by provincial health officials prompted Coleman Collieries to commission a scrubber for the tipple's coal dryer. The company was forced to incur this expense at a time when its finances were precarious.[13]

Between 1963 and 1966, there was a doubling of the amount of coal exported to Japan by Coleman Collieries. Mined at Vicary Creek north of Coleman, on any day of production from fifty to sixty loads of coal were trucked over roads in the east end of Coleman as they headed to the tipple. One source of dust in 1966 was the road dust kicked up by the trucks. To try to suppress this source, Coleman Collieries poured between 6,000 and 8,000 gallons of oil on the roads around the plant. A second source stemmed from coal stockpiled near the tipple as the company waited for railcars. A company official estimated that in a windstorm (a regular occurrence in the Crowsnest Pass) "2,000–3,000 tons of coal is blown away and lost."[14]

The dust in Coleman in the spring of 1966 was again so bad that town council wrote to Coleman Collieries, "asking that steps be taken to cut the coal dust problem in town." A company official stated in a subsequent council meeting that Coleman Collieries was considering building a new tipple "closer to their coal fields which would remove the dust problem from the town."[15] Figure 6.1 shows that the company eventually located its new tipple right beside the old tipple. Nevertheless, the citizens of Coleman were widely seen as having waged a successful campaign against coal dust pollution in the mid-1960s. In 1967, when discussing a more extreme and persistent coal dust problem in Natal and Michel, members of the Sparwood district council pointed to "public actions of protest" as the reason that Coleman's problem had been rectified.[16]

In the mid-1960s, the residents of Natal and Michel likewise had to deal with emissions of a great deal of dust associated with the production of finer textured coal for the Japanese steel industry. This problem was compounded by "coke ovens [that] spew[ed] forth a quantity of dust, smoke, gasses and other noxious elements." Paul Chala, born in 1913 in Middletown (the cluster of houses between Michel and Natal), worked at Michel Collieries for almost fifty years, and lived in Natal in the 1960s, and he recalled that, when the wind blew from the cleaning and by-products plants toward Natal, it carried a black cloud. Clotheslines had to be cleaned with a rag before hanging clothes out to dry, "and if it got windy, I'm telling you, ... you better take them clothes off, because you wouldn't know if they were black clothes or what they were." Chala also remembered that every morning Natal residents had to sweep coal dust off the wooden sidewalks in front of their houses. His recollections align with an observation made by Commissioner Joe Gaal at the 23 September 1963 meeting of Natal's council: the dust coming from CNPC's cleaning plant was "worse than a thick fog on occasion."[17]

Area residents also confronted two other significant environmental hazards at that time. First, sludge ponds filled with tarry waste from the by-products plant. These ponds were a drowning hazard for children and frequently overflowed, spoiling nearby ground. In November 1967, the Pollution Committee of the Association of Kootenay and Boundary Municipalities called on "the coal company [to] cease the dumping of the waste sludge near the Michel Creek as it was found that seepage resulted in sludge polluting Michel Creek." Three months later the Fernie rod and gun club asserted that the waters of Michel Creek and Elk River were being heavily blackened by overflows from the coal company's sludge ponds as well as coal slides.[18] Second, the ancient septic systems in Natal were contaminating a well that the village's water system had to use when its other source, a reservoir on a pristine creek to the north, ran dry or became turbid. The water system also suffered from low pressure. Hence, one reason that the village's leaders were strong backers of the resettlement scheme was that depopulating Natal would solve a very dangerous water pollution problem. Fortunately, a clean water supply was secured in 1966 when Crows Nest Industries dug a new well for the village in exchange for the water rights to the creek that had been the community's source of good water.[19]

CNPC/CNI did not respond straightforwardly to the litany of environmental grievances voiced by the residents of Michel and Natal.

The company would sometimes promise to act (e.g., at a meeting with Natal Commissioner Siro Cimolini on 20 April 1964) but fail to follow through. By the spring of 1965, the Natal council was starting to realize that it was getting the run around. A letter from J.E. Morris, CNPC's resident manager, not only claimed "that there was no solution to date on the problem of trucks hauling mine products through the village limits" but also "implied that the village had only a dust problem whereas they had a financial problem." Despite the insensitive and disparaging tone of Morris's letter, the Natal council decided to "attempt for the last time to get cooperation."[20]

When Natal was first incorporated as a village in 1960, its council had embraced a deferential posture toward CNPC. For instance, when Morris estimated in 1963 that it would cost $50,000 to solve the coal dust problem, "council put it on record that it appreciated the efforts of the coal company, agreeing that the industry provides the community's 'bread and butter' and that even with a large company, the $50,000 expenditure is 'tremendous.'"[21] Yet CNPC was grumbling about $50,000 to solve a coal dust problem seriously threatening the health of over 1,000 people less than a year after it had blown ten times that amount on a failed exploratory well (see Chapter 5). Evidently, CNPC prioritized business growth and diversification ahead of environmental stewardship and human well-being.

In the spring of 1967, when the District of Sparwood council abandoned appeasement toward Crows Nest Industries once and for all, it explained its past approach in these terms: "[We] had cooperated with CNI ... with hopes of forming good public relations. [We] had hoped that [we] would be granted the land at Sparwood more easily if there was cooperation." Around the same time, Reeve Orlando Ungaro started to criticize CNI unambiguously, claiming that the entire community had been "toyed and played with for years."[22]

The urban renewal scheme first proposed by the BC government in 1964 had the support of the Central Mortgage and Housing Corporation (CMHC) and CNPC. This was before the coal company had mapped the northward extension of the Balmer coal seam. Hence, the land that CNPC coveted for industrial growth in 1964 was restricted to Michel and

Natal, and it was happy to see residents relocated to an expanded Sparwood, with government money subsidizing the process. In keeping with this vision, an initial presentation to the Natal council by Everett Brown, the BC deputy minister of municipal affairs, promised that the current owners of houses and small businesses in Natal and Michel would be "offered a fair price for their properties" and that "land [would] be available to them in the new Sparwood urban area for re-establishing themselves." He further promised that "for old-age pensioners or people wishing to rent the necessary accommodations [would] be constructed by the different levels of government."[23]

As soon as CNPC/CNI started to make plans for the exploitation of the high-grade metallurgical coal in the northward extension of the Balmer seam, it had second thoughts about resettling Michel and Natal residents at Sparwood. Its main fear was that new, expanded coal production facilities (including a new tipple located less than a kilometre from Sparwood), and the dust-creating potential of the coal slack that would have to be piled around the tipple each year, might pollute the air at Sparwood just as the old facilities had polluted Michel and Natal. According to a provincial planner, the coal company was concerned that the pollution would spark "protests from local residents [that] would be as great as they are now." Therefore, Crows Nest Industries began promoting the relocation of Michel and Natal residents to Fernie beginning in 1965, a campaign that lasted until it sold its coal business to Kaiser Steel.[24]

Whereas Crows Nest Industries reimagined its corporate future in light of the magnificence of the Balmer coal seam, it dragged its heels on reducing the pollution suffocating Michel and Natal. In response, groups of residents – including large contingents of women – initiated contentious protests, elected municipal officials abandoned their failed strategy of conciliation in favour of adversarial action, and Michel Local 7292 joined the growing movement for environmental justice. The inaction of Crows Nest Industries was as puzzling as it was infuriating. In a speech in the BC legislature in early 1967, MLA Leo Nimsick suggested that there was a logic behind how the company handled the pollution crisis: "The coal company did very little – practically nothing – to try and stop that dust. Their attitude appears to be if you won't move willingly, we'll force you out anyway."[25]

The pollution crisis in Michel and Natal continued unabated. Its ongoing severity was documented in letters by Michel's United Church minister and MLA Nimsick in the fall of 1966. In the spring of 1967, Sparwood's council provided the following update: "The pollution is steadily increasing and CNI always has excuses ready. Presently their scrubbers, which broke down some months ago, are still not repaired. They occasionally water the haulage roads when actually they had promised to oil or hard surface these roads and keep them as dust free as possible." In the late fall of 1967, the Pollution Committee of the Association of Kootenay and Boundary Municipalities provocatively likened the area to the "Black Hole of Calcutta."[26]

At exactly this time, small-business owners and homeowners in Natal had the option of selling their properties to the regional government and using the proceeds to relocate far away from the pollution. The initial plan outlined in 1964 had involved land development and new building at Sparwood in tandem with the purchase of houses and commercial buildings in Natal. In early 1967, it looked as if this plan would finally be implemented: the Central Mortgage and Housing Corporation approved a grant of just over $1 million toward purchasing the homes and businesses in Natal and the few privately owned structures in Michel. Meanwhile at Sparwood, planning for the new water and sewer systems was nearing completion, surveys of the new townsite continued, and, after much equivocation, Crows Nest Industries finally offered to sell 400 acres for development.[27]

Hopes for a seamless resettlement of most of the residents of Michel and Natal to Sparwood were dashed on 12 May 1967 when Kaiser Steel secured its option to purchase Michel Collieries and the coal rights on nearby land. Kaiser's initial plans called for a strip mine and new coal plant that might well pollute Sparwood. Consequently, early in June 1967, representatives of Kaiser Steel and Crows Nest Industries, along with provincial and CMHC officials, met the residents of Natal and Michel to deliver "the sad news" that they would have to move to Fernie.

Furthermore, Deputy Minister Everett Brown, anticipating that all existing houses at and near Sparwood would have to be moved as well, privately asked Crows Nest Industries and Kaiser to cover this cost.[28]

The people of Michel and Natal again resisted the idea of resettling to Fernie and refused to abandon the hope of remaining in the area. In turn, Everett Brown gave Sparwood council an ultimatum on 13 July 1967: either immediately proceed with land assembly at Fernie or "leave the matter of land assembly in abeyance until Kaiser Steel has completed its master plan." Council members were unanimous in choosing the second option. As a result, it was impossible for anyone leaving Michel and Natal in 1967 to contemplate moving to Sparwood – no rental or subsidized housing was being built, and no new lots were for sale. Nevertheless, plans to purchase properties in Natal using government funds continued apace. The first cheque for a Natal property was handed out on 2 October 1967, and, by the end of the year, the regional government had acquired almost half of the 310 eligible properties.[29] The continuing pollution problems caused many property owners to sell out and leave the area even though doing so meant abandoning the possibility of reconstituting the social networks of Michel and Natal at Sparwood.

"This was truly the beginning of the end," wrote a lifelong resident of Natal whose family relocated to Kelowna in 1968. "Now we began to see the phasing out of the residents of Michel-Natal. The money was now available for their present homes, no building lots were available in Sparwood and restlessness was ever present." Arlene Gaal believed that "no one truly wanted to move away, but they felt the inevitable may never come and life was too short to waste valuable years in almost continuous depressed spirits."[30] Along the same line, in October 1967, Stan Grocutt of Michel Local 7292 noted that, "because of the lack of land at Sparwood," many retired union members were "moving away who might otherwise have remained." In turn, the growing depopulation undermined the business community of Natal; businesses, reported the Chamber of Commerce, were having trouble "maintaining an income" since "more and more people [were] moving away because the lots [were] not available."[31]

Therefore, a major cost of the growth of the coal industry in the Elk Valley was not just the demolition of the historic villages of Natal and Michel but also the unravelling of many social bonds; this transpired because those who could not stand the pollution in 1967 had no option but to move away. Crows Nest Industries was responsible for the pollution, and both it and Kaiser were guilty of not being willing to work their expansion plans around the promise made in 1964 that Sparwood would be available for residential resettlement.

More problems with resettlement emerged after development at Sparwood was finally given the go ahead in the spring of 1968 once Kaiser Steel determined that its strip mine and coal plant could coexist with people living at Sparwood after all. In subsequent years, many of the residents of Michel and Natal who wanted to move with their neighbours to Sparwood could not do so. For one thing, the different levels of government failed to construct affordable rental units except for seniors.[32] More importantly, the prices paid for properties and businesses in Natal fell far short of what was required to relocate to Sparwood. Valerie Podrasky estimated that the cost of building a house at Sparwood was "three and four times the amount you got for the old one." John Desjardins remarked that what Natal owners "were getting for their homes would barely build the doggone home basement [in Sparwood]." Podrasky sketched the consequence of this inequity: "We lost a lot of older residents at that time because they just couldn't afford to buy a new home or to build a new home in Sparwood. A lot of them bought up the Pass [in Alberta] or in Fernie or we lost a lot of them to Creston."[33] Surprisingly, the economics of relocating a business from Natal to Sparwood were even worse. Joe Altomare continued to operate the BC Bakery in Natal long after most residents and businesses had moved out. He sold bread to the growing population in Sparwood but could not afford to re-establish his business there. "What they offered me for my home, my business and my land," remarked Altomare in mid-1975, "was less than 10 per cent of what it would cost me to set up an operation in Sparwood." This explains why only a couple of Natal businesses would be re-established at Sparwood.[34] Things could have been much different.

In 1967, Altomare argued that "if Mr. Brown had lived up to his promises most of [Natal's eighty businesspeople] would have taken up residence in Sparwood."[35]

The fate of the residents of Natal and Michel is a glass-half-full/glass-half-empty story. The resettlement process can be judged as a failure because many of the residents who would have preferred to move to Sparwood were forced to move elsewhere. Yet the resettlement process simultaneously can be judged as a success since about half of the residents ended up in Sparwood despite years of strong pressure from the provincial government and Crows Nest Industries to shift resettlement to Fernie. This fight was won because of environmental justice activism by contingents of local women, the tenacious advocacy of elected municipal leaders, and the decision by Michel Local 7292 late in the game (1967) to use its considerable associational power to get behind the demand for relocation to a pollution-free Sparwood.

Prior to 1966, complaints about the pollution in Natal and environs were routed through a village council that remained committed to "playing nice" with both Crows Nest Industries and the provincial government (for reasons explained above). For instance, a petition signed in April 1965 by 200 residents that asked council "to take immediate action regarding the deplorable state of affairs regarding coal dust within the Village" merely resulted in Orlando Ungaro being assigned to talk to the mine manager.[36]

The persistence of severe problems of pollution in Natal in 1966 started to draw local women into the political process. In April, Deputy Minister Everett Brown responded to a petition in which mothers threatened to keep their children at home in September if the coal dust problem was not improved. Brown offered no immediate help, so the next month a group of mothers attended a meeting of the school board and issued the same threat. They pointed out that children needed two changes of clothes each school day and that "recently when the school became hot and stuffy because of warm weather, a window was opened and at least one of the children became slightly ill from the coal fumes."[37] Later that year Mr. E. Ungaro wrote to the minister of municipal affairs not only to provide an update on the extreme pollution in Natal (including photographs) but also to complain about the delay in organizing the resettlement to Sparwood. The letter exposed a new cause of pollution: "The coal company is dumping their coal right in the centre of the town, creating dust conditions which are almost unbearable."[38]

Residents and elected municipal officials expected fast action on the resettlement plan in 1966, especially given the urgency of the pollution crisis in Michel and Natal. However, Crows Nest Industries and the provincial government blocked progress. The coal company refused to sell the land needed for Sparwood's expansion unless it was granted an easement for its planned railway, an exemption from municipal taxation on production facilities, and a further exemption from any municipal bylaw that might attempt to control pollution.[39] For its part, the provincial government slowed proceedings by insisting on two governance changes (including the creation of the District Municipality of Sparwood) that brought progress on other parts of the resettlement scheme to a standstill.[40]

Deputy Minister Brown visited Natal immediately after the incorporation of the district municipality; he announced that the installation of services at Sparwood was expected by the end of 1966, thus making possible the sale of lots at the end of 1966 and into 1967.[41] Toward the end of 1966, however, it became apparent that this timetable would not be met. This failure, along with the unabating pollution crisis, caused the district council to take a new adversarial stance toward both Crows Nest Industries and the provincial government. In early December, Orlando Ungaro travelled to Vancouver to get legal advice on whether the residents of Natal had grounds to sue Crows Nest Industries for damages caused by pollution; a few days later the council retained the services of a Vancouver law firm. Then in February 1967, the district council asked the federal government to cover 50 percent of the cost of land development at Sparwood, which would match the CMHC contribution to the cost of purchasing and demolishing buildings at Natal and Michel. This request was summarily refused. Furthermore, after Reeve Ungaro was quoted by MLA Nimsick in the BC legislature as describing the provincial government as "dragging its feet and throwing sand in the gears of the SNM [Sparwood-Natal-Michel] project," the minister of municipal affairs presented Sparwood council with an ultimatum: accept the current financial terms, or see "the entire project be dropped." On 6 March 1967, council acceded to this threat.[42]

The next month it became apparent that an environmental justice movement, led by local women, had emerged to tackle the pollution issue using contentious tactics. The meeting on 24 April 1967 of Sparwood council had been called "solely to discuss ... commercial planning." However, the first part of the meeting was devoted to addressing the "numerous letters of complaint regarding the increased dust conditions of Natal and area" that had been submitted recently to council. A delegation of twenty-four local women supported the letters.[43] Prior to this meeting, Reeve Ungaro had proactively discussed the current dust conditions with a CNI official who maintained that, after the fine-cleaning plant was "put back in proper working order" (a process estimated to take over two months), "the only other thing that CNI could do was to close up the operations." This comment demonstrated that the coal company continued to treat the dust in Natal and Michel as an inconvenience with which residents would just have to learn to live. It just so happened that Crows Nest Industries was holding its annual corporate meeting in Vancouver at that time. Sparwood council voted to send a night letter to the company's president "voicing the strong complaints presented by the delegation."[44]

Later that week forty local women marched as a group to the CNI offices and had a closed-door meeting with manager J.E. Morris. Unnamed "spokesmen" for the group were interviewed by Vern Decoux. "The women said it is next to impossible to keep homes clean and hang out wash," he reported. "Windows in homes can never be opened without a layer of dust filtering into rooms. During the summer, gardens become covered with coal dust. Leafy vegetables cannot be used."[45] These complaints support the idea that one reason for women's dominant role in environmental justice protests is the extra burden of domestic labour created by pollution. From this perspective, activism will be gendered whenever the household division of labour is strongly gendered.[46] Unsurprisingly, Morris promised only minor remedial actions – oiling roads and cleaning trucks and buildings. Sparwood's clerk, Loretta

Montemurro, gave the protesters permission to use Natal's town hall as a meeting place and served them coffee and sandwiches immediately after the meeting. She recalled the protesters marching to the CNI office as a determined, united group but straggling back, telling her on their return, "oh, the poor guy, he's got so many problems ... We should think about what he's got to put up with." Montemurro thought that the protesters were too easily disarmed by Morris's tale of company woe and promises of inconsequential corrective actions. Nevertheless, the march and confrontation sparked additional activism that encompassed a wider swath of the community.[47] Seemingly energized, Ungaro made the militant statement quoted at the beginning of this chapter just a few days after the march by forty local women to the CNI office. In subsequent months, he and the other members of the district council would be unflinching in their fight against pollution and advocacy for resettlement to Sparwood.

Another large delegation of women appeared at the 5 June 1967 meeting of Sparwood council. This time the group raised concerns not just about pollution but also about the future of the resettlement scheme. In an interesting reversal of roles, council members asked the thirty-five women "what they would do if the project fell through. They replied with various answers such as suing the coal co., renting to anyone for any price and leaving town, [and] a march on Victoria stating the premier had backed out on them. CNI wants all the Valley but haven't paid anything." Twenty of the women "definitely agreed" to march on Victoria, reflecting the militancy and determination in the room.[48] This was the point at which the environmental justice movement transitioned from a movement of "activist mothers" whose caring role had expanded to include the broader community[49] to a community movement for environmental justice. Convincing and inspiring men to commit to the struggle was a notable accomplishment of the protesting women.

The rise of a community movement was evident in the strong participation in meetings and protests later in June. Sixty citizens attended the meeting on 6 June at which authorities tried to convince everyone that resettlement to Sparwood was now out of the question because of Kaiser Steel's big plans. Then, on 15 June, "well over 200 people in a truculent mood jammed into the UMWA hall in Natal to protest the decision ...

to close Michel Elementary School." The *Fernie Free Press* described the crowd as "hostile," and school board officials were heckled with lines such as "we want to stay where we are" and "why didn't you ask us first?" In a related mobilization, a group of parents demonstrated at Sparwood School on 21 June in opposition to the plan to bus high school students to Fernie starting in September.[50]

On 22 June, the district council met to discuss how best to tackle ongoing pollution from the CNI operations. Attending were council's new lawyer and representatives of the East Kootenay Health Board. The meeting recognized the importance of "public actions of protest" on pollution but noted that, despite the "strong delegation" that had approached J.E. Morris of Crows Nest Industries "not too long ago[,] ... actually very little has been done since then." Hence, council decided to initiate a set of aggressive actions: drafting an antipollution bylaw, installing air-pollution testing devices, and pursuing a public nuisance legal claim against Crows Nest Industries. The most interesting revelation from the meeting is that council recognized how the power dynamics of the situation had shifted since Kaiser Steel was about to assume ownership of Michel Collieries: "Such a company, with its vast holdings all over the continent, must be accustomed to operating under both anti-pollution and zoning by-laws and if they must abide by them they will."[51]

Environmental justice protests in the spring of 1967 gave residents of Natal and Michel some hope and a renewed commitment to fight for resettlement at Sparwood. Public unity of purpose was a key factor in Sparwood council's decision on 13 July to reject the provincial government's proposal to immediately begin a resettlement process at Fernie.[52]

As summer turned to autumn, Kaiser Steel's plans for the area came into focus. A Japanese trade mission visited Michel Collieries just after Labour Day. It learned that Kaiser's test pits on Harmer Ridge to the north had exposed two significant coal seams, the first fifty feet thick and the second sixty-five feet thick, described by a CNI spokesperson as "one of the unique coal seams in the world." Then, on 6 October, Kaiser officials revealed production plans that appeared to offer hope for resettlement to Sparwood: a strip mine at the top of Harmer Ridge was quite distant from Sparwood, the location of the new tipple was farther away than previously anticipated, and the company was committed to having at least "key personnel" reside at Sparwood.[53]

Orlando Ungaro's move at this crucial time was to channel the resolve of the environmental justice movement and commit to local democracy. At a council meeting on 2 October 1967, "the reeve declared the plans for expansion of coal mining should not be undertaken without full involvement of the people affected by the scheme." He criticized the coal companies on several grounds, including "a lack of interest in the welfare of their employees." Governments were indicted for "allowing industry to exploit the people of the community" and proceeding with urban renewal in Natal "without making arrangements or providing sufficient assistance for new accommodation."[54]

Council's next move was to organize a special meeting with a long list of local organizations to ascertain the range of things that needed to be addressed in the resettlement process. At this meeting, Stan Grocutt fully committed Michel Local 7292 for the first time to the community fight for environmental justice. He acknowledged "that everyone was lax years ago" when it came to the pollution problem. Most significantly, he suggested that Local 7292 would "if necessary [launch] a strike for better living conditions."[55]

At the end of January 1968, Kaiser Steel signed a fifteen-year contract to supply metallurgical coal to seven Japanese steel companies. It was set to begin on 1 April 1970 and was for 45,750,000 long tons. Kaiser simultaneously announced that it would proceed to purchase Michel Collieries and the coal rights on nearby lands. The initial expected investment by Kaiser in mine development was $55 million, but this increased by $25 million when the company signed a supplementary contract with the Japanese cartel in late 1968 that committed it to producing 5 million tons of coal per year for the three years starting in 1970. The long-hoped-for coal boom was at hand: "It's the biggest thing to happen in Fernie area in 50 years," wrote the *Fernie Free Press*, "and the community is still reeling from the delightful shock."[56]

The size of Kaiser Steel's planned investment gave the company a great deal of political capital, which it used to solve the transportation issues that had bedevilled Crows Nest Industries for years. Just days after finalizing its purchase of Crows Nest Industries, Kaiser's president journeyed to Ottawa to meet with federal cabinet ministers and CPR executives. By the spring of 1968, the federal government had agreed to build the Roberts Bank Superport south of Vancouver for the efficient loading of coal on large ocean freighters and to have it ready for the beginning of the new contract in 1970. In exchange for this substantial government investment in infrastructure, Minister of Transport Paul Hellyer insisted that coal be shipped from the Elk Valley to Roberts Bank on an all-Canadian rail route, torpedoing the option of shipping it through the United States using the Great Northern Railway. For its part, the Canadian Pacific Railway agreed to drop its transportation rate from $5.28 per short ton in effect in 1968 to just $3.50 for delivery to Roberts Bank. This reduction meant that the federal rail subvention for coal exported to Japan could be ended once Roberts Bank became operational.[57]

Just three days before Kaiser Steel's new subsidiary, Kaiser Coal, took over the operation of Michel Collieries on 29 February 1968, the provincial government made its final pitch to Sparwood council for resettlement to Fernie. Kaiser executives took part in the meeting but were at pains to distinguish their company's position from that of the province. According to Kaiser's public relations officer, Gene Clemmer, he had never said that "there would be a great deal of pollution in Sparwood." This explains why neither Kaiser nor the provincial government saw a problem with the existing residents of Sparwood remaining where they were, thereby undermining the case for resettlement of Natal and Michel residents to Fernie instead of Sparwood. The logical hole in the province's argument was revealed by a question posed by Councillor Earle Tabor. Why was Sparwood "good enough for some to live [in] and not others?" Recognizing that the environmental case against resettlement to Sparwood was now weak, its elected representatives fought back. Reeve Orlando Ungaro insisted that any plan for resettlement at Fernie had to be put to a plebiscite, and Councillor John Thomson informed Kaiser managers that Local 7292 intended to negotiate for acceptance of the Sparwood townsite.[58]

The following Sunday, Sparwood council organized a public meeting on the latest proposal for resettlement to Fernie. The *Fernie Free Press* reported that the 300 residents in attendance appeared to be unanimous in rejecting the proposal. The next day (4 March) council met to work out its next moves in the effort to secure the right to resettle at Sparwood. A tactic that it had initiated at the previous day's public meeting was to get as many residents as possible to write letters to the BC minister of municipal affairs. Thirty-five of the letters were read out at the council meeting. They were described as "highly-emotional ... [T]he thought of leaving friends and associations was mentioned by almost every letter."[59] This pattern confirms that the protest movement in Natal and Michel in 1967–68 was at its heart an environmental justice movement, as defined by Luke Cole and Sheila Foster: "The notion of 'environment' for environmental justice groups and networks has come to mean home and community. These are the places that need to be preserved and protected from pollutants and other harms."[60]

It took Kaiser a couple of months to find its bearings and commit to the expansion of Sparwood. Shortly afterward, the BC minister of municipal affairs approved new development at Sparwood. This, he said, turned on a promise from Kaiser officials to limit noise, blasting tremor, and dust fallout.[61]

The CMHC began selling lots at Sparwood in July 1969; that month construction of Sparwood's first apartment building began. As noted earlier, only half of the population of Natal and Michel ended up in Sparwood. Among those who moved elsewhere were community leaders such as Orlando Ungaro, who packed up his family in the summer of 1968 to take up a teaching position in Kelowna. More commonly, those on fixed incomes and/or with limited savings moved away because they could not find affordable housing at Sparwood. This dispersal of the population and the concomitant fraying of long-standing bonds of friendship, kinship, and solidarity were social costs of the growing coal industry. On top of this, for those strongly attached to Michel and Natal as historical places, their obliteration was an additional psychic cost. As Francis Travis remarked in an interview in 1991, "yes, the town [Sparwood] is nice now but it could've been just as nice for the older section and history would've still been standing had it not been [for] a

whim of a company that wanted the property." That sentiment was especially poignant in 1991 since, by then, it had become apparent that the
land on which Natal had been constructed was no longer needed for coal
production.[62]

Political Realignments and NDP Victories in Provincial Elections

The first section of this chapter documented the development of a for-
midable environmental justice movement that re-established the worker
movement as a leading political force in the coal-mining villages of
Sparwood-Natal-Michel. In contrast, beginning with the closing of Elk
River Colliery in 1958, and the concomitant waning of the influence of
Fernie Local 7310, members of the small-business class drove the political agenda in Fernie. They commanded a local growth coalition that
sought not only to grow the economy but also to spruce up and morally
reform a down-on-its-luck blue-collar community. Nonetheless, as
shown in Chapters 3 and 5, a sizable proportion of Fernie's citizens were
unimpressed with the patronizing tone and business stumbles of the
growth coalition. In 1961, the founding president of the Snow Valley Ski
Association, Telfer Dicks, was defeated in the aldermanic election, and
in 1964 Vernon Uphill easily outpolled a former Chamber of Commerce
president in a mayoral by-election after launching populist attacks on the
local business elite.[63]

Despite these ripples of opposition to the business-dominated local
growth coalition, in the 1960s Fernie continued to migrate away from the
trade union city that it had been prior to 1958. This is seen in the results
of successive municipal elections. In the mid-1960s, two long-time labour
aldermen suffered surprise defeats. In 1963, Jack Sweeney, a past leader
of the fire bosses union, was defeated in his re-election bid after having
served as an alderman for sixteen consecutive years. A former Local 7310
executive member, Mike Nee, suffered a similar fate in 1964; at the time,
he had served as a Fernie alderman for eight consecutive years. A staunch
supporter of Thomas Uphill in the Fernie District Labour Party, Nee
diligently tried to regain a place on city council on each available oppor-

tunity over the next thirty-two months (two regular elections and a by-election); however, he was handily defeated each time. Nee was finally returned to council in 1967, squeaking into the last aldermanic position by just two votes.[64]

Although opposition to its agenda was routine, most of the time the business community in Fernie was able to set the political agenda because it was by far the city's best organized and resourced organization. The leading but one-dimensional role of the Fernie Chamber of Commerce was demonstrated by an event that it initiated and organized in the summer of 1964 aimed at drawing tourists and media outlets to the city and possibly to "boost local morale." The event was a "curse-lifting ceremony," organized to mark the sixtieth anniversary of Fernie's municipal incorporation.[65] The following rendition of the curse is taken from a postcard: "Old legends tell of Captain William Fernie courting an Indian Princess of the Kootenay Indian band to learn the source of her necklace's 'sacred black stones.' Upon learning the location of the Morrissey coal seams, Fernie jilted his Indian bride. Her angry mother then placed a curse on the Elk Valley."[66]

The idea for a curse-lifting ceremony originated at a Chamber of Commerce meeting in June 1964. The group quickly lined up the participation of Mayor James White and Ktunaxa leaders. The initial public announcement of the event included a picture designed to grab the attention of potential attendees – a former chief, Joe Dennis, in traditional regalia, with a ceremonial pipe in his mouth, standing alongside the wife of a current chief, likewise in traditional regalia. The picture's caption stated that "Chief Dennis has promised to lift the legendary curse off Fernie Aug. 15."[67]

The Chamber of Commerce saw the curse-lifting as an opportunity to generate free publicity and attract tourist dollars. The main proponent believed that the event would help Fernie to make "hay" from its legend, just as communities on Okanagan Lake had done with the legend of the Ogopogo lake serpent. The Ktunaxa were treated as a means to a commercial end in the initial discussion of the curse-lifting, and the plan was to offer material inducements to encourage their participation: free barbecued beef to all Ktunaxa participants and prizes "for the best-dressed

Indian Brave, [for] the best-dressed squaw and for the best-dressed boy and girl."[68] The stereotypical language of "Indian Brave" and "squaw" revealed that the Ktunaxa were meant to participate in roles "that reified people in a timeless past of normalized conflict."[69] For Fernie's business community, the curse-lifting ceremony was to be a type of Wild West show in which traditional Ktunaxa cultural practices (dress, music, and sacred ceremony) were the main act, simultaneously unusual but following a familiar colonial narrative.

The curse-lifting on 15 August attracted a crowd of 600 people as well as "almost coast-to-coast publicity," including CBC and national magazine reporters. However, the *Fernie Free Press* expressed disappointment at the parade that preceded the curse-lifting "for which there just were not enough Indians to go around." It also deployed a slightly mocking, don't-take-this-too-seriously tone in its coverage of the curse-lifting itself. It is notable that none of the Chamber of Commerce organizers addressed the colonial history obfuscated by what the newspaper called "the whiteman's version" of the curse. Mayor White, however, rose to the occasion with remarks that acknowledged the unfair treatment of Indigenous peoples "by the early settlers" and called for reconciliation. In turn, the mayor was honoured with the title of Chief Big Eagle by the Ktunaxa.[70] In my view, Mayor White mistakenly imagined that a new, mutually prosperous pattern of Indigenous-settler relations could be willed into existence without fully appreciating and actively counteracting the contemporary dimensions of colonialism.[71] To his credit, however, White demonstrated a respectful approach to the Ktunaxa generally lacking in a small-business class fixated on economic growth and commercial success.

The diverging politics of Fernie and Sparwood-Natal-Michel in the mid-1960s, and the implications of that divergence for the success of NDP candidates, can be seen in the results of provincial elections held in September 1963 and September 1966. The data in Table 6.1 are organized so that the voting patterns in Fernie and Sparwood-Natal-Michel in each of the two elections can be directly compared even though the Fernie Electoral District disappeared after the 1963 election, absorbed into the larger Kootenay Electoral District that included Kimberley and Cranbrook.

After Thomas Uphill's retirement from provincial politics in 1960, a prominent member of Fernie's local growth coalition, lawyer Harry McKay, was elected to the provincial legislature from the Fernie Electoral District, one of only four Liberal Party representatives elected to the legislature that year. McKay had come to prominence in 1958 immediately after CNPC announced the closure of Elk River Colliery – he took on chairing the Chamber of Commerce industrial committee tasked with attracting replacement industries and institutions to Fernie, and he was the committee's main promoter of Fernie as a potential site for a new federal prison (see Chapter 3).[72] Two additional factors facilitated his victory in 1960: McKay had strong social ties in both Fernie, where he practised law, and Michel, where he had grown up; and, as noted in Chapter 3, there was no labour candidate on the ballot.

In the subsequent provincial election (1963), the NDP candidate was twenty-five-year-old Ezner De Anna. Born and raised in Natal, where his father worked as a coal miner, De Anna came to identify with labour unions and the Cooperative Commonwealth Federation at an early age, strongly influenced both by his father's circle of left-wing friends and by his older brother, who worked at CNPC's unionized sawmill at Natal while finishing high school. After a year of university studies in Vancouver, Ezner was hired at Michel Collieries but soon laid off because of the downturn in the steam coal industry at the end of the 1950s. He then worked at a sawmill in Cranbrook before moving to CNPC's sawmill at Natal in 1961. At that mill, he was quickly elected as an International Woodworkers of America (IWA) job steward, and in 1963 he was appointed as the representative of the Fernie area on the IWA board. In the meantime, he had built a home just outside Natal on land leased from the coal company, and he and his wife had three young children.[73]

In the early 1960s, there were still enough jobs in the Sparwood-Natal-Michel area to keep some of the younger generation around. This was crucial to the revitalization of the union and CCF/NDP movement. "[There were] more young people interested in those days than there are today," recollected De Anna in 2011. "There were quite a few people like me in there ... The grandfathers used to call us – what the hell was that Ukrainian name that this Ukrainian gave us – because we were always pushing hard. And we were proud of what we did. We didn't back down."

Both in securing the NDP nomination and in campaigning for election, De Anna received a great deal of support from the older generations of CCF/NDP members. After he won the nomination, one of the elders who voted for him told him that "we've all had our time, but we've got to encourage guys like you."[74] The election campaign in 1963 turned into an opportunity for De Anna and his fellow young leftist activists to learn how socialists had organized in the region in past decades. Without any prompting, he told me this story about the campaign:

> I had an old fellow here. He wasn't my campaign manager, but I called him "the wise guy." He had been around politics since before the CCF was formed ... He said, "kid, I've never lost an election in this area ... We've got to hold our zone [Sparwood-Natal-Michel] and hold it big. If you want, I'll help you, but you have to do what I tell you." So I looked at his record, and the son of a gun had never lost. And he'd won big. He was a Tom Uphill supporter originally. So I says, "okay, go at it. Just tell me what you want to do." Basically, he was campaign manager ... And we won big in this area ... "Fernie is going to be a different ball of wax," he said. "But if we can win big enough here and get close in Fernie, [in] the south country [the rural, southern part of the Fernie Electoral District], we should break even."

When I asked De Anna for the name of the "wise guy," it turned out to be Simeon Weaver (see Figure 6.2), the long-time (1924–57) secretary-treasurer of Michel Local 7292 mentioned frequently throughout this book. Weaver was a CCFer whose political orientation was a product of the milieu of socialist and syndicalist ideas that swirled through this coalfield society in the first two decades of the twentieth century.[75] Therefore, De Anna and his friends received a unique political education in the 1963 NDP campaign from an eighty-year-old socialist labour activist. One of the striking features of the campaign was the bilingual (English-Italian) election advertisement that it ran in the *Fernie Free Press*.[76]

The results of the 1963 election are recorded in Part (A) of Table 6.1. The New Democratic Party managed "to hold big" Sparwood-Natal-Michel, winning 50 percent of the popular vote compared with the incumbent McKay's 33 percent. It fell a little short of breaking even in the south country, however, with McKay winning 40 percent compared with 30 percent each for De Anna and the Social Credit candidate.[77] Nevertheless, if the New Democratic Party had managed to "get close in Fernie," which Weaver

FIGURE 6.2 Simeon Weaver with his wife, Florence, and son, Wilfred, at home in Natal, British Columbia, circa 1948.
| Courtesy of daughter Florence Reeve.

had identified as an objective, De Anna would have been elected to the legislature. What happened instead is that McKay "won big" in Fernie (by 19 percent over De Anna), paving the way for his relatively comfortable victory across the whole district (42 percent to 35 percent, with the Social Credit at 23 percent). This result is additional proof of the eclipse of the labour movement by the local growth coalition in Fernie in the years after the closure of Elk River Colliery.

By the time of the next BC provincial election, the Fernie Electoral District, with only 3,505 registered voters in 1963, had been absorbed into the larger Kootenay Electoral District. The 12,050 registered voters in this new district in 1966 were concentrated in the cities of Cranbrook and Kimberley. Between them, Fernie and Sparwood-Natal-Michel had just 23 percent of the electors.[78]

Redistribution completely changed the calculus for electoral victory. Leo Nimsick, a long-time CMS employee at Kimberley, had been the CCF/NDP representative for the Cranbrook Electoral District (which included Kimberley) since 1949; he was the obvious choice to carry the NDP banner in the 1966 election. The party's strength in Cranbrook and

TABLE 6.1 Elk Valley popular vote (%), 1963 and 1966 BC provincial elections

Polling stations	NDP	Liberal	Social Credit	Valid votes
(A) 1963 candidates	De Anna	McKay	O'Rourke	
Sparwood-Natal-Michel	50	33	17	859
Fernie	29	48	23	1,410
All other votes	30	40	30	673
Overall result	35	42	23	2,942
McKay (Liberal) elected as MLA for Fernie Electoral District				
(B) 1966 candidates	Nimsick	McKay	Jones	
Sparwood, Natal, Michel	54	17	28	759
Fernie	29	36	35	1,283
Other polling stations in 1963 Fernie District	32	31	37	537
Subtotal for former Fernie District	37	30	33	2,579[a]
All other votes in 1966 Kootenay District	43	22	36	6,219
Overall result	41	24	35	8,798
Nimsick (NDP) elected as MLA for Kootenay Electoral District				

NOTE: [a] "Fernie District" residents who voted in the advance poll or cast an absentee ballot are included in the "All other votes in 1966 Kootenay District" row.

SOURCES: British Columbia. Chief Electoral Officer, 1963 and 1966.

Kimberley was demonstrated by the nomination meeting/picnic that the Kootenay New Democratic Party organized in Cranbrook on 14 August 1966: it was attended by a crowd of 1,000. De Anna volunteered to run Nimsick's campaign in Sparwood-Natal-Michel.[79]

In the Elk Valley, Nimsick's share of the popular vote almost mirrored what De Anna had achieved in 1963 (see Part B of Table 6.1). Nimsick actually did slightly better than De Anna in Sparwood-Natal-Michel (54 percent versus 50 percent), and Nimsick praised his election workers in the area: "They really went to town ... very conscientious, and they worked very hard."[80] The NDP share of the popular vote in Fernie was the same in 1966 as in 1963, and Nimsick finished in third place in the city.

In the other Fernie Electoral District polls, Nimsick's result (32 percent) was just slightly ahead of De Anna's (30 percent). Overall, in the old Fernie Electoral District part of the new Kootenay Electoral District, Nimsick's popular vote in 1966 was slightly better than what De Anna had achieved in 1963 (37 percent versus 35 percent). Interestingly, this was enough to make Nimsick the leading vote getter in the old Fernie Electoral District since the rest of the popular vote was split evenly between Harry McKay (30 percent) and Robert Jones, the Social Credit candidate (33 percent). Jones was a railway worker based in Cranbrook who had been the Social Credit candidate in Cranbrook in the 1963 election. Between 1963 and 1966, McKay lost 12 percent of his vote in the old Fernie Electoral District, with 10 percent of it shifting to Jones and just 2 percent to Nimsick. This result confirms a judgment made by the *Fernie Free Press* immediately after the 1963 election: De Anna and the New Democratic Party would have won that election if Social Credit had nominated a stronger candidate and run an organized campaign, thereby allowing it to "pull ... a few more [votes] away from Mr. McKay."[81]

Fernie was the only major centre in the Kootenay Electoral District that Nimsick lost in the 1966 election, although in both Cranbrook and Kimberley his margin of victory over the Social Credit candidate was fairly small (with McKay running a distant third). Upon his electoral victory, Nimsick immediately became a key ally of the elected municipal leaders for the District of Sparwood during the environmental justice struggles of 1966–68.[82]

The results of the BC provincial elections of 1963 and 1966 confirmed that Fernie and Sparwood-Natal-Michel were on divergent political paths in the mid-1960s. This divergence was a consequence of three factors: (1) the closing of Elk River Colliery in 1958, which sidelined Fernie Local 7310 at a time when Michel Local 7292's power was growing; (2) the fact that Fernie had been able to reap some benefits from the modest economic growth in the first half of the 1960s while avoiding the pollution problems that befell Natal and Michel; and (3) the important role of the local growth coalition in promoting pro-business values in Fernie.

In the years after the 1966 election, the political fortunes of Leo Nimsick and the New Democratic Party would benefit from the growing strength of the union movement among both public sector and forestry workers in the Elk Valley. Outside workers employed by the City of Fernie had achieved union representation in 1962, and employees of Fernie's school district followed suit in 1966. These two bargaining units joined forces in 1968. Meanwhile, the class consciousness of lumber workers and loggers was sharpened by a massive IWA strike across the southern BC Interior that lasted from October 1967 to May 1968. All of the sawmills in the Elk Valley were idle. The forty-five lumber companies engaged in sectoral bargaining with the International Woodworkers of America used large advertisements in local newspapers to try to convince workers to abandon the union and return to work as strike breakers. This union-busting effort failed. It was a testament to the strength of the labour movement in the Elk Valley that, among those forty-five lumber companies, two local companies (Crows Nest Industries and Crestwood) "were the only employers who did not attempt to ship lumber or operate portions of the plants by using supervisory personnel."[83]

The class consciousness that underpinned this collective action was demonstrated in an open letter to the lumber operators printed in the *Fernie Free Press* shortly before the strike began. Submitted by the wife of one of the IWA members, the letter objected to the wage increase proposed by the lumber companies and asked "what are you trying to do? Starve people or make living conditions like the hungry 30's?" The letter writer made a strong case that "the basic rate at present leaves quite a gap in the family budget." She also argued that the operators were underinvesting in safety, thereby endangering her husband's life: "I guess a man's life means very little compared to dollars and cents." Finally, she captured the humanistic crux of the lumber workers' struggle in this remarkable sentence: "I fear for our children's future if we are not treated more like humans with a brighter future ahead."[84] Of the major political parties in the 1960s, only the New Democratic Party had a program that would appeal to someone with such a strong pro-worker perspective. Therefore, the IWA strike of 1967–68 can be seen as a leftist political antidote to the pro-business politics pushed by Fernie's local growth coalition.

Leo Nimsick's victory in 1966 occurred less than a month before the historic by-election in Pincher Creek–Crowsnest that elected the first-ever NDP representative to the Alberta legislature. In the general election that preceded the by-election, held in 1963, the long-standing Social Credit MLA, William Kovach, had won 54 percent of the popular vote in the constituency, whereas the NDP candidate had managed only 13 percent.[85] Indeed, Social Credit had won Pincher Creek–Crowsnest in every election since the creation of the constituency in 1935, and not since 1944 had a leftist candidate challenged for victory.[86] Therefore, Garth Turcott's victory in the 1966 by-election was a surprise to almost everyone, including Premier Ernest Manning.

At the time of this by-election, economic growth in the Alberta Crowsnest Pass was keeping up with, and perhaps even exceeding, that across the provincial boundary. Michel Collieries produced more coal than Coleman Collieries that year (a net production of 837,000 tons versus 633,000 tons), but the latter company sold 144,000 more tons to the customer whose sales would determine the long-term future of the coal industry in the region – the cartel of Japanese steelmakers (compare Tables 5.2 and 5.3). In 1966, Michel Collieries had just 103 more employees than Coleman Collieries, whereas in 1963 the gap in employment had been 322.

When it came to other industries, the Alberta segment of the region was also on par with the BC segment in 1966. Whereas the Elk Valley had a more robust forestry industry, the promising Snow Valley ski hill at Fernie was beset by financial problems. Meanwhile, only Alberta Crowsnest Pass communities could boast new manufacturing companies, notably Phillips Cables, Becker Drills, and the sour gas and sulphur plants at Sentinel.

Most of the economic growth in the Alberta Crowsnest Pass in the mid-1960s was at Coleman or nearby Sentinel. Hence, though the town of Coleman experienced a 24 percent drop in its population between 1951 and 1966, with almost half of the net decline occurring between 1961 and 1966 (see Table 2.1), the Oldman River Planning Commission's anticipation of "a population explosion over the years to come" did not seem to be farfetched.[87] Turcott's success in the economically rebounding Coleman was key to his surprising by-election victory. The growth of Coleman Collieries' coal business by 1966, and the early success of the

Phillips Cables factory, meant that Coleman workers could pursue an oppositional political path without having to worry about how the Social Credit government's response might affect their economic future.

Garth Turcott was a well-respected Pincher Creek lawyer when he was recruited by Grant Notley, the Alberta NDP secretary, to run in the 1966 by-election. Turcott had landed in Pincher Creek, a small ranching town just to the east of the Crowsnest Pass, in 1956 after articling in Calgary. In his first decade in Pincher Creek, he not only established his legal practice but also jumped into community service, having been a member of the board of the Pincher Creek School Division for eight years by 1966. Turcott was not the only member of his family who was politically active: his wife, Joan, shared his social democratic values and was a member of Pincher Creek town council, the first woman to hold this elected office.[88]

His public profile in Pincher Creek helped Turcott to gain votes from people who otherwise never would have dreamt about voting for the New Democratic Party. He also had the ability to connect with miners and their families since he had grown up in hard-rock mining communities in Manitoba before moving to Wawa, Ontario, where, prior to his legal career, he had spent a year working underground mining iron ore. As an outsider to the Crowsnest Pass, however, Turcott might have had trouble gaining high vote totals if the incumbent Social Credit had nominated a popular, local candidate. Fortunately for the NDP campaign, Social Credit put forward a candidate with considerable baggage. A district foreperson with the provincial government's Department of Highways, Joseph Hanrahan had been living and working in Lethbridge immediately prior to the death of William Kovach. However, Hanrahan had lived in Coleman for many years before then and had drawn the ire of miners for some of his hiring decisions after the closing of the International mine in 1954 (see Chapter 2). After this, his track record in local elections was spotty: he had failed in two bids to be elected to the Coleman school board in 1956 and been defeated in a bid for election to Coleman town council in 1961 before finally winning election to it in 1962. Nevertheless, Hanrahan had an inside track on the nomination because he had been the campaign co-chair for Kovach in 1963.[89]

Garth Turcott was nominated as the NDP candidate at a convention attended by "an enthusiastic audience of over 175;" in contrast, the Social Credit nomination meeting, although it featured a contest between two candidates, drew only 75 voting members.[90] At the outset of the campaign, Premier Manning and his inner circle treated the outcome of this by-election as a foregone conclusion even though, in a by-election in Edson the previous year, the Social Credit candidate had been outpolled by both the victorious Liberal candidate and the runner-up NDP candidate.[91] The by-election proved to be highly competitive, however, with both the Liberal and the Progressive Conservative parties running strong candidates. Furthermore, the Alberta New Democratic Party, with the help of the federal party, threw virtually all of its organizational resources into the by-election. The New Democratic Party opened campaign offices in Coleman, Blairmore, Bellevue, and Pincher Creek, each with a paid staff member. The key organizational innovation was voter contact and personal persuasion through a painstaking door-to-door canvass of the constituency: by 1 October, the party had "completely canvassed the riding twice," and homes in Blairmore were apparently canvassed four times by the end of the election. Such a labour-intensive campaign would not have been possible without the volunteer labour of dozens of New Democrats who journeyed to Pincher Creek Crowsnest to help, usually on weekends. Furthermore, the party published four issues of an election paper distributed by canvassers, advertised extensively in local newspapers, and brought in federal NDP leader Tommy Douglas on 30 September for a campaign rally in Blairmore.[92] This rally, attended by "more than 700 people," was described by the *Pass Herald* "as the largest political meeting in the history of the Crowsnest Pass." Social Credit responded by bringing Premier Ernest Manning to Blairmore on 4 October to deliver a two-hour speech; he drew a crowd of 500.[93] The New Democratic Party countered with a final rally in Coleman on the eve of the by-election; the guest speakers included just re-elected BC MLA Leo Nimsick.[94]

The results of the by-election are found in Part (A) of Table 6.2. Garth Turcott won 44 percent of the votes in the Crowsnest Pass, fully 14 percent clear of Joseph Hanrahan. Turcott won a healthy 63 percent of the

TABLE 6.2 Crowsnest Pass popular vote (%), 1966 Alberta by-election and 1967 provincial election

Polling stations	NDP	Social Credit	PC	Liberal	Valid votes
(A) 1966 candidates	Turcott	Hanrahan	Wells	Murphy	
Crowsnest Pass – all polls[a]	44	30	18	8	2,996
Coleman/Sentinel	44	38	10	8	883
Bushtown	63	26	6	5	180
Blairmore/Frank	39	26	26	9	961
Bellevue/Passburg	48	22	22	8	579
Hillcrest	43	42	6	8	206
Pincher Creek	24	39	13	23	1,229
All other polls	18	29	24	29	841
Total	35	32	18	15	5,066[b]

Turcott (NDP) elected as MLA for Pincher Creek–Crowsnest

	NDP	Social Credit	PC	Liberal	Valid votes
(B) 1967 candidates	Turcott	Drain	Wells	Murphy	
Crowsnest Pass – all polls[c]	42	42	14	2	2,953
Coleman/Sentinel	44	43	11	3	873
Bushtown	62	31	5	2	176
Blairmore/Frank	34	47	18	1	988
Bellevue/Passburg	46	33	19	2	585
Hillcrest	39	50	8	2	305
Pincher Creek	27	55	11	7	1,321
All other polls	24	45	20	11	818
Total	35	46	14	5	5,092[d]

Drain (Social Credit) elected as MLA for Pincher Creek–Crowsnest

NOTES: [a] Includes 133 votes cast at the advance polls in the Crowsnest Pass.

[b] Based upon poll-by-poll results, corrected for adding mistakes, found in *Lethbridge Herald*, 7 October 1966. The vote total of 896 for Wells in this source (after correcting an adding mistake) is 55 votes short of the number found in Alberta, Chief Electoral Officer, *Report on Alberta Elections*, 180. This discrepancy is not large enough to change the pattern of results found in this table.

[c] Includes twenty-six votes cast at the Crowsnest Pass hospital.

[d] Based upon poll-by-poll results, corrected for adding mistakes, found in *Lethbridge Herald*, 24 May 1967. For this source, the vote totals for two candidates match the official vote totals, and for each of the other two candidates the vote totals are only one vote different from the official vote totals.[95]

votes in Bushtown, a working-class enclave just to the east of Coleman (and the site of the Ukrainian Labor Temple pictured in Figure 4.4). He also won a majority of votes at the polling stations in southeast Blairmore and came out ahead of Hanrahan in every other Crowsnest Pass community. Overall, Turcott had 407 more votes than Hanrahan after all of the votes cast in the Crowsnest Pass were counted, with the Progressive Conservative and Liberal candidates trailing badly.

The final result in the by-election then hinged on whether Hanrahan could overcome this fairly large deficit in the polls outside the Crowsnest Pass, where 2,070 total votes would be cast. For a couple of reasons, he failed to do so. First, Turcott managed to win 24 percent of the votes in Pincher Creek, finishing second to Hanrahan. Second, although Turcott won only 18 percent of the votes in rural polls, and finished last among the four candidates, the remaining 82 percent of the rural vote was fairly evenly split among his opponents (see Table 6.2). Therefore, over the entire constituency, Turcott's lead of 407 votes in the Crowsnest Pass was enough to withstand Hanrahan's margins of victory by 185 and 86 votes, respectively, in Pincher Creek and the rural polls.

For a couple of decades prior to the elections in 1966, the labourist/leftist vote on the BC side of the region had held up while the comparable vote on the Alberta side had withered. The audacious NDP campaign in support of Turcott in 1966, however, upended this pattern. His share of the popular vote across the three larger communities in the Alberta Crowsnest Pass ranged from a low of 39 percent in Blairmore and Frank to a high of 48 percent in Bellevue and Passberg. In comparison, Nimsick outdid Turcott by winning 54 percent support in Sparwood-Natal-Michel in 1966, but he also underperformed by finishing last among three candidates in Fernie, securing only 29 percent support. At this point, Fernie's shift away from its roots as a trade union city had been more pronounced than the political changes in the Crowsnest Pass communities in Alberta, which likewise had experienced devastating mine closures. The local growth coalition had promoted a new, pro-business path in Fernie that secured considerable popular support even though its practical achievements were slim. No parallel ideological campaign had been waged in the Crowsnest Pass communities in Alberta that had lost their mines.

Furthermore, the economic pain in Fernie was less than that on the Alberta side of the region, as demonstrated by Fernie's loss of only 3 percent of its population between 1961 and 1966 (see Table 2.2), compared with losses in the range of 10–13 percent in Blairmore, Coleman, and Bellevue (see Table 2.1).

Turcott's successful campaign in 1966 capitalized on the strong sense of economic hardship that persisted in Alberta Crowsnest Pass communities even with the recent growth of employment at Phillips Cables and Coleman Collieries. The New Democratic Party distributed its last campaign flyer the day before people went to the polls. It concluded that, "if Social Credit has done such a good job, why has the Crowsnest Pass become a depressed area??? GO TURCOTT." This message would have resonated with the many middle-aged and older workers who had remained in the area after losing their jobs when mines closed. I surmise that Premier Manning's long-standing unwillingness to provide financial support to the coal industry, as documented in Chapters 2 and 3, finally netted political retribution in this election.

Although most rookie MLAs or MPs are invisible while they become acclimated to their new duties, within months of his election Garth Turcott had become a household name in Alberta because of his challenges to Manning on the issue of ethical accountability. In the fall of 1966, questions about possible ministerial misconduct by Ted Hinman and Alf Hooke had been aired in Alberta and indeed across Canada[96] for some time. Manning himself had sparked many of these questions when he forced Hinman's resignation as provincial treasurer on 28 July 1964. With hints of corruption and intrigue in the air, Neil Reimer, leader of the Alberta New Democratic Party, made conflict of interest the party's main strategic issue. When Turcott was elected in 1966, he willingly took up the cause of ethical accountability, and, since Reimer did not have a seat in the legislature, Turcott became the public face of the NDP attack campaign.

The ins and outs of how Turcott pursued this issue in the fall of 1966 and winter of 1967 lie beyond the scope of this book.[97] He eventually forced the Manning government to appoint a royal commissioner to conduct a public inquiry into the charges of misconduct levelled against

Hinman and Hooke. Four days later Alberta's fifteenth legislature was dissolved so that a general election could be held on 23 May 1967.

In the 1967 election, four key factors worked against Turcott's re-election. First, in the months preceding the election, Turcott poured his heart and soul into the issue of the Manning government's ethical accountability, to the detriment of strengthening relationships and building loyalty in his constituency.[98] Second, the Alberta New Democratic Party spread its resources across the province and, consequently, provided Turcott with only a small fraction of the support that he had received in the by-election. Third, Premier Manning and the Social Credit League put extra efforts and resources into winning back Pincher Creek–Crowsnest, including convincing the unpopular Joseph Hanrahan to drop out of the contest to be the party's candidate. Charlie Drain, a Blairmore contractor and town councillor, won the nomination contest.[99] Fourth, on his first day in the Legislative Assembly, Turcott had inadvertently insulted the leader of the opposition, Liberal Michael Maccagno, by trumpeting the New Democratic Party as "the real opposition in Alberta." Furthermore, Maccagno disapproved of Turcott's persistent temerity in challenging the judgment and authority of Manning, the undisputed centre of Alberta's political universe at the time. Presumably because of these strained relations, the Liberal Party did not run an effective campaign in Pincher Creek–Crowsnest in 1967, a fact publicly noted by the Progressive Conservative candidate at an election forum.[100] The practical effect of the weak Liberal campaign in 1967 was to lessen the vote splitting that had helped to elect Turcott in the by-election.

The results of the 1967 election are reported in Panel (B) of Table 6.2. Garth Turcott won the same percentage (35) of the popular vote in 1967 as he had in 1966. As might be expected given that Charlie Drain's hometown was Blairmore, Turcott's share of the popular vote in Blairmore and Frank fell from 39 to 34

FIGURE 6.3 Garth and Joan Turcott at a gathering of supporters on the evening of 23 May 1967 after Garth failed to win re-election in Pincher Creek–Crowsnest.

| Courtesy of Joan Turcott.

percent. Yet, across the Crowsnest Pass, Turcott won 42 percent of the popular vote, close to the 44 percent that he garnered in the by-election. He also slightly improved his share of the vote in Pincher Creek and the rural polls.

The determining factor in the 1967 election in Pincher Creek–Crowsnest, however, was the decrease in the Liberal and Progessive Conservative shares of the vote. The Liberal Party's noncampaign yielded just 5 percent of the popular vote, down from 15 percent in 1966. The Progressive Conservative candidate saw his vote share decrease by a more modest 4 percent (from 18 to 14). In total, Drain's share of the popular vote in 1967, at 46 percent, was 14 percent more than Hanrahan had achieved in 1966 and gave him a comfortable margin of victory over Turcott.

The electoral victories of Leo Nimsick and Garth Turcott in 1966, and the latter's considerable electoral support in the 1967 election, reflected a re-energized worker movement that had emerged from the ashes of the mine closures and depopulation of the 1950s and early 1960s. This worker movement was considerably different from the worker movement in the Crowsnest Pass and Elk Valley in the years immediately after the Second World War. Most notably, there were now far fewer coal-mining jobs and only two active UMWA union locals; many young people had left the area over the preceding fifteen years in pursuit of other opportunities; many ethnocultural organizations with predominantly working-class memberships had folded up; and the Communist Party had disappeared as an organized political force that could be counted on to push the worker movement to the left. Nevertheless, there was a large reserve of sympathy for social democratic thinking in the region in the mid-1960s effectively mobilized in Sparwood-Natal-Michel by Ezner De Anna's crew of activists and in Alberta by the swarm of NDP employees and out-of-town volunteers who bolstered the work of local NDPers. These provincial election campaigns, and the local struggles upon which they built, asserted that mismanaged economic growth could be just as ruinous as the economic contraction stemming from mine closures. The NDP victories reflected desires for democratic control over the contours of economic expansion, improved protection and compensation for workers, and environmental justice.

Conclusion

Lessons and Opportunities for a Future beyond Coal

This case study of deindustrialization ends in 1968 with the Crowsnest Pass and Elk Valley on the verge of a massive reindustrialization in coal after the two surviving coal producers signed long-term contracts to supply metallurgical coal to Japanese steel companies. Economic recovery, however, would turn out to be very uneven across the region. Although five strip mines at the tops of mountains would thrive for decades in southeastern British Columbia, by 1980 Coleman Collieries had ceased mining coal, leaving Alberta's Crowsnest Pass without any active coal mines – a state that persisted into the 2020s and might well extend indefinitely into the future after a joint federal-provincial review panel in 2021 rejected an Australian mining company's proposal to renew strip mining on Grassy Mountain.[1] Therefore, the fight against mine closures and economic ruin that roiled the region in the 1950s and 1960s is not without contemporary reverberations for communities such as Bellevue, Blairmore (see Figure C.1), and Coleman (united administratively in the Municipality of Crowsnest Pass since 1979), which have continued to struggle to find ways to maintain a modicum of a tax base and population, let alone prosper.

The lessons from this case study are also pertinent wherever and whenever citizens and governments confront major job losses. Deindustrialization has been a common phenomenon in the Global North over the past forty-five years or more because of fierce competition in the globalized, neo-liberal economy, which has frequently resulted in the closing of factories as corporations have shifted manufacturing to lower-wage and less-regulated jurisdictions. Furthermore, given the climate emergency

FIGURE C.1 Blairmore, Alberta, December 2009. Crowsnest Mountain rising above downtown stores and the CPR line looking toward Frank and Bellevue. | By Tom Langford.

caused by rising levels of greenhouse gases in the atmosphere, during the upcoming decades deindustrialization can be expected to haunt coal-, oil-, and natural gas–producing regions. Government regulations and taxes aimed at reducing greenhouse gas emissions will be one driver of a decline in new investment in fossil fuel production and the shutdown of some existing wells and mines; a second will be the development and refinement of low-carbon technologies such as electric vehicles powered by batteries or hydrogen fuel cells that will play a significant role in reducing demand for fossil fuels. Metallurgical coal has long been thought to be immune from such competitive pressure because it is essential to the traditional blast furnace/basic oxygen furnace method for making steel, and it is hard to imagine a world of the future without steel. Nevertheless, as I noted at the end of the introduction, the successful piloting of new technologies that produce steel out of iron ore utilizing natural gas and electricity, or hydrogen and electricity, have opened the door to the rapid decarbonization of the global steel industry in coming decades. "Green steel" manufacturing will result in a drop in demand for metallurgical coal and eventually push the Elk Valley and Crowsnest Pass into yet another economic downturn. The lessons from the deindustrialization crisis documented in this book should be instructive to those who will confront this anticipated future crisis.

In the last section of this conclusion, I collate the major lessons from the fight against economic ruin in the Crowsnest Pass and Elk Valley in the 1950s and 1960s with lessons from other struggles over deindustrialization and the inspiring campaign by the Haida Nation to assert Aboriginal title to and significant control of their traditional territory on the Haida Gwaii archipelago. The Haida example is pertinent because the Ktunaxa, Piikani, and Kainai, whose voices were muted by colonial strictures in the nineteenth and twentieth centuries, can be expected in the twenty-first century to assert their legal and moral rights and demand full participation in decisions on the future of their traditional territories. As coal mining winds down, I expect that these First Nations will anchor a counterhegemonic movement aimed at building a truly sustainable future for the Crowsnest Pass and Elk Valley. Before turning to the discussion of lessons, I return to the sociological and political questions posed in the introduction. Some of these questions were answered in the flow of the historical narrative of previous chapters and need no further attention. Questions that have not yet been addressed, however, I will consider here. I organize my answers under three headings: "The Worker Movement," "The State," and "Left Politics."

THE WORKER MOVEMENT

A majority of this study's research questions problematized how the worker movement in the Crowsnest Pass and Elk Valley responded to and shaped the course of the deindustrialization crisis of the 1950s and 1960s and how that crisis in turn changed the worker movement. Before turning to my answers to specific questions, it will be helpful to identify the major changes in the worker movement between the late 1940s and the mid-1960s. These changes are summarized in Table C.1. The political mission of the movement of the late 1940s was counterhegemonic in that it aimed to build alternatives – economic, cultural, and political – to the status quo. The pragmatism of this counterhegemonic project is shown in the leadership of the Coleman, Blairmore, and Bellevue UMWA locals in establishing a modern, community-financed hospital in 1949. In contrast, the movement in the mid-1960s had a narrower political mission: to defend jobs and the way of life of working-class communities. The broader political project in the mid-1960s was social democratic electoralism, a distinct contrast to the rank-and-file, socialist activism that fuelled the counterhegemonic politics in the late 1940s.

Following the lead of David Featherstone, I see the political orientations and capacities of worker movements as being generated through the networks of solidarity in which they act. In this conceptualization, "solidarities are ... transformative political relations" rather than "something which just binds already formed communities together."[2] The entries on such networks in Table C.1 encapsulate just how much the worker movement in the Crowsnest Pass and Elk Valley changed between the late 1940s and the mid-1960s. In general terms, the earlier movement was well connected, with numerous strong ties of solidarity within the region complemented by a large variety of weak ties of

TABLE C.1 Key characteristics of the worker movement in the Crowsnest Pass
and Elk Valley, late 1940s versus mid-1960s

Characteristic	Late 1940s (peak of railway steam coal sales)	Mid-1960s (modest sales to Japanese steelmakers)
Political mission	Counterhegemonic but pragmatic	Defending jobs and way of life Social democratic electoralism
Networks of solidarity		
General pattern	Well connected, strong local ties; numerous weak ties across distant scales	Isolated, diminished local ties; much fewer weak ties across distant scales
Crowsnest Pass and Elk Valley	Five UMWA locals working together in two subdistricts and on yearly May Day celebrations	Two UMWA locals no longer in joint contract negotiations; no more May Day celebrations
Western Canada	Interconnected with more than forty UMWA locals (9,500 members) in District 18; part of IFL of Alberta	District 18 with six locals (1,750 members); not part of AFL
Canada	CCL member; opposed to Cold War raiding/expulsion of communist unions	Outside CLC from founding (1956) to 1970
International	International causes and connections reflecting pro-Soviet focus of CPC	No discernible international connections other than within the UMWA
Infrastructure of dissent	Dense with overlapping sources: ethnocultural groups, democratic union locals, and socialist/labour parties	Thin since power of union locals diminished; ethnocultural groups much less important; CPC and Fernie District Labour Party gone
Collective protests	Miners' wildcat strikes common; ethos of collective struggle throughout region; district-wide miners' strikes in 1946 and 1948	Wildcat strikes constrained by UMWA; Local 7292 miners' strikes in 1965 and 1967; environmental justice protests by groups of women in Sparwood-Natal-Michel in 1967
Coal policy orientation	Protectionism from American coal imports to help secure sales in Ontario	Subsidized export sales to Japan and creation of new steel plants in western Canada
Miners' working-class identity	Male, white, cosmopolitan-European	Male, now stretched to include those with Japanese ancestry

solidarity across different geographical scales and labour organizations. Most significantly, as an active member of the Canadian Congress of Labour and the Industrial Federation of Labour of Alberta, the earlier movement opposed the Cold War attacks on leftist unions such as the International Union of Mine Mill and Smelter Workers and maintained international labour connections through the work of communist militants inside the movement. In contrast, the movement in the mid-1960s was relatively isolated: not only was the number of connections of solidarity within the region diminished by the decline in the coal industry, but also the celebration of May Day had been abandoned, the isolationism of the International UMWA meant that its Canadian affiliates were forbidden from belonging to provincial or national labour organizations, and the international connections of the past had fizzled out alongside the ruin of the Communist Party.

Alan Sears's notion of an "infrastructure of dissent"[3] provides a conceptual approach to worker movements that complements David Featherstone's stress on connections of solidarity. The entries in Table C.1 indicate that there was as large a change in this infrastructure between the late 1940s and mid-1960s as there was in networks of solidarity. The virtual disappearance of leftist ethnocultural groups and the ruin of the Communist Party were crucial transformations.

There was a strong ethos of collective struggle in the Crowsnest Pass and Elk Valley in the years immediately following the Second World War. The high points included a political strike in 1946 against the composition of the Workmen's Compensation Board of Alberta, regular wildcats by miners, and a strike by Blairmore high school students in 1948 over the poor physical condition of their school. It is significant that this ethos persisted into the 1960s even though the International UMWA cracked down on wildcat strikes by disciplining the leadership of Michel Local 7292 in 1955 and the infrastructure of dissent had withered. The most notable of the collective actions in the mid-1960s were environmental justice protests by groups of women in Natal and Michel that galvanized the entire community into action.

The last two characteristics listed in Table C.1 capture additional ways in which the worker movement changed in significant ways between the late 1940s and the mid-1960s. At the beginning of the coal crisis (and carrying on until the Royal Commission on Coal in 1960), the movement saw protectionist measures as the answer to survival, ignoring the economic inefficiencies associated with using tariffs and quotas to create a domestic market for Canadian-mined coal. Starting in the late 1950s, however, the movement began to change its policy thrust by asking governments to subsidize the development of new, promising markets for coal from the Crowsnest Pass and Elk Valley. My research identified Sam English, who ran for the Labor-Progressive Party in the federal election of 1953 and was a long-time leader of Michel Local 7292, as being at the forefront of working-class leaders who made this important shift in thinking about coal policy. In doing so, English contradicted the stereotype of a communist leader stuck in the industrial past and wedded to the old ways of doing things.

Finally, in both time periods, the coal miner was the normative centre of the worker movement in the Crowsnest Pass and Elk Valley. Miners' working-class identity in the late 1940s was gendered as male and racialized as white; simultaneously, it was cosmopolitan, seeded by the diverse European ethnocultural groups organized in the region. In the mid-1960s, miners' class identity remained uncompromisingly male (women were still legally barred from underground employment in coal mines), but Japanese Canadian men were now employees and hence members of the UMWA. I interpret this important change in working-class identity as an extension of the reduction of ethnocultural stratification observed in the postwar years: as noted at the beginning of Chapter 2, by the late 1940s those of Eastern European ancestry were less likely to be negatively stereotyped and had been reracialized as white. Less than two decades later, the notion of a coal miner had been stretched to include the Japanese Canadian men who had lived in the Crowsnest Pass since their release from internment after the Second World War. This stretch was also promoted by the broader, progressive shift in thinking about human rights in the years after the war. During those years, however, the worker movement in the region became less cosmopolitan as ethnocultural organizations disappeared or diminished in importance because of generational change and the intertwined economic and political crises of the

1950s. Simultaneously, the worker movement lost its counterhegemonic orientation. The result was a miners' class identity in the mid-1960s considerably closer to being conventionally Anglo-Canadian than what had existed in the late 1940s.

This discussion of Table C.1 has addressed several of the research questions on the worker movement posed at the beginning of this book. To conclude this section, I consider two outstanding questions.

First, I posed two counterfactual questions related to the absence of a militant response to mine closures in the 1950s: if workers in the Crowsnest Pass and Elk Valley had engaged in a contentious collective protest (e.g., an underground occupation and hunger strike), would they have gained anything like the level of support enjoyed by protesting coal miners in south-central France in 1962, and would such militancy have been successful? In solidarity with the miners of Decazeville, France, farmers in the area blockaded roads, over 300 mayors resigned, and citizens participated in a regional general strike (see the introduction). It is hard to imagine such a widespread show of regional support if miners at the International mine at Coleman, Greenhill mine at Blairmore, or Elk River Colliery at Coal Creek had similarly stayed underground and engaged in a hunger strike. The political divide between the unionized coal miners and the conservative Alberta ranching communities to the east of the Crowsnest Pass would have been one barrier to extensive regional solidarity across southwestern Alberta. Nevertheless, strong, across-class support within the Crowsnest Pass and Elk Valley could have been mobilized, and it is not inconceivable that the International Union of Mine Mill and Smelter Workers locals at Kimberley and Trail would have engaged in a sympathy protest. Such actions would have been sufficient to garner a great deal of provincial and national media coverage and force the senior levels of government to engage with the protesters. It is hard to know which concessions might have been won in this scenario. Yet I am confident that a contentious collective protest at least would have leveraged something better than bus tickets, moving expenses, and seasonal make-work projects.

Second, I asked whether the worker movement in the Crowsnest Pass and Elk Valley during the years covered in this book was a flawed exemplar because of its marginalization of women. This is another area where the ruin of the Communist Party was consequential: through initiatives such as the Housewives Consumers Association in the late 1940s, local women were encouraged by the Labor-Progressive Party to become active in politics, and the party featured senior female leaders such as Annie Buller, who spent considerable time in the Crowsnest Pass during the provincial election campaign in 1948 (see Chapter 4). These positive examples of women's political involvement and leadership were lost in the 1950s as LPP membership and activism declined precipitously. In the absence of a strong communist presence, the worker movement during the 1953–54 and 1957–61 downturns was largely a movement of men. Nevertheless, there is evidence of ongoing women's engagement with working-class struggles, including the public protest by the Crowsnest Pass chapter of the Alberta Association of Registered Nurses in 1956 over the dismissal of their head nurse and the publication of Florence Del Rio's poem "Three Days a Week" (see Chapter 2).

As the story shifts to the 1960s, the participation rate of women in the labour force grew, and more women became union members with the successful unionization of municipal and school board employees as well as the Phillips Cables plant. Although the worker movement in the region was still dominated by the all-male UMWA locals, women's voices were increasingly heard. Two important examples from 1967 are the compelling letter to the editor from a lumber worker's wife just prior to the IWA strike and collective protests for environmental justice by women living in Natal and Michel. What stands out is that these women activists were not participating in a secondary role under the direction of male movement leaders but initiating action that, in the case of the environmental justice movement in Natal and Michel, stirred male municipal and union leaders to commit to the struggle. This significant development leads me to conclude that, despite the virtual absence of women from leadership roles prior to the 1960s, many still identified with the movement through their family and friendship ties and developed a working-class consciousness rooted in everyday struggles. As a result, although the worker movement in the region was flawed because its formal marginalization of women echoed that of major social institutions, it was simultaneously exemplary because women were engaged at the margins and over time developed a class consciousness that, in subsequent years, could be activated to spark and help guide the movement.

THE STATE

The introductory chapter posed three sets of questions about the actions of governments during the crisis investigated in this book. The first set points to the broader implications of the Alberta government's refusal to subsidize the coal industry. The second focuses on the private ownership of the mines in the Crowsnest Pass and Elk Valley, querying whether state ownership would have resulted in different approaches to the crisis and better outcomes for workers. The third set asks why one government intervention (transportation subventions for coal exported to Japan) proved to be so successful in boosting the industry while other interventions fell short.

In the view of Premier Ernest Manning, the coal industry's decline in Alberta was simply because coal could not compete with natural gas and oil in many markets where it had previously dominated. In 1951, Manning argued that, "in endeavouring to protect or assist one industry we must not do so to the point which will discourage progress and development in other fields and progress generally."[4] The premier offered virtually the same opinion in response to the closing of the Greenhill mine at Blairmore in the spring of 1957. At that time, his government refused an appeal to help sustain coal mining in the Crowsnest Pass by providing a modest subvention to boost coal sales in Ontario.[5] Three years later a senior federal civil servant reported that the Alberta government "had shown no particular concern as to the fate of the [coal] industry."[6]

The Manning government was fully committed to the unfettered development of the oil and natural gas industries in Alberta, not least because of the windfall that flowed into provincial coffers from land leases, royalties, and taxes. Nevertheless, in the late 1950s and early 1960s, when the province was flush with oil and gas revenue, it easily could have provided some financial support to the struggling coal industry – a point highlighted by the Royal Commission on Coal in 1960. Did the government fail to act because it relished the opportunity to destroy communities that housed militant workers who had been among its fiercest opponents in years gone by, as suggested by Alvin Finkel (see the introduction)? Or was it because of the government's ideological aversion to interfering with competition among fuels?

My research indicates that the Manning government remained very sensitive to, and quite intolerant of, leftist criticisms of its policy approach to the economic crisis in the Crowsnest Pass in the mid-1950s. This was revealed in a dressing down administered by the chair of the Miners' Rehabilitation Committee several months after the closure of the International mine in 1954. John Ferguson complained to the secretary-treasurer of Local 2633 about a "small group in Coleman," apparently "influenced by propaganda agents," "finding fault with every endeavour put forth by the Committee."[7] Significantly, Social Credit MLA William Kovach participated in the meeting, suggesting the Manning government's guiding hand.

At the same time, Manning well recognized that the Crowsnest Pass was hardly a hotbed of opposition to his government. Over the four provincial general elections between 1952 and 1963, Kovach secured a solid majority of all votes cast in Pincher Creek–Crowsnest, with his vote share ranging from 76 percent in 1952 (when he faced but one opponent) to 54 percent in 1963 (against a roster of three opponents).[8] A large proportion of mining families in the Crowsnest Pass consistently supported the Social Credit government through these lean years. If the government had been even slightly inclined toward extending a helping hand to the coal industry in the 1950s, then the solid electoral support that it received in the Crowsnest Pass should have pulled it toward proffering such aid.

The reality is that Premier Manning rejected on principle helping an old industry (coal) getting squeezed out by new industries (oil and natural gas) that had turned around Alberta's economic fortunes in a few short years. His thinking was driven by a combination of market fundamentalism and a desire to remain in the good books of the oil and gas companies investing heavily in Alberta. I contend that the provincial government was so committed to letting market competition decide the

fate of the coal companies in the Crowsnest Pass that its political con-
siderations – solid electoral support coexisting with a rump of leftist
critics – were beside the point. Manning rejected the solidaristic moral
economy principles favoured by many mid-twentieth century Canadian
politicians, including Progressive Conservatives, and therefore felt no
compulsion to keep the coal industry and its employees afloat. In taking
this stance, he anticipated the neo-liberal revolution of Margaret Thatcher
and Ronald Reagan that likewise pushed commitments to working
people's security aside in favour of unleashed capital accumulation.
Manning's approach in the 1950s and 1960s, like that of Thatcher and
Reagan in the 1980s, shifted the burden of the costs of deindustrialization
onto workers and their communities.[9]

Two of the comparative cases presented in the introduction –
Decazeville in south-central France and the Rhondda in South Wales –
were in countries where the coal mines had been nationalized shortly
after the Second World War. Consequently, the mines in each of these
regions were operated by state-owned corporations in the 1950s and
1960s during deindustrialization crises that paralleled what occurred in
the Crowsnest Pass and Elk Valley. I asked whether state ownership
changed the economic and political reasoning behind the decisions to
close coal mines and whether workers at the state-owned mines were accorded greater rights and better treatment than the workers in the
Crowsnest Pass and Elk Valley employed by Coleman Collieries, West
Canadian Collieries, or Crow's Nest Pass Coal.

In France, there was a moratorium on closing uncompetitive, state-
owned coal mines between 1946 and 1958. During these years, however,
managers employed in Decazeville by the state-owned coal company,
Les Charbonnages de France, paved the way for the closure of the area's
underground mines by routing new capital investments into open-pit
rather than underground operations, thereby making the coal coming
out of the underground mines even more uncompetitive. After the moratorium ended, all underground mines and many open-pit mines in
Decazeville were phased out by Les Charbonnages in a process that took
until 1966; at that time, only 500 coal miners were still employed, down
from a labour force of 2,750 in 1959. The reasoning behind the mine

closures in Decazeville was identical to the reasoning extended by West Canadian Collieries for closing its Greenhill and Bellevue mines in 1960–61: the high cost of producing a ton of coal made the mines money losers at market prices at which lower-cost competitors could thrive. It is therefore apparent that, when operating in a capitalist market system, both national and private companies ultimately must apply the same sort of bottom-line reasoning when confronted with a decision on higher-cost, unprofitable mines.

At the same time, there is no doubt that the treatment of displaced miners by the nationalized coal corporations in France and Wales was qualitatively superior to the treatment of miners who lost their jobs in the Crowsnest Pass and Elk Valley in the 1950s and early 1960s. For example, one concession gained by the protest movement in 1962 in the Decazeville region was the extension of partial pension benefits to miners aged from fifty to fifty-five who lost their jobs. In comparison, in the Crowsnest Pass and Elk Valley, only miners sixty-two and older qualified for a re-tirement pension from the District 18 Welfare and Retirement Fund, with a large percentage of miners who lost their jobs in the late 1950s being in the age bracket of fifty to fifty-nine (shown in Figure 3.1). Hence, partial pension benefits for miners who fell just a few years short of the pension-qualifying age of sixty-two would have been a popular and hu-mane policy when mines closed. My best guess is that, if the mines in the region had been nationalized, then workers and their union at least would have won partial pensions for workers approaching retirement age. This is what happened at the Sydney Steel plant in 2000 when the Nova Scotia government agreed to prorated pensions for workers with between twenty-five and twenty-nine years of seniority during an unsuccessful effort to facilitate the sale of the state-owned plant to a Swiss firm.[10]

In Ron Berry's novel *Flame and Slag*, the fictional Caib underground mine in South Wales is closed by the National Coal Board in 1967 be-cause of a geological fault that eliminates the working coal faces. Young, able-bodied miners are offered transfers to another mine, given the opportunity to sell their houses to the National Coal Board, and given money for relocation expenses. This fictional outcome aligns with the two principles that guided Coal Board pit closures in Scotland at the time, as explained by historian Jim Phillips: "The agreement of workers and their representatives and the guaranteed economic security of the men affected, through transfer to nearby pits or local provision of comparably paid, alternative employment."[11] In contrast, as documented in Chapters 2 and 3, decisions on mine closures were taken unilaterally by coal companies in the Crowsnest Pass and Elk Valley in the 1950s and 1960s, and laid-off workers were offered nothing close to economic security – only low-paid temporary work or (in Alberta) moving expenses if they could find jobs elsewhere.

Yet not all was sweetness and light when a mine run by the National Coal Board was closed, as illustrated by Berry's novel. In the case of the Caib colliery, one-third of the workforce does not qualify for the assistance package, including the novel's protagonist, Rees, who suffered a badly broken pelvis in a rock fall a few years before and, after a long recovery, was classified as "twenty-five per cent compo." Rees notes that "I was redundant, along with a third of the men belonging to Caib, men over sixty, near sixty, men disabled, the ailing, the worn-out and the half-broken."[12] Hence, top-down nationalization was no panacea for the working class even in a setting (mid-twentieth-century Britain) where a moral economy based upon solidarity governed decisions on mine closures.[13]

This book has shown that transportation subventions provided by successive federal governments in the late 1950s and 1960s were essential to the eventual reindustrialization of coal in the Elk Valley and Crowsnest Pass. When Coleman Collieries (1967) and Kaiser (1968) signed long-term contracts for large yearly tonnages of metallurgical coal, the federal government was among the winners – it could phase out the subventions once the new contracts began and take credit for giving the new export industry a lifeline during its formative years.

It is noteworthy that the federal government provided transportation subventions for coal exported to Japan without knowing what it would take to create a strong, self-sufficient metallurgical coal industry. The eventual success of the government's policy on subsidization depended on two unanticipated, fortuitous developments: CNPC's discovery of a high-quality seam of coal and Japanese steel companies' willingness to sign contracts that paid a premium for Canadian metallurgical coal in order to ensure that lower-cost Australian producers would not hold a monopoly as suppliers (see Chapter 5). In the absence of these developments, the subventions would have gone for naught.

Although the subventions for coal exported to Japan were a resounding, long-term success, other forms of government subsidization fell short of providing pathways to stable economic expansion. Three examples are transportation subventions for Crowsnest Pass and Elk Valley coal sold in Manitoba and northwestern Ontario "directed towards the displacement of United States bituminous by Canadian bituminous"; [14] a federal government directive to keep burning Canadian coal in government buildings even when it cost more than American coal; and the BC government's subsidization of new pig iron and steel factories at Kimberley that utilized coal and coke from Michel Collieries. The first two examples are forms of protectionism that enabled a more expensive commodity (Canadian coal) to win some sales from a less expensive rival (American coal) but did not offer any hope of closing the competitive price gap between them. The subsidization of the pig iron and steel factories at Kimberley, in contrast, was a government gamble on a new industry that theoretically could have become competitive in western Canadian steel markets over time. Nevertheless, the gamble did not pay off since Cominco (the new moniker of CMS) closed its iron and steel plants in 1971. [15]

These examples demonstrate that government subsidization can be part of a long-term plan to grow fledgling endeavours or a protectionist move that, though it might alleviate hardship and keep some domestic operations in business, is driven by political optics rather than economic logic. Furthermore, even strategically directed government subsidies are risky propositions, with long-term success far from guaranteed. In the future, strategic investments by the federal and provincial governments will be essential to building a sustainable regional economy in the Crowsnest Pass and Elk Valley. Most importantly, as I discuss below, large sums of money will be needed for environmental remediation and to establish a new Indigenous Protected and Conserved Area (IPCA) and/or national park reserve in the Flathead Valley as the centrepiece of an expanded conservation economy.

LEFT POLITICS

The interpretive questions on left politics posed in the introduction arose from my comparative study of the history of the Rhondda coalfield in South Wales. In Chapter 4, I showed that left internationalism was as strong a tendency in the Crowsnest Pass and Elk Valley in the 1930s as in the Rhondda, as measured by the rate of miners who volunteered to join the fight against fascism in Spain. The two regions also shared the reputation for being highly cosmopolitan since, when jobs opened as the coalfields were being developed, there was an influx of workers with a diverse range of European ethnocultural backgrounds. I queried whether the left-internationalist tendencies in each region grew out of the cosmopolitan social composition. Furthermore, following from the insights of Raymond Williams, I asked whether the left internationalism in the Rhondda was fundamentally different from that in the Crowsnest Pass and Elk Valley because of the backdrop of Welsh culture and national struggle in the Rhondda.

Compared with left nationalism, left internationalism is more likely to find fertile ground in a cosmopolitan social setting. This is because people coming from different ethnocultural backgrounds might well agree on a left-internationalist political project while harbouring different nationalist imaginaries connected to their backgrounds. Furthermore, once left internationalism is widely accepted in a cosmopolitan society, the logic of a left-nationalist project can seem to be retrograde. This accounts for the difficulty that Plaid Cymru, the Welsh nationalist party, faced when trying to mobilize an electoral following in the Rhondda in the mid-twentieth century. Rees, the protagonist in *Flame and Slag*, contemptuously rejects Welsh nationalism by denying the idea of national superiority: "Can you prove it's superior to be born Welsh than, say, Spanish, or Greek, or Hindu? Where's the goodness in being Welsh?"[16]

In discussing changes in the worker movement in the Crowsnest Pass and Elk Valley earlier in this conclusion, I noted that miners' typical class identity shifted from cosmopolitan-European in the late 1940s to conventional Anglo-Canadian in the mid-1960s. An implication of this assertion is that leftist organizing had a tougher row to hoe in the 1960s since a large proportion of miners now identified with the ethnocultural mainstream in western Canada – their diminished sense of ethnocultural difference, subordination, and grievance tended to lessen their openness to oppositional political ideas. This process is distinct from what transpired in the Rhondda, where, in similar conditions of cosmopolitan diminishment, a strong, subaltern Welsh movement could serve as an oppositional counterpoint to the dominant English culture. The left-nationalist movement in Wales, therefore, was in a position to inherit the sympathies of a Rhondda working class that for several decades had been more attuned to left internationalism. In contrast, in the Crowsnest Pass and Elk Valley, workers could more readily drift away from leftist politics toward mainstream perspectives. Contrary to the poetic image of Raymond Williams outlined in the introduction, it was not sheep grazing on Welsh mountaintop pastures that reinforced the class consciousness of workers in the Rhondda during the era of mine closures and deindustrialization; rather, it was the underlying Welshness of the Rhondda and the persistent organizing of Plaid Cymru to build a left-nationalist movement. Given the settler-colonial origins of the Crowsnest Pass and Elk Valley coalfield society, nothing like the Rhondda transition from left internationalism to left nationalism was ever possible.

Lessons and Opportunities for a Future beyond Coal

Five significant problems undermined the fight against economic ruin in the Crowsnest Pass and Elk Valley in the 1950s and 1960s. First, the region's geographical isolation hampered efforts to recruit manufacturing firms and land a new federal prison. Second, attempts to rebuild the region's economy after mine closures were helter-skelter rather than well considered with a distant time horizon in mind. Third, municipalities rarely worked together on regional solutions. Fourth, the federal government's use of tax incentives to increase manufacturing employment in the Crowsnest Pass and Elk Valley yielded just one flawed success – a Phillips Cables plant that mainly offered low-skill, low-pay employment and closed in 1985 after nineteen years of operation. Fifth, private corporations controlled the significant pools of invested capital. In the good times, profits flowed out of the region to distant shareholders, and the regional economic multiplier effect from coal mines or the Phillips Cables factory was low. In the tough times, CNPC, West Canadian Collieries, Coleman Collieries, and Phillips Cables exercised unilateral power when they closed operations.

Nevertheless, starting in 1968, the scourge of deindustrialization was beaten back by a coal boom as long-term contracts with Asia-Pacific steelmakers drove the development of new mines. The phase of reindustrialization was short lived on the Alberta side of the region but has persisted for over half a century in the Elk Valley, where the four mountaintop strip mines are slated to produce 25–26 million tonnes of coal annually between 2023 and 2025 (almost an order of magnitude higher than the 3.7 million tons produced at the height of the railway steam coal industry in 1949; see Figure I.2).[17] In years when the price of metallurgical coal is high, the profit from these mines is huge. For instance, in 2021, Teck Resources reported a gross profit (after depreciation and amortization) of $2.8 billion from its steelmaking coal operations, with gross profit making up 45 percent of every dollar of revenue from coal sales.[18]

As successful as the reindustrialization of the Elk Valley has been, it is best viewed as an interlude in a conjuncture of deindustrialization that began in the 1950s and likely will last well into the twenty-second century because of the decades of complex environmental remediation that will be necessary after the mining of coal ceases. As a nonrenewable resource, coal has always been the foundation for a regional economy with a looming expiry date. However, recognition of the pressing need to stabilize the concentration of greenhouse gases in the atmosphere has stimulated the development of new "green steel" technologies and advanced the date when the mining of metallurgical coal in the Elk Valley will end. Furthermore, once metallurgical coal production at existing mines in the Elk Valley starts to decline, it is unlikely that a company will invest in a new coal mine on either side of the continental divide since falling demand will put downward pressure on the price and profitability of metallurgical coal. That said, there is uncertainty about when the demand for steelmaking coal from Asia-Pacific countries will begin to decrease.

Based upon projections of the International Energy Agency, Queensland's treasury department estimated in 2020 that worldwide trade in metallurgical coal will grow by 16 percent between 2018 and 2040 under national policies in place in 2018 but fall by 23 percent "if global policies and actions were to align closely with the key Sustainable Development Goals of the United Nations."[19] Splitting the difference between these scenarios suggests that the demand for seaborne steelmaking coal will be steady until 2040, keeping the Elk Valley's mines more or less humming. After then, the pace of the fall in demand for metallurgical coal from the Elk Valley will depend on how quickly steelmakers in Japan, South Korea, India, and China abandon the coal-dependent blast furnace/basic oxygen furnace system in favour of "green steel" manufacturing. It is hard to envision a scenario in which production cutbacks and mine closures will not be headlines in the Crowsnest Pass and Elk Valley in the second half of this century. Consequently, long-term planning for the next phase of the struggle against economic ruin cannot begin too soon.

As a starting point, planning must be cognizant of two fundamental changes in Canada's economy and politics that have altered the parameters of a fight against economic ruin resulting from mine closures. The first is the ascendancy of a globalized neo-liberal economy with far fewer restrictions on the movement of capital and goods across national borders and the shift of much consumer goods production to lower-wage and less-regulated jurisdictions. This change precludes the regional development strategy of using subsidies to lure large manufacturing firms to far-flung corners of Canada such as the Crowsnest Pass, Elk Valley, and Cape Breton; simply put, no reasonable subsidy can overcome the cost advantages of manufacturing in the Global South.

Second, a legal ruling has fundamentally altered the politics of development in rural Canadian regions: the Supreme Court's recognition of Aboriginal title to land that "derives from prior occupation and use, not from ownership."[20] Once legally established, Aboriginal title becomes a property right that coexists with the property rights of the Crown or private landowners. Furthermore, it is a unique property right since it "is closer to stewardship than ownership, as it assumes a sustainability ethos that prohibits any use of the land that would threaten the food security of the community, while safeguarding the cultural integrity of the land for future generations."[21] Hence, holding Aboriginal title "is in essence the right of land management"[22] and a legal foundation for the efforts of First Nations to reverse the colonial dispossession of traditional territories.

One way that the concept of Aboriginal title has been implemented is through the creation of Indigenous Protected and Conserved Areas. The first three IPCAs, established in the Northwest Territories in 2019, include Thaidene Nëné, managed by three Akaitcho Dene First Nations at the eastern end of Great Slave Lake, and this IPCA doubles as a national park reserve.[23] Since 2020, the Ktunaxa Nation Council has negotiated with the BC and federal governments on the establishment of an IPCA for a segment of their traditional territory in the central Purcell Mountains; it will include Qat'muk, a sacred Ktunaxa place believed to be grizzly bear's spirit home, centred on the glacier in the Jumbo Valley. The Ktunaxa and their allies fought for thirty years to stop a ski resort from being constructed in the Jumbo Valley; with financial contributions from governments and private organizations, all development rights in this valley were extinguished in early 2020, thereby protecting Qat'muk in perpetuity.[24] IPCAs and national park reserves are potential components of a sustainable development plan for the Crowsnest Pass and Elk Valley that includes prominent conservation roles for First Nations.

Assertion of Aboriginal title decisively changes the balance of power in rural regions with a strong Indigenous presence since it means that environmental stewardship and sustainability must guide decisions on the uses of renewable and nonrenewable resources. It is an avenue that will allow the Ktunaxa, Piikani, and Kainai to have important voices in planning discussions on the future of the Crowsnest Pass and Elk Valley beyond coal. The Haida and their allies on Haida Gwaii[25] have demonstrated the monumental political and economic changes that can follow from a determined struggle to define and assert the rights of Aboriginal title.

In the face of growing environmental devastation from clear-cut logging, in the mid-1970s the Council of the Haida Nation and non-Indigenous environmentalists began to organize to protect the southern portion of the archipelago from such destruction. Protracted struggles and negotiations eventually produced an agreement in 1993 to create Gwaii Haanas (Islands of Beauty) as a national park reserve co-managed by the Council of the Haida Nation and Parks Canada.[26] This was an important accomplishment in a political process in which the Haida asserted their rights of Aboriginal title throughout Haida Gwaii and built up their capacity to govern according to the principle of Yah'guudang – respect for all living things.[27]

Instructive developments on Haida Gwaii during the early years of this century include the following:

- A commitment to long-term planning. In 2001, the Haida House of Assembly called for the Council of the Haida Nation to develop a thousand-year plan for the management of trees on the islands (since old-growth cedar are culturally important and the foundation for Haida carving).[28]
- Joint BC-Haida planning and management of land use. A strategic land use agreement was signed in 2007, and a management council for statutory land use decisions was set up in 2009.[29]
- Haida ownership of key assets. The Council of the Haida Nation purchased the largest forest tenure on Haida Gwaii from Western Forest Products in 2012, making the archipelago "multinational-free." It also bought a former bear-hunting lodge and a network of fishing lodges.[30]

A crucial dimension of politics on Haida Gwaii since the 1970s is the collaboration of settlers with the Haida in what researcher Louise Takeda calls a "grassroots indigenous-environmental-community movement."[31] The Haida Gwaii model is organized around the values and priorities of a First Nation exercising Aboriginal title; however, because it includes commitments to environmental stewardship and economic self-determination, the model has won the support of settlers who share those commitments. Takeda argued in 2015 that, "although still in their early phases, the political and economic models unfolding on Haida Gwaii may be a preview of what could emerge in rural communities across British Columbia."[32] At the least, developments on Haida Gwaii demonstrate that it is possible to curtail the power of multinational corporations and distant governments over what happens in a rural region and that considerable associational political power is created when non-Indigenous residents join with Indigenous groups to assert the primacy of environmental stewardship and sustainability.

Notably, it might be the Haida approach to planning rather than Haida political and economic models that will prove to be the most useful to Indigenous groups and their allies in other rural communities. "Rather than moving from the 'traditional past' into the unknown future," anthropologist Joseph Weiss argues, "Haida people are drawing just as much on possible futures as a way of interpreting the past, of clarifying what can be taken as 'traditional,' and of marking the boundaries of what 'fits' into ongoing Haida life."[33] In applying this future-centred approach to planning, the Haida deny the settler-colonial notion that time has passed Indigenous people by. "The Haida people are actively retaking control of their own temporalities," Weiss contends. "Indeed, ... they are asserting the capacity to determine possible futures for settler *as well as* Haida subjects, fundamentally inverting the order of colonial temporality."[34]

I conclude with suggestions for how to plan for and organize the fight against economic ruin in the Crowsnest Pass and Elk Valley that will ensue from the expected decline and eventual end of metallurgical coal mining later this century. The suggestions are organized into three sections: "Principles," "Governance," and "Strategies." I draw from lessons identified in recent studies of deindustrialization and the Haida Gwaii experience to supplement my own research findings.

1. Principles
  1.1 Respect for all living things, environmental stewardship, sustainability
  1.2 Reconciliation, decolonization

1.3 Just transitions for coal workers and communities
1.4 Restoration, reclamation, remediation
1.5 Connect to the history of labour struggles
1.6 Relocalization

Some 125 years of coal·mining in the Crowsnest Pass and Elk Valley have created a legacy of environmental disturbance, destruction, and pollution, including elevated levels of selenium in the Elk River watershed, along with a history of social dislocation. This region is one of the "sacrifice zones" of Canada's modern economy, zones that serve, in the words of researchers John Sandlos and Arn Keeling, "as a barometer of the ecological and social consequences of modernity at the margins of Canada's settled geography."[35] Principle 1.1 (respect for all living things, environmental stewardship, sustainability) envisions a much different future for the region; implementation will require a plan to rejuvenate and sustain ecosystems over hundreds of years while creating jobs consistent with environmental stewardship. Recognition of the Aboriginal title of the Ktunaxa, Piikani, and Kainai is fundamental to the pursuit of Principle 1.1; indeed, enacting the first principle will be how Principle 1.2 (reconciliation, decolonization) can be realized in practice. Decolonization in the Crowsnest Pass and Elk Valley will mean that Indigenous peoples have moved from the margins to the centre of the regional power structure and society. In this scenario, a more equitable social order will be built on the ashes of the unjust mining economy. Such a change has already occurred in Cape Breton, where the Membertou First Nation, a Mi'kmaq community near Sydney, has experienced an "economic miracle" in recent years after its members were largely denied employment opportunities during the heyday of the steel and coal industries. Historian Lachlan MacKinnon observes that "the collapse of industrial employment has opened the door to a more equitable social order."[36]

A corollary of Principle 1.1 is that humans should prioritize stewardship and conservation ahead of wealth generation. This challenges the logic of capital accumulation – a logic also challenged by the coal miners of past generations who viewed coal mines and mining jobs as community resources.[37] Enoch Williams, the Local 7295 secretary-treasurer, District 18 Executive Board member, and mayor of Blairmore who retired in 1951, eloquently expressed this idea in an interview in 1969:

> All of this here comes from the resources of the country, the resources of the world, and God, if there is a God, he never put it there for the benefit of a few. He put it there for the use of all of his people. At least, I'm simple enough to think that. And the only way we're ever going to get to the bottom is say, "NO, there's no more oil, fellow, and there's no more gold, there's no more copper, there's no nothing anymore – all things that's in the ground belongs to the people. And it's going to be not for profit, but for use for and by people."[38]

Both his view that "all things that's in the ground belongs to the people" and Principle 1.1 imply control of productive assets in the public interest. Principle 1.1 goes further than Williams' working-class socialism, however, by expanding the domain of "public interest" to include all living things – hence, it posits an eco-socialist philosophy.

On the question of public control of assets, however, two caveats are important. First, private pools of capital aimed at generating profits for owners could exist in an eco-socialist political economy as long as the owners work within the limits of a strong regulatory framework. Second, public ownership does not mean state ownership since an unsympathetic government can turn a nationalized company against workers and their communities, as happened in Britain in the 1980s "when the nationalised [coal] industry came to cast a dark shadow across the landscape and lives, undermining local government and democracy."[39] Alternative forms of public ownership (e.g., by cooperatives, municipalities, trusts, or First Nation enterprises) are preferable when they are based in the region, accountable to local residents, follow democratic procedures, and are constrained by legal checks and balances such as the rights of Aboriginal title. Public ownership is a means of preserving societal order, a way to limit the power and disruptive latitude of capitalist firms following market signals instead of the public interest.[40]

Just transitions for coal workers and communities (Principle 1.3) involve providing "meaningful alternative employment" for workers as coal mining winds down,[41] protecting communities from outsized de-population and creating a new regional identity.[42] In the Crowsnest Pass and Elk Valley, there will be a need for restoration, reclamation, and re-mediation (Principle 1.4) work for decades after the end of coal mining because of the scale of environmental destruction and degradation. Hence, there should be ample job opportunities in this field, not only for former coal workers remaining in the region but also for new recruits with specialized scientific or engineering skills. It will be the responsibil-ity of senior levels of government and the former operator(s) of mines to adequately fund this important work; their investments will provide a bridge for communities while a new sustainable economy is built and a new regional identity solidified.

The rough outline of a new regional identity can be seen in the first two principles. This identity will take root through widespread partici-pation in a grassroots Indigenous-environmental-labour-community movement committed to environmental stewardship and building a sustainable economy. A communitarian ethic underpins this movement, quite unlike the "possessive-individualism-inflected democratic partici-pation" that the Cape Breton Development Corporation tried to culti-vate for regional development in the 1970s.[43]

Principle 1.5 (connect to the history of labour struggles) recognizes the similarities between the late-1940s worker movement with a counter-hegemonic but pragmatic political mission (see Table C.1) and the counterhegemonic coalition of groups that could build a long-term, decolonized, sustainable future for the Crowsnest Pass and Elk Valley. Emphasizing these similarities will make it easier for local residents to feel pride in how a sustainable future after the end of coal mining builds upon the sacrifices and hopes of previous generations of mining families. This will be an application of historical interpretation unlike what is often seen in deindustrialized areas. For example, in his study of Minnesota's Iron Range, Jeffrey Manuel noted that "history became a vehicle for moving deindustrialization out of the realm of politics and into an apolitical realm of nostalgia." The "romanticized story of the Iron Range" that Manuel observed in museum displays "depoliticize[d] industrial change in northeastern Minnesota."[44] In contrast, connecting to the history of labour struggles in the Crowsnest Pass and Elk Valley will stress that the fight for a sustainable and decolonized future follows the same political path as miners' militant struggles for health and safety, economic advancement, workers' control, and universal social security.

Finally, relocalization (Principle 1.6) aims to "reduc[e] reliance on costly and environmentally damaging food chains ... while increasing sustainable agriculture and energy security and creating local jobs that cannot be outsourced."[45] Relocalization is a way to demonstrate a commitment to sustainability and resource conservation; it also creates new jobs and a larger regional market.

2. *Governance*

    2.1 Regional devolution of significant powers

    2.2 Regional government for southeastern British Columbia and southwestern Alberta

    2.3 Public engagement and democratic decision making

    2.4 Nested regional and community planning processes

In their recent study of two of Britain's former coalfields, Durham and South Wales, Huw Beynon and Ray Hudson document how "these two thoroughly industrialised and deeply politicised areas" had been transformed "into deindustrialised backwaters."[46] Both coalfields experienced "failed regeneration strategies" after mine closures. Beynon and Hudson argue that the major weaknesses in the regeneration efforts – a lack of resources, inadequate political determination, few opportunities for residents to have meaningful involvement, and "policy development characterized by official obfuscation and delay" – could have been overcome by a change in governance ("a much greater degree of devolution to Scotland, Wales and the regions of England") alongside a commitment by a national government to provide "the resources for change." They add that, "with a more devolved political structure within the UK, it would be easier for new forms of ownership to be encouraged and developed."[47]

A problem for the Crowsnest Pass and Elk Valley is the split provincial jurisdiction that creates disparities in policies and regulations and discourages regional cooperation. Regional devolution in this case will involve significant transfers of power from both British Columbia and Alberta to a unique regional government for southeastern British Columbia and southwestern Alberta (Governance 2.1 and 2.2). An obvious argument for such a devolution of political power is the shared interests of the people and communities on either side of the boundary. A second argument is the fact that the traditional territories of the Ktunaxa, Piikani, and Kainai flow across the boundary. A new regional government would allow the people of the region to better participate in shaping their own future and experiment with new approaches (Governance 2.3). It would also give them a louder voice in negotiations with senior levels of government for adequate strategic investments. Furthermore, participation by First Nations would add gravitas to the arguments of the regional government just as support from settler communities would give weight to Ktunaxa, Piikani, and Kainai assertions of the rights of Aboriginal title. The geographic range of any regional government will be a matter for discussion and democratic decision making. A larger geographic range encompassing more communities might be somewhat unwieldy but would have greater political weight and more opportunities for developing sustainable businesses. Finally, a regional government is not meant to displace the development initiatives of communities; its role would be to support communities while initiating distinctive regional initiatives (Governance 2.4).

The literature on deindustrialization indicates that public engagement is a common feature of successful efforts at rebuilding economies. A cross-national study of four shrinking mining cities recommended that planning "needs to embrace the public in a much more vigorous manner"; it not only gives residents "some control over their own destiny" but also can yield better planning solutions.[48] A comparison of the experiences of Youngstown, Ohio, and Allentown, Pennsylvania, after the closure of steel mills found that Youngstown "languished" because it failed "to establish the habit of civic collaboration with other elements of the community," thereby making "cooperation and innovation much more difficult when economic changes demanded it."[49]

3. Strategies

    3.1 Ensure that the wind-down of the coal industry does not compromise long-term goals

    3.2 Secure long-term funding for coal industry restoration, reclamation, remediation

    3.3 Identify and build upon regional and community assets

        3.3a. Conservation and wilderness economy

        3.3b. Heritage economy

        3.3c. Mountain sports and recreation

        3.3d. Sustainable logging

        3.3e. Renewable energy production (wind and solar)

        3.3f. Green hydrogen production from renewable energy

        3.3g. Land for sustainable agriculture

    3.4 Invest in infrastructure and cultural amenities

    3.5 Attract young people, working-age families, and retirees

Building a new sustainable economy in the Crowsnest Pass and Elk Valley will be impossible if coal mining is not wound down in a systematic fashion (Strategy 3.1) and a large sum (in the billions of dollars) is not set aside to address the legacy of environmental problems in this "sacrifice zone" of Canada's economy (Strategy 3.2). Beyond these necessary preliminary steps, the primary strategic task for rebuilding a deindustrialized economy is to identify regional and community strengths. In a book on small rust-belt cities in the United States, James Connolly states that "communities, experts agree, need to determine what assets they have – institutions, geographic advantages, unique amenities, clusters of businesses in a particular industry, and so forth – and build upon them" (Strategy 3.3).[50]

I have listed seven categories of assets (Strategies 3.3a–3.3g) to illustrate that the region has abundant sustainable assets upon which to build a diverse economy. Nothing in the list will come close to generating the tens of billions of dollars in profits secured by Teck Resources and earlier operators of mountaintop strip mines in the Elk Valley. However, the list promises the creation of sustainable and satisfying jobs that will create useful goods and services in line with Principle 1.1 (respect for all living things, environmental stewardship, sustainability) and Principle 1.2 (reconciliation, decolonization).

Perhaps the most outstanding asset is the only wilderness area remaining in southern Canada that has no permanent human settlement, the Flathead Valley, located in the southeastern corner of British Columbia and bordering both Waterton Lakes National Park in Alberta and Glacier National Park in Montana. The Flathead Valley is a prime candidate for an IPCA/national park reserve. It is notable that a similar idea was proposed in 1958 just after the closure of Elk River Colliery. James Lancaster, a long-time resident of Fernie, queried "why not ask for something big?" His "big ask" was for the establishment of a national park to the east and southeast of Fernie to the Alberta and Montana borders – a massive area that includes the Flathead Valley.[51] A new IPCA/national park reserve would enhance ecotourism and might well encourage the establishment of a permanent mountain ecology research centre.

One regional asset already the source of considerable economic activity is winter skiing and snowboarding. The Fernie Alpine Resort, whose origins in the 1960s I discussed in Chapters 2, 3, and 5, is known for its excellent powder skiing and attracts customers from around the world as well as those who live within driving distance. A second notable skiing/boarding area is Castle Mountain Resort, located in Alberta due south of the Crowsnest Pass and near the continental divide; it caters mainly to southern Alberta visitors. Unfortunately, as the climate warms in coming decades because of elevated levels of greenhouse gases in the atmosphere, these two resorts will face shortened seasons and declining business prospects.

Strategies 3.4 and 3.5 are complementary: investments in infrastructure and cultural amenities will aid in attracting new residents across a range of ages just as increasing the region's population base will make further investments in infrastructure and amenities possible. Prospective migrants include outdoor recreation enthusiasts and those who support the region's proposed political emphases on environmental stewardship and decolonization. The present-day ability of many employees to work remotely and the availability of reliable satellite internet make it much more feasible to attract those of working age as permanent residents. An ethos of sustainability should also appeal to a segment of retirees.

It is hoped that regional development beyond coal will protect land, water, air, and all living things; provide a wide variety of sustainable livelihoods, with jobs treated as a community resource; experiment with different forms of public ownership in order to enhance regional self-determination; embrace the rights of Aboriginal title held by the Ktunaxa, Piikani, and Kainai; and work toward reconciliation through ongoing political and economic dialogue in grassroots activism and democratic forums. This is a vision of a future in which Robert Lilley could have transitioned to new, meaningful work, his dignity intact, after the lights on the tipple were extinguished.

Acknowledgments

My historical research on the Crowsnest Pass and Elk Valley began in the mid-1990s, jumpstarted by a student's engaging undergraduate research study on "class consciousness and labour politics in Blairmore, Alberta, 1944–1953." That student, Chris Frazer, later worked as a research assistant with me on a project, "The Collapse of the Workers' Movement in the Crowsnest Pass: Shrinking Coal Orders, Cold War Politics, and Communist-C.C.F. Rivalry," supported by a University of Calgary Research Grant Committee Short-Term Grant. I learned a great deal from Chris's political acumen as we coauthored a conference paper that was subsequently revised for publication in *Labour/Le Travail* in 2002. Chris Frazer has gone on to bigger and better things (a Brown University Ph.D. and a professor's job in the history department at St. Francis Xavier University), but traces of Chris's excellent archival research and historical analysis can be found in the current manuscript, particularly Chapters 1 and 2.

My very first publication coming out of my newfound research interest in the Crowsnest Pass and Elk Valley, "'Workers of the World, Unite': Celebrating May Day," appeared in a local history collection in 1998. The book launch in Fernie, British Columbia, for *The Forgotten Side of the Border: British Columbia's Elk Valley and Crowsnest Pass* was memorable because I met for the first time several people who had the local historical knowledge and insights that would help to ground my developing research program, most notably Grace Arbuckle Dvorak, John Kinnear, and the collection's lead editor, Wayne Norton. *The Forgotten Side* was a runaway best seller (at least for a local history collection). This caused Wayne to envision a follow-up collection that would equally balance historical stories from the Alberta and British Columbia communities in the region. I was all on board when Wayne asked me to coedit the new collection, *A World Apart: The Crowsnest Communities of Alberta and British Columbia*, that appeared in 2002. My work on *A World Apart* deepened my knowledge of local historical sources and sensibilities and, to my extremely good fortune, established a strong working relationship and friendship with Wayne Norton that has continued to the present day. Wayne's enthusiasm for and commitment to rigorous research and writing on the history of the Elk Valley have inspired me over the past twenty-plus years. I also thank Wayne for a careful read of a close-to-final version of the book, important recommendations for additions to the photographic line-up, and helpful advice on the book's title.

Most of the research for this book happened in the archives listed in the bibliography and at microfilm readers in libraries where I could examine editions of the newspapers also listed in the bibliography. Fortunately, the main archival collections (originally located at the Glenbow Museum's Glenbow Library and Archives but later transferred to the Glenbow Western Research Centre at the University of Calgary) are close to my home; this allowed me to pick away at the research whenever my schedule allowed over many years. In addition, with research funds provided by the University of Calgary, at different points I was able to hire students to assist with the archival and library research in Calgary. I thank Louis Grenier, Krista McEwen, Rachel McKendry and Matt Godfrey for their conscientious and dedicated contributions.

I spent hundreds of hours in archives across Canada while researching this book. Invariably I was impressed by the knowledge of the archivists at each institution and their commitment to public service. I thank them all but reserve a special accolade for Doug Cass of Glenbow Library and Archives who ensured that union and company records were preserved from the era of underground coal mining in the Crowsnest Pass and Elk Valley. Doug retired in 2020 after an amazing forty-six-year career at the Glenbow. I also thank Terry Melcer, chief administrative officer of the District of Sparwood, 2010–18, for going out of her way to provide digital files of the historical records of the villages of Sparwood and Natal and the District of Sparwood, and to arrange my interview with Loretta Montemurro in 2013. For help in pulling together the photographs, I thank Chris Matthews, Michelle Cavanagh, and Christopher Fairman at Crowsnest Museum and Archives; Lindsay Vallance at Fernie Museum and Archives; Nadia Singleton at Glenbow Museum; Andrew Chernevych at Galt Museum and Archives | Akaisamitohkanao'pa; Allison Wagner at Archives and Special Collections, University of Calgary; and Kelly-Ann Turkington at Royal BC Museum.

Over the years, I discussed the research that appears in this book in two of the undergraduate courses I taught regularly at the University of Calgary: Worker Movements & Labour Unions, and Alberta Society. I thank the students who took these courses for their patience with my interminable references to the Crowsnest Pass and Elk Valley, and for their many questions and comments that sharpened my thinking. My colleagues at the University of Calgary, as well as colleagues at academic conferences, likewise endured quite a few presentations and conversations on different dimensions of the research. I thank them for their supportive engagement with my work.

It would be impossible to undertake an historical analysis like this one without a sense of how events from the mid-twentieth century are connected to the present. During a research leave in the fall of 2009, I rented the University of Lethbridge's Gushul Writer's Cottage in Blairmore, Alberta, and took the opportunity to learn more about the contemporary economy, society, and politics of the Crowsnest Pass and Elk Valley. Both during that residency and over the course of the ensuing decade, I learned a great deal about labour struggles and labour politics in the Elk Valley from Local 9346 of the United Steelworkers, the union for hourly employees at the large strip mine on a mountain ridge near Sparwood, BC. I thank in particular local president Chris Nand for being so candid in interviews conducted in 2009 and 2011; the Local 9346 executive of that era for granting me permission to copy issues of the local's newsletter published during Local 9346's early years (1993–2000); the many members of Local 9346 who patiently explained the ins and outs of the union's 67-day strike in the winter of 2011 during a visit to a picket line and the union office by one of my university classes; and the team of local president Alex Hanson and grievance/WCB chair Troy Cook who, during the 2012–18 era, not only graciously hosted occasional visits by my university classes and fielded all sorts of questions from me on the union's strategic plan and diverse initiatives, but also produced and hosted the phenomenal *Steel Megaphone* podcast that balanced entertaining banter, labour news, and leftist critiques on the issues of the day.

It was a pleasure working with UBC Press on this book. I thank two anonymous reviewers and the press's publication board for excellent guidance on how to strengthen the manuscript. I also thank acquisitions editor James MacNevin for expertly marshalling the manuscript through the peer-review and publication-grant processes; and the production staff who skillfully worked to bring everything together, notably production editor Meagan Dyer, copyeditor Dallas Harrison, and cartographer Eric Leinberger.

I have two messages for those interested in undertaking research on the Crowsnest Pass and Elk Valley. First, I expect to archive at the Glenbow Western Research Centre, University of Calgary, the original data I generated for this book (notably, digital recordings of interviews), the annotated timelines of events I constructed to aid historical analysis, and copies of my unpublished writing (including an early and more lengthy draft of this book). Second, some of the archival reference codes reported in this book are out of date because of new coding schemes recently introduced by the Glenbow Western Research Centre and Library and Archives Canada. If this makes it difficult to locate a document in one of these archives, please contact me (langford@ucalgary.ca) since I have paper or digital copies of almost every document I cite.

One unfortunate consequence of taking so long to complete this project is that some of those who were interested in reading the finished product died before publication. My book is dedicated to the memories of Eric Cameron, Troy Cook, Grace Arbuckle Dvorak, Barry Fowlie, Doug MacFarlane, Bob McDonald, Loretta Montemurro, Gillian Ranson, Alan Rimmer, Garth Turcott, Joan Turcott, and Beth Wiwchar, each a trailblazer in their own right.

Finally, I thank Evelyn McCallen for enduring yet another book project that consumed such a significant quotient of my time, attention, and brain power in recent years; her support was crucial to the peace-of-mind I needed to see the project to completion.

Notes

Introduction | INTERPRETIVE AND COMPARATIVE PERSPECTIVES ON
DEINDUSTRIALIZATION IN THE CROWSNEST PASS AND ELK VALLEY, 1945–68

1 Glenbow Western Research Centre (hereafter GWRC), M-6000, file 883, Local 7310 minutes, 12 December 1954.

2 Ibid., 3 November 1956; *Fernie Free Press*, 3 January 1957.

3 *Fernie Free Press*, 14 March 1957.

4 GWRC, M-6000, file 883, Local 7310 minutes, 16 November 1957.

5 I borrow this term from historian Steven High, "Deindustrialization," 279.

6 GWRC, M-6000, file Fernie 1962, memo by Edward Boyd, secretary-treasurer of District 18, 4 November 1957, on an inspection tour of the new mine.

7 GWRC, M-6000, file Fernie 1962, memo by William Ure, District 18 representative, 28 January 1958; *Fernie Free Press*, 16 January 1958; GWRC, M-6000, file 250, William C. Whittaker to Edward Boyd, 21 February 1958.

8 Maund, "Japanese Resource Procurement," 150.

9 GWRC, M-6000, file 681, Joseph Kary arbitration decision, 28 March 1958.

10 GWRC, F1844, District Executive Board (hereafter DEB) minutes, 11 April 1958

11 *Fernie Free Press*, 3 September 1959.

12 *Fernie Free Press*, 31 March and 2 June 1960; GWRC, M-6000, file Fernie 1959–62, Robert Lilley to William Ure, 14 and 27 May 1960; *Fernie Free Press*, 10 January 1963.

13 GWRC, M-6000, file 883, Local 7310 minutes, 23 June 1961.

14 *Fernie Free Press*, 21 May 1959 and 4 July 1963; GWRC, M-6000, file Fernie 1959–62, Edward Boyd to Fred Dawson, president of Local 7310, 11 October 1961.

15 *Fernie Free Press*, 4 July 1963.

16 Gibbs, *Coal Country*, 252.

17 *Fernie Free Press*, 11 July 1963.

18 Dublin and Licht, *Face of Decline*, 4.

19 Lucas, *Minetown, Milltown, Railtown*, 193.

20 For example, High and Lewis, *Corporate Wasteland*.

21 Brown and Webb, *Stranded Coal Towns*; CBC Citizens' Forum, "The Pass."

22 Waddington and Parry, "Managing Industrial Decline," A49.

23 Kirk, "Representing Identity," 195.

24 Linkon and Russo, *Steeltown U.S.A.*, 47, 53.

25 High, *Industrial Sunset*, 67.

26 High, MacKinnon, and Perchard, *Confronting Ruination*, 8.

27 Reid, *Decazeville*, 201–4.

28 Sears, *Next New Left*.

29 Featherstone, *Solidarity*, 55.

30 Harvey, "Militant Particularism," 91.

31 Franz, "An Affront"; Miles, "Is This a Soviet?"

32 Macintyre, *Little Moscows*; see also Knotter, "Revisited" and "Small-Place Communism."

33 Adams, "Tear Down a Mountain." Adjusting for inflation to 2022, Kaiser's capital investment was over $900 million.

34 Gunton, "Natural Resources." One of the strip mines was shut down by Teck Resources in 2019; see "Coal Mountain Mine."

35 *Globe and Mail*, 1 November 1983.

36 Finkel, "Cold War, Alberta Labour," 138.

37 See Ragin, *Constructing Social Research*, on these contrasting research strategies.

38 Berger, "Working-Class Culture," 8.

39 Woodrum, *Alabama Coalfields*, 85, 119 (statistics), 52–53 (quotation).

40 Ibid., 150, 158.

41 Ibid., 189.

42 Bowden, "Pan-Pacific Coal Trade," 7.

43 Bowden, "Heroic Failure," 7, 9.

44 Ibid., 8–9.

45 Dublin and Licht, *Face of Decline*, 23. Coal breakers are surface plants where hard anthracite is broken into different sizes.

46 Ibid., 203 (Table 3).

47 Ibid., 130–34.

48 Ibid., 88–90.

49 Bowden, "Heroic Failure," 7.

50 Reid, *Decazeville*, 193.

51 Ibid., 190–95.

52 Quoted in ibid., 195.

53 Ibid., 199, 208.

54 Ibid., 206–7.

55 Williams, *Democratic Rhondda*, 18–19.

56 Ibid., 19, 25–26. The Tower Colliery, the last underground coal mine in the Rhondda, and indeed in all of South Wales, finally closed in 2008 after workers had purchased the mine from British Coal in 1994 and successfully operated it until the coal ran out. See "Coal Mine Closes."

57 Macintyre, *Little Moscows.*
58 Cooke, "Radical Regions," 38.
59 Berger, "Working-Class Culture," 20–22.
60 Ibid., 21.
61 Davies, *Best of Rhys Davies*, 100–9.
62 Berry, *Flame and Slag*, 106.
63 Davies, "The Last Struggle."
64 Quoted in Smith, *Aneurin Bevan*, 90.
65 Berger, "Working-Class Culture," 18.
66 Knight, "Rhys Davies's Fiction," 60.
67 Ibid., 61.
68 Williams, "Welsh Industrial Novel," 222–23.
69 Nisbet, *Mapmaker's Eye.*
70 MacPherson, "Ktunaxa History," 12–13, 56–57, 85.
71 Whitney, "Preface," xi.
72 Hildebrandt, "Treaty 7," 198.
73 McIvor, *Standoff*, 160.
74 Taylor, "Capitalist Development," 162–63.
75 Crowshoe and Manneschmidt, *Akak'stiman*, 9–11; Harris, *Making Native Space*, 191.
76 Dempsey, *Red Crow*, 82–92.
77 MacPherson, "Ktunaxa History," 89.
78 Ibid., 42–46.
79 Harris, *Making Native Space*, 210. The fourth Ktunaxa reserve, Yaqan Nukiy, just south of Creston, was established in the early 1900s (222).
80 Lutz, *Makúk*, 279, 284, 307.
81 Ibid., 287, 305.
82 Regular, *Neighbours and Networks*, 71–102.
83 See Narine, "Blood Member."
84 Hawthorn, Belshaw, and Jamieson, *Indians of British Columbia*, 148–50.
85 Ibid., 148, 135.
86 MacPherson, "Ktunaxa History," 83.
87 Hoffmann, Van Hoey, and Zeumer, "Decarbonization Challenge for Steel."
88 See "Dofasco"; Province of Ontario, "Province Invests in Clean Steelmaking."
89 Blank, "Green Steel"; Riley, "Cutting Out Coal."
90 *Edmonton Journal*, 2 March 1960.

Chapter 1 | THE WORKING CLASS ON THE RISE

1 *Fernie Free Press*, 12 April 1945; *Coleman Journal*, 12 April 1945.
2 Carroll, Morrison, and McLaurin, "Report," 296.

3   *Calgary Albertan*, 3 April 1945; GWRC, M-1601, file 2169, WCBCOA Brief to the Royal Commission on Coal, Calgary Sittings, 3–7 April 1945.

4   Carroll, Morrison, and McLaurin, "Report," 579.

5   Richards and Pratt, *Prairie Capitalism*, 43–46, 159–62.

6   *Coleman Journal*, 18 April 1946.

7   Alinsky, *John L. Lewis*, 35.

8   Black and Silver, *Building a Better World*, 58.

9   Cousins, *Crow's Nest Pass*, 120, estimated that "there were between one hundred and one hundred and fifty men on military service from each town during this period."

10   Ibid.

11   Carroll, Morrison, and McLaurin, "Report," 540; *Coleman Journal*, 2 November 1944 and 7 June 1945. The emergency order also "reduced the age of employment in coal mines to 16 years for males, and permitted the employment of females 18 years of age or more in surface work in the Alberta mines"; Carroll, Morrison, and McLaurin, "Report," 548. There is no evidence of women being hired in production jobs at the mines in the region during the war. Because of the general shortage of male labourers, however, women were recruited for other nontraditional jobs such as bringing in the hay crops on local farms (as told to me by a leader of the Michel-Natal-Sparwood Heritage Society).

12   Ibid., 541.

13   GWRC, M-1601, file 571, WCC, "Labour Situation" report, 19 November 1945.

14   Cousins, *Crow's Nest Pass*, 135. These figures include supervisory staff. In 1945, the number of working UMWA members at the five Crowsnest Pass and Elk Valley locals was 2,618; see GWRC, M-6000, file 616, "Per Capita Tax Received, 26 November 1945."

15   GWRC, M-1601, file 571, WCC, "Labour Situation" report, 4 September 1948.

16   Crowsnest Pass Historical Society, *Crowsnest ... Millennium Ed.*, 248–51.

17   GWRC, M-1601, file 571, WCC, "Labour Situation" report, 6 December 1947; *CJ*, 27 March 1947.

18   GWRC, M-1601, file 571, WCC, "Labour Situation" report, 6 November 1947. For the ten years ending in 1945, the number of fatalities per million man hours worked was 36 percent higher in Alberta coal mines than in Nova Scotia coal mines. See Carroll, Morrison, and McLaurin, "Report," 296; *Coleman Journal*, 4 November 1948.

19   GWRC, M-1601, file 571, WCC, "Labour Situation" report, 7 October 1948.

20   Cousins, *Crow's Nest Pass*, 107.

21   Crowsnest Pass Historical Society, *Crowsnest ... Millennium Ed.*, 260; Library and Archives Canada (hereafter LAC), RG 33/42, vol. 18, file Alberta Bituminous Coal, chart "Alberta Bituminous Coal Production by Colliery and District."

22 GWRC, M-1601, file 571, WCC, "Labour Situation" report, 20 May 1946; LAC, RG 33/42, vol. 18, file Alberta Bituminous Coal, chart "Alberta Bituminous Coal Production by Colliery and District"; GWRC, M-1601, file 569, WCC, "Other Mines" report, 12 November 1946; GWRC, M-6000, file 234, "Memorandum Joint Conference," 3 May 1948 (lists the WCC surface operations).

23 *Fernie Free Press*, 28 July 1949; *Coleman Journal*, 20 January 1949.

24 LAC, RG 81, vol. 75, file 58-1-5-1, District 18 contract demands to WCBCOA, 23 December 1947; GWRC, M-6048, file 2, Local 2633 minutes, 10 October 1948. The collective agreement in effect in 1948 had a more limited prohibition: stripping operations could not work a sixth day in a week unless the underground operations had worked five days that week.

25 *Coleman Journal*, 6 November 1947.

26 Cousins, *Crow's Nest History*, 104, 106–7; GWRC, M-1601, file 569, WCC, "Other Mines" report, 12 November 1946; *Coleman Journal*, 10 March 1949; GWRC, M-6000, file 234, union-management joint conference on the pay rate for miners operating a mechanical loader in the York Creek mine, 27 November 1948.

27 Carroll, Morrison, and McLaurin, "Report," 533–34.

28 Seager, "Proletariat in Wild Rose," 471–72.

29 GWRC, M-1601, file 2169, WCBCOA Brief to the Royal Commission on Coal, Calgary Sittings, 3–7 April 1945.

30 Alinsky, *John L. Lewis*, 282–321.

31 GWRC, M-6000, file 616, "Unauthorized Strikes in District 18, UMWA – During Last Three Years," 23 October 1945.

32 Seager, "Proletariat in Wild Rose," 478.

33 Ibid., 479–80.

34 GWRC, M-6000, file 899, DEB minutes, 5 and 6 November 1943.

35 Seager, "Proletariat in Wild Rose," 481.

36 Carroll, Morrison, and McLaurin, "Report," 549.

37 GWRC, M-6000, file 199, WCBCOA brief to a board of arbitration, 2 February 1948.

38 LAC, RG 81, vol. 45, file 58-1-5-1, response to District 18 contract proposals by the WCBCOA, 17 August 1946; *Coleman Journal*, 19 September and 24 October 1946.

39 Dubofsky and Van Tine, *Lewis Abridged*, 332; Mulcahy, "Welfare and Retirement," 21.

40 GWRC, M-6000, file 899, DEB minutes, 3 August 1946; *Blairmore Graphic*, 9 August 1946.

41 *Blairmore Graphic*, 11 October 1946.

42 In beginning its strike in this precipitous fashion, District 18 ignored the rules governing strikes found in Alberta labour law, an option available because the district

had never bothered to certify its union locals with the province. From the outset, the provincial government stated that the strike was illegal (*Calgary Albertan*, 14 January 1948), but it never attempted to legally enforce this opinion.

43 LAC, RG 81, vol. 75, file 58-1-5-1.2, Notice of Termination of Agreement, 29 August 1947; *Labour Gazette*, January–February 1948, 58–59, Submission of WCBCOA, 2 February 1948; *Calgary Albertan*, 9 February 1948; *Calgary Herald*, 9 February 1948; *Blairmore Graphic*, 20 February 1948.

44 GWRC, M-6000, file 197, "Results of Ballot on New Agreement," 23 February 1948.

45 CNPC signed an initial contract with the UMWA locals at its mines in 1905; see GWRC, M-6000, file 663, arbitration award by L.R. Lipsett, 20 August 1945.

46 GWRC, M-6000, file 616, "Unauthorized Strikes in District 18, UMWA – During Last Three Years," 23 October 1945.

47 GWRC, M-6000, file 899, DEB minutes, 8–9 October 1945; *Coleman Journal*, 17 January 1946; GWRC, M-6000, file 616, "Data re Stoppage of Work in Protest of Inadequate Meat Ration," 22 October 1945.

48 GWRC, M-1601, file 571, WCC, "Labour Situation" report, 9 December 1946.

49 LAC, RG 81, vol. 45, file 58-1-5-1, response to District 18 contract proposals by the WCBCOA, 17 August 1946.

50 GWRC, M-6000, file 616, letter to the membership on unauthorized strikes, 8 November 1945.

51 GWRC, M-2239, file 137, Agreement between District No. 18, UMWA, and the WCBCOA, 1 October 1946–31 March 1948. A final draft of the language added to the contract is found in GWRC, M-6000, file 230, page dated 27 September 1946.

52 GWRC, M-6000, file 624, joint negotiating conference, 8 January 1952.

53 GWRC, M-6000, file Susnar 1946–48, DEB minutes, 11–14 November 1946.

54 GWRC, M-6000, file 317b, "Memorandum of Joint Conference Held in the Office of the Hillcrest Mohawk Collieries Ltd., Bellevue, 28 July 1949."

55 GWRC, M-6000, file 234, "Memorandum on Conference," 3 May 1948.

56 GWRC, M-6000, file 686, an index to the grievance arbitration cases in District 18 between 1946 and 1963 that includes eighteen cases from Crowsnest Pass and Elk Valley mines for 1946 to 1949. The records of seven additional grievance arbitration decisions in 1945 are found in GWRC, M-6000, file 663 (six cases) and file 542 (one case).

57 GWRC, M-2239, file 137, Agreement between District No. 18, UMWA, and the WCBCOA, 1 October 1946–31 March 1948.

58 GWRC, M-1601, file 1374, arbitrator John W. Hugill's decision for the case heard on 5 May 1949. One of the discharged workers was Isaac Rae, then seventy years of age, whose daughter Isobel was married to Communist Party labour organizer Harvey Murphy (see Text Box 4.1).

59 GWRC, M-6000, file 592, District 18 brief on compensation cases, 6 November

1944. Farmilo was a long-time member of the executive of the Alberta Federation of Labour (AFL) when appointed to the Workmen's Compensation Board; he served concurrently as a WCB commissioner and an AFL executive between 1941 and 1944; see Finkel, *Social Credit Phenomenon*, 78. At that point, the AFL included only craft unions and was affiliated with the Trades and Labour Congress (TLC). In contrast, industrial unions such as the UMWA were affiliated with the Canadian Congress of Labour (CCL).

60 *Edmonton Journal*, 15 February 1945.

61 Devine, "Equitable and Sympathetic," 60.

62 GWRC, M-6000, file Susnar, 1946–48, letter of 18 June 1946 on the plan to strike on 26 June. The Blairmore detachment of the RCMP recorded the number of persons involved in the strike in Coleman, Blairmore, and Bellevue as 2,507 and answered "no" to the question "any communistic influences ascertainable?" LAC, RG 27, volume 448, microfilm reel T-4081, file 122, Department of Labour strike and lockout file: "Coal Miners - Bellevue, Coleman, Blairmore, Alberta."

63 Devine, "Equitable and Sympathetic," 60.

64 Alberta, Chief Electoral Officer, *Alberta Elections*, 14.

65 See the biographical sketch produced by the Provincial Archives of Alberta, "Alfred Farmilo Fonds."; and Devine, "Equitable and Sympathetic," 61.

66 *Blairmore Examiner*, 22 March 1946.

67 *Fernie Free Press*, 12 July 1945.

68 Crowsnest Pass Historical Society, *Crowsnest and Its People*, 760; Seager, "Proletariat in Wild Rose," 139n117.

69 Franz, "An Affront."

70 *Lethbridge Herald*, 28 August 1949.

71 *Coleman Journal*, 8 April 1948.

72 Norton, "Trusteeship," 144; *Fernie Free Press*, 30 May and 25 July 1946.

73 Langford and Frazer, "Cold War," 62–63.

74 Ibid., 69.

75 *Fernie Free Press*, 28 April 1949.

76 Langford, "Alternate Vision," 154; *Fernie Free Press*, 26 December 1946.

77 *Coleman Journal*, 19 December 1946. A major fire destroyed the hall in 1948; see *Coleman Journal*, 26 February 1948.

78 *Coleman Journal*, 2 March 1944, 22 June 1944, and 13 March 1947; Crowsnest Pass Historical Society, *Crowsnest ... Millennium Ed.*, 79.

79 Crowsnest Pass Historical Society, *Crowsnest ... Millennium Ed.*, 80–81.

80 See *Coleman Journal*, 2 July 1952, for an advertisement for "hospital contracts for resident non-ratepayers."

81 *Fernie Free Press*, 9 May 1957. Among the thirteen directors on the Fernie Memorial Hospital Board in 1959 were three prominent labour leaders; see *Fernie Free Press*, 14 May 1959.

82 Monod, "End of Agrarianism."

83 GWRC, M-6048, file 8, Sub-District 5 documents 1946–54, minutes of Sub-District 5 board meeting, 17 September 1946. There is no record of whether this support broadcast was aired before the strike ended on 6 October 1946.

84 GWRC, M-6048, file 2, Local 2633 minutes, 13 March 1947; *Fernie Free Press*, 10 October 1946.

85 LAC, MG 28-I103, vol. 33, file 33-4, Enoch Williams to Pat Conroy, 8 December 1948.

86 See Langford, "Alternate Vision" and "Union Democracy."

87 Dublin and Licht, *Face of Decline*, 107.

88 Zajicek and Nash, "Lessons," 223.

89 GWRC, M-6048, file 2, Local 2633 minutes, 14 March 1948.

90 GWRC, M-6000, file 899, DEB minutes, 22–24 April 1948.

91 LAC, MG 28-I103, vol. 33, file 33-6, A.J. Morrison to Pat Conroy, 5 February 1944.

92 LAC, RG 145, vol. 13, file 751:103:44, contract between Western Canada Firebosses Association, District Number 1, and the five Crowsnest Pass coal companies.

93 Relations between fire bosses and miners were strained prior to the strike in 1950, and as a result most miners refused to honour fire bosses' picket lines. This caused the strike to collapse and quickly led to the destruction of the fire bosses' union at the Alberta mines in the Crowsnest Pass. *Calgary Albertan*, 4 March 1950; GWRC, M-1601, file 864, William Bird to Jean Albert Brusset, 4 and 6 March 1950.

94 Cousins, *Crow's Nest Pass*, 122.

95 *Coleman Journal*, 10 November 1948; *Blairmore Graphic*, 12 November 1948 [mistakenly listed as 29 October 1948].

96 *Coleman Journal*, 8 April 1948.

97 LAC, RG 27, volume 473, microfilm reel number T-4101, file 36, Department of Labour strike and lockout file: "Sawmill Workers – Blairmore, Alberta."

98 *Coleman Journal*, 27 January 1949; *Fernie Free Press* story reprinted in *Coleman Journal*, 3 February 1949; *Calgary Herald* story cited in *Coleman Journal*, 28 April 1949.

99 LAC, RG 81, vol. 75, file 58-1-5-1, WCBCOA submissions, 6 January and 17 January 1949.

100 *Coleman Journal*, 24 February 1949.

101 GWRC, M-6048, file 2, Local 2633 minutes, 12 June 1949.

102 GWRC, M-1601, file 571, WCC, "Labour Situation" report, 27 June 1949.

Chapter 2 | A CRISIS BEGINS

1 *Coleman Journal*, 24 and 31 March 1954.

2 *Michel-Natal Spectator*, 2 April and 15 October 1954; GWRC, M-1601, file 571, WCC, "Labour Situation" report, 8 March 1954.

3 GWRC, M-1601, file 1361, Wage Negotiations 1954–60; copy of *The Lamp* 5, no. 2 (May 1955), 4.

4 I am unaware of any evidence sustaining the "dumping" assertion. Rather, favourable mining conditions, mechanization of production, and proximity to markets accounted for American coal imports being much less expensive in Ontario than coal from the Crowsnest Pass and Elk Valley.

5 Cousins, *Crow's Nest History*, 120.

6 Ibid., 123. However, some new houses were being built in Sparwood, a "fully serviced" subdivision that CNPC had created so that its employees (especially management and supervisory staff) could live at some remove from coal production facilities; see *Coleman Journal*, 29 May 1947.

7 *Coleman Journal*, 20 January 1949.

8 Cousins, *Crow's Nest History*, 123.

9 *Fernie Press Press*, 30 January 1964.

10 Cousins, *Crow's Nest History*, 115.

11 Ibid., 117.

12 Dvorak, "Childhood Remembered," 189.

13 Cousins, *Crow's Nest History*, 116.

14 Ibid., 118.

15 Alberta Labour History Institute (hereafter ALHI), group interviews in Coleman, including Pauline Griegel, 10 November 2005, 2–3, and Liz and Steve Liska, 9 November 2005.

16 Cousins, *Crow's Nest History*, 117–18.

17 Hawthorn, Belshaw, and Jamieson, *The Indians of British Columbia*, 136.

18 "Indian Chiefs to Be Honored" was one of the few stories that acknowledged the presence of Indigenous peoples. It reported on how "leading chiefs of the major Indian tribes in Alberta," as well as "all Alberta treaty Indians who were born during or prior to 1905," would be presented with medallions as part of the province's fiftieth-anniversary celebrations; see *Coleman Journal*, 6 July 1955.

19 Robertson, *Imagining Difference*, 166–67.

20 Despite the absence of Ktunaxa, Piikani, and Kainai from the employment rolls of coal mines, it is possible that other Indigenous peoples had migrated to the region by the 1950s and secured work in the mines without ever announcing their Indigenous ancestry. A student of mine offered this conjecture after reviewing a list of the names of miners killed in Elk Valley mine disasters and noting that several of the surnames are common among Manitoba Métis.

21 Interview with a former resident of the Crowsnest Pass, 26 October 2001.

22 Gill, "Story and Stereotype," 21.

23 This assertion is supported by data from the Census of the Prairie Provinces 1936, "Alberta Table 34," 976, 978. Of a population of 4,069 in Blairmore, Coleman, and Frank, 60 people were counted as "Asiatic Races," 0 were counted as "Indian," and

1 was slotted in the category "Others and Not Stated." The remainder were almost evenly divided between "British Races" (1,952) and "European Races" (2,056).

24 This failure has endured. In 2004, after having worked as a high school English teacher in the Crowsnest Pass for almost three decades, Gill, "Story and Stereotype," 20–21, noted that "my loyalty to the Pass causes me to want to paint it as a place where different ethnicities grew to forget their differences and form a strong community. When I hear the racist attitudes of some of my students, I am ashamed that they could grow up in this community and value other human beings so little."

25 *Coleman Journal*, 11 December 1947.

26 Norton, "Music and Musicians."

27 Cousins, *Crow's Nest History*, 1.

28 *Coleman Journal*, 23 October 1947; GWRC, M-6000, file 883, Local 7310 minutes, 19 February 1956.

29 *Coleman Journal*, 3 April 1947; GWRC, C0059, Tape IT0106, Alrik Tiberg interview, 13 April 1980.

30 Cousins, *Crow's Nest History*, 122.

31 GWRC, M-6000, file 223, Edward Boyd memo to convention delegates, 2 April 1956; GWRC, M-6000, file 392, "Summary of Operations [of the Welfare and Retirement Fund] from Inception to August 31, 1970." The criteria to qualify for a pension are specified on the application form; see GWRC, M-6047, file 261.

32 *Coleman Journal*, 6 March 1956.

33 GWRC, M-6000, file 899, DEB minutes, 8–9 December 1955; GWRC, M-6000, file 392, Welfare and Retirement Fund, "Summary of Operations from Inception to August 31, 1970."

34 In April 1954, working miners in the Crowsnest Pass and Elk Valley constituted approximately 40 percent of all working miners in the twenty-nine UMWA locals in District 18; see GWRC, M-6000, file 228, average membership of locals in District 18, 5 April 1954.

35 GWRC, M-1601, file 571, WCC, "Labour Situation" report, 2 June 1953.

36 *Calgary Herald*, 10 October 1957.

37 GWRC, M-6048, file 8, Sub-District 5 documents 1946–54, minutes of Sub-District 5 board meeting, 24 September 1951.

38 GWRC, M-1601, file 571, WCC, "Labour Situation" report, 10 September 1953.

39 *Coleman Journal*, 2 December 1953 and 26 May 1954.

40 GWRC, M-6000, file 624, coal operator – District 18 negotiation conference.

41 Cousins, *Crow's Nest History*, 129.

42 Provincial Archives of Alberta (hereafter PAA), Manning, file 1659, BC Minister of Mines R.C. MacDonald to Alberta Minister of Mines and Minerals N.E. Tanner, 19 March 1951.

43 LAC, RG 33/42, vol. 18, file Alberta Bituminous Coal, chart "Alberta Bituminous Coal Production by Colliery and District."

44 GWRC, M-1601, file 569, WCC, "Other Mines" report, 10 September 1951; GWRC, M-1601, file 571, WCC, "Labour Situation" report, 30 November 1951; GWRC, M-1601, file 1161, WCBCOA special meeting minutes, 2 October 1951; *Coleman Journal*, 14 October 1953 (reprint of a *Star Weekly* story).

45 *Coleman Journal*, 17 March 1954. English's slogan was not original: "Put Canada First" was promulgated at the fifth national LPP convention in March 1954; see Penner, *Canadian Communism*, 232–33; GWRC, M-6048, file 2, Local 2633 minutes, 23 March 1952.

46 *Fernie Free Press*, 21 September 1957.

47 *Globe and Mail*, 3 December 1951; *Coleman Journal*, 16 January 1952.

48 GWRC, M-6048, file 3, Local 2633 minutes, 8 November 1953.

49 Reprinted in *Coleman Journal*, 14 October 1953.

50 *Fernie Free Press*, 21 August 1969. Employment numbers for 1965 are found in a report on a strike by Michel Local 7292; see LAC, RG 27, microfilm reel T-3414, file 6, Department of Labour strike and lockout file: "Crow's Nest Pass Coal – Michel and Fernie, British Columbia."

51 GWRC, M-1601, file 1233, Jean Albert Brusset to Charles A. Dunning, Ogilvie Flour Mills, 18 October 1952.

52 In the mid-1950s, LPP leaders (e.g., *Michel-Natal Spectator*, 18 December 1953) as well as IFL leaders (GWRC, M-6048, file 3, Local 2633 minutes, 28 November 1954) also called for the development of a steel industry.

53 *Coleman Journal*, 23 March and 26 October 1955; PAA, Manning, file 1812, "Progress Report, Crowsnest Pass," attached to John Ferguson's memo to Deputy Minister J.E. (Jack) Oberholtzer, 20 September 1955.

54 *Coleman Journal*, 18 January 1956; *Calgary Herald*, 28 March 1956; *Coleman Journal*, 27 June 1956.

55 *Coleman Journal*, 14 November 1956 (citing the *Calgary Albertan* story of 12 November 1956).

56 *Michel-Natal Spectator*, 22 January 1954; *Coleman Journal*, 20 January 1954 (reprinting a *Calgary Herald* story).

57 The coal companies in the Crowsnest Pass and Elk Valley were members of the WCBCOA up to the fall of 1952. At that time, it amalgamated with the Domestic Coal Operators' Association of Western Canada (hereafter DCOAWC) to form the COAWC; see *Coleman Journal*, 5 November 1952.

58 *Coleman Journal*, 3 October 1956.

59 Crowsnest Pass Historical Society, *Crowsnest and Its People*, 243–44.

60 *Coleman Journal*, 5 November 1952.

61 Swankey, "Alberta People"; PAA, Manning, file 1628, T.A. Collister, Secretary-

Treasurer of Coleman, to Premier Manning, 17 January 1951, and Manning's reply, 1 February 1951; *Calgary Herald*, 14 November 1951.

62 LAC, RG 81, vol. 75, file 58-1-5-1.2, William C. Whittaker's report on the founding of the Western Coal Federation; GWRC, M-1601, file 1161, William C. Whittaker's report to the annual meeting of the WCBCOA, 9 January 1951; minutes of WCBCOA meeting, 17 May 1951; and minutes of joint meetings of representatives of District 18, WCBCOA, and DCOAWC, 7 and 8 June 1951.

63 GWRC, M-1601, file 1161, minutes of WCBCOA meeting, 17 May 1951.

64 *Calgary Herald*, 3 April 1954 (Prowse); *Edmonton Journal*, 12 March 1953 (Roper); *Coleman Journal*, 22 June 1955 (Swankey).

65 After immigrating to Canada from Britain in 1952, Collins worked for mainstream media outlets for many years. Later in life, he became known for anti-immigrant and racist columns in the Vancouver-area *North Shore News*. Robert Fulford wrote of Collins in the *National Post* on 3 November 2001 that, "if he was not a Holocaust denier, he was certainly a Holocaust trivializer." These elements of his ideology were not evident in his series on the coal crisis.

66 Reprinted in the *Coleman Journal*, 28 October 1953.

67 LAC, RG 81, vol. 12, file 4-2-15.2, Order-in-Council PC 1953–64; LAC, MG 28-I103, vol. 33, file 33-5, Chris Pattinson, "Crisis in Western Coal Industry," unsourced and undated [approx. 1950–51] newspaper story; *Coleman Journal*, 15 September 1954.

68 GWRC, M-1601, file 1144, details on the vote to renew the contract supported by all five union locals in the Crowsnest Pass and Elk Valley. Livett's comment is quoted in the *Coleman Journal*, 2 June 1954. The *Lethbridge Herald* story was reprinted in the *Coleman Journal*, 6 January 1955.

69 Azzi, *Walter Gordon*.

70 GWRC, M-6000, file 285, report attached to a letter addressed to the prime minister and his cabinet, signed by Robert Livett and Edward Boyd of District 18, 22 November 1954.

71 *Coleman Journal*, 8 December 1954; LAC, RG 33/42, vol. 28, file DCB ..., "Total Monies Spent by the Federal Government in Support of and in Assistance to the Canadian Coal Industry."

72 GWRC, M-6000, file 524, COAWC contract requests, 15 January 1953, and "Memorandum Showing Total Vote on Agreement – 1953"; file 194, 8 June 1953 memo on the 29 May 1953 contract ratification vote in District 18; file 762, Edward Boyd to John L. Lewis, 20 July 1953.

73 GWRC, M-6048, file 3, Local 2633 minutes, 21 June 1953.

74 GWRC, M-6048, file 8, minutes of Sub-District 5 board meeting, 31 January 1954; *Coleman Journal*, 17 March 1954; GWRC, M-6000, file 899, DEB minutes, 3–4 December 1953.

75 *Coleman Journal*, 17 and 24 March 1954; GWRC, M-6000, file 730, John Ferguson to J.E. (Jack) Oberholtzer, "Re: Unemployed Coal Miners, Coleman, Alberta," 6 May 1954.

76 GWRC, M-1601, file 1161, minutes of WCBCOA meeting, 17 January 1950.

77 GWRC, M-6048, file 3, Local 2633 minutes, 25 March 1954; *Coleman Journal*, 31 March 1954; GWRC, M-1601, file 1350, "Private Report to Mr. W. Bird on Union Meeting at Coleman – March 25, 1954."

78 GWRC, M-6048, file 3, Local 2633 minutes, 25 March 1954.

79 LAC, RG 33/42, vol. 19, file Alberta – Miners Rehabilitation, "Miners Rehabilitation Alberta," approximately June 1955.

80 *Coleman Journal*, 7 April 1954.

81 PAA, Manning, file 1625, "CONFIDENTIAL – Directive to Miners' Rehabilitation Committee," 15 April 1954; GWRC, M-6000, file 730, John Ferguson to J.E. (Jack) Oberholtzer, "Re: Unemployed Coal Miners, Coleman, Alberta," 6 May 1954.

82 GWRC, M-6048, file 8, Sub-District 5 board meeting, 17 April 1954; GWRC, M-6048, file 3, Local 2633 minutes, 25 April 1954.

83 *Fernie Free Press*, 6 May 1954.

84 PAA, Manning, file 1812, memo from John Ferguson to J.E. Oberholtzer, 13 July 1954.

85 *Coleman Journal*, 19 May 1954; GWRC, M-6048, file 3, Local 2633 minutes, 30 May 1954. Opposition to the employment of married women would also be voiced in Fernie in 1964 (see Chapter 5). These incidents suggest that the gender order in the Crowsnest Pass and Elk Valley in the 1950s and 1960s was every bit as patriarchal as the gender orders in other prominent coalfield societies (see the introduction).

86 PAA, Manning, file 1812, John Ferguson report on the Miners' Rehabilitation Committee, 21 February 1955.

87 Crowsnest Pass Historical Society, *Crowsnest and Its People*, 737–39; GWRC, M-6000, file 730, John Ferguson to Owen Distributing of Lethbridge, authorizing the move, 16 August 1954.

88 GWRC, M-6000, file 296, F.J. Lote, Blairmore National Employment Service (hereafter NES) office, to John Stokaluk, 17 June 1955.

89 GWRC, M-6000, file 730, John Ferguson to J.E. Oberholtzer, "Re: Unemployed Coal Miners, Coleman, Alberta," 6 May 1954; LAC, RG 33/42, vol. 19, file Alberta – Miners Rehabilitation, "Miners Rehabilitation Alberta," approximately June 1955.

90 GWRC, M-6000, file 296, F.J. Lote, Blairmore NES office, to John Stokaluk, 17 June 1955; PAA, Manning, file 1812, "Progress Report, Crowsnest Pass," attached to John Ferguson's memo to Deputy Minister J.E. Oberholtzer, 20 September 1955.

91 *Coleman Journal*, 26 May 1954.

92 LAC, RG 33/42, vol. 19, file Alberta – Miners Rehabilitation, "Miners Rehabilitation Alberta," approximately June 1955; obituary for Joseph Peter Robutka, *Lethbridge Herald*, 9 February 1980.

93 GWRC, M-6000, file 253, meeting of the Crowsnest Pass Special Seasonal Unemployment Committee, 4 May 1955.

94 *Coleman Journal*, 15 June 1955.

95 GWRC, M-6000, file 253, meeting of the Crowsnest Pass Special Seasonal Unemployment Committee, 4 July 1955; PAA, Manning, file 1812, "Progress Report, Crowsnest Pass," attached to John Ferguson's memo to Deputy Minister J.E. Oberholtzer, 20 September 1955; PAA, Manning, file 1812, John Ferguson to J.E. Oberholtzer, 23 September 1955, and F.J. Lote to John Ferguson, 24 November 1955; GWRC, M-6000, file 253, John Ferguson to District 18, "Re: Miners' Rehabilitation Committee," 28 February 1959.

96 Dubofsky and Van Tine, *Lewis Abridged*, 356–58.

97 *Coleman Journal*, 11 July 1956.

98 GWRC, M-6048, file 8, minutes of Sub-District 5 board meetings, 12 August and 18 September 1952.

99 GWRC, M-6000, file 816, statement on unauthorized strikes, UMWA, 24 October 1951; GWRC, M-6000, file 524. COAWC contract demands to District 18, 15 January 1953.

100 Fudge and Tucker, *Labour before the Law*, 228–301.

101 Quoted in Langford, "Coal Miners' Resistance," 237.

102 LAC, RG 27, microfilm reel T-4130, file 130, Department of Labour strike and lockout file: "Crow's Nest Pass Coal Co. Ltd. – Michel, BC."; *Michel-Natal Spectator*, 22 October 1954; GWRC, M-6000, file 762, Robert Livett to John L. Lewis, 22 October 1954; *Calgary Herald*, 25 and 26 October 1954.

103 From an undated *Calgary Herald* story, likely April 1955, found in the RG 27 materials on the strike.

104 GWRC, M-6000, file 18, Correspondence with International Headquarters, letter to Sim Weaver, Local 7292 secretary, 10 May 1955, on the decision of the International Commission as approved by the International Executive Board, 3 May 1955.

105 Langford, "Coal Miners' Resistance," 239.

106 Ibid.

107 GWRC, M-6048, file 8, Michel Local 7292 circular letter, 8 March 1954; GWRC, M-6048, file 3, Local 2633 minutes, 28 February 1954; GWRC, M-6000, file 815, Robert Livett to John L. Lewis, 19 April 1954.

108 GWRC, M-6000, file 251, Edward Boyd letter to sixteen coal companies, 5 May 1954.

109 GWRC, M-6000, file 656, "Personal and Confidential Ancillary Instructions to Executives and Field Representatives Implementing Declaration of Policy by the International Executive Board," 17 May 1956.

110 GWRC, M-6048, file 3, Local 2633 minutes, 10, 24, and 31 January, 14 February 1954.

111 GWRC, M-6048, file 3, Local 2633 minutes, 13 June 1954; 27 February and 31 July 1955; 29 January 1956.

112 GWRC, M-6000, file 762, Robert Livett to John L. Lewis, 10 June 1953; GWRC, M-2239, file 43, "Proceedings of Special District Convention, April 5th, 1954– April 9th, 1954," Resolution 206.

113 GWRC, M-6000, file 899, DEB minutes, 16 March 1955; GWRC, M-1601, file 1361, Wage Negotiations 1954–60; copy of *The Lamp*, 5, no. 2 (May 1955), 3.

114 GWRC, M-6048, file 3, Local 2633 minutes, 17 April 1955; GWRC, M-6000, file 815, John Owens to Robert Livett and Edward Boyd, 9 May 1955; GWRC, M-6000, file 763, Mahaffy & Howard to District 18, 15 April 1955.

115 Sofchalk, "District 50."

116 GWRC, M-6000, file 899, DEB minutes, 8–9 December 1955; *Financial Post*, 17 September 1955.

117 GWRC, M-6000, file Correspondence with International Headquarters, Edward Boyd to John Owens, 2 August 1955, and Owens's reply, 8 August 1955.

118 GWRC, M-6048, Local 2633 minutes, 28 August 1955; GWRC, M-6000, file 815, Sim Weaver to John Owens, 23 August and 19 October 1955.

119 Sofchalk, "District 50."

120 GWRC, M-6000, file 899, DEB minutes, 8–9 December 1955.

121 GWRC, M-6048, Local 2633 minutes, 9 December 1951 (file 2), 25 March and 30 May 1954 (file 3); GWRC, M-6000, file 815, letter from Mercoal Local 5453, 12 August 1955, and reply from John Owens, 30 August 1955; GWRC, M-6048, file 3, Local 2633 minutes, 28 August 1955.

122 GWRC, M-6000, file 815, Edward Boyd to John Owens, 25 October 1956; *Coleman Journal*, 14 November 1956.

123 *Michel-Natal Spectator*, 2 April 1954.

124 PAA, Manning, file 1812, "Progress Report, Crowsnest Pass," attached to John Ferguson's memo to Deputy Minister J.E. Oberholtzer, 20 September 1955; *Coleman Journal*, 7 December 1955.

125 LAC, RG 27, microfilm reel T4126, file 125, Department of Labour strike and lock-out file: "Various Hotels - Bellevue, Blairmore and Coleman, Alberta;" the file in-cludes the Legion petition and a *Lethbridge Herald* story, 1 October 1953.

126 *Coleman Journal*, 31 October and 28 November 1956.

127 CSIS AIR, 96-A-00189, CPC Coleman, 517–24, copy of *The Lamp* 1, no. 6, May 1951, 3.

128 Langford and Frazer, "The Cold War," 68–69, 73.

129 *Coleman Journal*, "Coal Built Coleman" supplement, approximately July 1953.

130 *Coleman Journal*, 3 February 1954 and 29 February 1956.

131 ALHI interview with Tets Kitaguchi, 28 October 2005, Hinton, Alberta, 8–9; *Coleman Journal*, 29 February 1956. Kitaguchi left Summit Lime Works in the

summer of 1956 on doctor's orders since lime dust was breaking down the membranes inside his nose. He also resigned from the school board. See *Coleman Journal*, 15 August 1956.

132 GWRC, M-6000, file 193, J.D. Woods & Gordon, "A Survey of the Market for Underground Mined Coal, June 1956."

133 *Coleman Journal*, 9 May and 1 August 1956.

134 *Coleman Journal*, 3 October 1956.

135 GWRC, M-2239, file 44, Proceedings of Special Wage Scale Convention of District 18, 9–13 April 1956.

136 GWRC, M-1601, file 1350, tentative agreement, 22 June 1956; GWRC, M-6000, file 227, "Result of Referendum Ballot on Proposed Wage Agreement, July 24th, 1956."

137 GWRC, M-6000, file 815, District 18 report to the 42nd Constitutional Convention; GWRC, M-6000, file 193, Arbitration Board report, 1 October 1956; *Coleman Journal*, 9 November 1956; GWRC, M-6000, file 250, Edward Boyd to William C. Whittaker, 5 November 1956; GWRC, M-1601, file 571, WCC, "Labour Situation" report, 7 November 1956.

138 *Edmonton Journal*, 19 October 1956; GWRC, M-6000, file 274, letter to Edward Boyd reporting on the results of the supervised strike vote, 23 November 1956; *Coleman Journal*, 28 November 1956.

139 GWRC, M-1601, file 571, WCC, "Labour Situation" report, 8 December 1956 and early January 1957; *Coleman Journal*, 12 December 1956.

Chapter 3 | GHOST TOWN FUTURE?

1 *Lethbridge Herald*, 3 May 1957. Brazeau Collieries in Nordegg, Alberta, shut down in early 1955. The closing of the last store in Nordegg in July 1955 received widespread press attention (see, e.g., *Coleman Journal*, 3 August 1955), cementing Nordegg's ghost town fate in the public's consciousness.

2 *Lethbridge Herald*, 27 April 1957; *Calgary Herald*, 9 October 1957.

3 *Fernie Free Press*, 19 May 1960.

4 CBC Citizens' Forum, "The Pass," available at LAC.

5 GWRC, M-1601, file 1229, WCC letter to the director of mines, Alberta, 19 August 1958; *Fernie Free Press*, 11 December 1958.

6 *Calgary Herald*, 13 July 1959.

7 *Coleman Journal*, 13 and 20 March 1957.

8 GWRC, M-6048, file 3, Local 2633 minutes, 31 March 1957.

9 GWRC, M-6000, file 516, Mike Susnar memorandum, 5 April 1957, with attached "Brief – Re Assistance to the Coal Mining Industry of Alberta, Blairmore, 26 March 1957."

10 *Coleman Journal*, 8 May 1957; *Lethbridge Herald*, 3 May 1957.

11 LAC, RG 81, vol. 34, file 9-4-61, William C. Whittaker to Wilbur E. Uren, 30 April 1957; *Calgary Albertan*, 29 April 1957; *Lethbridge Herald*, 27 April 1957; GWRC, M-1601, file 571, WCC, "Labour Situation" report, 6 February 1957.

12 *Coleman Journal*, 15 May 1957; GWRC, M-6000, file 253, John Stokaluk, memo on a conversation with John Ferguson, 8 May 1957; GWRC, M-1601, file 571, WCC, "Labour Situation" report, 4 November 1957.

13 GWRC, M-1601, file 571, WCC, "Labour Situation" report, 17 March 1958. On the May 1958 layoff, see GWRC, M-6000, file 281, District 18 Brief to Minister of Mines Comtois, 6 August 1958; and GWRC, M-1601, file 1374, William Bird to William C. Whittaker, 30 June 1958. On Grassy Mountain, see *Coleman Journal*, 24 December 1958 and 7 January 1959. On developments in Bellevue in 1959–61, see PAA, Municipal, box 171, file 1235a, William Bird to Village of Bellevue, 3 February 1961.

14 *Calgary Herald*, 10 October 1957.

15 *Coleman Journal*, 10 December 1958 and 20 January 1960.

16 *Fernie Free Press*, 8 and 23 April 1959, 18 February 1960; *Coleman Journal*, 10 December 1958, 29 April 1959, 2 and 16 March 1960; GWRC, M-1601, file 1229, application to renew mining at Greenhill, 4 May 1959.

17 GWRC, M-1601, file 1254, WCC internal memo to William Bird, 18 November 1960; GWRC, M-1601, file 1253, layoff notice.

18 GWRC, M-1601, file 1253, unsigned, handwritten WCC memo, 30 July 1960.

19 GWRC, M-1601, file 1254, *Western Canada Coal Review*, January–February 1961; GWRC, M-1601, file 208, William Bird's cancellation of the WCC membership in the COAWC, 20 January 1961.

20 PAA, Municipal, box 171, file 1235a, William Bird to Village of Bellevue, 3 February 1961; *Coleman Journal*, 20 July 1960; GWRC, M-1601, file 1252, WCC, general superintendent's reports for 20 May 1960 and 20 January 1961.

21 GWRC, M-1601, file 45, "Rapport annuel de l'administrateur – Delegue, ANNEE 1952."

22 *Fernie Free Press*, 7 April 1960; *Calgary Herald*, 12 April 1961.

23 GWRC, M-1601, file 569, WCC, "Other Mines" report, 11 January 1957; *Coleman Journal*, 13 March and 31 July 1957.

24 GWRC, M-1601, file 569, WCC, "Other Mines" report, 11 January 1957; LAC, RG 33/42, vol. 32, file Financial Statements – Coleman Collieries Ltd., Financial Statements 30 June 1957.

25 *Coleman Journal*, 5 September 1956, 15 May and 27 November 1957.

26 *Coleman Journal*, 13 February and 14 May 1958; *Fernie Free Press*, 17 April 1958. The export tonnage for 1958–59 is from a report prepared by MP Lawrence Kindt; see *Coleman Journal*, 25 March 1964.

27 Alberta Energy Regulator, "Coal Mine Atlas."

28 *Fernie Free Press*, 7 January 1960; *Coleman Journal*, 29 April 1959, 2 March 1960, 1 February and 6 April 1961, 15 October 1962; LAC, RG 33/42, vol. 18, file Alberta Bituminous Coal, chart "Alberta Bituminous Coal Production by Colliery and District."

29 GWRC, M-6000, file Coleman 1959–61, John Ramsay to William Ure, 3 September 1959.

30 GWRC, M-1561, Series 11, file 530, list of shareholders of capital stock of Crow's Nest Pass Coal Co. Ltd., as of 9 November 1959 (generated for a dividend payment). On that date, American citizens owned 80 percent of the capital stock of CNPC, whereas Canadian citizens owned 19 percent.

31 *Fernie Free Press*, 30 January and 6 February 1958, 28 May 1959.

32 *Fernie Free Press*, 23 January 1958; GWRC, M-6000, file 62, Ure's memo of 3 February 1958 on the initial meeting with cabinet ministers and a written copy of White's presentation to the cabinet on 24 January.

33 GWRC, M-6000, file 62, Ure's memo of 3 February 1958 on the initial meeting with cabinet ministers; *Fernie Free Press*, 30 January 1958; *Coleman Journal*, 12 February 1958.

34 GWRC, M-6000, file 62, Ure's memo of 3 February 1958 on the initial meeting with cabinet ministers and White's presentation to the cabinet on 24 January.

35 GWRC, M-6000, file 62, Ure's memo of 3 February 1958 on the initial meeting with cabinet ministers.

36 *Fernie Free Press*, 13 February 1958; GWRC, M-6000, file 883, Local 7310 minutes, 14 February and 26 April 1958.

37 GWRC, M-6000, file 883, Local 7310 minutes, 22 February and 26 April 1958; *Coleman Journal*, 13 February 1958.

38 *Fernie Free Press*, 30 April and 13 August 1959.

39 *Fernie Free Press*, 24 November 1960 and 2 February 1961; *Lethbridge Herald*, 14 November 1960; BC Archives (hereafter BCA), MS-250, Cominco Ltd. finding aid, "Historical Summary of Cominco" includes entries on pig iron and steel production at Kimberley, https://search-bcarchives.royalbcmuseum.bc.ca/ Document/Finding_Aids_Atom/MS-2001_to_MS-2500/ms-2500.pdf.

40 *Fernie Free Press*, 18 December 1958; 8 January, 30 April, and 1 October 1959; 7 July 1960.

41 *Fernie Free Press*, 17 July 1958, 12 February 1959.

42 *Fernie Free Press*, 22 January and 10 September 1959.

43 *Fernie Free Press*, 28 March, 16 April, and 2 June 1959.

44 *Fernie Free Press*, 14 April 1960.

45 Rand, "1960 Report," 57, 61–67.

46 Ibid., 20.

47 Ibid., 6, 3.

48 Ibid., 20.

49 Ibid., 37, 53.

50 Ibid., 34–37.

51 LAC, RG 33/42, vol. 2, file Hearings Held at Calgary Alberta – Volume 9, Calgary Hearings Transcript, 241–48.

52 Ibid., 256–57.

53 Ibid., 260–62.

54 Ibid., 264.

55 Ibid., 268–69.

56 *Coleman Journal*, 13 April 1960; *Fernie Free Press*, 14 April 1960; *Calgary Herald*, 9 April 1960; *Lethbridge Herald*, 11 April 1960; *Pass Herald*, 13 April 1960 (the last three clippings were found in LAC, RG 33/42, vols. 6 and 7).

57 GWRC, M-1601, file 1209, COAWC special meeting minutes, 20 May 1960.

58 GWRC, M-7422, file 8, William C. Whittaker, "Memo of Meeting with Mr. W.E. Uren" found within "Report on Eastern Trip re Japanese Export, 30 January to 2 February 1961."

59 GWRC, M-1601, file 1192b, William C. Whittaker to Edward Boyd, 30 December 1960, with attachment "Confidential Developments Arising out of the Report of the Rand Royal Commission on Coal."

60 GWRC, M-1601, file 1211, Tom Ewart to William C. Whittaker, 4 October 1960.

61 GWRC, M-6001, file 510, COAWC, "Statement for Press and Radio," 28 September 1960, and "Memo for the Honourable Paul Comtois," 7 October 1960; GWRC, M-1601, file 1192b, William C. Whittaker to Edward Boyd, 30 December 1960, with attachment "Confidential Developments Arising out of the Report of the Rand Royal Commission on Coal."

62 GWRC, M-1601, file 1192b, William C. Whittaker to Edward Boyd, 30 December 1960, with attachment "Confidential Developments Arising out of the Report of the Rand Royal Commission on Coal."

63 GWRC, M-6000, file 804, Edward Boyd to the secretary-treasurers of local unions in District 18, 16 June 1961; LAC, RG 33/42, vol. 2, file Hearings Held at Calgary Alberta – Volume 9, Calgary Hearings Transcript, 223; LAC, RG 33/42, vol. 24, file Welfare and Retirement Fund, District 18, "The Welfare and Retirement Fund of District 18, UMWA."

64 Based upon data reported in convention proceedings, 1958 (GWRC, M-6000, file 222) and 1962 (GWRC, M-6000, file 217).

65 LAC, RG 33/42, vol. 24, file Welfare and Retirement Fund, District 18, "The Welfare and Retirement Fund of District 18, UMWA."

66 *Michel-Natal Spectator*, 18 May 1953; GWRC, M-6000, file 770, DEB minutes, 23–24 May 1957.

67 GWRC, M-6000, file 222, District 18, 1958 convention proceedings; GWRC,

M-6000, file 221, Collective Agreement, 3 July 1958–2 July 1960, and Conciliation Board award, 4 August 1958.

68 On the occasion of each increase, the District 18 office informed locals that the amount of the monthly retirement benefit would be reduced by a sum equal to the increase in Old Age Security; Local 2633 minutes, 28 July and 24 November 1957.

69 GWRC, M-6000, file 223, Welfare and Retirement Fund of District 18, Summary for the Year 1955; LAC, RG 33/42, vol. 24, file Welfare and Retirement Funds, UMWA District 18, breakdown of those in receipt of WRF benefits as of 31 December 1959.

70 GWRC, M-6000, file 899, DEB minutes, 2 April 1954; GWRC, M-6000, file 770, DEB minutes, 23–24 May 1957; GWRC, M-2239, file 43, District 18 convention proceedings, 5–9 April 1954.

71 GWRC, M-6000, file 769, Edward Boyd to Donald McDonald, 3 February 1960: a union representative position was left unfilled after President Robert Livett's retirement at the end of 1957, and the vice-president position went unfilled after John Stokaluk retired at the end of 1959. GWRC, M-6000, file 769, Edward Boyd to International President Thomas Kennedy, 31 August 1961: union representative Donald McDonald was laid off in 1961.

72 GWRC, M-1601, file 569, WCC, "Other Mines" report, 12 March 1953. Information on the Forestburg mine is found in GWRC, M-1601, file 1233, Jean Albert Brusset to Charles A. Dunning, 18 October 1952.

73 *Calgary Herald*, 9 October 1957; *Coleman Journal*, 22 September 1954.

74 Piper and Green, "Province Powered by Coal," 558.

75 GWRC, M-6000, file 537, Donald McDonald's memos of 29 October 1959, 28 March 1960, and 7 February 1961, detailing District 18's organizing efforts; information on the Alberta Strip Miners Union is found in Mike Susnar's memo, 25 June 1962.

76 The "mortally scared" observation was by Boyd as quoted in Ramsey, *Noble Cause*, 191. On the Saskatchewan strip mine assessment, see LAC, RG 33/42, vol. 24, file Welfare and Retirement Fund, District 18, "The Welfare and Retirement Fund of District 18, UMWA," 4.

77 *Fernie Free Press*, 18 September 1958.

78 GWRC, M-6000, file 219, District 18 letter to the secretary-treasurers of local unions, 4 November 1960, for conciliation board vote results.

79 GWRC, M-1601, file 1209, COAWC minutes, 14 November 1960.

80 GWRC, M-6000, file Fernie 1959–62, CNPC letter to employees, 21 November 1960.

81 GWRC, M-6000, file Bellevue 1960, WCC letter to employees, 22 November 1960; GWRC, M-6000, file Coleman 1959–61, Coleman Collieries letter to employees, 21 November 1960.

82 *Lethbridge Herald*, 14 November 1960.

83 GWRC, M-1601, file 1209, COAWC minutes, 25 November 1960, for strike vote results; *Fernie Free Press*, 1 December 1960.

84 GWRC, M-6000, file 219, District 18 to the secretary-treasurers of local unions, 4 November 1960.

85 GWRC, M-6000, file 526, COAWC contract proposals, 15 May 1962, and result of contract ratification vote, 14 June 1962; GWRC, M-6000, file 454, signed tentative agreement, 4 June 1962.

86 *Fernie Free Press*, 10 January and 7 March 1957; *Coleman Journal*, 13 March 1957. On the recruitment of miners from Nova Scotia, see GWRC, M-6000, file 821, UMWA District 26 to William Ure, 9 November 1960; and *Fernie Free Press*, 24 November 1960. On the return migration of mining families, see *Lethbridge Herald*, 17 November 1960.

87 Crowsnest Pass Historical Society, *Crowsnest ... Millennium Ed.*, 152.

88 *Coleman Journal*, 12 November 1958.

89 *Fernie Free Press*, 25 February 1960; *Lethbridge Herald*, 22 September 1960.

90 *Coleman Journal*, 27 February 1957 and 26 October 1960.

91 GWRC, M-6000, file 883, Local 7310 minutes, 22 February 1958, 7 November and 5 December 1959; *Fernie Free Press*, 30 June 1949, 24 December 1959, 5 August 1965.

92 Franz, "An Affront" and "Alberta's Red Democrats."

93 Crowsnest Pass Historical Society, *Crowsnest and Its People*, 93.

94 Norton and Langford, "Politicians"; *Fernie Free Press*, 11 and 18 August and 15 September 1960.

95 *Coleman Journal*, 5 July 1961.

96 *Fernie Free Press*, 22 January and 13 August 1959, 6 June 1961.

97 Local 2633 minutes, 23 November 1957; GWRC, M-6000, file Coleman 1961 and 1962, Donald McDonald memo, 15 May 1961.

98 GWRC, M-6000, file Michel 1958–60, J.H. Newton to Edward Boyd, 10 October 1959, and Sam English to Edward Boyd, 20 October 1959; GWRC, M-6000, file Michel 1960–1962, William Ure memo, 21 June 1961.

99 McKay, "Springhill, 1958."

100 Local 2633 minutes, 5 November 1958; *Coleman Journal*, 12 November and 24 December 1958.

101 *Lethbridge Herald*, 16 August 1960.

102 Garside, "Very British Phenomenon," 190–91.

103 Harvey, "Militant Particularism," 91.

104 *Coleman Journal*, 18 January 1961.

105 McDonald, "Tom Uphill."

106 *Fernie Free Press*, 22 February and 1 March 1962.

107 *Coleman Journal*, 14 May 1959; *Fernie Free Press*, 14 May 1959.

108 *Fernie Free Press*, 9 March and 15 April 1958; *Coleman Journal*, 7 May 1958.
109 *Coleman Journal*, 27 April and 9 June 1960, 5 July 1961.
110 *Fernie Free Press*, 10 January 1957, 7 May 1958, and 7 April 1960; *Coleman Journal*, 16 January 1957 and 7 May 1958.
111 *Coleman Journal*, 6 August 1958.
112 *Coleman Journal*, 5 October 1955.
113 *Fernie Free Press*, 24 April 1958; 8, 15, 22, and 29 May 1958; 17 July 1958; 25 October 1958; and 18 December 1958.
114 *Fernie Free Press*, 10 April and 5 June 1958.
115 Linkon and Russo, *Steeltown, U.S.A.*, 63.
116 Herod, "Local Political Practice," 387.
117 *Fernie Free Press*, 29 May and 14 August 1958.
118 *Fernie Free Press*, 16 October 1958 and 12 March 1959.
119 *Fernie Free Press*, 14 July 1960 and 14 June 1962.
120 Dublin and Licht, *Face of Decline*, 447.
121 *Lethbridge Herald*, 17 November 1960. In 2012, Devon Canada announced that it would close the plants because of low gas prices and the fact that the plants had "long surpassed" their lifespans; *Pass Herald*, 10 April 2012. The gas plant was torn down in 2014; see "(De) Construction Time-Lapse."
122 Crowsnest Pass Historical Society, *Crowsnest ... Millennium Ed.*, 213.
123 *Coleman Journal*, 6 December 1961.
124 *Fernie Free Press*, 30 April 1959.
125 *Fernie Free Press*, 25 June 1959; 9, 16, 23, and 30 July 1959; 6 August 1959; 29 June 1961.
126 *Fernie Free Press*, 17 March 1960.
127 *Fernie Free Press*, 28 April and 4 August 1960.
128 *Fernie Free Press*, 25 August, 13 October, 10 and 17 November, and 8 December 1960.
129 *Fernie Free Press*, 5 January and 27 April 1961.
130 *Maclean's*, 8 April 1961, 1.
131 *Fernie Free Press*, 13 and 27 April 1961.
132 *Fernie Free Press*, 14 September 1961; 2 and 25 November 1961; 29 March, 19 July, 13 August, and 27 September 1962; 25 June 1964.
133 GWRC, M-6000, file 526, William C. Whittaker to the District 18 policy committee, 15 May 1962.
134 *Coleman Journal*, 18 July 1962; *Fernie Free Press*, 24 October 1963.
135 Crowsnest Pass Historical Society, *Crowsnest ... Millennium Ed.*, 238–40.
136 CBC Citizens' Forum, "The Pass." Census data demonstrate that young adults were overrepresented among those who left Coleman. In 1951, the cohort aged ten to nineteen made up 13 percent of Coleman's population of 1,961 people (Census of

Canada 1951, 23–73). Fifteen years later the same cohort, now aged twenty-five to thirty-four, made up only 7 percent of Coleman's population of 1,507 people (Census of Canada 1966, *Population Specified Age Groups*, 109).

137 *Edmonton Journal*, 3 March 1962.
138 *Lethbridge Herald*, 26 February 1962.

Chapter 4 | WE WERE CONTINUALLY LOSING MEMBERSHIP AND LOSING
PUBLIC SUPPORT

1 Langford and Frazer, "Cold War," 66. As strong as support for the Labor-Progressive Party was in the Crowsnest Pass and Elk Valley in 1945, it was very patchy in other parts of the ridings. Reverend E.G. Hansell won Macleod for Social Credit (Norton and Langford, "Politicians"), and James Matthews, a Fernie minister, won Kootenay East for the Cooperative Commonwealth Federation (*Fernie Free Press*, 14 June 1945).

2 Langford and Frazer, "Cold War," 67–70. In 1934, Uphill travelled to the Soviet Union as part of a delegation of labour leaders and workers. He returned to Canada impressed by what he had seen, declaring it to be a model for what the BC legislature should be doing; see McDonald, "Tom Uphill," 106.

3 CSIS AIR, 96-A-00189, CPC Coleman, 71–73, report by RCMP Insp. F.J. Vaucher, 16 May 1961; *Fernie Free Press*, 4 May 1961; GWRC, M-6000, file Michel 1960–62, Donald McDonald memo, 3 May 1961. The close political ties between Murphy and Uphill went back decades. In 1935, Uphill had actively worked in support of Murphy's campaign for election to the Alberta legislature; see Seager, "Proletariat in Wild Rose," 460–61.

4 Charlie O'Brien served as the Socialist Party of Canada member of the Alberta legislature for Rocky Mountain between 1909 and 1913; see Norton and Langford, "Politicians."

5 Seager, "Proletariat in Wild Rose."

6 Berger, "Working-Class Culture," 27.

7 CSIS AIR, 96-A-00189, CPC Coleman, 591, report by RCMP Cst. W. Henderson, 24 April 1933.

8 A contemporary Ukrainian spelling is Yasynuvata.

9 Smith, "Crossing." Smith died in 1947, his faith in the superiority of the Soviet Union presumably intact.

10 CSIS AIR, 96-A-00189, CPC Coleman, 632, report forwarded by F. Humby, commanding officer of RCMP East Kootenay Sub-District, to the commanding officer of RCMP Southern Alberta District, 20 April 1929; CSIS AIR, 96-A-00189, CPC Crowsnest Pass, 180, report by Insp. W.W. Watson, 27 September 1931.

11 Knotter, "Small-Place Communism," 492.

12 Swankey, interview with the author, 23 August 1997.

13 Langford, "Fighting Fascism."

14 Williams, *South Wales Coalfield*, 23–25.

15 Williams, *Democratic Rhondda*, 190.

16 Ibid., 25.

17 Cousins, *Crow's Nest Pass*, 110.

18 Ibid., 72–73.

19 Endicott, *Workers' Unity League*, 116; Knight, "Harvey Murphy," 41–42.

20 Cousins, *Crow's Nest Pass*, 74.

21 Ibid., 73.

22 PAA, Theo Serra fonds, PR0438, handwritten summary of interview with Gustaf Erikkson. Eriksson contributed an autobiographical note to Crowsnest Pass Historical Society, *Crowsnest and Its People*, 522–23.

23 ALHI interview with Steve and Liz Liska, 9 November 2005, Coleman, Alberta, 7, 15.

24 Quoted in Morgan, "Bastions," 197.

25 Miles, "Is This a Soviet?," 22. Released on 24 November 1934, Buck would have seen Tim Buck Boulevard for himself during a trip to western Canada in early 1935; see CSIS AIR, 96-A-00189, CPC Blairmore, 490–91, report by RCMP Sgt. J.A. Cawsey, 24 March 1935.

26 CSIS AIR, 96-A-00189, CPC Crowsnest Pass, 95–97, report by RCMP Cst. I.B. Bailey, 26 April 1938.

27 Ibid., 158–60, 128–29.

28 CSIS AIR, 96-A-00189, CPC Blairmore, 350, report by RCMP Cst. J.S. Connors, 21 April 1942.

29 Whitaker and Marcuse, *Cold War Canada*; Penner, *Canadian Communism*, 219–20.

30 *Canadian Tribune*, 30 April 1962, 8.

31 Langford and Frazer, "Cold War," 57. On-to-Ottawa trek veteran Syd Thompson assisted with the drive to unionize lumber workers in 1947; Swankey, interview with the author, 23 August 1997.

32 Langford and Frazer, "Cold War," 57–59.

33 Ibid., 57; Sangster, *Dreams of Equality*, 185–89; Guard, *Radical Housewives*.

34 Swankey, interview with the author, 23 August 1997.

35 CSIS AIR, 96-A-00189, CPC Crowsnest Pass, 128–29, report by RCMP Sgt. J.A. Cawsey, 9 February 1937.

36 Langford and Frazer, "Cold War," 59.

37 CSIS AIR, 96-A-00189, CPC Blairmore, 200, report by RCMP Cst. F.A.E. Ward, 16 August 1948.

38 Whitaker and Marcuse, *Cold War Canada*, 311–55.

39 Marcuse, "Labour's Cold War."

40 GWRC, M-6000, file 899, DEB minutes, 19–21 May 1949. I suspect that English, who had begun working for CNPC in the early 1940s, was "refused employment" in 1949 because of a severe leg injury that he had suffered in a mining accident in 1945 (*Fernie Free Press*, 29 November 1945) that at some point resulted in an amputation and the use of a prosthesis.

41 Swankey's "united labour" call appeared in a letter to the editor, *Blairmore Graphic*, 18 June 1948.

42 CSIS AIR, 96-A-00189, CPC Blairmore, 180, report by RCMP Cpl. J.S. Connors, 8 January 1949.

43 GWRC, M-6000, file 899, DEB minutes, 19–21 May 1949.

44 White had been a key organizer of a strike-breaking company union in Coleman during the strike in 1932 (Endicott, *Workers' Unity League*, 117) and in 1948 managed Lloyd's CCF provincial election campaign (*Blairmore Graphic*, 13 February 1948).

45 CSIS AIR, 96-A-00189, CPC Coleman, 511–12, report by RCMP Cst. F.A.E. Ward, 14 May 1951; 517–24, copy of *The Lamp* 1, no. 6, May 1951, 7.

46 GWRC, M-6048, file 2, Local 2633 minutes, 13 April 1952.

47 GWRC, M-6048, file 2, Local 2633 minutes, 12 March 1950; LAC, MG 28-I103, vol. 33, file 33–3, Local 7295 to Pat Conroy, CCL Secretary-Treasurer, 12 March 1950.

48 CSIS AIR, 96-A-00189, CPC Blairmore, 171–72, memo by RCMP Supt. G.W. Curleigh, 22 July 1949; ibid., 274, report by RCMP Sgt. T.E. Mudiman, 27 June 1944.

49 Ibid., 116–17 (material originally published in *National Affairs Monthly*, February 1952, 60–61, under the by-line of Adolph Pothorn, BC Provincial Executive member); ibid., 121, report by RCMP Cst. F.A.E. Ward, 4 April 1952; CSIS AIR, 96-A-00189, CPC Coleman, 492, 496–97; three reports by RCMP Cst. F.A.E. Ward, 3 September 1953, 29 October 1952, 4 April 1952.

50 CSIS AIR, 96-A-00189, CPC Fernie-Michel club, 398, report by RCMP Insp. H. Spanton, 27 January 1955; ibid., 404, report by RCMP Cpl. D.E. McRae, 20 September 1954; ibid., 491, report by RCMP Cst. D.M. McRae, 26 May 1952.

51 Levine, "Labor-Progressive Party," 164.

52 Whitaker and Marcuse, *Cold War Canada*, 144.

53 CSIS AIR, 96-A-00189, CPC Blairmore, 102, report by RCMP Cst. F.A.E. Ward, 2 March 1953; ibid., 190–91, report by RCMP Cpl. J.S. Connors, 24 September 1948; ibid., 206, report by RCMP Cst. W.A. Shields, 10 August 1948.

54 Ibid., 143, report by RCMP Cpl. J.S. Connors, 20 July 1951; ibid., 121, report by RCMP Cst. F.A.E. Ward, 4 April 1952. Responses to Ward's report: ibid., 122, RCMP Supt. F.A. Regan, 16 April 1952; and ibid., 118, RCMP A/Commr. S. Bullard, 23 April 1952.

55 Swankey, interview with the author, 23 August 1997.

56 Ibid.

57 Ibid.

58 Langford and Frazer, "Cold War," 63.

59 *Blairmore Graphic*, 20 August 1948; *Coleman Journal*, 10 August 1944; Alberta, Chief Electoral Officer, *Alberta Elections*.

60 CSIS AIR, 96-A-00189, CPC Blairmore, 193–94, report by RCMP Cpl. J.S, Connors, 25 August 1948.

61 Langford and Frazer, "Cold War," 66.

62 CSIS AIR, 96-A-00189, CPC Blairmore, 89, report by RCMP A/Cpl. F.A.E. Ward, 20 January 1955; CSIS AIR, 96-A-00189, CPC Fernie-Michel club, 404, report by RCMP Cpl. D.E. McRae, 20 September 1955.

63 University of Toronto, Robert S. Kenny Collection, MSS 179, box 9, "On Party Organization," report to the twelfth convention of the Alberta Labor-Progressive Party, 15–17 June 1956.

64 GWRC, M-1601, [for 1951] file 1143, wage negotiations, 1950–51; [for 1955] file 1361, wage negotiations, 1954–60.

65 Levine, "Labor-Progressive Party," 166; Penner, *Canadian Communism*, 242.

66 University of Toronto, Robert S. Kenny Collection, MSS 179, box 9, "On Party Organization," report to the twelfth convention of the Alberta Labor-Progressive Party, 15–17 June 1956; Swankey, interview with the author, 23 August 1997.

67 Langford and Frazer, "Cold War," 70–71.

68 Palmer, "Canadian Communism," 152.

69 Levine, "Labor-Progressive Party," 172–73.

70 McIlroy and Campbell, "Coalfield Leaders."

71 Although the leader of Scotland's union for coal miners, Abe Moffat, who had a Stalinist view of the Soviet Union's invasion of Hungary (Moffat, *My Life*, 144–53), undertook a speaking tour of Canada in early 1957 that included a talk in Fernie (*Fernie Free Press*, 7 March 1957).

72 *Fernie Free Press*, 18 May 1950.

73 CSIS AIR, 96-A-00189, CPC Blairmore, 148-155; copy of *The Lamp* 1, no. 7 (June 1951): "In the U.S.S.R." page of stories (5), including "Free Medical Care" and "Old Age Pensions at 55 and 60;" GWRC, M-1601, file 1143, Wage Negotiation, 1950–51; *The Lamp* 1, no. 8 (September 1951): "Drumheller Miner to U.S.S.R.," (1 and 8). A report on Roberts's talk at Natal is found in CSIS AIR, 96-A-00189, CPC Fernie-Michel club, 509, report by RCMP Cst. D. M. McRae, 28 December 1951.

74 CSIS AIR, 96-A-00189, CPC Coleman, 441, report by RCMP A/Cpl. F.A.E. Ward, 28 January 1955; *Fernie Free Press*, 5 October 1961; CSIS AIR, 96-A-00189, CPC Fernie-Michel club, 91–95, RCMP report by redacted, 7 November 1961.

75 Levine, "Labor-Progressive Party," 170–72.

76 Ibid., 162–63.

77 Ibid., 163, 180.

78 Ibid., 178–82.

79 English, letter to the editor, *Fernie Free Press*, 20 March 1958.

80 Footage of the talk in Blairmore on 14 February 1962 is found in *Tim Buck, Mr. Communism*; see also CSIS AIR, 96-A-00189, CPC Blairmore, 26, RCMP report by redacted, 28 May 1963; it stated, "The last known C.P. of C. activity at Blairmore, Alberta, was a public meeting on 14 February 1962 at which time Tim Buck was the guest speaker."

81 Sallant worked as a contract miner for Coleman Collieries and nominated Garth Turcott as the NDP candidate in Pincher Creek–Crowsnest; *Lethbridge Herald*, 12 September 1966. On his commitment to communism, see "An Old Communist Has a Warning for Generation X," *Vancouver Sun*, 4 July 1994, A11; and Gary Taje's remarks in ALHI, Crowsnest Pass Group 2 interview, 10 November 2005, Coleman, Alberta.

82 Langford and Frazer "Cold War," 66.

83 Whitaker and Marcuse, *Cold War Canada*, 109, 170, 176, 267.

84 On the importance of leftist caucuses and parties for rank-and-file struggles, see Nyden, "Democratizing Organizations"; Sears, *Next New Left*; and Langford, "Union Democracy."

Chapter 5 | PURSUING ALTERNATIVES FOR GROWING THE ECONOMY

1 *Fernie Free Press*, 4 April 1963; LAC, RG 81, vol. 134, file 4-2-42-1, "Production, Days Worked and Number of Men Employed, 1963," and William C. Whittaker to Colin L. O'Brian, 29 January 1964; *Coleman Journal*, 13 March 1963.

2 *Fernie Free Press*, 10 January and 28 March 1963.

3 *Fernie Free Press*, 16 and 23 May 1963, 16 January 1964; Crowsnest Pass Historical Society, *Crowsnest ... Millennium Ed.*, 297.

4 Minister of Finance Walter Gordon, speech in Parliament, 13 June 1963, as quoted in Kenward, "Political Manipulation," 100; *Fernie Free Press*, 12 September 1963.

5 *Fernie Free Press*, 4 July and 18 July 1963; LAC, RG 81, vol. 134, file 4-2-42-1, "Production, Days Worked and Number of Men Employed, 1963," and William C. Whittaker to Colin L. O'Brian, 29 January 1964; BCA, MS-2500, "Cominco Ltd.," Cominco Ltd. finding aid, "Historical Summary of Cominco" includes entries on pig iron and steel production at Kimberley http://search-B.C.archives.royalB.C.museum.B.C..ca/Document/Finding_Aids_Atom/MS-2001_to_MS-2500/ms-2500.pdf.

6 *Fernie Free Press*, 7 November 1963; *Coleman Journal*, 11 and 25 March 1964.

7 *Fernie Free Press*, 7 and 14 November 1963.

8 *Fernie Free Press*, 6 and 13 February 1964.

9   *Fernie Free Press*, 30 July and 10 September 1964; Langford, "Hanging of Peter Abramowicz."

10   Molotch, "The City as a Growth Machine," 318.

11   Dublin and Licht, *Face of Decline*, 118–21.

12   *Fernie Free Press*, 27 June and 6 September 1963.

13   Quoted in Kenward, "Political Manipulation," 100.

14   Galley, "Canadian Heavy Water Production," 5.

15   GWRC, M-7422, file 9, COAWC minutes, 12 November 1964.

16   *Fernie Free Press*, 4 March 1965, 28 April and 18 July 1966. Village of Natal minutes, 2 May 1966 (digital copy, provided by the District of Sparwood, available from the author on request); Galley, "Canadian Heavy Water Production," 5.

17   Galley, "Canadian Heavy Water Production," 6–7; *New York Times*, 11 March 1985.

18   *Fernie Free Press*, 27 February 1964, 6 May 1965.

19   *Coleman Journal*, 29 April 1966; Kenward, "Political Manipulation," 104; Crowsnest Pass Historical Society, *Crowsnest ... Millennium Ed.*, 210.

20   LAC, RG 124, vol. 68, file 718-1-0, part 1-1, Jess Succamore to Jean Marchand, 9 June 1969; Kenward, "Political Manipulation," 105–6, indicated that the hourly paid workforce was as high as 150 between 1968 and 1971.

21   *Lethbridge Herald*, 25 April 1968.

22   Crowsnest Pass Historical Society, *Crowsnest ... Millennium Ed.*, 210–12. Universal Reel and Recycling ceased operations in 2003.

23   LAC, RG 124, vol. 68, file 718-1-0, part 1-1, Jess Succamore to Jean Marchand, 9 June 1969.

24   Ibid.

25   Kenward, "Political Manipulation," 107.

26   The Canadian Electrical Workers Union merged with the Canadian Association of Industrial, Mechanical and Allied Workers in December 1969. The new organization used the latter name.

27   *Coleman Journal*, 4 May 1966, 29 May 1968 (reprinted from the *Alberta Commercial Report*).

28   LAC, RG 124, vol. 68, file 718-1-0, part 1-1, Jess Succamore to Jean Marchand, 9 June 1969.

29   Kenward, "Political Manipulation," 104–6.

30   Betty Dodds, letter, *Crowsnest Pass Promoter*, 25 August 2010; Dublin and Licht, *Face of Decline*, 134.

31   Kenward, "Political Manipulation," 117–18.

32   Ibid., 124, 115–16.

33   Ibid., 104–5, 121.

34   Dublin and Licht, *Face of Decline*, 121–22.

35 *Fernie Free Press*, 24 October 1963, 6 January, 19 March, and 18 June 1964.

36 *Fernie Free Press*, 27 August, 1 October, and 5, 12, and 19 November 1964.

37 *Fernie Free Press*, 12 November 1964.

38 *Fernie Free Press*, 19 September 1963, 23 January and 25 June 1964.

39 Crows Nest Industries became the new corporate name of CNPC in the summer of 1965; *Fernie Free Press*, 19 August 1965.

40 *Fernie Free Press*, 11 August and 3 November 1966.

41 Information on Heiko Sochar's life is found in his obituary in 2016, https://fernie.com/blog/2016/10/fernies-legendary-heiko-socher/.

42 *Fernie Free Press*, 3 December 1964; *Vancouver Sun*, 7 January 1965.

43 *Fernie Free Press*, 4 February 1965.

44 *Fernie Free Press*, 9 July 1965, 14 April 1966.

45 *Fernie Free Press*, 21 July and 29 September 1966, 24 December 1968.

46 *Fernie Free Press*, 4 April 1968. On Island Lake cat-skiing, see "Island Lake Lodge." https://en.wikipedia.org/wiki/Island_Lake_Lodge.

47 *Coleman Journal*, 14 June 1967.

48 Bowden, "Pan-Pacific Coal Trade," 7.

49 Ibid., 4.

50 GWRC, M-7422, file 9, COAWC minutes, 27 November 1964; LAC, RG 81, vol. 153, file 4-2-41-1, R. Guy C. Smith to Ottawa, 22 January 1965. In a meeting at the Canadian embassy in Tokyo, a delegation from a Japanese steel producer implied that the Canadian government should follow Australia's lead and subsidize a modern coal-handling facility for exports to Japan.

51 Bowden, "Pan-Pacific Coal Trade," 5–6.

52 LAC, RG 81, vol. 153, file 4-2-42-1, notes by Arthur Brown, adviser to the Dominion Coal Board, from a meeting of the members of the Board with the Minister of Energy, Mines, and Resources, Jean-Luc Pépin, 22 November 1966. Brown had been the Deputy Minister of Labour up until 1960 when he retired at age 65; *Labour Gazette*, January 1961, 12.

53 Bowden, "Pan-Pacific Coal Trade," 12–14.

54 *Coleman Journal*, 11 March 1964; GWRC, M-7422, file 9, COAWC minutes, 16 February 1965, and "Notes re Export Freight Rate," 19 February 1965; *Fernie Free Press*, 18 March 1965; *Coleman Journal*, 9 October 1965.

55 British Columbia Minister of Mines and Petroleum Resources, *Annual Report*, 1967, 450–51.

56 GWRC, M-6000, file 351, minutes of management-union meetings at Coleman Collieries, 3 April and 29 May 1965; *Coleman Journal*, 3 November 1965.

57 GWRC, M-6000, file 351, Robert Grant to Mike Susnar, 7 January 1966.

58 *Fernie Free Press*, 29 October 1964, with data from the *Financial Post*. Controlling for inflation, a $1,000 investment in CNPC in 1944 yielded a 360 percent return by 1964.

59 *Fernie Free Press*, 19 August 1965.

60 GWRC, M-6000, file Coleman 1961–62, William Ure, memo re 14 December 1962 union-company meeting.

61 GWRC, M-6000, file Michel 1963–64, Stanley Grocutt to William Ure, 15 April 1964.

62 GWRC, M-6000, file Coleman 1963–64, William Goodwin to John Ramsay, 10 February 1964.

63 GWRC, M-6000, file Coleman 1963–64, William Ure to John Ramsay, 4 February 1963, and John Ramsay to William Ure, 16 September 1964.

64 GWRC, M-6000, file Michel 1963–64, unsigned memo on Local 7292 stationery.

65 Derickson, "Nuisance Dust," 246.

66 Derickson, "Occupational Respiratory Diseases," 787.

67 Alberta Department of Mines and Minerals, *Annual Report of the Mines Division*, 1963–68; British Columbia Minister of Mines and Petroleum Resources, *Annual Report*, 1963–68.

68 British Columbia Minister of Mines and Petroleum Resources, *Annual Report*, 1966.

69 Ibid., 1967 (government investigation of the explosion 420–31).

70 Kinnear, "Balmer Mine Disaster," 155.

71 British Columbia Minister of Mines and Petroleum Resources, *Annual Report*, 1967, 430.

72 Kinnear, "Balmer Mine Disaster," 154–56.

73 Michel-Natal-Sparwood Heritage Society (hereafter MNSHS), interview with John Desjardins, conducted by Janice Talarico and Butch Archibald, 2 July 1992, 7–8, 16). Transcripts of MNSHS interviews were obtained from the District of Sparwood and are available from the author on request.

74 British Columbia Minister of Mines and Petroleum Resources, *Annual Report*, 1967, 423.

75 Quoted in Kinnear, "Balmer Mine Disaster," 156.

76 *Lethbridge Herald*, 4 April 1967; *Fernie Free Press*, 13 April 1967; MNSHS, interview with Frank and Francis Travis, conducted by Dan Tanaka and Christine Beranek, 1 August 1991.

77 *Fernie Free Press*, 13 April 1967.

78 Ibid.

79 *Lethbridge Herald*, 3 May 1967. GWRC, M-6000, file Michel 1967–69, Stanley Grocutt to William Ure and Mike Susnar, 18 May 1967.

80 GWRC, M-6000, file 211, wage scale convention proceedings, District 18, April 1964.

81 GWRC, M-6000, file 191, District 18 contract requests, 26 May 1964, and COAWC reply, 29 May 1964; GWRC, M-6000, file 790, William Ure to W.A. Boyle, 15 September 1964; GWRC, M-7422, file 9, COAWC minutes, 24 November 1964;

GWRC, M-6000, file Michel 1963–64, William Ure to policy committee, 27 November 1964.

82 GWRC, M-6000, file 351, F.J. Harquail to Local 2633 proposing a contract settlement, 6 January 1965; GWRC, M-7422, file 9, COAWC minutes, 27 November 1964.

83 LAC, RG 81, vol. 153, file 4-2-42-1, R. Guy C. Smith to Ottawa, 5 January 1965.

84 GWRC, M-7422, file 9, COAWC minutes, 27 November 1964.

85 *Coleman Journal*, 30 December 1964; GWRC, M-6000, file 351, F.J. Harquail to Local 2633 proposing a contract settlement, 6 January 1965; GWRC, M-7422, file 9, COAWC minutes, 5 January 1965; GWRC, M-6000, file 790, William Ure to W.A. Boyle, 29 December 1964.

86 GWRC, M-7422, file 9, COAWC minutes, 5 January 1965.

87 GWRC, M-6000, file 351, F.J. Harquail to Local 2633 proposing a contract settlement, 6 January 1965.

88 LAC, RG 27, microfilm reel T-3414, file 7, Department of Labour strike and lockout file: "Coleman Collieries – Vicary Mine, Coleman, Alberta;" *Fernie Free Press*, 14 January 1965; GWRC, M-6000, file 810, Mike Susnar to John Owens, 9 July 1968.

89 By 1969, F.J. Harquail and his wife, Helen (seated on the right in Figure 2.6), had relocated to the Cayman Islands, where he was known as a "wealthy, self-made Canadian businessman" who had "interests in mining, heavy construction and ranching." The extent of Harquail's involvement in the coal industry in the Crowsnest Pass is elided by these words, although it is safe to say that his multidecade career as a mining executive in the region significantly enhanced his personal wealth. Interestingly, a good chunk of that wealth was eventually turned into public goods through major donations to the performing and visual arts by Helen Harquail after her husband's death. Unfortunately, the Crowsnest Pass did not benefit from this largesse; today the national theatre in the Cayman Islands is known as the F.J. Harquail National Theatre, and there is an F.J. Harquail Exhibition Hall in the British Overseas Territory's national gallery. In honour of her significant donations to the arts, in 1987 Helen Harquail was appointed as an officer of the Order of the British Empire. See "Cultural Benefactor"; Owbewcirk, "Minister"; and Wilson, "Service."

90 *Fernie Free Press*, 14 January 1965.

91 LAC, RG 27, microfilm reel T-3414, file 6, Department of Labour strike and lockout file: "Crow's Nest Pass Coal – Michel and Fernie, British Columbia"; *Fernie Free Press*, 4 and 11 February 1965; GWRC, M-6000, file 124, Local 2633 contract, 3 July 1964–2 July 1967; GWRC, M-6000, file 810, Mike Susnar to John Owens, 9 July 1968.

92 LAC, RG 81, vol. 153, file 4-2-42-1, R. Guy C. Smith to Ottawa, 5 January 1965.

93 The seam and mine were named after Thomas Balmer, a former vice-president and

large shareholder of CNPC who died in 1959. Balmer, like his brother-in-law Thomas Gleed, president of CNPC/CNI in the 1960s, was based in Seattle.

94 Regional Planning Division ..., *Natal-Sparwood Urban Renewal Scheme Report*, III-5; *Fernie Free Press*, 7 October 1965.

95 *Fernie Free Press*, 7 October 1965.

96 *Fernie Free Press*, 18 November 1965, 21 July and 10 November 1966.

97 *Fernie Free Press*, 8 February 1968.

98 *Fernie Free Press*, 14 October 1965. In the early twentieth century, the Great Northern Railway had used coal from the mines at Michel and Coal Creek to run its trains in the United States; it shipped the coal along a spur line, abandoned in stages in the 1920s and 1930s, that joined the GNR line at Rexford, Montana.

99 *Fernie Free Press*, 18 August 1966; GWRC, M-7422, file 10, William C. Whittaker, annual report, 14 April 1967.

100 LAC, RG 81, vol. 153, file 4-2-42-1, Arthur Brown memo to DCB chair Colin O'Brian, 14 February 1966.

101 *Coleman Journal*, 29 June 1966; *Fernie Free Press*, 22 September and 3 November 1966, 12 January 1967.

102 GWRC, M-6000, file 210, wage scale convention proceedings, 14–16 September 1966.

103 GWRC, M-6000, file 582, CNI reply to Local 7292 contract demands, 4 October 1966.

104 For OAS rates over time, see "Old Age Security"; GWRC, M-7422, file 164, WRF 1966–70, "Welfare Fund Amendments since 1952," November 1968.

105 GWRC, M-7422, file 163, letter from Robert Grant, Secretary-Treasurer, WRF, to William C. Whittaker estimating financial impact of ten-dollar monthly increase in WRF rates, 24 July 1964.

106 GWRC, M-7422, file 164, WRF 1966–70, "Welfare Fund Amendments since 1952," November 1968; GWRC, M-6000, file 535, Local 7292 contract demands for Crows Nest Industries, 3 October 1966.

107 GWRC, M-7422, file 164, Welfare and Retirement Fund of District 18, summary of benefits, May 1967, and summary of the numbers in receipt of retirement and disability pensions, 1963–68, 19 March 1968.

108 GWRC, M-7422, file 164, WRF 1966–70, "Welfare Fund Amendments since 1952," November 1968; GWRC, M-7422, file 164, review of the operation of the Welfare and Retirement Fund, District 18, 10 June 1968.

109 GWRC, M-6000, file 255, board of conciliation report, 18 January 1967.

110 GWRC, M-6000, file 190A, William A. Prentice, executive vice-president of Crows Nest Industries, leaflet addressed "To All Employees and Their Friends," undated but distributed on 20 February 1967; *Fernie Free* Press, 23 February 1967 – the leaflet compared the terms of the tentative agreement and the conciliation

board's recommendations; *Lethbridge Herald*, 20, 22, and 24 February and 4 March 1967; *Fernie Free Press*, 23 February 1967; GWRC, M-6000, file 790, William Ure to W.A. Boyle, 7 March and 19 December 1967; GWRC, M-6000, file 810, Mike Susnar to John Owens, 9 July 1968.

111 Bowden, "Pan-Pacific Coal Trade," 9.

112 *Fernie Free Press*, 23 March 1967.

113 *Lethbridge Herald*, 12 April 1967; *Fernie Free Press*, 12 April 1967; *Coleman Journal*, 3 May 1967; GWRC, M-7422, file 10, COAWC managing director's annual report, 19 April 1968.

114 *Fernie Free Press*, 4 May and 27 July 1967, 4 and 31 January 1968; *Lethbridge Herald*, 12 May 1967.

115 GWRC, M-6000, file 535, contract demands from District 18 to Coleman Collieries, 2 May 1967; GWRC, M-6000, file 790, William Ure to W.A. Boyle, 19 December 1967; GWRC, M-6000, file 810, Mike Susnar to John Owens, 9 July 1968.

Chapter 6 | GROWTH AT WHAT COST?

1 Quoted in *Fernie Free Press*, 6 May 1965.

2 Quoted in *Fernie Free Press*, 4 May 1967.

3 Molotch, "Growth Machine," 318.

4 Pellow and Brulle, "Power, Justice."

5 *Fernie Free Press*, 28 April 1966; Village of Natal minutes (digital copy, provided by the District of Sparwood, available from the author on request), 21 April 1966.

6 Loretta Montemurro, the District of Sparwood's first clerk, estimated that "50 per cent or a bit more" ended up moving to Sparwood (interview with the author, 31 July 2013).

7 *Lethbridge Herald*, 22 March 1960; *Calgary Herald*, 22 March 1960.

8 Sparwood council minutes (digital copy, provided by the District of Sparwood, available from the author on request), 24 May 1966; *Fernie Free Press*, 3 November 1966.

9 See the 1970 documentary film *That's the Price* for an early dissection of these problems.

10 GWRC, M-6000, file Coleman 1966–69, John Ramsay to William Ure, 9 April and 5 June 1968; *Coleman Journal*, 2 October 1968.

11 *Coleman Journal*, 5 June and 20 November 1963, 3 November 1965, 17 April 1968.

12 Ezner De Anna, interview with the author, 7 July 2011; *Coleman Journal*, 5 June 1963.

13 *Coleman Journal*, 14 August 1963.

14 *Coleman Journal*, 29 June 1966.

15 Ibid.

16 Sparwood council minutes (digital copy, provided by the District of Sparwood, available from the author on request), 22 June 1967.

17 GWRC, M-1561, file 180, Sparwood 1966–68, A.T. (Tom) Campbell, CNPC lawyer, to Minister of Municipal Affairs, 16 May 1966; MNSHS interview with Paul Chala, conducted by Christine Beranek, 7 August 1991; *Fernie Free Press*, 26 September 1963.

18 *Fernie Free Press*, 1 August and 26 September 1963, Village of Natal minutes (digital copy, provided by the District of Sparwood, available from the author on request), 30 April, 3 May, and 7 June 1965; *Fernie Free Press*, 23 November 1967, 29 February 1968.

19 *Fernie Free Press*, 22 August 1963, 16 and 23 January 1964; Village of Natal minutes (digital copy, provided by the District of Sparwood, available from the author on request), 21 March and 4 April 1966; District of Sparwood minutes (digital copy, provided by the District of Sparwood, available from the author on request), 6 February 1967.

20 Village of Natal minutes (digital copy, provided by the District of Sparwood, available from the author on request), 20 April 1964, 5 April 1965.

21 *Fernie Free Press*, 10 October 1963.

22 Sparwood council minutes (digital copy, provided by the District of Sparwood, available from the author on request), 22 June 1967; *Fernie Free Press*, 4 May 1967.

23 Village of Natal minutes (digital copy, provided by the District of Sparwood, available from the author on request), 2 November 1964.

24 *Fernie Free Press*, 24 June 1965, 14 April 1966; BCA, Municipal Affairs, box 12, file Department of Planning – Planning, 1965, W.J. Tassie to J. Everett Brown, 4 May 1965.

25 *Lethbridge Herald*, 18 February 1967.

26 BCA, Municipal Affairs, box 16, file Incorporation and Change of Status, 1966, Reverend J.D.E. Watts to Premier W.A.C. Bennett, 25 September 1966; BCA, Municipal Affairs, box 17, file MLAs, 1966, Leo Nimsick to Minister Dan Campbell, 29 September 1966; Sparwood council minutes (digital copy, provided by the District of Sparwood, available from the author on request), 5 June 1967; *Fernie Free Press*, 23 November 1967. An analysis of the many retellings of the story of the Black Hole of Calcutta, centred on the alleged suffocation of 123 Europeans in a cramped prison cell in Kolkata in 1756, is found in Chatterjee, *Black Hole of Empire*.

27 *Fernie Free Press*, 5 January 1967; Sparwood council minutes (digital copy, provided by the District of Sparwood, available from the author on request), 1 May 1967. The total cost of purchasing and demolishing the privately held dwellings in Natal and Michel was split among the CMHC (50 percent), BC government (25 percent), and regional government (25 percent), although the federal government loaned the

latter $287,359. *Fernie Free Press*, 24 August 1967; GWRC, M-1561, file 180, Sparwood 1966–68, Draft Land Sales Agreement, 5 May 1967.

28 GWRC, M-1561, file 180, Sparwood 1966–68, John Cleeve memo, 7 June 1967, and Alex Fisher memo, 16 June 1967.

29 Sparwood council minutes (digital copy, provided by the District of Sparwood, available from the author on request), 13 July 1967; *Fernie Free Press*, 4 January 1968.

30 Gaal, *Memoirs of Michel-Natal*, 180–82.

31 *Fernie Free Press*, 5 October 1967; Sparwood council minutes (digital copy, provided by the District of Sparwood, available from the author on request), 11 October 1967.

32 *Fernie Free Press*, 16 May 1968; Sparwood council minutes (digital copy, provided by the District of Sparwood, available from the author on request), 14 April and 16 October 1969. On the limited affordable housing in Sparwood in the early 1970s, see Langford, "Class and Environmental Justice," 52.

33 MNSHS interviews with Valerie Podrasky, conducted by Dan Tanaka and Christine Beranek, 18 July 1991, 13; and John Desjardins, conducted by Janice Talarico and Butch Archibald, 2 July 1992, 6.

34 Langford, "Class and Environmental Justice," 51.

35 Sparwood council minutes (digital copy, provided by the District of Sparwood, available from the author on request), 18 October 1967. See Langford, "Class and Environmental Justice," 50, on the gap between what Natal homeowners received when expropriated and what it cost to rebuild at Sparwood.

36 Village of Natal minutes (digital copy, provided by the District of Sparwood, available from the author on request), 20 April 1965; *Fernie Free Press*, 22 April 1965.

37 Village of Natal minutes (digital copy, provided by the District of Sparwood, available from the author on request), 4 April 1966; *Fernie Free Press*, 12 May 1966.

38 BCA, box 16, file Incorporation and Change Status, 1966, E. [likely Emilio] Ungaro letter, 26 September 1966.

39 GWRC, M-1561, file 180, Sparwood 1966–68, Tom Campbell, CNPC lawyer, to Minister of Municipal Affairs, 16 May 1966; Sparwood council minutes, 6 September 1966; *Fernie Free Press*, 13 October 1966.

40 *Fernie Free Press*, 1 April, 19 May, 1 August, 29 September, and 4 October 1966; Village of Natal minutes (digital copy, provided by the District of Sparwood, available from the author on request), 21 April and 2 May 1966; District of Sparwood minutes (digital copy, provided by the District of Sparwood, available from the author on request), 6 September 1966.

41 *Fernie Free Press*, 19 May 1966.

42 District of Sparwood minutes (digital copy, provided by the District of Sparwood,

available from the author on request), 5 December 1966, including notes on the legal advice secured by Ungaro in Vancouver; 20 February 1967, with a report on a letter sent by Ungaro to Nimsick that had "voiced council's dissatisfaction with all the delays and changes which took place to the original proposition;" and 6 March 1967. District of Sparwood archived digital file, 330-001.tif (available from the author on request), Reeve Orlando Ungaro to Minister John Nicholson, 21 February 1967, 132, and Nicholson's reply, 2 March 1967, 135–36.

43 *Fernie Free Press*, 27 April 1967.

44 District of Sparwood minutes (digital copy, provided by the District of Sparwood, available from the author on request), 24 April 1967.

45 *Lethbridge Herald*, 29 April 1967.

46 Gugliotta, "Coal Smoke," 166, 175, 183; Broto and Carter, "Coal Ash Pollution," 210, 214.

47 *Lethbridge Herald*, 29 April 1967; Loretta Montemurro, interview with the author, 31 July 2013.

48 District of Sparwood minutes, (digital copy, provided by the District of Sparwood, available from the author on request), 5 June 1967.

49 Bell and Braun, "Environmental Justice Activism," 797.

50 District of Sparwood minutes, (digital copy, provided by the District of Sparwood, available from the author on request), 6 June 1967; *Fernie Free Press*, 8 and 22 June 1967.

51 District of Sparwood minutes (digital copy, provided by the District of Sparwood, available from the author on request), 22 June 1967; *Fernie Free Press*, 28 September 1967.

52 *Fernie Free Press*, 20 July 1967.

53 *Fernie Free Press*, 14 September 1967; District of Sparwood minutes (digital copy, provided by the District of Sparwood, available from the author on request), 11 October 1967.

54 *Fernie Free Press*, 5 October 1967.

55 District of Sparwood minutes (digital copy, provided by the District of Sparwood, available from the author on request), 11 October 1967.

56 *Fernie Free Press*, 31 January and 19 December 1968; GWRC, M-7422, file 10, COAWC managing director's annual report, 19 April 1968.

57 *Fernie Free Press*, 8 February, 23 May, 17 October, and 19 December 1968.

58 *Financial Times of Canada*, 5 May 1968; District of Sparwood minutes (digital copy, provided by the District of Sparwood, available from the author on request), 26 February 1968; *Fernie Free Press*, 29 February 1968.

59 *Fernie Free Press*, 7 March 1968; District of Sparwood minutes (digital copy, provided by the District of Sparwood, available from the author on request), 4 March 1968.

60 Cole and Foster, *From the Ground Up*, 16–17.

61 *Fernie Free Press*, 16 May 1968, 13 February 1969.

62 *Fernie Free Press*, 25 April and 3 July 1969; District of Sparwood minutes (digital copy, provided by the District of Sparwood, available from the author on request), 10 June 1968; MNSHS, interview with Frank and Francis Travis, conducted by Dan Tanaka and Christine Beranek, 1 August 1991.

63 *Fernie Free Press*, 14 December 1961, 5 November 1964.

64 *Fernie Free Press*, 12 December 1963, 17 December 1964, 15 December 1966, 31 August and 14 December 1967.

65 *Fernie Free Press*, 25 June 1964.

66 Recorded in Robertson, *Imagining Difference*, xxviii–xxix.

67 *Fernie Free Press*, 25 June 1964.

68 *Fernie Free Press*, 25 June and 20 August 1964.

69 Robertson, *Imagining Difference*, 161.

70 *Fernie Free Press*, 20 August 1964.

71 Anthropologist Leslie Robertson, *Imagining Difference*, 159, has a more critical view of Mayor White's speech at the curse-lifting ceremony, seeing it as an effort "to get rid of the story of colonialism."

72 *Fernie Free Press*, 23 and 30 January and 19 June 1958.

73 Unless otherwise noted, information on Ezner De Anna comes from his interview with the author, 7 July 2011.

74 *Fernie Free Press*, 20 June and 29 August 1963.

75 Seager, "Proletariat in Wild Rose," 202–361.

76 *Fernie Free Press*, 12 September 1963.

77 De Anna and Weaver campaigned together through the south country in 1963. De Anna noted that south country farmers often would recognize Weaver since "a lot of these people had worked in the mines, and they knew him from the mines." This connection helps to explain the decent NDP share of the rural vote in 1963.

78 British Columbia, *Chief Electoral Officer, 1966*.

79 *Fernie Free Press*, 18 August 1966; De Anna, interview with the author, 2011.

80 BCA, Nimsick interview, transcript reference copy 12-2, 13.

81 *Fernie Free Press*, 3 October 1963.

82 *Fernie Free Press*, 15 September 1966; De Anna, interview with the author, 2011.

83 *Fernie Free Press*, 5 October 1967, 7 March, 11 April, and 16 May 1968.

84 *Fernie Free Press*, 14 September 1967.

85 Alberta, Chief Electoral Officer, *Report on Alberta Elections*, 90.

86 Langford and Frazer, "Cold War," 62–63.

87 *Coleman Journal*, 6 October 1965.

88 Unless otherwise noted, all information about Garth Turcott's life and political career is taken from copies of campaign materials provided to the author by Garth

and Joan Turcott in 2001 or from an interview conducted by the author with Garth Turcott that year.

89 *Coleman Journal*, 25 October 1961, 24 October 1962, 13 March 1963; *Lethbridge Herald*, 7 October 1966.

90 NDP election advertisement, *Coleman Journal*, 21 September 1966; *Pincher Creek Echo*, 1 and 15 September 1966.

91 Alberta, Chief Electoral Officer, *Report on Alberta Elections*, 180.

92 Information on the Turcott by-election campaign is taken from NDP campaign materials provided by the Turcott family; author interview with Garth Turcott; Leeson, *Grant Notley*, 98–99; Pratt, "Grant Notley: Politics as a Calling," 25; *Lethbridge Herald*, 1 October 1966.

93 *Pass Herald*, 5 October 1966. *Lethbridge Herald*, 5 October 1966.

94 Rally advertisement, *Coleman Journal*, 5 October 1966.

95 As recorded in Alberta, Chief Electoral Officer, *Report on Alberta Elections*, 95.

96 *Maclean's*, 16 November 1964, 16–20, 65.

97 See Langford, "So Dauntless."

98 *Pincher Creek Echo*, 1 June 1967.

99 "Turcott Must 'Cut 'Em Off at the Pass," *Lethbridge Herald*, n.d. (week of 16–20 January 1967); *Pincher Creek Echo*, 9 February 1967.

100 *Edmonton Journal*, 17 November 1966; *Lethbridge Herald*, 17 May 1967.

Conclusion | LESSONS AND OPPORTUNITIES FOR A FUTURE BEYOND COAL

1 The joint review panel maintained that the proposed Grassy Mountain strip mine would have produced "significant adverse environmental effects" and only limited positive economic benefits; see "Report of the Joint Review Panel," viii–ix.

2 Featherstone, *Solidarity*, 16, 246.

3 Sears, *Next New Left*.

4 PAA, Manning, file 1628, Ernest Manning's 1 February 1951 reply to a letter from T.A. Collister, Secretary-Treasurer of Coleman, 17 January 1951.

5 *Lethbridge Herald*, 3 May 1957.

6 GWRC, M-1601, file 1192b, William C. Whittaker to Edward Boyd, 30 December 1960, with attachment "Confidential Developments Arising out of the Report of the Rand Royal Commission on Coal."

7 PAA, Manning, file 1812, memo from John Ferguson to J.E. Oberholtzer, 13 July 1954.

8 Alberta, Chief Electoral Officer, *Report on Alberta Elections*.

9 Phillips, "Moral Economy," 314.

10 MacKinnon, *Closing Sysco*, 172–74.

11 Phillips, "Deindustrialization," 101.

12 Berry, *Flame and Slag*, 176, 199.

13 Phillips, "Moral Economy," 318.

14 LAC, RG 33/42, vol. 28, file Railway Coal Subvention Sales, "Total Subventions Paid by Colliery 1959–60" and "Coal Subventions" historical summary.

15 At an all-candidates' meeting during the provincial election in 1966, NDP candidate Leo Nimsick asserted that Cominco had received $594,208 in provincial subsidies for its steel operation (*Fernie Free Press*, 1 September 1966). Controlling for inflation to 2023, this equals $5.3 million. On the closure of the Kimberley plants, see Teck, "Sullivan Mine."

16 Berry, *Flame and Slag*, 90.

17 See "Teck Reports Unaudited Third Quarter Results for 2022." A metric tonne (1,000 kilograms) is slightly heavier than a short ton by a factor of about 1.1; 25.0 million tonnes is equal to approximately 27.6 million tons.

18 See Teck, "2021 Annual Report."

19 Queensland Treasury, *Study*, 3, Table 5.1.

20 Dowie, *Haida Gwaii Lesson*, 61. The Supreme Court's important decisions on Aboriginal title are *Calder v Attorney General of BC* (1973) and *Delgamuukw v British Columbia* (1997); see Gill, *All that We Say*, 38–40, 186–88.

21 Dowie, *Haida Gwaii Lesson*, 64.

22 Ibid., 65.

23 Wood, "Indigenous Protected Areas."

24 *Nelson Daily*, 18 January 2020.

25 An archipelago that starts about 250 kilometres northwest of Vancouver Island and whose northern extremity is due south and within sight of islands in the Alaska Panhandle.

26 Gill, *All that We Say*, 147–48, 158–59.

27 Dowie, *Haida Gwaii Lesson*, 17–18; Weiss, *Life beyond Settler Colonialism*, 161.

28 Gill, *All that We Say*, 193–94.

29 Ibid., 222; Takeda, *Islands' Spirit Rising*, 184–86.

30 Takeda, *Islands' Spirit Rising*, 197–98.

31 Ibid., 4. See Thom Henley's memoir, *Raven Walks*, on the role of environmentalists.

32 Takeda, *Islands' Spirit Rising*, 192.

33 Weiss, *Life beyond Settler Colonialism*, 21.

34 Ibid., 14.

35 Sandlos and Keeling, *Mining Country*, 212, 85.

36 MacKinnon, *Closing Sysco*, 9.

37 Gibbs, *Coal Country*, 258.

38 LAC, MG 31-B6, vol. 2, file Enoch Williams, interview with David Millar, 10–11.

39 Beynon and Hudson, *Shadow of the Mine*, 285.

40 Gibbs, *Coal Country*, 9–10.

41   Ibid., 4.
42   Diluiso, "Coal Transitions," 26.
43   W. Langford, *Global Politics*, 184.
44   Manuel, *Taconite Dreams*, 219–20.
45   Tumber, "Small, Green, and Good," 223.
46   Beynon and Hudson, *Shadow of the Mine*, 18.
47   Ibid., 283–86.
48   Martinez-Fernandez et al., "Shrinking Mining City," 256.
49   Connolly, "Small Rust-Belt Cities," 9–10.
50   Ibid., 5.
51   *Fernie Free Press*, 27 February 1958.

Bibliography

ARCHIVAL SOURCES

BC Archives, Victoria (BCA)
Cominco Ltd., M-2500
Leo Nimsick interview by Andrew Petter and Derek Reimer, 1978, accession T3224
Municipal Affairs executive records, 1964–67, GR-0239

Glenbow Library and Archives, Calgary
This collection includes historical photographs of the Crowsnest Pass and Elk
    Valley that did not transfer to the University of Calgary upon the creation there
    of the Glenbow Western Research Centre.

Glenbow Western Research Centre, University of Calgary (GWRC)
Coal Association of Canada fonds, F0544 (formerly M-7422)
Crowsnest Resources Ltd. fonds, F0617 (formerly M 1561)
Tom Kirkam Oral History Project collection, C0059
United Mine Workers of America, District 18 fonds, F1844 (formerly M-2237,
    M-6000)
United Mine Workers of America, Local 2633 fonds, F1845 (formerly M-2239,
    M-6048)
West Canadian Collieries Ltd. fonds, F1896 (formerly M-1601)

Library and Archives Canada, Ottawa (LAC)
Canada Labour Relations Board, RG 145
Canadian Labour Congress fonds, MG 28-I103
Canadian Security Intelligence Service (CSIS), RG 146
CBC Citizens' Forum, "The Pass" (episode aired on CBC TV, 4 February 1962),
    consultation copy V1 8410-0055, item number 286547, CBC accession 1984-0286
CSIS Access-to-Information Request (AIR), 96-A-00189
David Millar fonds, MG 32-B6
Department of Labour, RG 27

Department of Regional Economic Expansion, RG 124
Dominion Coal Board, RG 81
Royal Commission on Coal (1959–60), RG 33/42

Provincial Archives of Alberta, Edmonton (PAA)
Alfred Farmilo fonds, PR0608
Department of Municipal Affairs, Accession 78.133
Ernest C. Manning fonds, Accession 1969.289
Theo Serra fonds, PR0438

Thomas Fisher Rare Book Library, University of Toronto (UT)
Robert S. Kenny Collection

NEWSPAPERS, MAGAZINES, AND NEWSLETTERS

Blairmore Examiner
Blairmore Graphic
Calgary Albertan
Calgary Herald
Canadian Mineworker
Canadian Tribune
Coleman Journal
Crowsnest Pass Promoter
Edmonton Journal
Fernie Free Press
Financial Post
Globe and Mail
Lethbridge Herald
Maclean's
Michel-Natal Spectator
Nelson Daily
New York Times
Pacific Tribune
Pass Herald
Pincher Creek Echo
Star Weekly
The Lamp
The Narwhal
Vancouver Sun
Windspeaker

ARTICLES, BOOKS, INTERNET, OTHER SOURCES

Adams, Ian. "When They Tear Down a Mountain What Do We Get? We Get the Pollution. The Americans Get a Fortune in Coal." *Weekend Magazine* 22, no. 42 (1972): 3–7.

Alberta. Chief Electoral Officer. *A Report on Alberta Elections, 1905–1982.* Edmonton: Government of Alberta, 1983.

–. Department of Mines and Minerals. *Annual Report of the Mines Division,* 1963–68. (Digital copies are available on the website of the Alberta Legislature Library: https://librarysearch.assembly.ab.ca/client/en_CA/internal/search/results?qu=u225318).

Alberta Energy Regulator. "Coal Mine Atlas Operating and Abandoned Coal Mines in Alberta." Serial Publication ST45. http://docplayer.net/42223833-Coal-mine-atlas-operating-and-abandoned-coal-mines-in-alberta.html.

Alberta Labour History Institute (ALHI). Group interviews in Coleman, AB, including Liz and Steve Liska, 9 November 2005; Pauline Griegel, 10 November 2005; and Gary Taje, 10 November 2005. http://albertalabourhistory.org/interviews.

–. Interview with Tets Kitaguchi, Hinton, AB, 28 October 2005. http://albertalabourhistory.org/interviews.

Alinsky, Saul. *John L. Lewis: An Unauthorized Biography.* New York: G.P. Putnam's Sons, 1949.

Azzi, Stephen. *Walter Gordon and the Rise of Canadian Nationalism.* Montreal and Kingston: McGill-Queen's University Press, 1999.

Bell, Shannon Elizabeth, and Yvonne A. Braun. "Coal, Identity, and the Gendering of Environmental Justice Activism in Central Appalachia." *Gender and Society* 24, no. 6 (2010): 794–813.

Berger, Stefan. "Working-Class Culture and the Labour Movement in the South Wales and the Ruhr Coalfields, 1850–2000: A Comparison." *Llafur: The Journal of Welsh People's History* 8, no. 2 (2001): 5–40.

Berry, Ron. *Flame and Slag.* 1968; reprinted, Cardigan, Wales: Parthian, Library of Wales, 2012.

Beynon, Huw, and Ray Hudson. *The Shadow of the Mine: Coal and the End of Industrial Britain.* London: Verso, 2021.

Black, Errol, and Jim Silver. *Building a Better World: An Introduction to Trade Unionism in Canada, Second Edition.* Black Point, NS: Fernwood, 2008.

Blank, Thomas Koch. "The Disruptive Potential of Green Steel Basalt, CO: Rocky Mountain Institute, 2019.

Bowden, Bradley. "Heroic Failure? Unionism and Queensland's Coal Communities, 1954–1967." *Labour and Industry* 11, no. 3 (2001): 73–94.

–. "A History of the Pan-Pacific Coal Trade from the 1950s to 2011: Exploring the

Long-Term Effects of a Buying Cartel." *Australian Economic History Review* 52, no. 1 (2012): 1–24.

British Columbia. Chief Electoral Officer. *Statement of Votes* (Victoria BC), General Election, September 12, 1966, p. 46, Kootenay Electoral District.

—. Chief Electoral Officer. *Statement of Votes (Victoria BC)*, General Election, September 30, 1963, p. 47, Fernie Electoral District.

—. Department of Mines. *Annual Report of the Minister of Mines*, 1945–59. https://www2.gov.bc.ca/gov/content/industry/mineral-exploration-mining/british-columbia-geological-survey/publications/annual-report-to-the-minister#1974-1950.

—. Minister of Mines and Petroleum Resources. *Annual Reports*, 1960–68. https://www2.gov.bc.ca/gov/content/industry/mineral-exploration-mining/british-columbia-geological-survey/publications/annual-report-to-the-minister#1974-1950.

Broto, Vanesa Castán, and Claudia Carter. "Environmental Justice within Local Discourses About Coal Ash Pollution in Tuzla, Bosnia and Herzegovina." In *Managing Environmental Justice*, edited by Dennis Pavlich, 199–221. Amsterdam and New York: Editions Rodopi, 2010.

Brown, Malcolm, and John N. Webb. *Seven Stranded Coal Towns: A Study of an American Depressed Area*. Works Projects Administration, Division of Social Research, Research Monograph 23. 1941; reprinted, New York: Da Capo Press, 1971.

Carroll, W.F., Angus J. Morrison, and C.C. McLaurin. *Report of the Royal Commission on Coal, 1946*. Ottawa: King's Printer, 1947.

Census of Canada 1951. *Volume 1 Population General Characteristics*. Table 23, "Population by Specified Age Groups, for census subdivisions, 1951," Ottawa: Dominion Bureau of Statistics, 1953. https://publications.gc.ca/collections/collection_2017/statcan/CS98-1951-1.pdf.

Census of Canada 1961. *Population Historical 1901–1961*. Bulletin 1.1-10. Ottawa: Dominion Bureau of Statistics, March 1963. https://publications.gc.ca/collections/collection_2017/statcan/CS92-539-1961.pdf.

Census of Canada 1966. *Population: Divisions and Subdivisions Western Provinces*. Vol. 1 (1–6). Ottawa: Dominion Bureau of Statistics, June 1967.

—. *Population: Specified Age Groups and Sex, for Counties and Census Subdivisions*, 1966. Bulletin S-2. Ottawa: Dominion Bureau of Statistics, August 1968. https://publications.gc.ca/collections/collection_2017/statcan/CS92-632-1966.pdf.

Census of the Prairie Provinces 1936. *Volume I Population and Agriculture*. Alberta Table 34. "Racial Origins Classified by Municipalities and Census Divisions, 1936." Ottawa: Dominion Bureau of Statistics, 1938. https://publications.gc.ca/collections/collection_2017/statcan/CS98-1936-1.pdf.

Chatterjee, Partha. *The Black Hole of Empire: History of a Global Practice of Power*. Princeton, NJ: Princeton University Press, 2012.

"Coal Mine Closes with Celebration." BBC News, 25 January 2008. http://news. bbc.co.uk/2/hi/uk_news/wales/7200432.stm.

"Coal Mountain Mine." Mining Data Online. https://miningdataonline.com/ property/29/Coal-Mountain-Mine.aspx.

Cole, Luke W., and Sheila R. Foster. *From the Ground Up: Environmental Racism and the Rise of the Environmental Justice Movement*. New York: New York University Press, 2001.

Connolly, James J. "Can They Do It? The Capacity of Small Rust-Belt Cities to Reinvent Themselves in a Global Economy." In *After the Factory: Reinventing America's Industrial Small Cities*, edited by James J. Connolly, 1–17. Lanham, MD: Lexington Books, 2010.

Cooke, Philip. "Radical Regions? Space, Time and Gender Relations in Emilia, Provence and South Wales." In *Political Action and Social Identity: Class, Locality and Ideology*, edited by Gareth Rees et al., 17–41. London: Macmillan, 1985.

Cousins, William James. *A History of the Crow's Nest Pass*. Lethbridge: Historic Trails Society of Alberta, 1981.

Crowshoe, Reg, and Sybille Manneschmidt. *Akak'stiman: A Blackfoot Framework for Decision-Making and Mediation Processes*. Calgary: University of Calgary Press, 2002.

Crowsnest Pass Historical Society. *Crowsnest and Its People*. Coleman, AB.: Crowsnest Pass Historical Society, 1979.

–. *Crowsnest and Its People. Millennium Ed., Book III*. Coleman, AB: Crowsnest Pass Historical Society, 2000.

"Cultural Benefactor Helen Harquail Dies." *Cayman Compass*, 14 August 2013. https://www.caymancompass.com/2013/08/14/cultural-benefactor-helen-harquail-dies/.

Davies, Rhys. *The Best of Rhys Davies*. London: David and Charles, 1979.

–. "The Last Struggle." In *A Rhondda Anthology*, edited by Meic Stephens, 123–33. Bridgend, Wales: Seren Books, 1993.

"(De) Construction Time-Lapse: Devon Energy – Coleman Gas Plant." Owlbox. http://www.owlbox.ca/portfolio/devon-energy-coleman-gas-plant-decommission-construction-time-lapse.

Dempsey, Hugh A. *Red Crow: Warrior Chief*. 2nd ed. Saskatoon: Fifth House Publishers, 1995.

Derickson, Alan. "'Nuisance Dust': Unprotective Limits for Exposure to Coal Mine Dust in the United States, 1934–1969." *American Journal of Public Health* 103, no. 2 (2013): 238–49.

–. "The United Mine Workers of America and the Recognition of Occupational

Respiratory Diseases, 1902–1968." *American Journal of Public Health* 81, no. 6 (1991): 782–90.

Devine, Jason Corey. "'In an Equitable and Sympathetic Manner': Alberta's Workmen's Compensation and the United Mine Workers of America, District 18's Welfare Fund." University of Calgary, 2011.

Diluiso, Francesca, et al. "Coal Transitions – Part 1: A Systematic Map and Review of Case Study Learnings from Regional, National, and Local Coal Phase-Out Experiences." *Environmental Research Letters* 16 (2021): 1–40.

"Dofasco Needs 14-Kilometre Natural Gas Pipeline Built for 'Green Steel' Project." *Hamilton Spectator,* 2 February 2023. https://www.thespec.com/news/hamilton-region/2023/02/02/dofasco-gas-pipeline.html.

Dowie, Mark. *The Haida Gwaii Lesson: A Strategic Playbook for Indigenous Sovereignty.* San Francisco: Inshares, 2017.

Dublin, Thomas, and Walter Licht. *The Face of Decline: The Pennsylvania Anthracite Region in the Twentieth Century.* Ithaca, NY: Cornell University Press, 2005.

Dubofsky, Melvyn, and Warren Van Tine. *John L. Lewis: A Biography, Abridged Edition.* Urbana: University of Illinois Press, 1986.

Dvorak, Grace Arbuckle. "Childhood Remembered: A Coal Creek Memoir." In *The Forgotten Side of the Border: British Columbia's Elk Valley and Crowsnest Pass,* edited by Wayne Norton and Naomi Miller, 189–94. Kamloops: Plateau Press, 1998.

Endicott, Stephen Lyon. *Raising the Workers' Flag: The Workers' Unity League of Canada, 1930–1936.* Toronto: University of Toronto Press, 2012.

Featherstone, David. *Solidarity: Hidden Histories and Geographies of Internationalism.* London: Zed Books, 2012.

Finkel, Alvin. "The Cold War, Alberta Labour, and the Social Credit Regime." *Labour/Le travail* 21 (1988): 123–52.

—. *The Social Credit Phenomenon in Alberta.* Toronto: University of Toronto Press, 1989.

Franz, Kyle R. "'An Affront to the Sensibilities of All Thinking Canadians!' The Makings of a Communist Town Council and the Community behind It, Blairmore, Canada." In *Radical Cultures and Local Identities,* edited by Krista Cowman and Ian Packer, 34–49. Newcastle upon Tyne, UK: Cambridge Scholars Publishing, 2010.

—. "Alberta's Red Democrats: The Challenge and Legacy of Blairmore Communism, 1921–1936." Queen's University, 2013.

Fudge, Judy, and Eric Tucker. *Labour before the Law: The Regulation of Workers' Collective Action in Canada, 1900–1948.* Don Mills, ON: Oxford University Press, 2001.

Gaal, Arlene B. *Memoirs of Michel-Natal, 1899–1971.* Self-published, 1971.

Galley, M.R. "Canadian Heavy Water Production – 1970 to 1980." In "Canadian Heavy Water Production – 1970 to 1980," companion papers for presentation at the Second World Congress of Chemical Engineering, Montreal, 1981, October 4–9, edited by M.R. Galley and A.R. Bancroft, ix-100. Chalk River, Ontario: Chalk River Nuclear Laboratories, 1981. https://inis.iaea.org/collection/NCLCollectionStore/_Public/13/680/13680421.pdf.

Garside, W.R. "A Very British Phenomenon? Industrial Politics and the Decline of the Japanese Coal Mining Industry since the 1950s." *Australian Economic History Review* 45, no. 2 (2005): 186–203.

Gibbs, Ewan. *Coal Country: The Meaning and Memory of Deindustrialization in Postwar Scotland*. London: University of London Press, Institute of Historical Research, 2021.

Gill, Ian. *All that We Say Is Ours: Guujaaw and the Reawakening of the Haida Nation*. Vancouver: Douglas and McIntyre, 2009.

Gill, Isabel. "Story and Stereotype: Aboriginal Literature as Anti-Racist Education." University of Lethbridge, 2004.

Guard, Julie. *Radical Housewives: Price Wars and Food Politics in Mid-Twentieth-Century Canada*. Toronto: University of Toronto Press, 2019.

Gugliotta, Angela. "Class, Gender, and Coal Smoke: Gender Ideology and Environmental Injustice in Pittsburgh, 1868–1914." *Environmental History* 5, no. 2 (2000): 165–93.

Gunton, Thomas. "Natural Resources and Regional Development: An Assessment of Dependency and Comparative Advantage Paradigms." *Economic Geography* 79, no. 1 (2003): 67–94.

Harris, Cole. *Making Native Space: Colonialism, Resistance, and Reserves in British Columbia*. Vancouver: UBC Press, 2002.

Harvey, David. "Militant Particularism and Global Ambition: The Conceptual Politics of Place, Space, and Environment in the Work of Raymond Williams." *Social Text* 42 (1995): 69–98.

Hawthorn, H.B., C.S. Belshaw, and S.M. Jamieson. *The Indians of British Columbia: A Study of Contemporary Social Adjustment*. Toronto: University of Toronto Press; Vancouver: University of British Columbia, 1958.

Henley, Thom. *Raven Walks around the World: Life of a Wandering Activist*. Madeira Park, BC: Harbour Publishing, 2017.

Herod, Andrew. "Local Political Practice in Response to a Manufacturing Plant Closure: How Geography Complicates Class Analysis." *Antipode* 23, no. 4 (1991): 385–402.

High, Steven. "Deindustrialization on the Industrial Frontier: The Rise and Fall of Mill Colonialism in Northern Ontario." In *The Deindustrialized World: Confronting Ruination in Postindustrial Places*, edited by Steven High, Lachlan MacKinnon, and Andrew Perchard, 257–83. Vancouver: UBC Press, 2017.

—. *Industrial Sunset: The Making of North America's Rust Belt, 1969–1984*. Toronto: University of Toronto Press, 2003.

High, Steven, and David W. Lewis. *Corporate Wasteland: The Landscape and Memory of Deindustrialization*. Ithaca, NY: ILR Press, 2007.

High, Steven, Lachlan MacKinnon, and Andrew Perchard. "Introduction." In *The Deindustrialized World: Confronting Ruination in Postindustrial Places*, edited by Steven High, Lachlan MacKinnon, and Andrew Perchard, 3–22. Vancouver: UBC Press, 2017.

Hildebrandt, Walter. "Treaty 7 in Its Historical and Political Context." In *The True Spirit and Original Intent of Treaty 7*, edited by Treaty 7 Elders and Tribal Council, Walter Hildebrandt, Sarah Carter, and Dorothy First Rider, 189–229. Montreal and Kingston: McGill-Queen's University Press, 1996.

Hoffmann, Christian, Michel Van Hoey, and Benedikt Zeumer. "Decarbonization Challenge for Steel: Hydrogen as a Solution in Europe." McKinsey and Company, 2020. https://www.mckinsey.com/industries/metals-and-mining/our-insights/decarbonization-challenge-for-steel#/.

"Island Lake Lodge." Wikipedia. https://en.wikipedia.org/wiki/Island_Lake_Lodge.

Kenward, John Kenneth. "Political Manipulation and Rewards in the Crowsnest Pass, Southern Alberta." Simon Fraser University, 1971.

Kinnear, John. "The Balmer Mine Disaster of 1967." In *The Forgotten Side of the Border: British Columbia's Elk Valley and Crowsnest Pass*, edited by Wayne Norton and Naomi Miller, 154–60. Kamloops: Plateau Press, 1998.

Kirk, John, Steve Jefferys, and Christine Wall. "Representing Identity and Work in Transition: The Case of South Yorkshire Coal-Mining Communities in the UK." In *Changing Working and Community Identities in European Regions: Perspectives on the Past and Present*, edited by John Kirk, Sylvie Contrepois, and Steve Jefferys, 184–216. London: Palgrave Macmillan, 2012.

Knight, Rolf. "Harvey Murphy: Reminiscences 1918–1943. Interviewed 1976–1977. Foreword by Mary Murphy." 2014. Downloaded from www.rolfknight.ca in 2016.

Knight, Stephen. "'Not a Place for Me': Rhys Davies's Fiction and the Coal Industry." In *Rhys Davies: Decoding the Hare. Critical Essays to Mark the Centenary of the Writer's Birth*, edited by Meic Stephens, 54–70. Cardiff: University of Wales Press, 2001.

Knotter, Ad. "'Little Moscows' in Western Europe: The Ecology of Small-Place Communism." *International Review of Social History* 56 (2011): 475–510.

—. "'Little Moscows' Revisited. What We Can Learn from French and German Cases." *Twentieth Century Communism* 5 (2013): 175–92.

Langford, Tom. "An Alternate Vision of Community: Crowsnest Miners and Their Local Unions during the 1940s and 1950s." In *A World Apart: The Crowsnest*

Communities of Alberta and British Columbia, edited by Wayne Norton and Tom Langford, 147–57. Kamloops: Plateau Press, 2002.

—. "Class and Environmental Justice Politics in the Demolition of Natal and Michel, 1964–78." *BC Studies* 189 (2016): 31–58.

—. "Coal Miners' Resistance to Industrial Legality in Western Canada, 1940–1955." *Prairie Forum* 31, no. 2 (2006): 233–44.

—. "Fighting Fascism in Spain: Volunteers from the Crowsnest Pass." In *A World Apart: The Crowsnest Communities of Alberta and British Columbia*, edited by Wayne Norton and Tom Langford, 125–30. Kamloops: Plateau Press, 2002.

—. "The Hanging of Peter Abramowicz and Father John Duplanil's Efforts to Save Him." *Alberta History* 59, no. 4 (2011): 1–9.

—. "'So Dauntless in War': The Impact of Garth Turcott on Political Change in Alberta, 1966–71." *Prairie Forum* 34, no. 2 (2009): 405–34.

—. "Union Democracy as a Foundation for a Participatory Society: A Theoretical Elaboration and Historical Example." *Labour/Le travail* 76 (2015): 79–108.

Langford, Tom, and Chris Frazer. "The Cold War and Working Class Politics in the Coal Mining Communities of the Crowsnest Pass, 1945–1958." *Labour/Le travail* 49 (2002): 43–81.

Langford, Will. *The Global Politics of Poverty in Canada: Development Programs and Democracy, 1964–1979*. Montreal and Kingston: McGill-Queen's University Press, 2020.

Leeson, Howard. *Grant Notley: The Social Conscience of Alberta*. Edmonton: University of Alberta Press, 1992.

Levine, Karen. "The Labor-Progressive Party in Crisis, 1956–1957." *Labour/Le travail* 87 (2021): 161–84.

Linkon, Sherry Lee, and John Russo. *Steeltown U.S.A.: Work and Memory in Youngstown*. Lawrence: University Press of Kansas, 2002.

Loch-Drake, Cynthia. "The Medalta Potteries Strike: An Appeal to the Pass." In *A World Apart: The Crowsnest Communities of Alberta and British Columbia*, edited by Wayne Norton and Tom Langford, 128–30. Kamloops: Plateau Press, 2002.

Lucas, Rex A. *Minetown, Milltown, Railtown: Life in Canadian Communities of Single Industry*. 1971; reprinted, Don Mills, ON: Oxford University Press, 2008.

Lutz, John Sutton. *Makúk: A New History of Aboriginal-White Relations*. Vancouver: UBC Press, 2008.

Macintyre, Stuart. *Little Moscows: Communism and Working-Class Militancy in Inter-War Britain*. London: Croom Helm, 1980.

MacKinnon, Lachlan. *Closing Sysco: Industrial Decline in Atlantic Canada's Steel City*. Toronto: University of Toronto Press, 2020.

MacPherson, Sean. "Rising and Remembering: Ktunaxa History and Settler Mythology in the East Kootenay." University of Victoria, 2020.

Manuel, Jeffrey T. *Taconite Dreams: The Struggle to Sustain Mining on Minnesota's Iron Range, 1915–2000*. Minneapolis: University of Minnesota Press, 2015.

Marcuse, Gary. "Labour's Cold War: The Story of a Union that Was Not Purged." *Labour/Le travail* 22 (1988): 199–210.

Martinez-Fernandez, Cristina, Chung-Tong Wu, Laura K. Schatz, Nobuhisa Taira, and José G. Vargas-Hernández. "The Shrinking Mining City: Urban Dynamics and Contested Territory." *International Journal of Urban and Regional Research* 36, no. 2 (2012): 245–60.

Maund, Jacqueline K. "The Implications of the Japanese Resource Procurement Strategy for Staple Resource Regions: An Examination of Coal Mining in Southeastern B.C." University of British Columbia, 1984.

McDonald, Robert. "'Simply a Working Man': Tom Uphill of Fernie." In *A World Apart: The Crowsnest Communities of Alberta and British Columbia*, edited by Wayne Norton and Tom Langford, 99–112. Kamloops: Plateau Press, 2002.

McIlroy, John, and Alan Campbell. "Coalfield Leaders, Trade Unionism and Communist Politics: Exploring Arthur Horner and Abe Moffat." In *Towards a Comparative History of Coalfield Societies*, edited by Stefan Berger, Andy Croll, and Norman LaPorte, 267–83. Aldershot, UK: Ashgate, 2005.

McIvor, Bruce. *Standoff: Why Reconciliation Fails Indigenous People and How to Fix It*. Gibsons, BC: Nightwood Editions, 2021.

McKay, Ian. "Springhill 1958." In *People, Resources, and Power: Critical Perspectives on Underdevelopment and Primary Industries in the Atlantic Region*, edited by Gary Burrill and Ian McKay, 162–85. Fredericton: Acadiensis Press, 1987.

Miles, Florence Elder. "Is This a Soviet?" *Maclean's*, 15 April 1935, 22, 56.

Moffat, Abe. *My Life with the Miners*. London: Lawrence and Wishart, 1965.

Molotch, Harvey. "The City as a Growth Machine: Toward a Political Economy of Place." *American Journal of Sociology* 82, no. 2 (1976): 309–32.

Monod, David. "The End of Agrarianism: The Fight for Farm Parity in Alberta and Saskatchewan, 1935–38." *Labour/Le travail* 16 (1985): 117–43.

Morgan, Kevin. "Bastions, Black Spots and Other Variations: In and beyond the Specificities of the Little Moscow." *Twentieth Century Communism* 5 (2013): 193–209.

Mulcahy, Richard. "In the Union's Service: The Political Economy of the U.M.W.A. Welfare and Retirement Fund." *Maryland Historian* 23, no. 1 (1992): 18–43.

Narine, Shari. "Blood Member Wants Entire 'Cows and Plows' Settlement Divided Evenly among Members." *Windspeaker.com*, 21 December 2021. https://windspeaker.com/news/windspeaker-news/blood-member-wants-entire-cows-and-plows-settlement-divided-evenly-among.

Nisbet, Jack. *The Mapmaker's Eye: David Thompson on the Columbia Plateau*. Pullman: Washington State University Press, 2005.

Norton, Wayne. "Music and Musicians: A Collection of Photographs." In *A World Apart: The Crowsnest Communities of Alberta and British Columbia*, edited by Wayne Norton and Tom Langford, 52–56. Kamloops: Plateau Press, 2002.

—. "Trusteeship: Public Administration in Fernie, 1935–46." In *A World Apart: The Crowsnest Communities of Alberta and British Columbia*, edited by Wayne Norton and Tom Langford, 131–46. Kamloops: Plateau Press, 2002.

Norton, Wayne, and Tom Langford. "Politicians of the Pass." In *A World Apart: The Crowsnest Communities of Alberta and British Columbia*, edited by Wayne Norton and Tom Langford, 89–98. Kamloops: Plateau Press, 2002.

Nyden, Philip W. "Democratizing Organizations: A Case Study of a Union Reform Movement." *American Journal of Sociology* 90, no. 6 (1985): 1179–1203.

"Old Age Security (OAS) – Maximum Monthly Amounts by Quarter and by Benefit Type." Government of Canada. https://open.canada.ca/data/en/dataset/ff1e4882-685c-4518-b741-c3cf9bb74c3e.

Owbewcirk. "Minister Pays Tribute to the Late Helen Harquail OBE." *Cayman iNews*, 15 August 2013. https://www.ieyenews.com/minister-pays-tribute-to-the-late-helen-harquail-obe/.

Palmer, Bryan D. "Canadian Communism at the Crossroads, 1956–1957: An Introduction." *Labour/Le travail* 87 (2021): 149–60.

Pellow, David Naguib, and Robert J. Brulle. "Power, Justice, and the Environment: Toward Critical Environmental Justice Studies." In *Power, Justice, and the Environment: A Critical Appraisal of the Environmental Justice Movement*, edited by David Naguib Pellow and Robert J. Brulle, 1–19. Cambridge, MA: MIT Press, 2005.

Penner, Norman. *Canadian Communism: The Stalin Years and Beyond.* Toronto. Methuen, 1988.

Phillips, Jim. "Deindustrialization and the Moral Economy of the Scottish Coalfields, 1947 to 1991." *International Labor and Working-Class History* 84 (2013): 99–115.

—. "The Moral Economy of Deindustrialization in Post-1945 Scotland." In *The Deindustrialized World: Confronting Ruination in Postindustrial Places*, edited by Steven High, Lachlan MacKinnon, and Andrew Perchard, 313–30. Vancouver: UBC Press, 2017.

Piper, Liza, and Heather Green. "A Province Powered by Coal: The Renaissance of Coal Mining in Late Twentieth-Century Alberta." *Canadian Historical Review* 98, no. 3 (2017): 532–67.

Pratt, Larry. "Grant Notley: Politics as a Calling." In *Essays in Honour of Grant Notley: Socialism and Democracy in Alberta*, edited by Larry Pratt, 1–39. Edmonton: NeWest Press, 1986.

Province of Ontario. "Province Invests in Clean Steelmaking Technology in Hamilton to Support Future of Ontario's Auto Sector." News release, 15

February 2022. https://news.ontario.ca/en/release/1001604/province-invests-in-clean-steelmaking-technology-in-hamilton-to-support-future-of-ontarios-auto-sector.

Queensland Treasury. *A Study of Long-Term Global Coal Demand*. https://s3.treasury.qld.gov.au/files/A-Study-of-Long-Term-Global-Coal-Demand.pdf.

Ragin, Charles C. *Constructing Social Research*. Thousand Oaks, CA: Pine Forge, 1994.

Ramsey, Bruce. *The Noble Cause: The Story of the United Mine Workers of America in Western Canada*. Calgary: District 18, United Mine Workers of America, 1990.

Rand, Ivan C. *1960 Report of Royal Commission on Coal*. Ottawa: Queen's Printer, 1960.

Regional Planning Division, Department of Municipal Affairs, Province of British Columbia, and Underwood McLellan and Associates. *Natal-Sparwood Urban Renewal Scheme Report*. Vancouver: Province of British Columbia and Underwood McLellan and Associates, 1966.

Regular, W. Keith. *Neighbours and Networks: The Blood Tribe in the Southern Alberta Economy, 1884–1939*. Calgary: University of Calgary Press, 2009.

Reid, Donald. *The Miners of Decazeville: A Genealogy of Deindustrialization*. Cambridge, MA: Harvard University Press, 1985.

"Report of the Joint Review Panel: Benga Mining Limited, Grassy Mountain Coal Project, Crowsnest Pass." 17 June 2021. https://static.aer.ca/prd/documents/decisions/2021/2021ABAER010.pdf.

Richards, John, and Larry Pratt. *Prairie Capitalism: Power and Influence in the New West*. Toronto: McClelland and Stewart, 1979.

Riley, Sharon J. "The End of an Era: How the Global Steel Industry Is Cutting Out Coal." *The Narwhal*, 1 May 2021. https://thenarwhal.ca/steel-coal-mining-hydrogen/.

Robertson, Leslie A. 2005. *Imagining Difference: Legend, Curse, and Spectacle in a Canadian Mining Town*. Vancouver: UBC Press.

Sandlos, John, and Arn Keeling. *Mining Country: A History of Canada's Mines and Miners*. Toronto: James Lorimer, 2021.

Sangster, Joan. *Dreams of Equality: Women on the Canadian Left, 1920–1950*. Toronto: McClelland and Stewart, 1989.

Sears, Alan. *The Next New Left: A History of the Future*. Halifax: Fernwood, 2014.

Seager, Charles Allen. "Memorial to a Departed Friend of the Working Man." *Bulletin of the Committee on Canadian Labour History* 4 (1977): 9–14.

–. "A Proletariat in Wild Rose Country: The Alberta Coal Miners, 1905–1945." York University, 1982.

Smith, A.E. "Crossing into USSR Thrilling Experience," *Canadian Tribune*, 2 November 1946.

Smith, Dai. *Aneurin Bevan and the World of South Wales*. Cardiff: University of Wales Press, 1993.

Sofchalk, Donald G. "District 50, Allied and Technical Workers of the United States and Canada; International Union Of." In *Labor Unions*, edited by Gary M. Fink, 76–79. Westport, CT: Greenwood Press, 1977.

Speisman, Stephen. "Antisemitism in Ontario: The Twentieth Century." In *Antisemitism in Canada: History and Interpretation*, edited by Alan Davies, 113–34. Waterloo, ON: Wilfrid Laurier University Press, 1992.

Swankey, Ben. "Alberta People Oppose Export of Gas." *Pacific Tribune*, 2 May 1952.

Takeda, Louise. *Islands' Spirit Rising: Reclaiming the Forests of Haida Gwaii*. Vancouver: UBC Press, 2015.

Taylor, Jeff. "Capitalist Development, Forms of Labour, and Class Formation in Prairie Canada." In *The West and Beyond: New Perspectives on an Imagined Region*, edited by Alvin Finkel, Sarah Carter, and Peter Fortna, 159–80. The West Unbound: Social and Cultural Studies. Edmonton: Athabasca University Press, 2010.

Teck. "Sullivan Mine: 111 Years of Community." N.d. https://www.teck.com/operations/canada/legacy/sullivan-mine/sullivan-mine-legacy.

—. "Teck Reports Unaudited Third Quarter Results for 2022." News release, 26 October 2022. https://www.teck.com/media/q3-2022-quarterly.pdf.

—. *2021 Annual Report*. 2021. https://www.teck.com/media/2021-Annual-Report.pdf.

That's the Price [documentary film]. Directed by Michael Scott. National Film Board, 1970. https://www.nfb.ca/film/thats_the_price/.

Tim Buck, Mr. Communism [archived CBC show]. https://www.cbc.ca/player/play/1861583166.

Tumber, Catherine. "Small, Green, and Good: The Role of Smaller Industrial Cities in a Sustainable Future." In *After the Factory: Reinventing America's Industrial Small Cities*, edited by James J. Connolly, 221–31. Lanham, MD: Lexington Books, 2010.

Verzuh, Ron. "#19. Trade Unionist Harvey Murphy." *BC BookLook*, 22 September 2016. https://bcbooklook.com/19-red-agitator-the-life-of-trade-unionist-harvey-murphy/.

Waddington, David, and D. Parry. 2003. "Managing Industrial Decline: The Lessons of a Decade of Research on Industrial Contraction and Regeneration in Britain and Other EU Coal Producing Countries." *Mining Technology* 112: A47–A56.

Weiss, Joseph. *Shaping the Future on Haida Gwaii: Life beyond Settler Colonialism*. Vancouver: UBC Press, 2018.

Whitaker, Reg, and Gary Marcuse. *Cold War Canada: The Making of a National Insecurity State*. Toronto: University of Toronto Press, 1994.

Whitney, Roy. "Preface." In *The True Spirit and Original Intent of Treaty 7*, edited by Treaty 7 Elders and Tribal Council, Walter Hildebrandt, Sarah Carter, and Dorothy First Rider, ix–xv. Montreal and Kingston: McGill-Queen's University Press, 1996.

Williams, Chris. *Capitalism, Community and Conflict: The South Wales Coalfield 1898–1947*. Cardiff: University of Wales Press, 1998.

—. *Democratic Rhondda: Politics and Society, 1885–1951*. Cardiff: University of Wales Press, 1996.

Williams, Raymond. "The Welsh Industrial Novel." In *Culture and Materialism: Selected Essays*, by Raymond Williams, 213–29, 1980; new edition, London: Verso, 2005.

Wilson, Colin. "Service of Thanksgiving for Helen Harquail." *Cayman iNews*, 27 August 2013. https://www.ieyenews.com/service-of-thanksgiving-for-helen-harquail/.

Wood, Stephanie. "The Promise and Peril of Canada's Approach to Indigenous Protected Areas." *The Narwhal*, 15 December 2022. https://thenarwhal.ca/indigenous-protected-areas-ipca-hurdles/.

Woodrum, Robert H. *"Everybody Was Black down There": Race and Industrial Change in the Alabama Coalfields*. Athens: University of Georgia Press, 2007.

Zajicek, Anna M., and Bradley Nash Jr. "Lessons from the UMWA." In *The Transformation of U.S. Unions: Voices, Visions, and Strategies from the Grassroots*, edited by Ray M. Tillman and Michael S. Cummings, 219–38. Boulder, CO: Lynne Rienner Publishers, 1999.

Index

mayor and council, 187; labour
control of town council, 57–58;
labour orientation of town council,
154; labour slate elected (1951), 117;
as a "Little Moscow," 14; mass
meetings in, 82, 96, 130; Tim Buck's
retirement-tour visit, 204. *See also*
Murphy, Harvey; RCMP, leadership
positions
Blairmore Local 7295, UMWA:
arbitration case, discharge of
elderly workers, 55; bulk purchase
of *Canadian Tribune* banned by
District 18, 192; involvement in
municipal government, 57, 154;
links to left-wing parties, 155, 185,
204; objection to CCL raiding of
Mine Mill locals, 61, 193–94
Bowden, Bradley, 225
Boyd, Edward: attempt to convince
hospital to keep burning coal,
137–38; concern about Michel
Local 7292 leaving UMWA, 115–16;
concern about UMWA withdrawal
from CCL, 113; on decision to
replace Robert Lilley on DEB, 7;
exchange with Rand at Royal
Commission hearing, 141; on
WRF assessments, 338n76
British Columbia government, policies
on coal industry: promoting iron
and steel plants at Kimberley,
138, 209, 299, 336n39, 357n15;
temporary work projects, 138
Brown, Everett, 258, 260–61;
relocation-to-Sparwood promises,
256
Buck, Tim, 197, 202, 342n25; and
Harvey Murphy, 184; talk in

Blairmore, 204, 345n80. *See also*
Tim Buck Boulevard
Buller, Annie, 197–98, 293

Canadian Congress of Labour (CCL),
324n59; coal policy lobbying, 94;
Cold War anticommunism, 61;
UMWA stops paying dues to,
113
Canadian Electrical Workers Union,
215(t), 216, 346n26
Canadian Labour Congress (CLC):
District 18 competing with, 149–50;
and UMWA unwilling to affiliate
with, 112–14
Canadian Legion, 116–17
Canadian Mineworker, 148–49
Canadian Pacific Railway (CPR), 65,
81, 225–26, 239
Canadian Tribune, 189, 192, 200
CANDU nuclear reactors, 212–13
Castle Mountain Resort, effects of
climate change on, 313
Catholic Church, 190, 192
Central Mortgage and Housing
Corporation (CMHC), 255–57,
261, 267, 352n27
class struggles at the mines: over
company crackdowns on absenteeism, 229; over increased risks
of accidents and occupational
diseases, 230–34; over intense
work scheduling, 229–30; over
pay reduction for pillar recovery
mining, 229
climate emergency, 32, 285, 287, 302
coal by-products, 83, 84, 85(f)
coal companies: cost-price squeeze,
169–70, 224–26, 239. *See also*

Coleman Collieries; Crow's Nest
Pass Coal (CNPC); Crows Nest
Industries; Hillcrest-Mohawk
Collieries; International Coal and
Coke; Kaiser; McGillivray Creek
Coal and Coke; West Canadian
Collieries (WCC)
Coal Creek, BC, 4(f), 160(f);
residential segregation, 73
coal imports from United States, 90
coal industry, government direction
during Second World War, 42
"Coal is King" discourse, 35–36
coal mine closures, 5, 84(t), 132(t);
impact on small-business owners,
123, 139; lack of protest against in
Crowsnest Pass/Elk Valley, 68–70,
114–15; protests of, 17, 19–20, 292;
resulting collapse in housing prices,
101; resulting unemployment, 100,
102, 126–27, 134; theft of copper
wire, 102–3
coal mine exploration and
development, 239–40
coal mines. *See specific mines*
Coal Operators' Association of
Western Canada (COAWC):
"Accident Prone Employees"
contract proposal, 152; and invalid
Fernie workers' seniority at Michel,
6; irritation at wildcat strikes,
105; labour negotiations, 235–37;
lobbying, 143–44, 169, 226
coal production, 6(f), 67, 145(t), 146,
227(t), 228(t), 238. *See also* strip
mining
coal workers' pneumoconiosis, 230
Cold War: anticommunism, 190–96,
206; beginnings in Canada, 189

Coleman, Alberta, 71(t), 280(t),
281–82; economic rebound (1966),
277–78; Local 2633 involvement on
town council, 58; reaction to coal
contract (1967), 244
Coleman Board of Trade, Crow View
Rodeo cancellation (1961), 161
Coleman Collieries: decline in
production and employment (1950s),
83, 130; ceased mining coal (1980),
285; contract with Japanese steel
companies (1967), 244; formation
of, 83; old and new tipples, 251(f);
production, sales, and employment,
1963–68, 226–28(t); survival of,
131; tenuous financial position, 228;
threat to close mines prior to strike
vote (1960), 151
Coleman Local 2633, UMWA: contract
negotiations, 237; and distribution of
dues money, 114; financial support
for Nova Scotia miners' strike, 60;
incumbent secretary-treasurer loses
re-election bid, 93; maintaining
funeral expenses fund, 110–11;
meeting on closing of International
mine, 94–96; opposing centralization
of dues administration, 109; split in
leadership, 1964–65; withdrawal
from regional May Day celebrations,
97–98, 192–93
collective agreements: (1938), 46;
(1946), 46–47, 49; (1948), 50;
(1949), 65–66; (1950–52), 92;
(1953), 92–93; (1954), 111; (1955),
111–12; (1956), 120–21; (1958,
1960, and 1962), 147–48, 150–52,
235; (1965), 236–37; (1967), 243,
245; (Coleman Local 2633), 237–38;

Printed and bound in Canada by Friesens

Set in AkzidenzGrotesk and Fournier by Julie Cochrane

Copy editor: Dallas Harrison

Proofreader: Jesse Marchand

Cartographer: Eric Leinberger

Cover designer: George Kirkpatrick

Cover images: *Front*: Miners coming off shift at the International mine,
Coleman, Alberta, circa 1952. By George Hunter. Courtesy of Crowsnest
Museum and Archives, Image CC-05-01. *Back*: Crowsnest Pass Mine
Closure, 2 May 1957. By Vern Decoux. Courtesy of Galt Museum &
Archives / Akaisamitohkanao'pa, Image P19752390501.